Performing Piety

(KARIN VAN NIEUWKERK)

Performing Piety

SINGERS AND ACTORS IN
EGYPT'S ISLAMIC REVIVAL

University of Texas Press AUSTIN

Requests for permission to reproduce material from this work should be sent to:
   Permissions
   University of Texas Press
   P.O. Box 7819
   Austin, TX 78713-7819
   http://utpress.utexas.edu/index.php/rp-form

♾ The paper used in this book meets the minimum requirements of ANSI/NISO
z39.48-1992 (R1997) (Permanence of Paper).

LIBRARY OF CONGRESS CATALOGING-IN-PUBLICATION DATA
Nieuwkerk, Karin van, 1960–
   Performing piety : singers and actors in Egypt's Islamic revival /
By Karin van Nieuwkerk.
      p.   cm.
   Includes bibliographical references and index.
   ISBN 978-0-292-74586-5 (cloth : alk. paper)
   ISBN 978-1-4773-0225-5 (paperback)
   1. Entertainers—Religious life—Egypt.   2. Entertainers—Egypt—
Biography.   3. Islamic renewal—Egypt.   I. Title.
PN2977.N535   2013
792.70962—dc23   2013000931

doi:10.7560/745865

Dedicated to my sons Ruben and Leander

Contents

Acknowledgments

Herein I would like to thank many people who have been important sources of support and inspiration. I would like to express my gratitude to all the people "in the field" who made this book possible. First of all, the artists and producers who gave their time and shared their thoughts with me. I hope I have conveyed their thoughts and stories correctly. I would also like to thank Amani and Hoda for their assistance in making appointments with artists and fans, digging in archival sources, and sharing insights. I would also like to show my gratitude to Sayyid and his family, as well as Nagah and her family, for providing me with a sense of belonging in Egypt. Since my research began in the late 1980s, I have always found their homes open and welcoming. Although this new topic was beyond the field of Sayyid's work, he has offered as much support and networking as possible. I am very grateful for this.

I would also like to express my appreciation for the reviewers and editors of the University of Texas Press, who—as always—have done a great job to improve the text. It is a great honor to have been working with the editors of the University of Texas Press for the fourth time!

Of course many people "at home" also—colleagues, relatives, and friends—have been important for completing this book. I would like to express my gratitude to my parents, who have always encouraged and enabled my academic career. My mother shared my happiness about the approval of the manuscript but was unfortunately not able to witness the actual launch. I know how happy she would have been for me. I am particularly grateful to my partner Hans Stukart. I am not only indebted for his assistance with many practical matters related to the book (and the family!), but likewise for his confidence. He is always full of pride with the birth of any new book or academic accomplishment. This encouragement and support are invaluable.

Performing Piety

Introduction

After conducting research in Egypt among singers and dancers of the Cairene street of entertainment, Muhammad 'Ali Street (Van Nieuwkerk 1995), I occasionally returned to visit friends. I particularly kept in contact with the family of my assistant Sayyid and my favorite dancer Ibtisam. After finishing fieldwork in 1989 I visited Ibtisam again in 1991. She was still active as a dancer in clubs and occasionally at weddings. She had tried to find other ways of earning money, for instance by opening a little shop for soft drinks in the basement of her house in the new district of Pyramid Street. She also sewed belly dancing costumes for other dancers and tried to establish herself as a teacher. But these activities did not provide her with sufficient means to raise her three daughters and two sons, for whom she had the sole responsibility after her divorce. The sign of the shop, *"Bint al-Balad,"* "daughter of the country," indicated the way she preferred to identify herself (see Van Nieuwkerk 1995, 111–116, 173–179) and was still on the wall outside the building. The eldest daughter, who at the time was one of the few veiled—and eventually face-veiled—young women originating from Muhammad 'Ali Street, was about to marry. The religious knowledge and veiling of Ibtisam's daughter were a source of pride to the family and the whole artists' community. "We are singers and dancers but know how to raise our children well" was the message they communicated, with Ibtisam's daughter as the prime example. Ibtisam's daughter gave her future husband a religious exam while I was having supper with Ibtisam and the mother of the bridegroom. He passed the exam, and they had a strict religious wedding without the customary form of entertainment such as belly dancing. In strict Islamic circles only religious songs, *anashid*, were permitted, accompanied by the *duff*, tambourine.

When I returned in 1996, I got lost in the neighborhood because of the large number of new buildings. I was eventually quite sure that I was facing the right building. I was hesitant, though, because instead of the "*Bint al-Balad*" sign there was an announcement on the door that "Sheikh Ahmad" lived there. Ibtisam's oldest son was named Ahmad, I remembered. No one was at home, and I asked people in the neighborhood whether Ibtisam was still living there. They queried me about Ibtisam's profession in order to find out whom I was looking for. I did not dare to mention her profession, particularly given the chance that it might taint her son's possible new reputation as a sheikh. I mentioned the names of her children instead. It took a while before the people were able to figure out who I was looking for, but fortunately someone knew Ibtisam as well as the place she was presently living: not that far away, on the other side of the crowded Pyramid Street. I found her at home, and she related that indeed her son Ahmad had become very religious. Besides working as a mechanic, he gave religious lessons. He was married, moved to another crowded part of the Pyramid district, and occasionally worked in Saudi Arabia to provide for his family. Ibtisam subrented the old house. She had stopped working as a dancer because she felt more and more uncomfortable under the religious pressure of her children. But before this pressure had forced her retirement, she had worn her shiny professional clothes under a black wide cloak when going out to work. This hypocrisy, coupled with her long-standing wish to step down from "the trade," had inclined her to respond positively to a marriage proposal. She continued sewing belly dancing costumes. I brought her the Dutch popularized version of my book featuring her prominently on the cover (Van Nieuwkerk 1996). She was initially shocked to see herself as a dancer again, but then started giggling, saying, "Was that me?!"

When I decided to do fieldwork in Egypt again after having done several studies in the Netherlands, I went to visit her in 2005. Living in an adjacent building, she appeared to have cut all ties with the entertainment trade. She started to follow religious classes and had visited Mecca the year before. Particularly the pilgrimage to Mecca had meant a lot to her religious commitment. She finally felt "purified" from all her former "sins" as a dancer. In the past, though she often complained about her difficult life and low status as a dancer, she always stressed that she loved dancing and actually was a talented dancer. She had always felt religious, but was not a regularly practicing Muslim, partly because she thought that her profession invalidated her prayers. She now severely regretted her former activities and regarded them as sinful. She also stopped sewing costumes, because she decided that if the profession is sinful for her, she should also not encourage others to continue dancing by sewing costumes or teaching them to dance. She still had suitcases full of costumes and suggested that maybe for non-Muslim dancers it was not sinful to dance. She asked me to sell the costumes abroad. With the money she would then be able to buy the dowry for her youngest daughter. She opened the suitcases and showed me about forty elaborate costumes. While spreading out a brown-gold costume, she picked up the accompanying dancing veil and remarked, "I can use this veil and change it into a *higab* to suit my new coat." The religious turn of Ibtisam, condensed and reflected in the decision to change the dancing veil into a headscarf, is, in a nutshell, what this study is about. The shifting use of the veil neatly portrays the influence of the "piety movement" on the field of art and entertainment. This personal story of creating a devout lifestyle transcends the artist's individual trajectory. The conversion also captures transformations in the religious climate in Egypt more generally.

Ibtisam is not an isolated case. When I was doing my fieldwork on Muhammad ʿAli Street, I interviewed several older former performers who, after long careers as a singer, dancer, or musician, decided to quit the trade and invest the time thus unencumbered in religious devotion. As with Ibtisam, a sense of guilt and trying to "make up for sins" were among the motivating sentiments, although on the whole they left the trade more because they had grown old and weary of the hardships of their profession than for religious reasons. After leaving the trade, though, they devoted their attention to the formerly neglected aspects of worship. This tendency to religious involvement in advanced age is not uncommon for many believers and certainly not for entertainers who feel they have been negligent in this respect.

Yet after I finished my research on female singers and dancers in Egypt, a new phenomenon was unfolding in the Egyptian scene of art and entertainment. Several famous singers, dancers, and acting stars suddenly left the scene in the early 1990s to devote themselves to religious study and worship. They were relatively young, still in the blossom of their careers, and working in the higher echelons of art. These celebrities were not facing the hardship of popular entertainers of Muhammad ʿAli Street, but left fame and richness for devotion. It was a different religious trajectory than I was acquainted with, because it apparently was more religiously motivated and meant a sudden rupture in their active professional lives. Besides, these famous performers were public personalities. Their stories were and are accordingly spread in the media and circulated on the Internet. Because of their high media profile, they are very influential as role models. Their life stories are followed by millions, and their sudden religious turn was shocking to secular fans and applauded by the fans who were influenced by the "Islamic Revival." Their personal decision to veil and to retire has accordingly had a huge impact on millions because of their status as stars. The importance of art and the film industry to Egypt's national interest and esteem further enhanced the sensitivity of this issue. Some of the performers eventually returned to the stage and screen in order to produce pious forms of art. The Egyptian government feared the religious power of the former celebrities and pious stars. I became intrigued by the life stories of these celebrities, the "repentant" artists, or "veiled" artists as they are often labeled in the media, and decided to have a closer look at this phenomenon.

In 2005, 2006, and 2008, and on two short visits in 2010 and 2011,[1] I returned to Egypt to study this new trend among famous performers: their motivations and stories, the impact of their pious turn, and the ensuing debates in the press among fans and critics, as well as their new productions. I started my research by returning to my acquaintances on Muhammad ʿAli Street to see if the phenomenon was unfolding in the lower echelons of art as well. It appeared that the scene of popular art had almost withered away. My former assistant Sayyid showed me around, and I had short conversations with many people in the street. The older generation of performers had kept their children out of the profession, and the trade was almost monopolized by "outsiders," developments which were already clearly discernible when I did my research between 1986 and 1989. Young dancers from outside the profession were now picked up by the "coiffeur," who also acted as impresario. Musicians were waiting idly in the few remaining coffee shops; their work had almost become redundant due to the introduction of the DJ at weddings. Instead of hosting a traditional wedding with popular artists in the streets and alleys of popular quarters, people danced to computer-based music in their homes or in clubs. Many performers had quit the profession but rarely because of religious reasons, although several cases of veiled female performers were brought to my attention.

I interviewed several of the veiled Muhammad ʿAli Street singers and dancers, but they all had stopped after a long professional career. Articulating their main reason for stepping down, they mentioned that they decided to "reject the trade before the trade rejected" them, indicating the difficultly for women to keep on working as performers in advanced age. They did not stop in the middle of their careers, because they simply could not afford to. Their experiences will not be central in the present study, but they indicate an important aspect of the pious turn of the stars: its class-based character. Popular performers might want to follow the example of stars—or not—yet their financial hardships do not allow for this step. So although my former acquaintances and friends from Muhammad ʿAli Street will not feature extensively in this book, they have provided me with an invaluable background for this research.

The phenomenon of the "repentant" artists and "veiled" actresses is thus a specific case study of middle- and upper-middle-class star performers. They are a small group of performers; yet as stars, they have had a great impact on millions. They have caused a great uproar in the field of art and in society at large. They were severely attacked by secularists and warmly embraced by Islamists who tried to capitalize on their stories to further their own visions for "the Egyptian Nation." I will start my analysis from the perspectives and the life stories of the retired performers themselves. Next, I will expand my analysis to the debates they have caused and finally to the various ways they have been influenced by and affected the "pietization" within Egypt more generally (Mahmood 2005; Turner 2008).

I have always felt that in writing the history of the entertainment trade, I was implicitly writing a history-in-miniature of Egypt more generally. The wider social, political, and religious developments have greatly impacted the field of art and entertainment: whether it was the ruler Muhammad ʿAli's opening to the West in 1834, which made him decide to banish all female dancers and singers to Upper Egypt, or Sadat's open-door policy in the mid-1970s, which caused a breakdown of the traditional monopoly of the community of entertainers of Muhammad ʿAli Street (Van Nieuwkerk 1995). So how has the pious climate that increasingly came to dominate the socioreligious landscape in Egypt since the 1980s affected the field of art and entertainment? How have the piety movement and different sociopolitical and religious developments in Egypt influenced artists and their artistic productions, and, conversely, how have the pious turns of celebrities affected the "pietization" in Egypt? At the level of the performers this study looks into questions such as: What is the reason behind so many celebrities' sudden decision to veil and to retire? How do they narrate these biographical turnarounds?[2] At the sociopolitical level it addresses the development of the piety movement and the changing discourses of sheikhs and scholars within the Islamist movements and their relationship with the state. Which competing views on religion, gender, and art have become hegemonic in the public arena from the 1980s onward? Can we discern a movement toward a post-Islamist public sphere? With regard to cultural-artistic issues the study investigates how the "repentance" and veiling of artists affect cultural production in present-day Egypt. Can we discern a "cultural sphere" (Van Nieuwkerk 2011a) in which aesthetics are developed in accordance with religious sensibilities? In that case, what are these "new Islamic aesthetics"? This book thus intends to portray a history of the religious revival in Egypt through the lens of the performing arts.

FIELDWORK AMONG CELEBRITIES

I first collected the names of the pious stars and reconstructed the history of retirement of the celebrities through media sources: actress Shams al-Barudi and her husband the actor Hassan Yusif had retired already in 1982, followed by the famous singer Shadia in 1986 and dancer Hala al-Safi in 1987. Around that time also actress Hana' Tharwat and her husband, actor Muhammad al-ʿArabi, retired, followed by actress Nisrin and her husband the actor Muhsin Muhiy al-Din, the singer Yasmin al-Khiyyam, and TV presenter Kamilia al-ʿArabi. From the early 1990s onward, especially after the earthquake of October 1992, a "caravan" of actresses, singers, and dancers stepped down: actresses ʿAfaf Shoʿib, Shahira, and Madiha Hamdi in 1992, and in 1993 comedienne Soheir al-Babli, together with the actresses Soheir Ramzi, Farida Saif al-Nasr, and Sawsan Badr, and dancer Sahar Hamdi. In the second half of the 1990s, another wave of young actresses and singers veiled and retired: the singers Mona ʿAbd al-Ghani and Hanan, actresses ʿAbir Sharqawi, ʿAbir Sabri, Miyar al-Bablawi, Sabrin, and lately Hanan Turk. Other cases were reported in the media as well, such as Hala Sheikha, Mona Liza, Mirna al-Muhandis, Ghada ʿAdil, and Wafa ʿAmir. Probably there are more performers who retired, but they received less media attention. I thus started to collect material about thirty "repentant," or veiled, artists.

After collecting the names and having a general idea about their stories, I tried to interview the "repentant" artists. It proved rather difficult to reach the famous former performers and to conduct interviews with the celebrities. Research among celebrities is quite different from doing interviews among the lesser stars, such as Muhammad ʿAli Street entertainers. I tried to reach the stars by means of the performers I knew, but none was "star" enough to be able to bring me into contact with them. The former dancer Hala al-Safi, for instance, began her career on Muhammad ʿAli Street and used to work with my former assistant's brother, who is a popular *tabla* player. They knew where she was living and could provide me with her address, but were reluctant to introduce me to her. They gave two reasons. First, Hala al-Safi had become such a celebrity that the social distance between them had become too big to visit her as "old friends." Second, her "repentance" made former colleagues insecure about whether they could drop by, because they were still working in the "shameful" trade.

I thus had to look for different ways of being introduced. Ibtisam's husband works at a subsection of the trade union of media employees and offered to help me. He gave me the address of the studio of Hassan Yusif, the husband of Shams al-Barudi. So I walked over to their place and had an interesting chat with his brother. He gave me the telephone number of singer-actress Mona ʿAbd al-Ghani, and he would ask his brother as well. I also went to the trade union of actors and was given an appointment with the 2005 head of the trade union, actor Yusif Shaʿban. I met him at the actors' club along the river Nile and was interrogated. I had to prove that I was not a spy from Bush or Sharon. Although this gave me a laughing fit, it was serious business. Conspiracy theories about spies infiltrating the art scene in order to destroy Egypt's primacy in art were looming large. As I was to learn later, not only "Americans" and "Jews," but also "radical Islamists" and "Salafi Saudis," were conspiring against the Egyptian art scene. The head of the trade union thus had to be sure about my intentions before he could provide me with telephone numbers and addresses. I managed to convince him I was an innocent anthropologist. I was given a contact at the union who could provide me with telephone numbers of actors or actresses I wanted to interview. The old generation of artists who had retired in the early 1980s and were out of touch with the art scene were out of his reach though.

I managed to collect several telephone numbers, but not a personal introduction. Although I could use Yusif Shaʿban as the person who provided me with their numbers, I had to convince the actors myself to have an interview with me. This, of course, was not an easy matter; most of them were either busy or traveling, or I had to call them next week, next month, etc. Some of them clearly did not want to have an interview at all, although they were too polite to tell me directly. Shams al-Barudi and her husband, as I was to learn later from a friend who is an Egyptian journalist, did not want to be interviewed by a non-Muslim, because they were convinced Westerners do not understand Islam and misrepresent Islam. After several phone calls it was agreed that I could send them my questions, which were never answered. Former actress Hanaʾ Tharwat, whom I called, first wanted to do an "*istikhara*" prayer, the special prayer in which God is consulted about whether an intended action is the right thing to do. If the answer was positive she would phone me back. Nothing came of it. Also when I called her the year after, she first wanted to do *istikhara*, which also did not yield any positive results for me. The celebrities with whom I managed to establish contacts were forced by their busy schedules to delay appointments several times. I sometimes felt like a paparazzo, chasing celebrities for the latest gossip. Although this was not my intention, from their point of view the distinction between a pulp journalist and a serious researcher is nil.

I eventually managed to meet and interview actress ʿAfaf Shoʿib at her home, and I was invited to visit her again to discuss in more detail her religious views. Actresses ʿAbir Sabri, Miyar al-Bablawi, and ʿAbir Sharqawi received me in their homes as well. Singer-actress Mona ʿAbd al-Ghani, singer Hanan, and dancer Amira are close friends, and I met them several times at one of the many "Islamic salons" that Amira, among others, organized in the posh neighborhood Muhandisin. I visited actress Madiha Hamdi and singer Yasmin al-Khiyyam at their charity organizations in Pyramid Street and 6th October City, respectively. Actress Sawsan Badr and Soheir al-Babli I interviewed in the studio during work, as I also tried to do with Sabrin. Only Soheir al-Babli really had time for an interview, whereas with Sawsan Badr I only had a short chat during her break. With the dancers Hala al-Safi and Niʿma al-Mukhtar, however, I had lengthy talks in their homes. After several failed appointments, I finally managed to interview Shahira at her villa in the Pyramid district. Retirement from art for religious reasons is not an all-female affair, although women form the majority and received the greatest media attention. Several men stepped down as well or decided to produce religious art or at least productions that do not go against religious sensibilities, such as Hassan Yusif. I interviewed the singers Ahmad al-Kahlawi and Mustafa Mahmud, actor Wagdi al-ʿArabi, and playwright, actor, and media man Ahmad Abu Haiba.

It not only took an enormous amount of time to arrange interviews with the celebrities, the interviews were also more formal than I was used to. They would certainly not speak their true minds and dealt with me as with any inquisitive journalist to whom they had told their stories before. Some of them preferred the interviews not to be recorded. The method of participant-observation, informal talks, joining them in daily activities — what I used with the Muhammad ʿAli Street performers — was impossible with the busy stars. Merely the simple fact that I mentioned the stars' names, or stage names, indicates already the difference between the research on Muhammad ʿAli Street and the present study. Where before I conformed to the anthropologist's usage of concealing the informants' identities — Ibtisam is accordingly a fictive name — the celebrities are not intending to conceal identities. On the contrary, they carefully orchestrate their public images.

Whereas all people "perform" their identities, embellish their life stories, present their choices as quite rational and coherent, etc., viewing them from the perspective of participant-observation provides glimpses at ambiguities, discrepancies, or straightforward contradictions. For instance, the self-presentation of popular singers and dancers as respectable women by denying any connection with "indecent" behavior such as drinking, flirting, or making obscene movements could be easily verified by observing their behavior on stage or traveling with them to weddings. With the religious stars I had to rely on their cautiously constructed and performed identities. In addition, they were promoted as lofty models of Islam by the Islamist press and as ideal representatives of "the Islamic woman." Moreover, since their behavior is watched and judged by millions, they themselves also felt a heavy responsibility to keep up their pious profile. Due to their "public and moral accountability," the pious stars were strongly aware that they had to uphold this presentation of moral virtue or at least should not publicly show any "breaches" that would be considered offensive to Islam. Accordingly, I could mainly collect material that gave insight into their self-presentations and religious discourses about virtuous selves.

As Schielke (2009) rightly observes, studies on Muslim piety have until now particularly analyzed the ideals and paradigmatic representatives of the piety movement. For that reason most studies do no justice to the "flaws of perfection" in everyday life and the ambivalent contradictory practice that can be the outcome of the striving for religious self-formation (2009, 34). In this study I also analyze epitomes of pious ideals, perhaps even more so because of the self-reported responsibility they feel as the public face of Muslim ideals for women. Thus, we have to study the material for what it is: discourses and self-presentation probably favoring coherence, ideals, and perfection, and not everyday experiences revealing "ambivalence, inconsistencies, and realistic imperfections." The staged presentations and constructed narratives provide insight into ideals and imaginations rather than daily realities. These ideals and imaginations are also reflected in the debates between Islamists and secularists about the veiled stars. The stars became touchstones for discussing the "moral good" in Islam and the favored direction for the Egyptian nation. Islamic morality and ideals were also acted out in the pious productions with which they made a comeback. Hence in this study I do not only deal with a small and specific group of (upper)-middle-class performers, but also with staged personae representing contested religious and nationalist worldviews. Yet, despite these disclaimers, it should be realized that the pious stars are quite powerful role models and moral touchstones that have a great bearing on everyday practices of large audiences. As models for emulation they present moral standards with which millions of fans—and critics—engage themselves.

Besides conducting interviews with the stars—which in broad strokes confirmed the stories I had read—I rummaged through religious book markets to search for the many booklets on the "repentant" artists and old magazines featuring their stories. I found the autobiographies of Shams al-Barudi and Kariman Hamza and many booklets in which the celebrities' stories of "repentance" were detailed. The genre of the "repentance" literature proved highly interesting in itself. I browsed around the archives of *al-Ahram* and

Dar al-Kutub to collect material about the reception of and debates on this phenomenon in the Islamist and secular press. It became clear that in the meantime many changes had occurred in the field of art. The profiled sheikhs who inspired the artists to retire had changed from conservative sheikhs such as Sheikh al-Sha'arawi and Dr. 'Umar 'Abd al-Kafi to young lay preachers such as 'Amr Khalid. The religious discourse on art transformed as well from "*haram* except" into "*halal* if"—that is, the starting point among several religious scholars fundamentally changed from prohibiting art to declaring it permissible, albeit conditionally. Therefore, I decided to study the changing religious discourse on art as well and asked the celebrities for their sources of inspiration on art and religion. I bought the books and audiotapes of the sheikhs they mentioned. I also collected quite a few recorded TV interviews with the veiled celebrities, such as Soheir al-Babli on 'Amr Khalid's talk show, and a videotape series in which 'Afaf Sho'ib, Zizi Mustafa, Hamdi Hafiz, and Madiha Hamdi tell their stories to 'Aliya Go'ar, a poetess who allegedly was influential in Shadia's withdrawal from art. This video series was banned in Egypt and produced in Saudi Arabia. Kamilia al-'Arabi, 'Abir Sabri, Hanan, and others were also interviewed on TV, and an Egyptian journalist friend provided me with a copy of these interviews.

It became clear in the midst of my research on the retired celebrities that many of them were actually trying or planning to make a comeback. Most of them had intentions of, or were involved already in, producing religious talk shows, historical plays about the golden age of Islam, religious soaps, pious songs such as *anashid*, and songs suitable for Islamic weddings. Whereas until the 1990s this had not been an easy matter, at the turn of the century the market for pious art had grown considerably, providing several pious performers with a specific market segment. For instance, in 2006, many veiled stars returned to produce Ramadan soaps, and it was a productive year for Islamic wedding songs as well. I decided to follow the "repentant" stars' new venture into pious art as well. I had a look at some of their productions and discussed them with fans and critics. In addition, I visited several Islamic weddings and interviewed the bandleaders and members of religious wedding bands. I also became interested in the discussions on "art with a mission" among Islamists, the discourse that intended to bridge art and religion, and encouraged the development of art that accords with religious sensibilities. I interviewed art journalists and film directors in favor of, or highly critical about, this "*fann al-hadif*" project.

The research thus developed over three periods of fieldwork that will also more or less structure the framework of the book. In the first part, "The 1980s: Celebrating Piety," I will highlight the narratives of the celebrities who retired in the 1980s and early 1990s. I will describe their spiritual journeys and elaborate their dreams and visions. The relationship of repentance and piety will be highlighted, as well as the intricate connection of the pious stars with the piety movement more generally. They were not only affected by the Islamic Revival in Egypt, but were influential in furthering this "pietization" among their fans, including the wealthy, relatively secular strata of Egyptian society (Van Nieuwkerk 2008b). On a more general analytical level, the importance of celebrities for the (religious) identifications of fans will be elaborated.

In the second part, "The 1990s: Debating Religion, Gender, and the Performing Arts in the Public Sphere," I will look at the discussions in the public sphere that took place in the mid-1990s, when the "caravan" of retired artists reached such a critical mass that it greatly disturbed the secular field of art, and the regime. I will provide some spiritual stories of veiled actresses of this period and look into the debates that their decision sparked in the media. I will analyze the way the "repentance" of artists was capitalized upon by the Islamist press and fulminated against by the secular critics. The coverage on the veiled celebrities in the public sphere, whether through TV, tapes, booklets, or magazines, will be central in this part. On a more theoretical level, I will delve into the contested place of Islam, gender, and art within the deliberations on and imaginings of "the nation" in the Egyptian public sphere of this period.

In the third part, "The New Millennium: Performing Piety," the comeback of the veiled stars will be central. The Islamist project of "art with a mission" will be analyzed. In Part Three some attempts to produce pious arts, such as religious soaps and religious wedding songs, will be highlighted. I will deal with the reception of these pious productions by fans and critics. Also the tremendous difficulties female celebrities encounter when they try to perform "pleasurable forms of pious arts" will be analyzed. On a more theoretical level the transformation of religious ethics into aesthetics will be discussed. The gendered nature of performing piety and the centrality of the body and the senses are central issues in the development of Islamic aesthetics. I will also investigate the influence of market forces on pious art productions and the development of "Islam lite"—that is, consumable versions. I will analyze the ambiguous outcome of the pious art project and discuss whether the greater effect has been to Islamize (popular) art or to popularize Islam.

Thus, this study has a historical and thematic trajectory, moving from the piety movement in the 1980s, to the emergence of a polemic public sphere in which secularists and Islamists debate Islam, art, and gender in the 1990s, to the production of pious performances after the turn of the century. From a study on "repentance" and "born-again" artists, the research grew into a project on social, religious, and political transformations in Egypt. It particularly examines the transformation of the Islamist movements through the lens of performing arts. Each chapter starts with a spiritual biography of one of the pious celebrities. The second section of each chapter deals with a specific analysis of the main themes: piety (Part One), the public sphere (Part Two), and religious ethics and aesthetics (Part Three). The final section of each chapter tries to link the biography and specific analysis with more general developments in the Islamist movement in Egypt during the last three decades. I thus try to interweave the personal narratives of the artists with the social, religious, and political changes by which they are influenced and which they have helped to bring about. I thus intend to give an intimate account of a specific history of the last thirty years in two fields that have a tremendous importance for Egypt: its art productions and the growing piety among its populace.

The 1980s

CELEBRATING PIETY

C elebrities reflect, reinforce, and have the power to transform the social, political, and cultural context in which they live. They are icons and trendsetters. Stars are not only entertainers, but also idols, models, and educators. They celebrate and legitimate certain lifestyles. Celebrities thus have a great impact on public consciousness and debate. Celebrities and celebrity culture have a cultural pervasiveness and have become integrated extensively into daily life (Turner 2004, 17). The huge importance of celebrities for everyday life is expressed in the concept of celebrification. Initially developed by Gamson (1994) to indicate the use by politicians of Hollywood presentational skills and codes, the concept has been widened by Rojek (2001). According to Rojek: "Celebrification proposes that ordinary identity formation and general forms of social interaction are patterned and inflected by the styles, embodied attitudes and conversational flows developed through celebrity culture" (2001, 16).

Celebrities have been studied as personifications of inauthentic media constructs and as superficial fabrications. Celebrity culture has been analyzed as a "pseudo-event" entirely staged by mass-mediated popular culture (see also Turner 2004, 5). Marshall (1997) and Turner (2004), though, have analyzed celebrities and celebrity culture as prime locations for the construction of cultural identity and as forms of cultural power. Celebrities not only influence lifestyle, fashion, consumption patterns, and cultural identity, but have also increasingly become touchstones for discussing political, social, and moral issues (Van den Bulck and Tambuyzer 2008). Celebrities are involved in political activities, fund-raising, and welfare, a development that Turner (2004) labels the "celebritisation" of politics. Celebrity culture is also an arena in which media and public engage in ethical discussions and negotiations. In the media, celebrities are no longer merely analyzed as "trivial" representatives of popular culture, they also figure in public discourses on ethical self-making and social engagements. The Egyptian stars are a clear example of this development. By veiling, distancing themselves from "immoral" arts, and promoting veiling and pious lifestyles, they have become a central means for discussing moral and religious issues in Egypt.

Most of the Egyptian performers with whom this book is concerned are celebrities. The literature sometimes distinguishes among celebrities, stars, and personalities. Stars are mainly related to the film industry and personalities to TV, whereas celebrity is a more generic term. Most of my Egyptian informants were stars, although it is not up to me to decide whether they belong—or used to belong—to the A, B, or C level within the Egyptian star system, and some have returned as veiled TV personalities. Most of them have been able to retain fame even after veiling, retiring, or (re)turning to the production of pious arts. According to some journalists, these activities have even added to their renown. Whereas I will use insights from celebrity studies, this book is not intended as research on celebrity culture as such. I will not delve into the historical process by which celebrities have become powerful as role models; rather, I will work from that assumption to investigate what changing messages and models they provide for emulation by discerning audiences. I am particularly interested in the ways they have come to celebrate piety and how they use their fame to spread a pious discourse and lifestyle. I will thus provide a specific example of the "celebritisation of piety."

Rojek (2001) distinguishes several approaches in the field of celebrity studies. These are subjectivism, structuralism, and poststructuralism. Subjectivist accounts of celebrities focus on the personal characteristics of stars and locate their fame in their unique talents. These studies often take the form of biographies of celebrities. I will also use a biographical approach and start every chapter with a life story of one of the stars. The performers' own narratives will be reconstructed based on personal interviews and media sources. However, I will focus on their religious transformations rather than their professional careers. I will briefly describe the way they have become star performers and provide some information on their professional lives, but I will particularly outline their spiritual journeys. For that reason I use the notion of spiritual biography instead of life story. The spiritual stories of the performers and their careers, though, are interwoven: their professional lives show radical ruptures and transformations upon their repentance and veiling. The performers' narratives on religious transformations will be deconstructed, and the devotional imagery will be analyzed. Their biographies will not merely be treated as unique expressions of individual personalities, but be situated in the changing social, cultural, and religious context of Egypt.

Structuralist studies of celebrities particularly concentrate on the inter-relations between stars and the social structures of society. Several structural-ist approaches have been developed in order to understand the development toward celebrity culture, but generally it is analyzed as a form of social con-trol. Several authors point to the powerful economic reach of the cultural and entertainment industries, particularly through mass consumption and pro-cesses of commoditization. They highlight the dominant ideologies dissemi-nated through celebrity culture and the various forms of subjectivities that are articulated and legitimated through celebrities. Forms of self-discipline and government are accomplished by providing role models and moral scripts. Marshall (1997), for instance, sees celebrity culture as an attempt to contain the masses by presenting preferred models of subjectivity with which audi-ences are encouraged to identify. Celebrities embody norms of individuality and personality within a given culture, subject positions that audiences can adopt or adapt (1997, 65).

These insights are important and also inform my analyses. I will analyze the debates on the celebrities and show how they have become the favored role models for the Islamist press to encourage piety among women. Yet this theoretical view lacks a dynamic approach. I rather analyze the transforma-tions within the lives of the stars and illustrate that celebrities are not attached to a fixed script or moral model but to multiple and contested models of subjectivities. From hegemonic secular forms of governmentality, the reli-gious stars have become part of Islamist counterhegemonic discourses and subjectivities. My approach does not deny the importance of social control over celebrities and affirms their powerful influence as role models over fans, but especially inquires into the changing, flexible, and contested character of power and social control. Where once models of fabulous fashion, the Egyp-tian "repentant" artists have become promoters of the veil. In the meantime, the veil has turned into a fashionable commodity as well. This is partly due to the new pious role models provided by the stars, which in turn transformed the form, meaning, and image of the veil.

Poststructuralist studies on celebrities and celebrity culture examine the codes of representation by which the star image is reproduced, developed, and consumed. Neither star biographies nor the social structures of society sufficiently explain the image, power, and influence of celebrities. Using a dispersed view of power, these studies concentrate on the way star images are modified by the mass media and by the active engagement of the audi-ence. In these studies, an intertextual approach is used by looking into films, biographies, autobiographies, interviews, critical studies, fanzines, and news-paper articles to analyze how celebrity images are produced and consumed.

Or in Rojek's formulation: "Post-structuralism both centres consciousness on the performer and decentres that consciousness by relating the presence and meaning of celebrity to a developing field of interests" (2001, 45). Celebrity is understood as a developing, relational field of power, and the flexibility of star images is emphasized. In my study also the transformations in the star images are essential, but one caveat is in order. I will particularly concentrate on the change toward piety and not that much on my subjects' changing images as stars. I will investigate the dynamics of the religious power of the stars.

The poststructuralist approach is important because it emphasizes that neither are the celebrities static icons, nor the fans passive consumers. They are what Turner (2004) calls "productive consumers." The star representations are mass-mediated and transformed. The audience also actively engages in consuming and selecting images and preferable lifestyle models. Barbas (2001), for instance, details that fans significantly influenced Hollywood and used their economic power as consumers to change the filmmaking process. I did not extensively study fans, and certainly not fans of particular celebrities, but I did discuss pious art productions with some fans. While talking with "pious consumers," it became clear that they were not only highly critical of mainstream "lowbrow" productions, but also of some of the "preachy" pious productions. The growing pious sensibilities among the Egyptian audiences and the emergence of pious taste cultures set in motion new demands in the art and entertainment market. The power of audiences to change directions in popular culture and entertainment also influenced the pious producers toward developing more pleasurable formats.

All three approaches, particularly poststructuralism, emphasize the centrality of the mass media. It is agreed upon that the growth of celebrity culture is intimately related to the spread of the mass media, particularly the visual media (Turner 2004, 10). The relationship between celebrities and mass media is a complex and reciprocal one in which economic interests play an important role as well. Mass media are the means by which stars present their changing image, by which these images are transformed in the public arena, as well as the means by which these (re)presentations are consumed and evaluated by different audiences. I will not deal with the "celebritariat" (Rojek 2001)—that is, all those involved in the mass media to fabricate and safeguard star images. Celebrity image-making and celebrity culture as such are not the focus in this book. I instead analyze what happens if stars suddenly turn pious and use their fame to spread pious lifestyles. How is this received and assessed in the mass media? The mediascape in Egypt, which is largely secular, is under strict state censorship. Yet due to the development of new media technology and satellite TV, religious media have become influential as well. They have become important channels for celebrating piety. The media have thus become a rather fragmented field. I will use different media sources to reconstruct the debates on the "repentant" artists and to evaluate the pious productions. It will become clear that the Egyptian public sphere is not a monolith, but consists of several competing parties and audiences that use the celebrities to discuss their normative views.

CELEBRITY AND PIETY

Research about celebrity and religion is relatively scarce (Rojek 2001 and 2006; Possamai 2005; Bakas and Buwalda 2006). Most attention has been given to the way devotion toward certain idols is close to religious worship. Death rituals and pilgrimages to burial sites such as to Elvis Presley's Graceland or the obsessive quest for reliquaries of the famous are clear examples of this devotion. Also public confessions by fallen stars—whether related to sexual abuse, drug addiction, or alcoholism—and the ritual of redemption to regain acceptability among fans have been given attention (Rojek 2001, 2006). Less attention has been given to idols who have turned religious. Although Madonna's interest in the Kabbalah, Tom Cruise's attachment to the Scientology Church, and rapper Kanye West's Christian lifestyle are known, they remain famous as performers rather than as religious personalities. Televangelists who have become celebrities have been given attention as well. Rojek analyzed to what extent the celebrity culture can be studied as a response of secular society to the decline of institutionalized religion. He sees a partial convergence and argues that organized religion has borrowed some of the forms and styles of celebrity culture. Celebrity culture also raises intense devotion and identifications. It is thus one of the possible secular replacements for a declining organized religion. Yet it forms a fragmented and unstable culture that is not able to sustain a grounded spiritual order (2006, 416–417).

This study about Egyptian pious (ex-)performers intends to add to the understanding of celebrity culture and religion in specific ways. It will particularly focus on the religious power of the celebrities. Some stars have now started careers as presenters of religious TV programs and have come close to the status of televangelists, while others have (re)turned to pious performing arts. Yet many of them have become famous for their piety rather than their performances. The Egyptian stars publicly confessed and repented of "their sins"—that is, working in the field of art and entertainment. Several of them initially intended to break with their lives as media stars. Their cases present an attempt at a qualitative turn away from the former source of fame toward another spring of values. They deliberately moved from the "secular" culture of celebrity into the "spiritual" domain of organized religion.[1] Yet the pious turn and journey to devotion became a topic of great media attention, and they have accordingly remained in the spotlight as public personalities. Some of them actively sought media attention to further the Islamic cause. On the one hand, the pious stars are part of the broader piety movement and reflect general religious developments. On the other hand, as celebrities, they have reinforced the Islamic Revival and helped to spread piety to the higher echelons of Egyptian society. By moving devotion up the social scales, they have influenced and reshaped devotion among members of the piety movement.

The Islamic Revival and piety movement in Egypt have been extensively studied by Mahmood (2001a, 2001b, 2005), Hirschkind (2001, 2006), Starrett (1995b, 1998), Wickham (2002), Bayat (1998, 2002a, 2002b, 2005a, 2005b, 2007b), and others. They point to the growing religiosity among the Egyptian populace. Instead of focusing on "political Islam," "Islamic fundamentalism," or "Islamism," they study the broad piety movement among different layers of society. It is fragmented and not a corporate organization, but rather to be understood as a dispersed movement. It consists of various activities and initiatives aimed at placing religion at the center of moral consciousness and action. The growing number of preachers, among them women trained in Islamic *daʿwah* institutes, invite people to religious reflection and incorporation of piety in daily life. Their views are disseminated by sermons, mediated by TV, the Internet, and cassettes. Theirs is a pedagogical project rather than an overtly political movement. It is aimed at ethically and morally reconstituting the self and the body and less focused on social and religious transformation of the body politic. The piety movement does not simply preach obeisance to religious rules and regulations as a purpose in itself, but promotes the formation of a pious self through the habituation of religious practices. As we will see, the pious artists provide clear examples of this process of ethical self-making.

Pious transformations usually have a radical effect on the everyday life of believers because they are encouraged to adapt their habits and lifestyle. Or, as Bryan Turner puts it, devotees are encouraged "to transform their habitus or dispositions and tastes towards the material world. Piety is about the construction of definite and distinctive life styles of new religious tastes and preferences" (2008, 2). It involves a pietization of the everyday world. The notions "pietization of everyday life" and "religious taste cultures" are interesting for the case studies I present. They draw attention to the all-encompassing and deep-seated character of the transformations in people's lives, involving minute details of their daily repertoires and comportment. We will come across many examples of radical transformations in the artists' lives in line with a pious habitus and religious sensibilities.

Bryan Turner (2008) describes piety as excellence in religious activities. Inculcating pious dispositions needs training in religious excellence, particularly in the sphere of morality. In the language of Foucault (2003), piety can be perceived as a technology of the self for producing religious excellence or virtues. Piety is described by the women of the Egyptian mosque movement as the "quality of 'being close to God': a manner of being and acting that suffuses all of one's acts, both religious and worldly in character" (Mahmood 2005, 122). Most women I interviewed used this expression to explain their understanding of piety: being close to God; love, devotion, and obeisance to God, as well as keeping away from everything that would displease God. They describe a state in which they continuously reflect on every single act as to whether it will please or displease God. It is thus close to fear of God. *Taqwa*, piety or devotion, is accordingly both love and fear of God (Mahmood 2005, 145). Virtuous behavior should be trained and become a natural and permanent part of a person's character. The body is the site for moral training and cultivation of the pious self. Like other members of the piety movement, the ex-performers try to reach complete *iltizam*, or (religious) commitment. Some of the ex-performers preferred to be labeled *fannanat multazimat* (from *iltizam*), but this label was not current.

In most cases the journey of Egyptian artists toward piety was combined with repentance, a strong feeling of remorse and regret about former activities. *Tawba*, repentance, or turning back to God, calls for a deliberate reassessment of one's priorities and values (Renard 2008, 43). It is close to the experience of conversion, reversion, or being born again. It can be gradual or more dramatic, but usually leads to a major refocusing of spiritual life. In the traditional Islamic hagiographical literature that is the topic of Renard's study, the conversion experience of the prophets and saints is often followed by a life of asceticism or withdrawal from life (*ʿuzla*), intensity of fasting, and generosity in charitable donations. The artists with whom this study is concerned are not only labeled *taʾibat* (from *tawba*, repentance), but also *muʿtazilat* (from *ʿuzla*). I will outline the artists' journey toward piety and ethical self-making in more detail in Chapter 1.

The stories of the "repentant" artists do not only illustrate forms of personal piety. The narratives also shed light on forms of engaged public piety (Deeb 2006). After gaining religious illumination, many artists have become active in *daʿwah*, Islamic outreach, and some have even turned into lecturers and preachers. *Daʿwah* is aimed at the renewal of faith by providing religious knowledge and the means to train pious dispositions. Organizing or, in some cases, giving religious lectures and religious education have been important ways of transforming the artists' selves and the selves of others. Their pious journeys thus contain clear elements of public outreach. Repentance, conversion, and striving for moral perfection through religious education and forms of *da'wah* will be central in Chapter 2.

Besides personal and public devotion, visible piety is another dimension of *taqwa*. Visible piety in the form of veiling has been an important moment in the female artists' pious journeys. The third label used for this group of female performers is *fannanat muhagabat*, veiled artists. Donning the veil was a crucial step toward complete *iltizam*, religious commitment. The veil not only signals the break with their former activities, but also constitutes a way of embodying the new self. Veiling keeps them straight on the pious path, prevents a relapse to former ways, and is an important means to cultivate a virtuous self. It is a way to train and habituate pious dispositions. Veiling, as Mahmood (2001a) has argued, should neither been understood exclusively in terms of submission nor of resistance. It should be comprehended as a modern and embodied form of piety that empowers women. Veiling has allowed women access to public spaces and fields from which they were previously barred such as religious education and instruction. Most artists became active advocates of the veil and helped spread the veil to the upper classes by preaching or inviting preachers to their homes at their "Islamic salons." They have become active agents of piety and moving forces in the pietization of the upper classes. They showed that piety is compatible with modern, urban lifestyles (Turner 2008, 5; Deeb 2006). The visibility and public demonstration of piety by veiling have drawn extensive attention from scholars. Yet women's charity is also an important way by which women's piety is brought into the public realm (Deeb 2006; Hafez 2003). Many women, the retired performers included, are actively engaged in religiously inspired charity and volunteerism. For middle- and upper-class women Yasmin al-Khiyyam, a former singer and present director of a huge charity organization in 6th of October City, provided a clear example of public piety. The importance of veiling and charity in attaining religious excellence and embodying piety will be the topic of Chapter 3.

Part One thus intends to follow the trajectories of pious artists, from their spiritual experiences, through learning, education, and pious instruction, to veiling and religious activism. It will analyze these different dimensions of piety against the backdrop of the general transformations in the socioreligious landscape of Egypt from the 1980s until the early 1990s.

1.1. *Former actress Shahira (gift of Shahira to the author)*

ONE

Dreams, Spirituality, and the Piety Movement

I n this chapter, I will present the life story of former actress Shams al-Barudi. Her story exemplifies a spiritual trajectory toward a pious lifestyle in which dreams and visions play a key role. The role of visions and dreams in the pietization of everyday life more generally will be dealt with in the second section. The final section provides background information on the development of the piety movement in Egypt in the early 1980s.

THE SPIRITUAL BIOGRAPHY OF ACTRESS SHAMS AL-BARUDI

Shams al-Barudi was the first famous performer to step down and veil in 1982.[1] I tried to interview her and went to the Islamic film company of her husband, Hassan Yusif. Although I had an interesting chat with Hassan Yusif's brother, Shams al-Barudi and Hassan Yusif were not willing to grant me an interview (for a picture of her, see the book cover shown in Figure 6.2). Later I had an introduction by actress 'Afaf Sho'ib and spoke to Shams al-Barudi on the phone. She would consider my request, but when I phoned her again she refused to be interviewed. She extensively questioned me about the theory I was going to use. The answer that my research was not about theories but about life stories of retired actresses was apparently not convincing. Later an Egyptian journalist friend explained that she and her husband did not want to speak to non-Muslims because the latter usually misunderstood and misrepresented Islam. As we will see, Shams al-Barudi and her "repentant" colleagues were regularly attacked in the secular press. She had accordingly become rather selective about whom to grant an interview.

The religious magazine *al-Nur* was among those selected as friendly, and she gave a lengthy interview telling her story of "guidance and repentance." This story was printed as a booklet entitled *Rihlati min al-dhulamat ila al-nur / My Journey from Darkness to the Light*, with an introduction by the Islamic preacher Zeinab al-Ghazali. This story circulates with some minor changes in several books.[2] Besides that, there are several other interviews in newspapers and magazines, most of which are collected in the book *Awraq Shams al-Barudi / The Dossier of Shams al-Barudi*, compiled by Siraj al-Din (1993). I will particularly use the parts that are traceable as views and opinions of Shams al-Barudi herself. Shams al-Barudi did not object to the word "repentance"—while some of her retired colleagues felt offended by the term—therefore I will use the word repentance without quotation marks.[3]

Shams al-Barudi was born in 1945, in a small village to the south of Cairo, and moved to Helwan at the age of five (Siraj al-Din 1993, 11). She described her parents as religious with a "simple ordinary form of religiosity" (*al-Nur*, February 10, 1998). She went to the preparatory and secondary school in Helwan. During her school career she enjoyed singing and acting, and participated in school contests (Siraj al-Din 1993, 12). After finishing her secondary school, she preferred to go to the law faculty or the Institute for Fine Arts, but the grades of her final exam did not allow for that. She entered the academy of dramatic art instead. She did not finish, because she started working before her graduation. In an interview with *al-Nur* that she gave shortly after her repentance, she stressed that she never dreamt of a career as an actress. She felt she was pushed into the profession, although she was also drawn to fame and glory. She explained this attraction as a lack of religious education and blamed the educational system for not teaching religion as a central topic.

Shams al-Barudi briefly worked for TV and soon after featured in several films. From the late 1960s onward, she worked in about thirty films. Most of her roles are characterized as seductive, and she is compared to Marilyn Monroe.[4] In 1972, she married the actor and director Hassan Yusif and worked with him. They were divorced for a few months but remarried. In interviews Hassan Yusif explained that the marital problems were related to Shams al-Barudi's work. He was not convinced that the genre she was specialized in was a form of art (Nasif and Khodayr n.d., 59). He preferred her to stay at home, particularly after the birth of their first two children.[5] The story of Shams al-Barudi's withdrawal from acting is usually concentrated on her *'umrah*, lesser pilgrimage, in 1982, which I will detail below. Yet, in the period before her pilgrimage, two other themes appear influential in her decision to retire. First, she increasingly felt uncomfortable with the attention that was attached mainly to her appearance instead of her talent. Second, she felt that her duties as a wife and a mother conflicted with her work as an actress.

With regard to the first theme she later reflected: "I felt that it was my beauty that brought me work in acting. When I started to refuse roles that were concentrated on the beauty that God had blessed me with, my work started to decrease" (Siraj al-Din 1993, 56). She felt there was a division between her real personality and the roles in which she acted. She had the feeling that she had "to step out of her skin." She likened this period to a coma and said she felt duped (Siraj al-Din 1993, 56).[6] When her daughter brought home a booklet with poems she was struck by a poem about the veil:

> I was at home preparing sweets when my little daughter Nariman came in. She was happy carrying her schoolbag. She kissed me and I hugged her lovingly to my breast. She said, "Mom, Mom, look at the present my teacher gave me for getting good grades." She was talking about a book of poetry. I kissed her and took the book from her. I skimmed through it and my eyes stopped at one poem that began this way: "Let them talk about my veil, I swear to God I don't care / My religion has protected me with the veil and deemed me lawful / Shyness will always be my makeup and modesty my capital."[7]

According to Nasif and Khodayr's reconstruction of the story, the same poet also quoted the verse "They cheated her by saying she is beautiful, the beautiful are duped with praise." Shams al-Barudi continued:

> When I read those verses I had a strange feeling. I sat down wearily and found tears falling from my eyes. I repeated what I'd just read. I said to myself, modesty and bashfulness don't describe me so I don't have any capital. At this moment I realized the secret behind the continuous anxiety that had spoiled the happy moments of my life. Those who told me that I was an actress of great beauty had cheated me. Those who had put my picture on the covers of magazines and in their pages had duped. It struck me in the heart and after that my life changed completely. I started hating acting and art. My pictures on the billboards disgusted me. I started thinking about everything . . . myself, my husband, my children, death.[8]

Shams al-Barudi started working with her husband Hassan Yusif in productions that were "closer to her personality." Between 1973 and 1981, she worked in nine films with him. He preferred to work in a "polite" way without any "indecency"—that is, kissing or physical contact between actors and actresses. She also felt attracted to a more "decent" lifestyle and—despite her former acting roles in a bikini—now waited until sunset when all people left the seaside before going into the water. She became shyer in her way of dressing as well, covering her short-sleeve dresses with a jacket. She also expressed the wish to play roles with a veil. She thus increasingly preferred a more "decent" way of life, which — in retrospect — becomes part of her religious trajectory.

The second theme that looms large in the period before retiring is marriage and motherhood. These topics are also retrospectively reconstructed in a religious frame. She refused roles not only because she did not like the scripts, but also because of caring for her husband, children, and the home. Already in an interview in 1979,[9] she explained that as an "Eastern woman" she could not bear the idea that her husband was waiting for her to return to the house at any time of the day or night. She stated also that an actress is first and foremost a woman and that being a wife and mother is more important than being a working woman. In *My Journey* the theme of motherhood is strongly present:

> I prefer to take care of the children. [. . .] With regard to acting, any other actress can take my place, but with regard to the role of the mother this is impossible. Motherhood is more important and powerful than acting and the most important place for a woman is in her house with her children and her husband. [. . .] When I married Hassan I was convinced that my first obligation is being a wife. (Siraj al-Din 1993, 31–32)

Shams al-Barudi mentioned the example of the famous actress Fatma Rushdi, who gave her whole life for art, which "brought her nothing" when she grew old. Art will only be a nice memory. In an interview in 1988, when she had developed herself into a kind of preacher, Shams al-Barudi further developed her views on gender and motherhood.[10] Her ideas were much in line with the conservative views of the late sheikh Mitwalli al-Sha'arawi, Dr. 'Umar 'Abd al-Kafi, and the preacher Zeinab al-Ghazali. In Chapter 6, I will go into the discourse on gender and art among retired artists and their religious sources of inspiration.

Shams al-Barudi described her feelings, in the period before her decision to retire, of unrest and anxiety, whereas she was supposed to be at the summit of happiness, glory, and material success (Nasif and Khodayr n.d., 54). The feeling of unrest put Shams al-Barudi on a spiritual path. She started to be committed to praying, while before she used to pray but not regularly and not on time. As an illustration of her devotion, but also of her "religious ignorance," Shams al-Barudi mentioned that she prayed with colleagues in the studio while wearing makeup and nail polish. They also fasted during work and continued film-shooting in Lebanon during Ramadan, in hindsight an impossible combination. She added regretfully that they were born after the 1952 Revolution, in a period of ignorance. She called this period the time of "the obedience of the ignorant and the worship of the disobedient."[11] She started reading the Qur'an, but due to her French school education, her Arabic was weak. For that reason, she had always refused productions in standard Arabic. Her husband, however, was well versed in Arabic and recited the Qur'an. When she tried to imitate him, he told her "*haram! haram!*, the way you read it." She read the Qur'an together with a group of friends from the secondary school during Ramadan. They got together and read the Qur'an, even if their recitation was incorrect. The eagerness but ignorance described here was an important preparation for the next stage of guidance, illumination, and repentance, the dramatic highpoint of her story.

The turning point is connected with her *'umrah* to Mecca in 1982. The year before, she had intended to accompany Hassan Yusif to Mecca, but decided to stay at home with the children because of their school examinations. They all fell ill, an event she interpreted as a punishment for not going on pilgrimage. She decided to go on pilgrimage with her father the next year. She felt a strange calmness while traveling to the sacred earth of Mecca and Medina. Whereas usually she was constantly anxious about the children, she now felt an inner calmness. The various reproductions of her story show slight variations. I will first present the most common version of the story:

> At night I felt a constricting of my chest as if all the mountains in the world were on top of me. My father asked me why I couldn't sleep. I told him I wanted to go to the Grand Mosque [Haram]. He was surprised but pleased that I requested this. When we got to the sanctuary and I greeted it and began to circumambulate, my body began to tremble. I started sweating. My heart seemed to be jumping out of my chest and I felt at that moment as if there was a person inside trying to strangle me. Then he went out. Yes, the Devil went out and the pressure that was like all the mountains of the world weighing on my breast lifted. The worries were gone. And I found my tongue burst forth with prayers for my children and my husband and I began crying so hard that it was as if a volcano had burst and no one could stop it.
>
> As I reached the shrine of the Prophet Ibrahim, I stood up to pray and recited the opening verse of the Koran as if for the first time. I started recognizing its beauty and meaning as if God had graced me. I felt there was a new world around me. Yes I was reborn. I felt I was a bride and that the angels were walking in my wedding march. Everything around me brought

me happiness. I felt I was a pure white bird who wanted to fly in the sky, singing and warbling, setting down on flowers and green branches. I felt the world around me had been created for me. I would no longer feel fatigue, anxiety, or misery.[12]

After this very special moment she finally decided not to unveil after returning from the pilgrimage.

The story of Shams al-Barudi's spiritual journey is concentrated on several issues connected to the body, its appearance, movements, and senses.[13] I will particularly discuss the importance of veiling, her spiritual experiences, and the strong physical experiences such as shaking, weeping, and bodily changes that accompany her turning points.

Veiling is of great importance. Before traveling, she discussed the necessity of veiling as a condition for doing the pilgrimage. Several friends told her that you can unveil after the pilgrimage and did so themselves, another sign of the widespread ignorance among her acquaintances according to Shams al-Barudi. She bought the white clothing for the 'umrah. She put it on without any makeup and looked at herself in the mirror. She deemed herself more beautiful than ever before in this pure clothing. This despite the fact—as she mentioned in this context—that she had just returned from Paris, where she had bought the latest fashion. Also during the pilgrimage she was regularly asked whether she would remain veiled after the 'umrah and was advised to refrain from this or to ask her husband's opinion first. She decided to wait for Hassan Yusif's opinion, not knowing that there was no "obedience in disobedience"—that is, she was not obliged to obey her husband if his wish was contrary to God's teachings. By the Haram mosque she met a sister who recited a poem about the veil she had composed. The poem struck the heart of Shams al-Barudi, made her cry, and strengthened her wish to remain veiled after her 'umrah. Veiling is described by Shams al-Barudi as an inner urge to obey God, yet it also constitutes an important break with her former life as an actress. It is a way of no return to her past. It is a change from the impure to the pure and the embodiment of a new life.

Several spiritual experiences accompany her religious transformations, such as the disappearance of the devil. An apparent metaphor of change is used for her conversion: from a "devil" inhabiting the body to "angels accompanying her wedding procession." The exorcist ritual is interesting in light of her description of acting as an unconscious activity. When acting she had the feeling it did not express her own self and that she "stepped out of her own skin." The idea of not owning her own body in acting, and the devil moving out of her body, powerfully link acting to an outside devilish force.

Acting is not her true self, but something that had possessed her and now finally left her body. She regained ownership of her body and could develop her genuine self.

The expulsion of the devil was not the only spiritual experience. Also her vision of the Prophet is important. In an interview with *al-Nur* in 1996, this vision had become the most important moment. In a short reconstruction of her story of 1982, it is mentioned that she met her uncle in Medina. He asked whether she had visited the tomb of the Prophet. She affirmed that she had visited it daily. Then he asked whether God had revealed himself to her, a question she did not understand. He then asked: "Did you cry?" Two or three days later she went to the Prophet's grave and felt something strange was happening. Suddenly she felt that she saw the Prophet with "her own eyes" and that he looked at her. Her body started trembling, she cried incessantly, and her tongue kept repeating "*ya habibi ya rasul Allah*," "oh beloved oh messenger of God." She was unable to walk on her own due to the overwhelming experience. The women around her exclaimed: "God has revealed himself to her" (Nasif and Khodayr n.d., 54; Siraj al-Din 1993, 59–60).

In a more elaborate story of Divine Guidance told in 1996, she described her visit to the tomb of the Prophet as the main moment, whereas the story of the devil is absent. She related that she was saying supplicatory prayers from a booklet and was reading the Qur'an with her face toward the *qibla*. Her tears were watering down her face from fear of the words of God. The Qur'an was more powerful than she had experienced before. Its verses and meanings were clear, apparent, and simple. The same questions about the revelation and weeping were asked by her uncle. Two days later, after the *fajr* prayer, she visited the grave with the booklet in her hand. She stopped saying the *du'a's*, and with her face toward the grave of the Prophet, looking at the door, she saw the Prophet, who was standing on a higher level than she was, near the door. Only the upper half of his body was visible, and the other part was like a mirage. She saw him "with her own eyes" while he was looking at her. She could no longer control her body and started trembling. The women who accompanied her tried to move her away from the grave, but she was unconscious of her surroundings and could not move, while her tears were running and her body was shaking. She lacked the power to stir, as she was overpowered by the vision. After some time, she realized that she was kneeling near a pillar of the mosque and silently moved out of the mosque with a woman who accompanied her. Her father asked what happened, and without Shams al-Barudi having told anything about her spiritual experiences, as she was speechless, the *hagga* who moved her out of the mosque told that

God had blessed her and that he had revealed himself to her (*al-Nur*, December 4, 1996, 8).[14]

The spiritual character of the experience is demonstrated by its physical impact. The stories are thus full of trembling, shaking, and quivering of the body. Shams al-Barudi's feelings are described as "a bursting volcano," "mountains upon her breasts," and an "earthquake shattering her being." The "streams of tears" that accompany reading poems, the expulsion of the devil from her body, and the vision of the Prophet point at dramatic spiritual and bodily experiences. Weeping was understood as a condition for having a true revelation, as is clear from the conversation with her uncle. Also the women who saw Shams al-Barudi's state of trembling, her inability to carry herself, and her incessant weeping understood this as a clear sign that God had revealed himself. She was either speechless or her tongue burst forth in prayers beyond her control. She was shaken to her bones and purified herself by tears before she was finally reborn.

The changes are profound. The most prominent is the transition from ignorance to understanding the word of God. Whereas previously she used to read Bergson, Sartre, and other Western philosophers, she now expressed the strong desire to read the Qur'an. Although her Arabic was weak, she now felt she understood the Qur'anic truth. After the revelation, she fully understood the *fatiha*, the opening verse of the Qur'an containing the declaration of faith, and "recited it as for the first time." She comprehended the content and meaning of every single character and word of the first *sura*. Besides showing the extent of her "illumination," the expression "reading the *fatiha* as for the first time" is a powerful metaphor for being born again as a Muslim.

Her rebirth was complete. Besides the mental changes after the religious illumination, she described herself as a completely different personality with a different appearance and identity. Veiling was the most visible change, which also meant the complete break with her former activity as an actress. In addition, she mentioned that even the timbre of her voice changed after her rebirth (Siraj al-Din 1993, 62). While in the story this is mentioned in the context of reciting the *fatiha*, it also indicates the totality of her change. Even within the smallest fibers of her being she was transformed. Also her unrest was gone, and she felt a complete calmness. She replaced her stage name with her birth name, Shams al-Muluk. The new name not merely indicates a change of identity, but also affirms the image of a total rebirth.[15]

DREAMS AND VISIONS

We will come across more dreams, visions, and spiritual experiences, for instance of dancer Hala al-Safi, who also saw the Prophet "with her own eyes" and received a piece of cloth to cover herself (see Chapter 2). Actress 'Afaf Sho'ib had several visionary and spiritual moments, including a visit by her deceased brother, who instructed her about the triviality of this world, and a vision of the earthquake that she would actually witness a few days later (see Chapter 5). According to some reconstructions of actress Shahira's story, she had a vision in which she saw a bookend suspended in the air. Her dream was explained as an encouragement to start reading the Qur'an and to follow the path of God (for a picture of her see Figure 1.1).[16] Both Shahira and 'Afaf Sho'ib were in the habit of doing supplicatory prayers before opening the Qur'an at random in order to find certain clues to questions they had raised in their prayers. Several actresses, like Hana' Tharwat, did *istikhara* prayers to seek spiritual advice.

The Islamist press detailed in particular those parts of the stories that were connected with spiritual guidance, visions, and dreams. The secular press, however, showed surprise over the extent of dreams and spiritual experiences among the celebrities. The attention by the Islamist press might come as a surprise, because the Islamists are known for their rationalist reformist approach and staunch opposition to anything that leans toward "popular religiosity" or forms of Sufism. Dreams, revelation, and divination are particularly related and studied in relation to Sufism (Schimmel 1998; Hoffman 1997; Katz 1997; Hermansen 1997; Renard 2008). According to Malti-Douglas (2001), the extent of spirituality in these stories is remarkable at a time in which more orthodox and legalist discourses among Islamists were dominant. Malti-Douglas analyzed these dreams and visions as a mystical bent in an otherwise heavily legalist revival (2001, 177). Although I think the stories are remarkable, there are reasons to analyze the spiritual experiences and dreams as embedded in the broader goals and spirit of the piety movement. In understanding the devotional commitment of the members of the piety movement, oppositions such as "Sufi versus Salafi" or "spiritual versus rational" are probably not very fruitful to work with.

First, visions and dreams fit in with a long-standing classical tradition of oneirocriticism, or dream interpretation. They are an integral part of Islam from its very beginning. The primary revelation of Islam came from Prophet Muhammad's visionary encounter with archangel Jabril (Green 2003, 298). Accounts of both Muhammad's and earlier prophets' visions are mentioned in the Qur'an. The validity of dreams is upheld in the Qur'an, in which it is mentioned that in dreams the soul is taken back into the presence of God. Further evidence for the validity of dreams and visions is provided by the *hadith*—that is, the records of the sayings and conduct of the Prophet Muhammad. Katz writes that "dreams were the ordinary Muslim's allotted share of prophecy as sanctioned by *hadith*," quoting the following saying of the Prophet: "There will not remain after me [anything] of prophecy except glad tidings. Then they said, 'And what are glad tidings, O Messenger of God?' He said, 'The righteous dream which the righteous man sees or appears to him. [It is] one forty-sixth part of prophecy'" (Katz 1997, 7). Or alternatively the Prophet is observed to have said: "A veracious dream is one fourth of prophecy" (Renard 2008, 72). Also interesting is the story about the dream of one of Muhammad's companions, 'Abd Allah ibn Zayd. He had encountered a man wearing two green garments who carried a clapper. He asked the man to sell the clapper to him and explained that he intended to use the clapper for summoning people to prayer. The man then said that there was a better way to do this and instructed 'Abd Allah ibn Zayd in the performance of the call to prayer. After ibn Zayd related the dream, the instructions were followed by the Prophet. One of the most characteristic elements of everyday Muslim life, the *adhan*, is thus believed to have been established through the intervention of a dream (Green 2003, 290; Schimmel 1998, 146).

Dreams and visions come in different shapes, as we have seen from the examples of the Egyptian stars above. It is not entirely clear whether, for instance, Shams al-Barudi had a dream or a wakeful vision. Hana' Tharwat's case also shows a lack of clarity as to whether it was a vision, dream, or another form of spiritual experience. 'Afaf Sho'ib was visited in a dream by a deceased relative, and Hala al-Safi saw the Prophet in her dream. Opening the Qur'an at random and seeking spiritual advice by *istikhara* are alternative forms of divination. *Ayat* (divine signs) is a word that also denotes verses of the Qur'an. Other ways of receiving spiritual messages are hearing voices, having an inner thought that is perceived as the voice of God, or hearing a voice speaking while asleep (Renard 2008, 83–84). The category of "visionary experiences" better captures the variety of spiritual events in the lives of ordinary believers and does not reserve them for experiences of saints and Sufi sheikhs only (Hoffman 1997, 45). Also in classical oneirocritical sources there is not a sharp dividing line between dreams and visions. The lack of distinction between them is apparent in the Arabic term *ru'ya*, expressing the concept of "sight," or "vision." For many Muslims the distinction is not of critical importance, since what is "real in the imaginal world of the dream is equally real in that of the vision in a state of wakefulness or in the state midway between sleeping and waking, in which so much visionary experience is related as taking place" (Sirriyeh 2000, 116).

Whereas the stars have met with skepticism on the part of some secular critics, the literature points at a long tradition vindicating the veracity of dreams. Invoking the appearance of the Prophet Muhammad in dreams and visions functions particularly to authenticate a claim to authority and legitimacy (Renard 2008, 72–73). The famous *hadith* of the Prophet "He who sees me in a dream truly sees me. For the devil does not impersonate me" is often cited by those claiming such authority (Malti-Douglas 2001, 59; Renard 2008, 72–73). The time of the day at which the dream takes place also adds to its veracity. The Prophet is quoted as having said that the dream that is most true is the one that is seen at dawn (Malti-Douglas 2001, 59). The cultural embeddedness of dreams and visions within Islam is also clear from the vast number of books on dream interpretation (Schimmel 1998; Green 2003; Katz 1997). The manuals help to interpret symbols such as angels, forecasting for instance a pilgrimage, salvation, and peace, whereas flying birds can indicate an approaching death, and a white dove symbolizes purity (Schimmel 1998, 83, 146). The manuals and oneirocritical literature point to the preponderance of certain images, symbols, and places encountered in the dreams and visions of the Egyptian performers: the importance of Mecca and the pilgrimage as site and time for dreams, the frequent appearance of the Qur'an in dreams, and the privileged character of seeing the Prophet. Seeing the Prophet and receiving an object such as a robe from the Prophet, as happened to Hala al-Safi, are particularly valued. Visionary experiences of the Prophet have formed one of the earliest and most lasting expressions of Islamic devotion (Green 2003, 291).

Second, in view of this theological, cultural, and historical rootedness of dreams and visions in the Islamic world, it should not come as a surprise that many devotees in present-day Cairo have visionary experiences. Hoffman conducted research among contemporary Sufis and Copts in Egypt and heard many accounts of dreams and visions. According to a sociological survey, some 50 percent of Egyptians interviewed said that their dead relatives had visited them in their dreams, usually to ask them to do specific things for them. This is not necessarily regarded as a religious experience, but when the appearing person is a saint, or when the person in the dream seeks or provides guidance, such dreams are religiously significant (1997, 47). This was the case, for instance, with ʿAfaf Shoʿib, who was told by her deceased brother to concentrate on the afterlife instead of mundane this-worldly affairs. Hoffman states that the ubiquity of dreams and visions among Muslims can be related to Sufis, since these latter groups continue to dominate "popular Islam" in Egypt. Yet there are reasons to deconstruct a clear-cut opposition between Sufi and Salafi devotees as regards the incidence of visionary experiences.

Interesting with regard to the ambiguity of Salafi skepticism regarding visions and dreams is Sirriyeh's study on the Syrian Salafi reformer Muhammad Rashid Reda (1865–1935). He was a famous critic of popular Sufism, although he had grown up in a traditional religious environment where dreams and visionary experience were taken seriously. Reda became more skeptical, due to the growing influence on him of the reformist thought of Jamal al-Din al-Afghani (1838–1897) and Muhammad 'Abduh (1849–1905) (Sirriyeh 2000, 126). With regard to seeing the holy dead in dreams, he tried to distinguish between pure imagination and genuine vision. Yet, according to Sirriyeh, despite "his demands for a strictly rational approach to seeking the truth, he is not above accepting a dream vision as valid evidence, when it suits him" (2000, 128). Reda argued that most ghosts that people saw in dreams were actually the spirits of devils associated with the dead rather than the dead themselves. A number of Sufis have in his view been misled, and their dreams were actually devilish delusions.

Rashid Reda's views on dreams of the holy dead as mainly dreams of unholy devils were influential and propagated extensively through the Salafi movement. Important for the argument here is that he did not deny the importance and communicative possibility of dreams, although he was critical and tried to dispose of false ones. The author Sirriyeh, therefore, considers Reda "traditional," since he believed in very much the same phenomena and did not undertake "a serious and consistent effort to dispel the old views by recourse to a more scientific investigation" (2000, 130). Sirriyeh holds that the position Reda finally reached showed "surprisingly little interest in making use of a rational, 'modernist' approach" (2000, 129). The assumed opposition between modernity and rationality versus dreams and visions is thus not necessarily part of Reda's thought and his Salafi legacy, but rather part of Sirriyeh's analysis.

The preponderance of visionary experiences, not only among Sufis, and the ambiguous reception of them even among Salafis point to their ubiquity. An interesting example showing the general acceptability of spiritual experiences and devices is the ritual of *istikhara* prayer. Dreams or spiritual experiences can be induced by certain acts, such as *istikhara*, and places. The shrine of Prophet Ibrahim and the tombs of other prophets and holy men, in Mecca, are particularly favorable places for receiving dreams and divine messages through prayer. This was, for instance, the case with Shams al-Barudi, and for many "repentant" artists the pilgrimage to Mecca was a turning point that they actively sought. Spending long hours in prayer is also a favorite way of actively seeking spiritual guidance. The clearest way of asking divine illumination is doing *istikhara* prayer, which is a common habit among many devotees. Also the "repentant" artists mentioned they did *istikhara* before important decisions in life, such as veiling. Hana' Tharwat used *istikhara* also to seek God's advice on smaller issues, such as whether or not to meet an anthropologist. This habit was perceived as a sign of great piety.

Istikhara is derived from the root *kh-y-r*, which expresses the idea of option or choice.[17] It refers to entrusting God with the choice between two or more possible options, motivated either by piety or the inability to decide oneself. Schimmel translates it as "Suchen nach Gutem," "seeking the right thing" (1998, 40–41). This latter description better fits with the way my Egyptian informants explained the practice, although this can mean they seek God's advice on the best choice. *Istikhara* is a practice believed to be taught by the Prophet and to generate true dreams and dream visitations. After ritual ablution and two cycles of prayer, the person recites a litany and requests some kind of divine guidance. Guidance can be asked for manifold matters, whether spiritual, material, or practical, or even, more generally, that a specific matter turns out for the best (Hermansen 1997, 26; Green 2003, 307–308). After the prayer, the seeker goes to sleep. The answer can come in the form of a dream. People also described a more diffuse understanding to me, like a feeling when waking up or "signs" during the following day. *Istikhara* thus allows for daily and active advice and spiritual guidance.

Third, dreams and visions can be analyzed as fundamental existential dimensions of religious life that provide a pietization of everyday life. As Graw (2005) argues for the Senegambia context, *istikhara* and other forms of divination should be understood as an encompassing and fundamental praxis of religious understanding and empowerment. Whereas this practice of *istikhara* and other spiritual activities can be understood in an instrumental way as helping the believer to settle for the best option, other interpretations of dreams, visions, and spiritual experiences are possible and probably better applicable in the case of "repentant" artists. In this light Katz's analysis of the autobiography of 'Abd al-Wahhab al-Sha'rani, a sixteenth-century Cairene sheikh, is interesting. Katz (1997) concludes that al-Sha'rani valued dreams not for their ability to foretell the future, but for their psychological merit as monitors of his spiritual condition. Katz argues that alongside the popular utilitarian approach to dreams as a means to divination, a less well-defined approach to the meaning of dreams exists. For the sixteenth-century sheikh, and I would argue for the "repentant" artists as well, dreams and visionary experiences mostly function as a guide for correcting behavior and to offer guidelines for improving observance of rituals. Dreams helped the Cairene sheikh to identify moral lapses and to regain moral equilibrium. Spiritual experiences can lead to introspection and moral edification. In the case of the "repentant" artists, their dreams and visions instruct them on their way to piety. These experiences initiate them on a journey to devotion and moral rectitude.

With these factors in mind, we can thus comprehend why the Islamist press promotes a genre of repentance literature in which dreams and visions loom large. They are part of the theological legacy and have a wide social and cultural acceptance that is not limited to Sufis. More important, dreams and visions are devices for moral edification and provide means to receive divine guidance on the road to devotion and commitment. This is not a preoccupation limited to Sufi believers, but constitutes the key objective of the piety movement. It is not that much the content of the dreams, although interesting in itself, that matters, but more what dreams do to the dreamer. Since visionary experiences provide the seeker with moral guidance and guidelines for moral perfection, dreams and visions are at the heart of the piety movement.

ISLAMIC REVIVAL AND THE PIETY MOVEMENT

Shams al-Barudi's new life was geared toward gaining religious knowledge and filling in the gaps of her religious education. For the first three years, she completely committed herself to religious study and buried herself in the Qur'an as her only pastime. Music, which she used to listen to with enjoyment, was now understood as the whistling of the devil (Abu Dawud and Bayumi 1994, 29). She gave her children an Islamic education, followed religious lessons, and eventually provided others with religious advice. Shams al-Barudi and other "repentant" artists were certainly not unique in their religious commitment and search for religious knowledge. They were part of a broad movement of Islamic activism that had developed in the 1980s. In this section, I will provide a general description of the development of Islamic movements in Egypt up to the early 1990s. In Chapters 2 and 3, the sectors of religious education and Islamic charity will be discussed in more detail.

First, a note on terminology is required. Several labels are current, of which the term "fundamentalism" has become more or less obsolete, as this is mostly associated with a scripturalist interpretation originating from the Christian tradition. "Political Islam" emphasizes the political aspects of the Islamic groups, whereas "revival" or "resurgence" stresses the religious character of these Islamic movements. Islamic Revival, or Islamic Resurgence, is criticized for its primordialist assumption (Bayat 2005a) — that is, it can transmit the idea that Islam is a primary force that resurfaces in identical manners over time. Bayat holds that the manifold and dynamic forces shaping the present Islamic movements need to be scrutinized instead. The notion of Islamic Revival, or Islamic Awakening, though, is often used as a mere translation of the Arabic *al-sahwa al-islamiyya*, the term used by many of those active in the Islamic trend. "Piety movement" is a more specific term that draws attention to important dimensions of the recent trend in Egypt in which the religious ethos and sensibilities are put in the forefront (Mahmood 2005). It is also called the *da'wah* movement, or the mosque movement, because of the great emphasis that is put on Islamic outreach by way of religious instruction and learning in the mosques. Finally, Islamic activism and Islamism[18] are two other labels that merit attention. As discussed by Bayat (2005a, 894), Islamic activism can refer to political, social, and cultural activities of Muslim activists. It does not refer that much to the "passive piety" that would aptly describe many believers touched by the piety movement, but rather to the extraordinary activities and missionary religiosity that aim to cause social change (2005a, 894). Bayat reserves "Islamism" for the overtly political aspects of the Islamic movements to distinguish the notion from the "apolitical" trends that center on individual self-enhancement (2005a, 894).

The lines between the political and apolitical are difficult to draw, though, and I will not make a clear-cut break between them. It is important to understand both the activist components and the more inwardly turned pious trends in the present landscape in Egypt. I thus propose to use "piety" and "piety movement" for the project of religious reform mostly aimed at correcting the self. Many of those involved have eventually taken on a more activist stance and are involved in Islamic activism, outreach, and charity. The active missionary form directed at social and/or political change can be caught by the term "Islamism," or "Islamic activism." The individual striving for commitment, or, for instance, following lessons aimed at perfecting one's religious understanding, on the other hand, can be better captured by the label "piety movement." This distinction is not that much based on its presumed political or apolitical aspect, but on the direction of change, inward or outward. Focusing only on activist aspects would leave out an enormous number of people who are less actively involved but profoundly influenced by the current Islamic movements in Egypt. In addition, these attitudes and positions can change over time.

This brings us to a second issue, the enormous breadth of the Islamic movements in contemporary Egypt. Sullivan and Abed-Kotob (1999) emphasize the plural and diverse character of the present movements, ranging from the state-sponsored Islam, the militant groups such as the Jihad and Jamaʿat Islamiyya and the accommodationist Muslim Brothers, to Sufism (1999, 20). This division is not strict and shows overlap. State-sponsored Islam means the official religious authorities of al-Azhar and the official preachers employed in the mosques under state control. State-sponsored Islam stands in contra-distinction to the Islamist opposition movement, whether militant or accom-modationist. Yet from both sides they encroach upon each other. The state tries to encapsulate and control part of the accommodationist strands, and, due to the general spread of religiosity, the vast state apparatus is permeated with Islamists of all sorts. The piety, or *daʿwah*, movement can be perceived as part of the acquiescent Islamic movement; however, it also encompasses activist Islamists. Sufism is perceived as a mystical and apolitical force, and for that reason the Islamist opposition has often adopted an anti-Sufi attitude. The members of the *daʿwah* movement also engage in this anti-Sufi rhetoric of the Salafi-modernist trends. We have seen, though, that pietists and Sufis can be close in the way they privilege pious ethics and religious edification (Hirschkind 2006, 120).

Also Bayat (2005a, 899–900) argues that the Egyptian Islamic move-ment is far from uniform. It can include radical Islamists engaged in armed struggle; the reformist and moderate Muslim Brothers; the state-controlled al-Azhar clergy, who are on an equal footing with the Muslim Brothers as regards religious conservatism; the massive Islamic welfare sector; religious education or lessons aimed at personal piety and virtue; and intellectual cur-rents such as *al-wasatiyya*, a moderate Islamist trend (Baker 2003; see also Chapter 7). Bayat regards all these disparate elements as part of the current religious and social trend because they share "general religious language and codes, advocating Islam as part of public life, and expressing a desire for some sort of religio-political change" (2005a, 900). Of these trends the militants and the Muslim Brothers, or, historically, Sufism (Gilsenan 1973), have drawn the greatest amount of attention. As Bayat also argues, however, the most significant development in Egypt since the 1970s and 1980s is the growth of religiosity in the form of Islamic welfare, religious teaching, mosque centers, and other civil institutions (1998, 155). In the present study, the piety move-ment and Islamic activists in the Islamic sector will be central. This is a trend that is difficult to locate and can better be studied as a religious discourse and code than as a well-defined movement. It is partly a counterforce to the state-controlled religious authorities, but not totally autonomous or outside the scope of the regime; it is anti-Sufi in rhetoric, but sometimes close to it through a shared emphasis on piety; it is partly activist and partly quietist.

This vast trend thus encompasses a multitude of political attitudes and religious trajectories. Yet they share an impetus to rescue religion from secular governance, compartmentalization or functionalization, and to restore Islam as the leading force that should inform all aspects of life: from daily comportment regarding the way of dressing, eating, and etiquette, to issues such as education, upbringing, and entertainment, to broader social and political issues.

There is a vast literature explaining the "resurgence" of Islam in the present era. Usually researchers point to the importance of both the 1967 Arab-Israeli War and the Iranian Revolution of 1979 as the starting point of the present "upsurge." Particularly the aftermath of the 1967 Arab-Israeli War caused a climate of intense and visible religiousness in Egypt not only among Muslims but also among Copts. It is in this mood and climate that the image of the Virgin Mary appeared to several inhabitants of the Zeitun area of Cairo. She appeared several months after the war and continued to reappear for several months thereafter (El-Guindi 1981, 481–482). El-Guindi analyzes this new intensity in religiousness, reaching the dramatic climax in the "miracle" of the Virgin Mary, as a phenomenon separate from the birth of the Islamic movement, which she connects with the 1973 Ramadan War. The Ramadan Crossing (al-ʿUbur) took place during the holiest Islamic month and was launched in the name of Islam. Instead of Nasser's battle cry "Land! Sea! Air!," Sadat's troops had shouted *"Allah akbar,"* "God is great," while crossing the Bar-Lev line (Gaffney 1994, 85). It was generally perceived as a victory and accordingly helped to affirm Islam's effectiveness and legitimacy for the people. The phenomenon of women's veiling began shortly after the 1973 Ramadan War. El-Guindi hypothesizes that two independent movements developed: one, male-oriented, underground, and of a religious-political nature; the other, of women, that was more open and religious-moral in character (1981, 481). At some point, as the movements found each other and discovered their overlapping aims, they merged.

Most studies look at the "revival" either from the vantage point of political economy or of cultural identity (Wickham 2002). To these approaches we can add a third cluster of theories, the social movement theory and theories on civil society, which has entered the field lately (Berman 2003; Bayat 2005a; Munson 2001). Whether locating the activism in the absence of economic development or in the reaction to Western domination, the first two approaches place the origins in the recruits and not that much in the Islamic message. The social movement theories (SMT) bring the agency of mobilizers as well as the content of the messages into focus (see Wickham 2002; Bayat 2005a). Wickham's study (2002) provides a useful SMT analysis of the development of Islamic activism, including the vast Islamic parallel sector of mosques and Islamic charity organizations, between 1960 and the early 1990s.

During Nasser's reign, a policy of both repression and co-optation was adopted. All political parties were banned in 1953, a policy expanded to the Muslim Brothers, formally a religious association at the time, after an attempt on Nasser's life in 1954. Student unions were dismantled as well in the mid-1950s. Potential opposition groups, such as urban-educated youth, were drafted in by a "social contract"— that is, by free higher education and the promise of a government job. Sadat continued the policy of co-optation and spent even more money on providing education and public employment. Sadat initiated the *infitah*, the open-door policy, from 1974 onward. It aimed to open the economy and encourage foreign and local private-sector initiatives, a policy that was followed up by other measures of economic liberalization during the rule of Mubarak. The ensuing rise of the private sector and foreign investment and decline in the role of the public sector resulted in a substantial gap of income between employees of the two sectors. In addition, although the *infitah* created opportunities for better jobs in the private sector, public education and state university degrees did not deliver the necessary competencies such as foreign language proficiency and computer skills, which were only available in expensive private schools. For (aspiring) employees in the public sector, it led to the well-known phenomenon of long waiting lists for public employment, and jobs that yielded only a meager salary and necessitated that an employee hold a second or third job to make ends meet. The *infitah* thus resulted in a split in the field of education and the job market: creating a vast group of well-educated youth without the necessary skills to compete in the lucrative private sector and a small group of higher-class youth that had been educated in private schools and universities (De Koning 2009). Moreover, the economic crisis that started in 1982, caused by low oil prices and the shrinking opportunities for outmigration, hampered the financing of the "social contract." During the oil boom of the late 1970s millions of Egyptians had migrated to the Gulf countries. Between 1974 and 1985 more than 3 million Egyptians were working as construction workers, laborers, or teachers, providing their families back home with the purchasing power to buy the newly available consumer goods. These new consumption patterns became important markers and symbols of their social advancement (Amin 2000, 19). The traditional middle class and those dependent on government salaries, however, suffered from inflation and the withdrawal of social services provided by the government.

As the Egyptian economist Galal Amin (2000) has also argued, the change in Egypt's social structure was especially crucial for understanding the economic and social crises in Egypt. It was particularly the group of "lumpen elite," raised with high expectations and ambitions, who constituted the basis of the Islamist movements (Wickham 2002, 46–63). Bayat also sees the impoverished and frustrated university graduates as the ones engaged in the Islamist movements, but according to him, political mobilization took place in the university clubs, professional associations, and syndicates rather than in the Islamic welfare sector (1998, 157). Most activists were thus located in the middle and lower middle class. They were well educated but not able to live up to the expectations that are tied to higher education. Materially, they were lower-middle-class, whereas they expected upward mobility and middle-class status. The "repentant" artists, with their, generally, middle- and upper-middle-class background and well-off status, were thus a rather exceptional phenomenon in the Islamist movement. They foreshadowed a development that would become more obvious in the 1990s: an increased pious commitment among the higher classes.

During the rule of Sadat, the space for political parties was increased, because he experimented not only with economic, but also with political, liberalization (Bayat 1998, 168; Wickham 2002, 64). The turn from closed to semi-open authoritarian rule led to a closely regulated form of opposition. Islamic political parties such as the Muslim Brothers and Islamic student unions were encouraged by the "Believer President." The open-door policy, the *infitah*, and the peace treaty with Israel, eventually leading to the assassination of Sadat by radical Islamists in 1981, ended the space for Islamic militancy. On the margins of government control, however, there emerged a large and decentralized network of Islamic associations and organizations. This Islamic sector was to expand enormously under his successor, Mubarak. In the first decade of his rule, Mubarak continued the strategy of Sadat, a policy also known as "selective accommodation" and "selective repression" (Bianchi in Wickham 2002, 103). The Muslim Brothers were officially illegal but allowed to participate in elections with the Wafd and Labor Parties in 1984 and 1987. Islamists also became strong in universities' unions and in professional organizations. Militants, however, were severely repressed.

The growth of the Islamic movement, together with the repression of opposition political Islamists, resulted in what Wickham describes as a political system "with a hollow core and a dynamic periphery, in which Islamists barred from contesting power within the formal party system diverted their activity to institutional outlets outside the regime's control" (2002, 64). Wickham makes it clear that many engaged in the Islamist movement were not politically active, but, foremost, religiously inspired. Even if not overtly political, the mosques and the Islamic welfare sector constituted a fertile ground for Islamist mobilization. Those who eventually became politically active mainly campaigned for the Muslim Brothers.

The enormous growth of private mosques is one of the clearest examples of the massive expansion of the Islamic sector. Several estimates are mentioned in the literature: in 1970 there were about 20,000 private mosques, in 1981, 46,000, and in the mid-1990s, 140,000 (Wickham 2002, 98, 107). Bayat mentions a growth from 40,000 in 1981 to 70,000 in 1989 (1998, 155). Mahmood mentions the total number of mosques expanding from 28,000 in 1975, to 50,000 in 1985, and to 120,000 in 1995. Of the 50,000 mosques in 1985, only 7,000 were established by the government (2005, 3). These local mosques were sometimes no more than a simple space in a basement. One of the factors that stimulated the growth was the exemption from taxes of any building containing a religious site (Wickham 2002, 98). These mosques were often financed by private donations from the neighborhood or by wealthy patrons from the Gulf. Members of the community selected the *imam*, who offered sermons and religious lessons. Many mosques also provided activities such as charity, health care, and kindergarten (see also Chapter 2).

Also the number of Islamic associations, quite often centered in the local mosques, expanded rapidly. Over 4,000 Islamic associations existed in the early 1990s, which is estimated to be a rise of over 100 percent since 1975 (Bayat 1998, 155). They accounted for one-third of all Egyptian private voluntary organizations (PVOs) in the late 1980s, and were estimated at 6,237 in the late 1990s. They were mostly outside the control of the government, although PVOs needed to be registered with the Ministry of Social Affairs (Sullivan and Abed-Kotob 1999). This enabled people to participate in public life without overtly competing for political power. The Islamic associations were more effective in distributing services to the local populations than the government's PVOs. They offered charity and health services to millions (Bayat 2002a, 12). Mubarak at first did not consider the Islamic welfare sector a serious threat. The social welfare and charity they provided were even contributing to social stability. The government development programs were not able to offer the vast array of services these PVOs provided in poor urban areas (see also Chapter 3).

Besides the private mosques, Islamic charity organizations, health clinics, and schools, a wide range of Islamic businesses developed, of which Islamic banking is the most famous case. Sadat's *infitah* had also opened up possibilities for Islamic investment companies (al-Awadi 2004, 68, 101). Their main distinguishing feature was that they did not charge interest, but used the principle of *musharaka*, partnership in profit or loss. In the 1980s, Islamic investment companies based on the same principle developed at a staggering speed.

The Muslim Brothers had started economic enterprises from the inception of the movement in order to provide an economic basis for their activities. By the 1980s, a number of Muslim Brothers had become wealthy entrepreneurs and had connections with the construction magnate Osman Ahmad Osman (Utvik 2006, 74). In particular, Egyptians who had worked in the Gulf and Libya, and had earned relatively large sums of money, invested their money in Islamic companies. These included enterprises in construction, manufacturing, trade, and tourism. In order to demonstrate the Islamic character of their companies, business owners established connections with Islamic sheikhs, such as, for instance, Sheikh al-Sha'arawi (Utvik 2006, 203–207). Al-Awadi gives the case study of one of the Islamist entrepreneurs, 'Ubayd. He used his organizational network to persuade members of the Muslim Brothers who worked in the Gulf and searched for safe and Islamic ways of investing their money to invest in his Islamic investment company al-Sharif. Islamic investment companies also employed members of the Brotherhood who were not able to travel to the Gulf (al-Awadi 2004, 68). Of the hundred Islamic investment companies in 1988, about fifty were considered large or medium in size. The total funds of the larger investment companies were estimated at more than US$4.3 billion (Sullivan 1994, 63).

Islamic banks were tolerated in the early 1980s, and the Islamic International Bank of Investment and Development and the Faisal Islamic Bank were founded in 1979. Both were developed and supported by the Muslim Brothers (al-Awadi 2004, 69). The growth of Islamic banking in the early 1980s was interrupted due to internal struggles and disputes (al-Awadi 2004, 134). In 1988, the government passed a bill that led to the demise of Islamic investment companies. The regime probably both feared links with the militant Islamist movement and worried about their material power. Besides, the companies had become dangerous competitors for the Egyptian national banking system that used to receive the foreign currencies repatriated by Egyptians working abroad (Utvik 2006, 211; see also Chapter 4).

The Islamo-business (Haenni 2005) also expanded to publishing and media companies. Islamic publishing houses and bookstores such as al-Dar al–Islami li al-Tawzi' wa al-Nashr, Dar al-Shuruq, Dar al-Wafa', and Dar al-I'tisam flourished (Wickham 2002, 101). The same holds true for the appearance of Islamic periodicals and journals, such as *al-Mukhtar al-Islami*, *al-I'tisam*, and *Liwa' al-Islam* (Wickham 2002, 101). A journal with an almost identical title, *Liwa al-Islami*, is a state-sponsored publication. This is evidence again of the government's strategy of co-optation and encapsulation of the Islamic trend (Starrett 1995b, 55). In the 1980s, the production and distribution of religious books surpassed that of books on all other subjects, such as literature, history, and social sciences (Starrett 1995b, 55). The price of books was very low, an encouragement to consumers. In addition, there was mass production of religious commodities, both for decoration and display and as pedagogical tools: Qur'ans; Qur'anic calligraphy; religious posters, cards, and stickers; prayer beads and caps; and jewelry. Veiling is, of course, the most noted development of the "resurgence," to which I will return in Chapter 3. Islamic fashion, including veils, has accordingly become another important Islamo-business. Men wearing a beard and an Islamic outfit were an equally salient symbol of the *sahwa al-islamiyya*, but they have received less scholarly attention. They were often nicknamed the "beardies," although the long beards have recently been replaced by well-trimmed small beards.

The growth of the *da'wah* movement was enabled by the number of well-educated Islamic activists. Not only the material advantages of the associations and mosques drew local activists and inhabitants to the mosques. As Wickham observed, the messages also made sense to the addressees. The study groups provided moral and spiritual gains. The movement enhanced social ties and solidarity in neighborhoods. It also provided the activists with a lifestyle that suited their economic circumstances by rejecting the pervasive materialistic values in overall society. Islamic outreach was seen as a moral duty. It was felt to be a religious obligation to engage in *da'wah*, to begin with friends and relatives and slowly target wider circles of neighbors and the community at large (Wickham 2002, 151). The enormous power of the mosques and Islamic sector became increasingly evident in the 1990s. By then the state had a hard job to contain this massive parallel sector. It began a heavy attack on all sorts of Islamists, and distinctions between militants and reformists were increasingly blurred. These developments took place after the early 1990s and will be discussed in Part Two.

(TWO)

Repentance, Da'wah, and Religious Education

I n this chapter, I will introduce the story of former dancer Hala al-Safi, who left her "sinful profession" and opened a religious school. Her story of remorse will be used to analyze an important aspect of piety: repentance, which will be the central concept in the second section. In the final section, I will describe the development of core activities of the piety movement in the 1980s: *da'wah*, Islamic outreach, and religious instruction.

THE SPIRITUAL BIOGRAPHY OF DANCER HALA AL-SAFI

As I mentioned in the volume Introduction, it was not easy to reach the stars. Despite my connections with musicians of the Muhammad 'Ali Street, who had worked with Hala al-Safi before she reached stardom, they could not introduce me to her. I eventually went to her house with my former assistant Sayyid, on the off chance that I might encounter her there, and met her son. He gave me her telephone number, but whenever I phoned she was busy, on trips, or about to travel. She apparently did not want to be interviewed. In 2006, I tried again and was surprised by her willingness to grant me an interview the same evening, on the condition that it was without filming or taking pictures. I was first led into the sitting room, which was just under construction and in the process of being restyled in a mosquelike fashion. Afterward, we sat in her large bedroom and had a pleasant, informal interview. While one of her cats joined us on her bed, she mentioned that she used to have dogs. After her "repentance" and "reversion" to Islam, she could no longer keep these "unclean" animals.[1]

I expected that talking about her former activities, which she now considers *haram*, would be a sore point to touch. Yet Hala al-Safi spoke without any hesitation about her past as a dancer:

> I loved art from a young age; at school I participated in the theater group. I sang and danced from an early age. [. . .] My father was a famous football player and he did not mind me entering the field. [. . .] I worked in all the famous hotels; I worked as an ambassador for Egypt and went to Denmark, Iceland, and Switzerland. The last trip was to London and then happened what happened. [. . .] I worked for about eighteen years. I made beautiful and new shows. I added things to the existing repertoire of Oriental dance. I raised the level of Oriental dance. I was at the top of fame. I had a good name and worked a lot for television.[2]

About her decision to retire at the pinnacle of her career, she said:

> I loved God more than art. Really, I always loved to be a good person and did charity; even as an artist I fasted the whole month of Ramadan. I did not work in that month. I distributed alms to the poor. I slaughtered and went to Sayyidna Nafisa or to Sayyid al-Badawi in Tanta to give meat to the poor. I did this without knowing that this was a religious duty. But *al-hamdulillah* on a day God knew me. Although I was an artist, I loved God a lot. I loved him more than anything else.[3]

She claimed ignorance about religious matters and stated that she did not know that dancing was *haram*. Like Shams al-Barudi, she described a period of doubt, unrest, and insomnia. She cried a lot and felt a sudden revulsion at wearing makeup or the belly-dancing costume. One evening she was no longer able to perform. She was touched by Umm Kulthum's song "Call Me to His House," to which she usually danced, but which now caused feelings of embarrassment. She dropped to the floor and felt very strange. She did the ablutions and prayed (Nasif and Khodayr n.d., 24, 25).

Knowing her story from booklets, I asked if something special happened that pushed her to her decision to step down. She continued:

> By God, I really was psychologically exhausted from my work; I did not want it anymore. On a day after work I went to take a bath and slept. I then had a vision. I dreamt that I was standing on a high spot from which I could see the *kaʿba* and all people were wearing white. I wanted to go to them. I went to the *kaʿba* and went in. There were many people around.

When I entered, I saw a man and a woman from afar gesturing that I should come to them. I went to them wearing only my revealing pajama and my hair loose. I kept on walking . . . the man was sitting on his knees as if praying and had a towel on his lap. He told me to cover myself with it. After that, we stood up and we prayed with him. I started crying and crying and felt happy. I was naked; he covered me and I felt so happy. I started trembling. I asked the woman where the man was. I finished praying and wanted to give him the towel back. He put his hand on my forehead and said: "Keep it and wear it." When I went out, I wept intensely. I asked: "Who is this man?" People answered: "Muhammad *rasul* Allah" [Muhammad the messenger of God]. I woke up and screamed: "Sayyidna Muhammad, Sayyidna Muhammad!" My mother came in and I told her it is over. "The Prophet Muhammad has covered me. I cannot reveal myself again." I took my mother's *galabiyya* and did the Friday prayer.[4]

After that dream, Hala al-Safi retired in 1987. Shortly afterward, she went to Mecca for the first time. This was not easy, because the Saudi authorities were not willing to give a permit to dancers to go to Mecca. The phenomenon of artists going on pilgrimage and afterward happily returning to their "sinful" activities was a thorn in their side. She managed to convince the Saudi consul of her genuine repentance and retirement. While putting on the white clothes for the pilgrimage, she felt they were the most beautiful clothes she had ever worn. In the holy land, she remembered the words of Umm Kulthum's song that had touched her so much. She wept incessantly in "His [God's] house" and asked for forgiveness for her enormous number of sins (Nasif and Khodayr n.d., 27).

Hala al-Safi described the tremendous change in her life as a transformation from darkness to lightness, from evil to goodness, from unrest and doubt to calmness and tranquillity. Hala al-Safi, the person who liked traveling, dancing, and going out, "had died; my name is Soheir Hassan 'Abdin" (interview, *al-Nur*, July 22, 1990). She no longer understood how "the devil had been able to steal her life" all those years. Her change from keeping dogs to cats is also significant. It not only symbolizes her change from impure to pure, but, as Malti-Douglas has argued, the dog is also a symbol of Westernization (2001, 65). Hala al-Safi mentioned that she devoted her new life to her two children and tried to give them a religious upbringing. Her daughter also commented on the change she experienced after her mother's repentance. Once the "daughter of a dancer," a heavy insult, she had become the daughter of Hagga Soheir and was finally respected (Nasif and Khodayr n.d., 35). Hala al-Safi now considers art and religion as mutually exclusive. Art is *haram* and an improper field for women. It inevitably means mixing with men, meeting people, and facing potentially incriminating situations. Knowing her comparison of dance to the devil, I was surprised she openly talked about her former profession and also claimed she made a valuable contribution to the field of dance. I asked her if she could also look back with pride on her successful career. She replied, though, that she regretted her former profession, since regret is part of repentance.[5]

She completely changed the rhythm of her life; instead of concluding her day after work in the early morning, she awoke early for the *fajr* prayer. She started reading religious literature, participated in religious classes, and met other "repentant" artists. She went five times on *hajj* and did the *'umrah*, the lesser pilgrimage, three times. After staying at home for about four years, she wanted to start a new project. She went to Sheikh Mitwalli al-Sha'arawi to ask his opinion on how to use her money. He told her that her money from dancing was *haram*. She could invest her money in a new project that would generate *halal* money, that is, income from a religiously permissible source. Hala al-Safi was not the only "repentant" artist who had to deal with the question of *haram* money. Other artists also decided to invest their money in Islamic businesses, because it was a way to produce *halal* money and perform good deeds at the same time. Hala al-Safi invested in religious education. Like Shams al-Barudi, she blamed a lot of her ignorance on her lack of proper religious education. As children of the Nasser era, they were brought up with religion being taught as any other secular subject matter. She decided to open a private religious school. She appointed religious scholars and supervised the management of the school (interview in magazine *Shabab*, November 1989, p. 48). The school was successful, and she has now terminated the project and lives off her *halal* money.

I will briefly introduce the TV presenter Kamilia al-'Arabi and actress Hana' Tharwat, because they have also been active in the field of religious instruction. They did not open religious schools, but became important as preachers. I got the telephone number of "Hagga Kamilia al-'Arabi" from Miyar al-Bablawi, a young actress who retired for a short while and is now presenting a religious program. She was fond of Hagga Kamilia and was sure she would be willing to talk to me. Kamilia al-'Arabi is regularly featured as one of the "repentant" artists in the literature. I knew that this label was sensitive and not liked by all. Thus, in introducing my research topic, I always explained it in different terms as "what they call *fannanat ta'ibat*, or *fannanat mu'tazilat*, or *fannanat muhagabat*,"[6] hoping the person with whom I was speaking would identify with at least one of the labels. Yet Kamilia al-'Arabi replied during the phone call that she did not belong to the target group of my research because she was not an artist. She continued, saying that she had nothing to say about art and its relationship with religion, and there was no incompatibility whatsoever between her profession as a presenter and religion. Although she stated this in a matter-of-fact way, I felt she was slightly insulted by the label "artist." This shows the sensitivity not only of the notion "repentance," but also of "*fannana*," artist. At least for women, art is a sensitive field. I also tried to interview former actress Hana' Tharwat. As I mentioned in the volume Introduction, she insisted twice on performing *istikhara* prayer beforehand. Already as reported in the book by Abu Dawud and Bayumi (1994) she insisted on doing *istikhara* before talking to the interviewers. They were luckier, because they were granted an interview. She is presently known among her colleagues as a very pious person who is "not of the world" any longer, preponderantly devoting herself to religion and asking God's approval for all her actions by way of *istikhara*. Her husband Muhammad al-ʿArabi is from a family of artists. He is the half brother of TV presenter Kamilia al-ʿArabi. I eventually interviewed their other brother, actor Wagdi al-ʿArabi.[7]

Hana' Tharwat claimed that she never did productions that would embarrass her children.[8] She always carefully selected the productions she would participate in and was modest in her clothing and demeanor. She worked particularly in TV serials and not in films. Yet she increasingly had the feeling that she compromised her moral standards and that the demand for easygoing actresses was increasing. She described a feeling of unrest about not veiling and lacking the courage to take the decision (interview, *Sabah al-Khayr*, February 15, 2000, p. 60). The turning point happened when her role contained—unspecified—words close to the immoral. While her colleagues used these expressions without further ado, Hana' Tharwat felt saddened and embarrassed to use them. She refused to do her part because she considered it disgraceful. For the first time she discussed with her colleagues whether art is *halal* or *haram*. One of them proposed to visit Sheikh al-Shaʿarawi, and, together with a few colleagues and her husband, they visited his house. Sheikh al-Shaʿarawi told them that art is like a knife. If you use it to cut meat to feed your children, it is *halal*; if you use it to cut the throat of a fellow human being, it is *haram* (interview, *Sabah al-Khayr*, February 15, 2000, p. 61). For women the most important thing is to follow Islamic education and to wear the Islamic garb (Abu al-ʿAynayn 1999, 142). Hana' Tharwat and her husband were immediately convinced, and she decided to veil. Yet she still had contracts that she could not cancel and had to continue for a while. Muhammad al-ʿArabi completed his last role in the serial *Awlad Adam / Children of Adam*. Hana' Tharwat, besides her role in *Awlad Adam*, also had some work to finish in Jordan and Kuwait. She already bought a veil, but in the evening she was on stage unveiled. The last evening she had to act, she cried intensely, thanking God for having given her the length of life to veil. She had been fearful to die before being able to repent from the sin of not veiling (interview, *Sabah al-Khayr*, February 15, 2000, p. 61). Although she already had given her first daughter, Iman, an Islamic name to express her piety, her son was born in the period of repentance when she was asking God for forgiveness. He was named "Ghafran," "Mercy" (al-Sayyid n.d., 79). Hana' Tharwat's final decision to retire was connected with her pilgrimage in 1986, the *hajj* she undertook together with her husband and his half sister Kamilia al-'Arabi. It was an important religious experience that made her feel very close to God. She realized that despite fulfilling many of her ambitions as an artist, she had never felt real happiness and tranquillity (interview, *Hiwar*, June 9, 2001).

About the experience of the pilgrimage was also important to Kamilia al-'Arabi, she did not decide to step down. She did not consider her work as a TV presenter *haram* and felt accordingly no need to retire. As a child she had always dreamt of working in the media. She was acquainted with the field of art and media through her father's work. She had a strong ambition to become famous and saw the field of media and art as the way to happiness (interview, *Hiwar*, June 9, 2001). She married and had three children. Her dream almost vanished. She finished her secondary education after her oldest son went to school. She continued to study at home and graduated from the Faculty of Commerce (Abu al-'Aynayn 1999, 147). In 1981, her dream came true, and she started to work in TV, particularly in children's programs and later on in more varied programs (Nasif and Khodayr n.d., 112).

About her religious education she mentioned that she was from a very religious family. Her father was strict, and his children had to pray at the age of six and to fast at the age of ten (interview, *Hiwar*, June 9, 2001).[9] He would beat them if they did not comply. He instructed her that her short sleeves were shameful, and if she phoned in a loud voice he told her it was "*'eb*," shameful. He obliged his children to give *zakat*, alms, from their earnings. Kamilia al-'Arabi described her saturation with religion as having occurred with no real understanding of Islam. She was unfamiliar with the religious content of rules and why certain things are *haram*, or obligatory (al-Sayyid n.d., 83; interview, *al-Nur*, April 1, 1992, p. 7). With regard to veiling, she mentioned that she did not know it was a religious duty. She believed that the right intention, *niyya*, is what really mattered. Also, when she started reading religious literature, she did not know whether veiling was a religious duty or *sunna*, following the example of the Prophet's wives.[10]

The final decision to veil was taken during Ramadan 1989 (Nasif and Khodayr n.d., 114–115). She was in the habit of not visiting any hairdresser during Ramadan. She had just returned from the hairdresser the last night of the month Sha'ban and would not visit the hairdresser until the first day of the 'Id al-Fitr. She found the house empty and went to her room to read the Qur'an. She then had a strong religious sensation variously described as "talking to God" (Nasif and Khodayr n.d., 114), "having the feeling God is with her," or a "vision" (Abu al-'Aynayn 1999, 146). She read passages in the Qur'an about the slaves of God and the believers and asked herself why she was not one of them. She prayed and did *salat al-tarawih*, special Ramadan evening prayers, for several hours and cried. She wept as she never had before and had the strange feeling that God "washed" her, "purified" her, and took her "to the lights." On this evening, described as a "rebirth," she came out of her room veiled and decided never to unveil. She finally understood the real "content of happiness," her hesitation transformed into "firm belief," and her unrest changed into "tranquillity" (Nasif and Khodayr n.d., 114).

A recurrent theme in the spiritual biographies of "repentant" artists is a strong feeling of unrest, unhappiness, and aversion before the spiritual transformation actually takes place. These feelings of anxiety and discomfort are changed into a sense of calmness and peace of mind. Reactions of remorse and regret are important in mediating the transformation from restlessness to serenity. These are important emotional states that accompany the process of repentance. For most artists, repentance was a crucial experience. Yet not all approved of the label "repentant" artists. Several positions were discernible. Some of them, like Hala al-Safi and Shams al-Barudi, used the concept to signal a total break with the life before. They did not mind being called repentant artists. They regretted their former activities and considered art *haram* and "of the devil," at least for women. Other artists, like Yasmin al-Khiyyam, strongly detested the concept of "repentance." Yasmin al-Khiyyam, whom we will meet in Chapter 3, refused to cooperate when Nasif and Khodayr wrote the second edition of their book. She was insulted by the title of the first edition, *Repentant Artists and the Sex Stars*. She forecasted that they "would enter hell" (Nasif and Khodayr n.d., 93). She objected not only to "Sex Stars," but also to the label "penitent." She did not consider her former career as a singer of mostly religious and national songs sinful. Actress Hoda Sultan also rejected the term "repentance" when she decided to act veiled (*Al-Liwa' al-Islamiyya*, May 6, 2003). She was totally committed to art and convinced of its potential to raise people's awareness. She saw no reason to retire and refrain from using her God-given talent as an actress. It is particularly the combination of "repentant" with "artist," suggesting that art is a sin from which one has to repent, that is repugnant to them. A third position among artists was taken by those who did not mind the concept "*tawba*," but used it in a more subtle and generalized way. They pointed at the habit of the Prophet to repent a hundred times a day. All people make mistakes and commit sins, and it is a lofty practice for anyone to repent. They sinned not as artists but as human beings. So the discussion among the artists about the label "repentant artists" is linked not only to their conception of art as sinful or not, but also to the concept of sin. The third group of artists that asserts the inevitability of sinning and thus the need for continual repentance is supported by many religious scholars.

REPENTANCE AND PIETY

The religious significance of the preparatory stage of discomfort or worry was made clear to me by a sheikh of al-Azhar, whom I visited twice to discuss my research topic.[11] His take on the repentance of artists had a psychological-religious twist. He explained that God had created human beings with *fitra*, a nature or disposition that connects them with their Creator. It is an essential and innate source of faith and spirituality existent in every human being. People who disobey the commandments of God, the sheikh continued, thus not only infringe on "God's right," but also act against their own disposition. This causes feelings of unrest, estrangement, and pain. The awareness of the disconnection of the *fitra* with actual comportments becomes increasingly unbearable and painful. This leads to an urge to reestablish the original balance between human nature and the divine. Once this balance is established, the pain is gone and transformed into tranquillity, *sakina*. Human beings, however, find it difficult to keep in touch with their spiritual nature and often relapse into distancing themselves from God (see Chapter 9). It was interesting to hear the sheikh explain what the artists told me about the process they had gone through. Many of them explained it in terms of unrest (*qal'a*) and pain (*alam*) that was finally replaced by feelings of calmness (*raha*) and tranquillity (*sakina*). The sheikh's account and the experiences of the repentant artists are in striking correspondence with the religious idiom of *tawba*, repentance.

Tawba literally means to (re)turn to God or to be converted to God (Denny 2000). The translation of *tawba* as repentance is according to Khalil (2006) not completely correct. It should be understood as a turn or return to and by God—that is, a movement from humans to God but also from God to humans. One of the names of God is the "*Tawwab*," describing the "oft-turning and relenting" character of God (Denny 2000). *Tawba* sub-sumes the notion of repentance and entails a broader process of returning or conversion. In addition, it implies a dialectical relationship between God and human beings (Khalil 2006). As we have seen in Chapter 1, the idea of "divine guidance," whether in the form of dreams, visions, or spiritual experiences, was important in the onset of the repentance process. It was the experience of God's turning to his servant that started off the transformation from ignorance to illumination, and from "sinning" to "*iltizam*," religious commitment.

The broad notion of *tawba* as a process of (re)turning explains why many of the Islamist booklets on repentance include a mixture of born-again Muslims, reverts, and converts. The stories of the repentant artists are thus combined not only with coreligionist penitent burglars, but also with Western converts to Islam. Among theories on conversion, models exist that compare the different forms of religious transitions: between and within religious institutions and traditions, as well as forms of religious intensification (Rambo 1993). In addition, there is a notion that "all humans are born Muslim," that is, in a state of "submission to God." For that reason Islam is the original and natural religion to which believers should revert. Many converts accordingly prefer to be called reverts. They do not embrace a new conviction, but return to the original message of unity and submission to God (see Van Nieuwkerk 2006a, 2006b). From that specific point of view, it does not really matter whether a person returns to God from a secular, Christian, or non-practicing Muslim background. Besides titles with *tawba*, such as *Dumuʿ al-Taʾibin / Tears of the Repenters* (ʿAbdallah 2004) or *Fannanat Taʾibat / Repentant Artists* (Nasif and Khodayr n.d.), other authors use the general notion of "return," "*ʿaʾida*": such as *Al-ʿAʾidun ila Allah / People Returning to God* (al-Sangri 1999), or *Nisaʾ ʿAʾidat ila Allah / Women Returning to God* (al-Sayyid n.d.).

There is a body of, predominantly, Sufi literature on *tawba*. The eleventh-century Sufi al-Hujwiri (d. 1063–1064) described *tawba* as the turning back from what God has forbidden out of fear (transl. Nicholson 1911, 294–300). A related concept is *nadam*, regret or remorse, and the Prophet is reported to have said, "regret is the act of returning," "*al-nadam al-tawba*." Regret, repentance, and the return to God are thus closely linked concepts, of which *tawba* is the most encompassing. Ibn al-ʿArabi, the thirteenth-century Andalusian mystic, emphasized the two-directionality of turning (Khalil 2006, 404). Imam al-Ghazali, who started to write his encyclopedic work *Ihya ʿUlum al-Din / The Revivification of the Science of Religion* in 1095, devoted a book to the concept and practice of repentance. According to him, *tawba* consists of three successive and joined elements: knowledge, the state of remorse, and action.

Knowledge is first, awareness second, and action third. Knowledge, regret, and the abandonment of sin are three successive steps within this process. *Tawba*, al-Ghazali explained, is frequently used for regret alone, as if making knowledge a precondition, and abandonment a consequence. According to him, though, the term *tawba* refers to the totality of the process.[12] Repentance is thus a highly valued and positive act, particularly among Sufis. Al-Ghazali tries to unify Sufism and traditional Islamic knowledge. He opened the fourth part of his encyclopedic work, which deals with the positive traits human beings must strive for, with a chapter on repentance. He regarded *tawba*—as do many Sufis—as a basic process and a prerequisite for attaining salvation. Repentance is the first stage "of pilgrims on the way to the Truth" (al-Hujwiri, transl. Nicholson 1911, 295).

As we have seen in the section on dreams and visions in Chapter 1, spiritual experiences that are often associated with Sufism accompany members of the piety movement in Egypt on their way to devoutness. The Islamist movement is embedded in the Wahhabi-inspired Salafi tradition, which is mostly understood as stressing legal reasoning and favoring scripturalism. Sufism is regarded by many Islamists as an apolitical quietist trend or as a form of mystical backwardness. Ibn al-ʿArabi is despised among many Islamists, and al-Ghazali is not considered the most authoritative or inspirational figure among contemporary Islamists (Lauzière 2005, 248–249). Not only contemporary Islamic activists, but also the official *ʿulama'* in Egypt, condemn popular Sufism. The artists whose spiritual biographies I outline are not Sufis, but part of the mainstream Islamist movement. This emphasis on *tawba* is not necessarily a contradiction, though. First, *tawba* also belongs to the religious, historical, and cultural legacy of Sunni mainstream orthodoxy. Despite its privileged position among Sufis, it is also encouraged by contemporary preachers who are important to the piety movement such as ʿAmr Khalid. Besides, not all forms of Sufism are in contradistinction to orthodox interpretations. Interesting in this regard is Moroccan sheikh Yassin's attempt to distinguish between "Salafi" Sufism and "philosophical" Sufism. In his attempt to create more space for spirituality within the Moroccan Islamist movement, he embraces "Salafi Sufist" thinkers (Lauzière 2005, 248).

Understanding the piety movement in terms of an opposition between Salafism and Sufism is not very helpful. Despite the discursive juxtaposition, a firm opposition between Salafism and Sufism should be deconstructed in order to understand the development of the piety movement. Spirituality rather than Sufism is perhaps a better term to capture the pious aspirations of the "repentant" artists. Although inflected by Wahhabi Salafi thought, the piety movement allows ample space for spirituality and renewal of faith. So spirituality is brought into the Islamic Revival by the piety movement. As Gaffney also observed, the strong appeal to moral arguments in public life is shared among Sufis, Islamic activists, and the piety movement at large (1994, 50).[13]

Whether in the artists' stories, the explanation of the sheikh of al-Azhar mentioned above, the lessons by the popular preacher ʿAmr Khalid, or the more Sufi-inspired literature of around the twelfth century, several points of convergence on the notion of repentance arise and are worth considering. I do not intend to trace the genealogy of the concept *tawba*. Nor do I want to give the impression that the concept has remained unchanged over the centuries or that there are no alternative interpretations or unconventional readings.[14] I will outline some consistencies that are relevant for the present-day piety movement and also shed light on the experiences of the "repentant" artists. These consistencies can be due to the framing by artists of their stories according to models of sincere repentance, "*tawba nasuha*," or, in other cases, to the religious authors reworking these stories according to the narrative form of the "authentic" repentance experience. I will outline important notions and affective states that, according to several sources, are part of the repentance idiom and recur in the stories of the artists.

First, an interesting point of conjunction in the material I consulted is the stress on the feeling of pain, uneasiness, and discomfort that sets in motion the process of repentance. Akin to the sheik's theory about the alienated *fitra*, Imam al-Ghazali explained that the first stage of repentance is knowledge, that is, the realization of the "magnitude of the sin's harm and its being a barrier between man and the divine. [. . .] [T]his realization will stir a heartache on account of the Beloved eluding him. For the heart, whenever it perceives the withdrawal of the Beloved, is pained. If the withdrawal be through man's own action, he is regretful of that alienating behaviour. Such grief of the heart over behaviour alienating the Beloved is called Regret. When this anguish becomes overpowering, another inner state is induced, termed volition and aspiration towards [new] behaviour connected with the present, the past, and the future."[15] So the distance to God, the Beloved, is the cause of the pain and the moving force for repenting and thus transforming the pain into an aspiration for renewed nearness. In a similar vein, the preacher ʿAmr Khalid asked his audience, in the talk show *Kalam min al-Qalb | Words from the Heart*, in what way one can recognize the start of the *tawba* process. The right answer is "pain of the heart." Also in a special lesson on *tawba*, he lectured that the heart tells the believers to repent in order to rededicate themselves to God.[16] The pain of the heart can be motivated by different factors such as fear of God's punishment, desire for God's favor and love, or shame before God (see al-Hujwiri transl. in Nicholson 1911, 295), yet it is often described as the distance or alienation from the Creator or Beloved that ultimately evokes a sense of guilt and loss. The ultimate aim of repentance is thus nearness to God, which is the essence of piety according to the women I spoke to (see also Mahmood 2005).

Second, this removal of the alienation from God presupposes knowledge of the acts, thoughts, and comportments that might endanger the relationship with God. For that reason al-Ghazali stressed that the first step is gaining knowledge about the right conduct and abstention from sins. It is the knowledge of the sources of sin and the awareness of actually committing sin that set in motion the process of repentance. Popular preacher 'Amr Khalid in his lesson on *tawba* repeats the three aspects outlined above by al-Ghazali: *tawba* starts with knowledge (*'ilm*), which is then translated into fear and regret for making mistakes and finally into actions or deeds (*'amal*) to rectify behavior. This partly explains the commitment of the artists to spreading religiously sound knowledge, as they felt they themselves had lacked correct religious instruction. They were not aware of the major sin of, for instance, not veiling, of which they became aware only after proper religious instruction. In the process of shedding their ignorance they realized the enormity of their sins and the reasons for their dormant anguish and anxiety.

Third, there is an elaborate theory of sinning in which authors provide examples fitting the historical context of their writing. Al-Ghazali discussed several divisions based on the sources and origins of sin. "Some of them [pertain] especially to the heart; such as unbelief, heresy, hypocrisy and harboring evil designs; others [pertain specifically] to the eye and ear, or to the tongue, or the stomach and genitals, or the hands and feet; some to the entire body" (Stern 1990, 56). A more common classification is dividing sins into those between man and God and those pertaining to the relation of man to man. Another recurrent distinction is between major sins and lesser sins. 'Amr Khalid, for instance, stressed as major sins not obeying parents and not praying on time, and as lesser sins not wearing the veil, as well as the sins of the eyes committed by boys who look at unveiled girls or engage in indecent "chatting." A third category of sins has to do with inattentiveness (*ghafla*). Negligence and lack of real attentiveness during prayer and failure to value God's bounty and blessings are even worse and more difficult to undo than most other sins, according to 'Amr Khalid.[17]

What is common in the literature on sin is its massiveness and ubiquity even among saints and prophets, let alone among the common believers. 'Amr Khalid lectured that many people do not fully realize the number of sins they commit daily, thinking of sins only in terms of major and obvious mistakes and offenses. Al-Ghazali also explained: "No man is free from sins by his limbs; for even the prophets were not free of them [. . .]. If a man, in some cases, is free of sin by commission, he is not free of thinking about sin in his mind. If he is free, sometimes, from such thought, he is not free of satanic temptation by instigation of sporadic thoughts distracting from invoking God's name. But even if he is free there from, he would not be free of heedlessness and shortcoming in the knowledge of God, His attributes and acts. [. . .] That is why the Prophet said: 'Verily my heart is beclouded so that I beg forgiveness of God seventy times in a day'" (Stern 1990, 46). Sinning is inevitable and part of human nature. Al-Ghazali posited, nonetheless, that man is created with a "sound heart" and that the correction of sins through repentance is also intrinsic to man's basic nature. Sinning, for human beings, is inevitable, but no one is inherently evil (Stern 1979, 590–591). Repentance, it is stressed by 'Amr Khalid, is a personal duty (*farida min al-fara'id*). It is obligatory for every believer.

Fourth, the danger of the habituation to sins and the importance of the habituation to repentance are recurrent in the literature. Al-Ghazali often used clear and mundane examples to clarify his points. He compared the persistent continuation of even small sins with drops of water falling, continuously, upon a stone until they wear it away. The same amount of water, poured onto the stone all at once, would not produce a similar effect. Al-Ghazali stressed the fact that human beings are highly subject to conditioning. The importance of habit is a trait that could reinforce negative behavior. Sins are to faith what toxic foods are to the body, al-Ghazali argued. "They keep accumulating inside [the body] until the component elements change, imperceptibly, until the composition deteriorates and suddenly the man falls ill, then, suddenly, dies. So it is with the sinner. Hurry, hurry, then, to repent before the toxic sins do their work on the spirit of faith" (Stern 1990, 42). *Tawba*, inversely, can strengthen the process of spiritual progress. Once used to repenting from sins and obeying God's commandments, believers will find it progressively easier to continue such a habit (Stern 1979, 594). It is important for them, once aware of the commission of a sin, to repent instantly. Also 'Amr Khalid urges his audiences to continuously repent from all minor and major sins, day and night. If the Prophet is doing it seventy times during one meeting or a hundred times a day, it must be a lofty practice. Continuous repentance is perceived as a key to constant renewal of faith; it means a recurrent way to approach God. During 'Amr Khalid's talk show, audience members were invited to tell about their experience of *tawba*. One of them recounted her quick temper toward her parents. When she realized the gravity of her sin and that it would undo all her good deeds, she repented and prayed two *raka'at al-tawba*, special prayers for repentance. Yet losing her temper happened again and again, but every time she prayed and repented. After some time she experienced that her heart was no longer able to commit this sin against her parents. She experienced this transformation as divinely inspired: God had changed her heart in such a manner that she was no longer able to commit this particular sin. As with the Prophet, who repented a hundred times a day, the recurrent *tawba* prayer ingrained a pious disposition in the young woman's heart. If repentance is continuously practiced, it is a profound instrument for developing a pious habitus.

Another aspect most authors stress is the relenting and merciful character of the Creator. Penitence is not only a lofty and important religious practice; it is also very simple and rewarding. God tries to make devotion as smooth and easy as possible for the believer. 'Amr Khalid in particular tries to convince his audience of the easiness of *tawba* and the compassion of God. After informing his audience about the severity and magnitude of their sins, he immediately clarified that it is not his intention to annoy the audience, but to show them a solution that is so easily at hand for every believer: repent! God is the *Ghafur al-Rahim*, the Compassionate One who forgives sins. Doubt about the acceptance of *tawba* by God is disbelieving in one of his names and attributes. Even if there is a relapse into the same sin, the previous sins of which one has repented are wiped away; one only has to repent for the newly committed sins. There is also no need to repent from all sins at the same time; one can repent from a specific sin. After the repentance, sins are changed into meritorious deeds, *hasanat*. Sins of twenty years not praying on time can be forgiven in one moment of sincere *tawba*, 'Amr Khalid explains.[18] Al-Ghazali also argued that partial repentance is possible. He based his argument on the *hadith* "One who renounces a sin is as one who has never sinned," reasoning that otherwise it would have been expressed as "One who renounces all sins" (Stern 1990, 98). Al-Hujwiri also mentioned several *hadiths* showing the extent of God's happiness about penitents: "There is nothing that God loves more than a youth who repents" (transl. Nicholson 1911, 294).

Another point of convergence in the literature illuminates Hala al-Safi's conviction that regret was a necessary part of repentance. She felt she could not be proud about her past fame, because this would call into question her sincere remorse. The importance of regret is congruent with the literature about sincere repentance. The formulated conditions of genuine *tawba* are rather consistent and can be summarized by the following three elements as mentioned, for instance, by Ibn al-'Arabi: "There are three conditions of *tawba* for it to be sound: remorse for the violations that have been committed [*al-nadam* . . .]; an immediate abandonment of the slip [. . .]; and a firm resolve not to return to similar acts of disobedience" (in Khalil 2006, 405). 'Amr Khalid reiterates the same three conditions in his lessons, and al-Hujwiri mentioned them as well (transl. Nicholson 1911, 294). Also, al-Ghazali mentioned that repentance consists of regret, which leads to determination and resolution. As we have seen, al-Ghazali understands regret to be caused by "knowledge that the offenses are a barrier between man and his Beloved" (Stern 1990, 86). Regret is characterized by a strong aversion to the original sin. Shams al-Barudi's dislike of acting and Hala al-Safi's aversion to the belly-dancing costume are signs of the sincerity of the wish to repent. Regret points to a process of changing sensibility on the way to sincere repentance. Al-Ghazali held that "Indeed, whenever man himself deems the sin as major, it becomes, in God's view, minor, because the apprehension of its magnitude stems from the heart's aversion to it and loathing of it" (Stern 1990, 83). Besides aversion, regret is also marked by grief, sorrow, tears, and excessive weeping. "The sign of the sincerity of regret is the mellowness of the heart and the profusion of tears" (Stern 1990, 86). And to clean, purge, and purify the heart, one needs to "wash it in the flow of tears and the burning of regret" (Stern 1990, 51). So the affective states we have seen in the artists' stories of repentance, such as aversion, weeping, and regret, are part of the repentance idiom. The same holds for the ensuing experiences of illumination and nearness to God that finally bring about the sense of calmness, serenity, and tranquillity.

Finally, consistent with the theory of al-Ghazali that repentance consists of knowledge, regret, and action, the literature points to the importance of good deeds to make up for former sins. There is not only an inward element to *tawba*, but also an active and outward aspect. Public confession of sins can be part of it, but also religious engagement. The third stage of action or resolution, according to al-Ghazali, concerns the will to rectify oneself. The penitents must show an abundance of good deeds. They should scrutinize their past and seek for each of these sins a corresponding good deed. "Listening to entertainments is atoned by listening to the recitation of the Koran and *dhikr* sessions. The consumption of wine is atoned by charitable donation of a licit beverage which is better and liked by him" (Stern 1990, 89). 'Amr Khalid instructed one of his auditors, who feared she had trespassed the rights of her deceased parents, to do many supplicatory prayers for them or to make an *'umrah* on behalf of them. There are many ways to make up for sins: religious acts to confirm faith on a personal level or more actively in the form of public outreach. Many of the former artists decided to use their fame and name to publicize their religious renewal. The granting of interviews by "repentant" artists to religious magazines and the publication of their stories of illumination and sincere repentance are examples of *da'wah*. Others were also engaged in forms of charity, donations of money, food, and clothing, or other good deeds (see Chapter 3). Some became active in the field of religious instruction as auditor or as preacher, crucial facets of the piety movement that will be described below.

DA'WAH AND RELIGIOUS INSTRUCTION

The stories of the "repentant" artists I have presented so far show that religious knowledge and practice were not wholly absent from their lives. Hala al-Safi mentioned her commitment to fasting and praying, and also to giving alms "without knowing it was a religious duty." Kamilia al-'Arabi also stressed the rigor of her father, even to the point of beating her, if she was negligent in religious duties. The "repentant" artists complained that they lacked "proper" knowledge and that they did not fully understand the religious importance and meaning of those religious rituals they performed. Hala al-Safi did not realize that dancing is "*haram*" and, like Kamilia al-'Arabi, did not know that veiling is a "religious duty." Shams al-Barudi related regretfully that they were raised after the 1952 Revolution in a "period of ignorance." Religion was taught as any other subject such as mathematics or science. She called this period the time of "the obedience of the ignorant and the worship of the disobedient."[19] Kamilia al-'Arabi was "saturated with religion," yet, at the same time, without a "real understanding of Islam."

It is this lack of real understanding of correct practice and Islam's importance for daily life that the piety movement intends to redress through lectures, sermons, and instruction. Mahmood (2005) has analyzed the aims of the female instructors belonging to the mosque movement. According to them the real problem is that religion has become marginalized under secular governance. The teachers warned against "secularization," "*almaniyya*." By this concept they meant that religion had fallen prey to a process of differentiation that made Islam into a separate sphere, whereas, they argued, religious sensibilities should be extended over all aspects of their lives. Islam was often either practiced out of habit and custom, or perceived as an abstract system of values that was largely inessential to daily life. Religion should be reinstated to its encompassing importance for regulating day-to-day life (Mahmood 2005, 44–47). Religion was a standard subject of the curriculum, and, as Starrett shows, the decline of time per year devoted to religion as a subject between 1930 and the 1980s was compensated for by the increase of the number of years in which religion was taught (1998, 80–81). He draws attention, though, to the "functionalization" of religion as a subject in the curriculum. That is, religion was "put to work" for different social and political projects, such as Sadat's ideas about "Science and Faith" or Mubarak's attempt to combat extremism, rather than for instilling religious values. The mosque movement intends to put religion back for its own sake into the center of the believers' lives.

In order to understand the difference in approach between the state and the members of the piety movement, it is instructive to compare the way ritual ablution and prayer are handled in school textbooks with religious lessons of the piety movement on this topic. In the school curriculum, cleanliness is described as a token of advancement and civilization. According to the sixth grade textbook: "Perhaps the *wudu*ʿ [. . .] clarifies best the scope of Islam's interest in cleanliness since it is part of prayer [. . .] and the modern physician has established that the *wudu*ʿ a number of times a day brings health and keeps away skin diseases" (in Starrett 1998, 140). In another primary school textbook, prayer is presented as a form of productivity and progress. The movement of prayer invigorates the body, increases production, and promotes the nation: "Prayer accustoms us to order, and the keeping of appointments, and the binding together of Muslims with cooperative ties and love and harmony" (in Starrett 1995a, 962). For the female instructors of the mosques, ablution and prayer are critical to the formation of a virtuous Muslim. Habitual prayer is something the believer cannot do without. It is a feeling and a practice through which pious dispositions are created. It is the way to reach nearness to God and a means to pious conduct. Prayer is not the outward sign of piety, but should become a desire for worshipping God. One does not pray because one is a virtuous Muslim, but one creates a pious self by habitually performing the *salat* (Mahmood 2005, 122–128). It is the functional take on religion, in which Islam is emptied of its vast significance for every aspect of life, that the pious instructors of the mosque movement try to rectify. This should be replaced by instruction on the performance and habitual completion of devotional practices.

Lessons, sermons, instruction, and other forms of *da'wah* to counter the compartmentalization of religion were the most crucial activities of the piety movement. The number of private or local mosques that provide lessons has accordingly increased enormously. In 1991, it was estimated that there were 91,000 mosques, of which 45,000 were private and 10,000 small prayer rooms (*zawiya*) (Wickham 2002, 98). The major source of finance for these private mosques was voluntary donations from Egyptians, as well as financial support from institutional and individual patrons in the Gulf. Besides daily and Friday prayer, and religious lessons (*durus dinniya*), the mosques often provided after-school and day-care activities for children, competitions in the memorization of the Qur'an, a library for Islamic books and cassette tapes, and—depending on the size of the mosque—health care and charity distribution. In the latter case the private mosque resembled an Islamic voluntary association. Some of these Islamic private voluntary organizations (PVOS) also provided classes for the memorization of the Qur'an and had day-care centers, schools, and job training (see Chapter 3).

Lessons were thus not only provided in official mosques, but even more in local mosques and in Islamic welfare associations. The teachers at neighborhood mosques and Islamic welfare associations were not the same as those working in the official mosques where official preachers gave sermons. Hirschkind (2006) underlines the difference between the state mosques and the local neighborhood mosques: those run by the Ministry of Religious Affairs and those run by nongovernmental associations or neighborhood committees. In the former *khutaba'*, that is, preachers who graduated from al-Azhar University and were appointed by the government, gave sermons; in the latter the *da'iyya*, the "lay preacher," preached (2006, 49, 57). Yet the two sectors can come together, as the label *da'iyya* became attached also to the graduates from al-Azhar *da'wah* institutes, institutes created by the government to get a firmer hold on the parallel Islamic sector.

The word *da'iyya* comes from *da'a*, to call or to summon. It refers to someone who calls on other Muslims to live in conformity to God's will, or someone who practices "*da'wah*," Islamic outreach. *Da'iyya* is the singular used for both male and female preachers, whereas in the plural *da'iyat* is used for female preachers and *du'at* for men. With the growth in the number of female preachers, there is a tendency to distinguish in the singular as well: *da'i* for men and *da'iyya* for women (Hirschkind 2006, 47; Mahmood 2005, 57).[20] Whereas the official preachers have been incorporated into the state, the *da'iyya* initially worked outside the state-administered religious bureaucracies. Nasser started to supervise, train, and certify religious specialists, a project that was continued by his successors. In the 1960s, steps were taken to bring all mosques under the control of the Ministry of Religious Affairs, a process that is still underway. Several "*da'wah* institutes" were founded by the Ministry of Religious Affairs to combat Islamic militancy, and in 1978 a "*da'wah* college" was set up for the same reason (Hirschkind 2006, 44). Those graduated from a *da'wah* institute or college were called *da'iyya* and employed by the state. Most preachers of the Islamic Revival, however, did not graduate from state-controlled *da'wah* institutes or from al-Azhar University. They regarded *da'wah* as a vocation rather than as employment. They mostly graduated from secular universities, as did 'Amr Khalid, who graduated in accounting from Cairo University. The *da'iyya* received specific religious education through mosque lessons and self-study, and through the *da'wah* institutes such as the Gama'iyya al-Shar'iyya. These *da'wah* institutes are organized by the parallel Islamist sector's nongovernmental organizations (Mahmood 2005, 64, 72).

The attempt of the government to gain control over the private mosques and Islamic PVOs was to crystallize more clearly in the 1990s. In 1989, the Ministry of Al-Awqaf (Religious Endowment) established several *da'wah* institutes, renamed into cultural centers, which offered postgraduate diplomas to non-Azhar graduates (*al-Ahram* weekly no. 614, November 28, 2002). This was linked to an attempt of the regime in the 1990s to speed up the surveillance over mosques and *da'wah* institutes of the parallel sector. Accelerating the nationalization of local mosques was a difficult task in view of their extensiveness. In 1992, the government announced a plan to put the mosques under the supervision of the Ministry of Religious Endowment at a speed of ten thousand mosques a year (Wickham 2002, 106). Several factors hindered the implementation of this plan. First, it was too expensive, as the incorporation of each mosque cost about six thousand pounds a year. Besides, there was an imam shortage. The government needed forty thousand new imams, and the number of graduates from al-Azhar University fell short by far. It was estimated that about 45 percent of the mosques were brought under control in 1994, yet this estimate is probably too high (Wickham 2002, 107). Other attempts at control were the stipulation of the topics that should be discussed each week in the sermon and the posting of government inspectors in all mosques. In 1997, a law was passed that made it illegal to give a sermon without a license from the Ministry of Religious Affairs (Hirschkind 2006, 49–50). This control over sermons, however, did not encompass the whole field of religious instruction and certainly not those lessons given outside the mosques in homes.

The first lessons in the 1980s were particularly aimed at public employees and Egyptians who returned from the Gulf states after having worked there during the oil boom. Also in poor neighborhoods mosque lessons became a common feature. Lessons in the posh neighborhood of Muhandisin, such as in the mosque–cum–charity organization of Mustafa Mahmud, started probably in the early 1990s. It is difficult to evaluate the precise content of the lessons between 1980 and 1990. Studies based on participant-observation of the mosque lessons are of a later date. They were mostly conducted in the mid-1990s, when the lessons had spread to all neighborhoods and became a salient feature of the religious landscape. Mahmood, who conducted fieldwork in 1996, analyzed the major themes of the lessons of that period. They were strikingly similar to the lessons I followed in the beginning of 2000 in the Netherlands among Dutch Moroccan immigrants (Van Nieuwkerk 2007, 2010). The *ʿibadat* as well as the *muʿamalat,* that is, the acts of worship as well as social transactions, were addressed. Religious concepts such as *taqwa,* piety or virtuous fear, *khushuʿ,* humility before God, *hubb Allah* and *hubb lilaah,* God's love and love for God, as well as sincerity, were discussed (Mahmood 2005; Van Nieuwkerk 2007, 2010). In 2005, I followed several lessons in the upper-middle-class neighborhood of Muhandisin and witnessed that the themes outlined by Mahmood were still highly relevant. Patience, *sabr,* *daʿwah,* and female modesty were also prominent themes. The topics were particularly aimed at the formation of a pious self through habitual practice of worship and developing the right disposition for devotion.

Whereas separate lessons for women started around the 1980s (Mahmood 2005, 42–43), lessons by female preachers were probably first delivered by the early 1990s and became more frequent in the mid-1990s. The entrance of women into the field of *daʿwah* is according to Mahmood (2005) related to two factors. First, there are sociological reasons connected to the general level of female literacy. Women's enrollment in universities has increased tremendously since the 1950s. Since 1961, al-Azhar admitted female students, and women have accordingly started to study religious subjects (Mahmood 2005, 66). The establishment of *daʿwah* institutes, which offered diplomas to non-Azhar graduates, encouraged this trend. Second, modern religious interpretations of *daʿwah* hold that all individuals who are observant of Islamic rules are qualified to practice outreach. This modern notion of *daʿwah* is connected to the founder of the Muslim Brotherhood, Hassan al-Banna. He saw propagation as a mode of action by which moral and political reform was to take place. Members of the Muslim Brotherhood went to schools, mosques, and other public places and discussed Islam in an effort to build a pious society (Hirschkind 2006, 113–114). *Daʿwah* was linked to the concept of "*amr bil maʿruf wal-nahi ʿan al-munkar,*" the injunction to command what is good and to prohibit what is evil (Mahmood 2005, 58; Wickham 2002, 128). "Commanding right and forbidding wrong"[21] is considered an individual obligation (*fard al-ʿayn*). This obligation can entail other forms, such as physical force; however, verbal admonition or encouragement constitutes the main field of *daʿwah.* This duty is thus not based on doctrinal knowledge or gender, but rather on moral uprightness and practical knowledge of the religious tradition. This conception opened up the field for female preachers (Mahmood 2005, 62–66). The growth of the number of female preachers is probably also related to the phenomenon of the Islamic salons, which were hosted in the private homes of (upper-)middle-class women.

One of the first and most well-known Egyptian *da'iyya* was Zeinab al-Ghazali, who wrote the introduction to Shams al-Barudi's *My Journey from Darkness to the Light*. Shams al-Barudi herself initially restricted her activities to advising her circle of relatives and those who actively sought her advice from outside the family, mostly artists, but was not actively engaged in extensive *da'wah* (Abu Dawud and Bayumi 1994, 30). Asked in 1988 about her missionary activities, she said she did not know when to consider someone a *da'iyya*, a preacher. But if a fellow Muslim asked her about something connected with the Qur'an and the *sunna* and she happened to have this knowledge, it would be *haram* to keep this knowledge to herself.[22] Hana' Tharwat and Kamilia al-'Arabi became famous preachers. There is only scarce information about the lectures they gave. According to an eyewitness account in the magazine *Ruz al-Yusif*, Kamilia al-'Arabi and Hana' Tharwat had become full-fledged preachers by 1993. The reporter for *Ruz al-Yusif* had visited the lectures of both women. They were accompanied by Hala al-Safi, all three covered in black *niqab*. The journalist compared their styles of preaching. Whereas Kamilia al-'Arabi preached about the blessings of heaven, Hana' Tharwat allegedly invoked fear of hell. According to the *Ruz al-Yusif* journalist, Hana' Tharwat preached that women are *fitna* and should hide themselves in order not to rival the devil. If even a small part of her body becomes visible, she will have to give "*sadaqa*," that is, voluntary donations of it, in hell (*Ruz al-Yusif*, March 1, 1993, pp. 54–55). Whereas Hana' Tharwat used the *tarhib* style, making people fearful of the afterlife, Kamilia al-'Arabi emphasized trust in God's mercy. The latter style is known as *targhib* ("awakening desire") or *wa'd* ("promise"), referring to God's promise of eternity for the righteous (Hirschkind 2006, 151). Initially the female audience came to listen to their lessons out of curiosity and to see the famous stars; they eventually stayed — according to Kamilia al-'Arabi — because of her message (in Abu al-'Aynayn 1999, 146). Kamilia al-'Arabi at first gave lessons to ten to fifteen women in a few neighborhood mosques in Ma'adi and gradually developed into a popular preacher giving lessons in seventeen different mosques to more than a thousand women (Abu al-'Aynayn 1999, 146; Nasif and Khodayr n.d., 117). During my fieldwork, Hana' Tharwat had retired from Islamic outreach, but Kamilia al-'Arabi was still active as a *da'iyya* in the media.

Weekly religious lessons inside elite homes, also called "Islamic salons," emerged from the mid-1990s onward (Haenni 2002). According to journalist Kamal Masri,[23] who was involved in the organization of the Islamic salons for the elite in Muhandisin, it started in the early 1990s. The well-known Egyptian family of the late Ahmad Mashar, an actor, provided the link to actors and actresses. In the beginning the preachers were all males, but from the mid-1990s there were also female instructors for women. From this first "Islamic salon" the phenomenon spread to other elite neighborhoods such as Heliopolis and Maʿadi. Shams al-Barudi, Hanaʾ Tharwat, Kamilia al-ʿArabi, Hala al-Safi, and a few other retired artists were active in this first stage as audience, and later on some of them, also, as preachers. The "repentant" artists have played a key role in this development. The establishment of mosque lessons in the Mustafa Mahmud mosque by Shams al-Barudi and her colleagues in 1991, as well as those given by Kamilia al-ʿArabi and Hanaʾ Tharwat in private homes for upper-middle-class women in posh neighborhoods such as Maʿadi, became a trend. These artists also attracted other actors and actresses to visit their salons. Whereas the initial stage was directed at imparting knowledge, later the emphasis was redirected toward *daʿwah* inside and outside the circles of art. At present, Islamic salons are very common among women in upper-middle-class neighborhoods. The importance of these lessons for ethical self-making among women becomes clear from an interview researcher Sherine Hafez had with Omaima Abu Bakr, a well-known female scholar of Islam. Asked why she attended lessons, despite being a scholar of Islam herself, she replied:

> Of course the information that is taught in the lessons is not new to me. I may not be challenged intellectually. But these lessons inspire me. Sherine Fathi [a female star preacher], for example, is an excellent speaker. What these lessons do is provide me with "roads to God." Every time I go it renews some aspect of faith that has become obscured in me by daily concerns. I leave with a sense of peace and satisfaction and a renewed religious vigor. (Hafez 2003, 36)

Whereas for less scholarly women, the information of the lecture is important, it was clear in the few Islamic salons I attended that the renewal of faith and religious inspiration was important as well. These Islamic salons in the well-to-do neighborhood Muhandisin were frequented by retired dancer Amira, former singer Hanan, and the veiled singer, actress, and TV presenter Mona ʿAbd al-Ghani, together with well-to-do women from the neighborhood. One of them opened her salon for religious lectures by female *daʿiyat*. Women were seated on couches and chairs while listening to the lesson. After the lecture and the *duʿa*, supplicatory prayer, there was time for socializing, and enjoying cakes, snacks, pizzas, and soft drinks. Around the abundantly filled table, the women decided where to attend the next Islamic salon. Some women open their houses on a fixed day. Besides being places for social talk and religious instruction, the Islamic salons are also a religious network for furthering *da'wah*. During one of the salons I visited, the owner of the salon, who also acted as *da'iyya* that day, provided us all with a book on "women in Islam," of almost seven hundred pages, for free. Those active in charity ask for donations for their organization or promote their next Islamic salon.

The "repentant" artists stood at the cradle of the Islamic salons, which became a new venue for religious learning and *da'wah* inside the homes of the elite. This pattern of holding religious meetings in private houses was adopted by other women of the upper-middle-class neighborhoods. Such meetings offered upper-middle-class women a comfortable way of Islamizing their lifestyles. They created a space for ethical self-making in accordance with the participants' consumption and socializing patterns. Whereas the "repentant" artists were, on the one hand, merely part of the Islamic trend, they have also helped to advance the piety movement up the social ladder into their own circles. Due to their celebrity status, the "repentant" artists, and their religious vigor, evoked curiosity among many female fans. Among them were women of the upper middle classes who until the 1990s had hardly been involved in the parallel Islamic sector. We will come across a related phenomenon, the involvement of upper-middle-class women in Islamic charity, in Chapter 3.

(THREE)

Veiling and Charity

I n this chapter, I will start with the life story of former singer Yasmin al-Khiyyam, who now runs a large charity organization. In the second part, I will discuss an important aspect of the trajectory toward piety for women—that is, veiling. Finally, I return to larger trends in the piety movement in Egypt and discuss the development of the Islamist parallel sector that provides religious service and charity.

THE SPIRITUAL BIOGRAPHY OF SINGER YASMIN AL-KHIYYAM

I obtained Yasmin al-Khiyyam's phone number from the veiled actress ʿAfaf Shoʿib, and she was immediately willing to talk to me.[1] I was invited to Gamaʿiyya al-Sheikh al-Hosari (Hosari Association), her charity organization named after her late father, in 6th of October City. She organized a guided tour through all the different projects of the organization, and in between the talks with several visitors we spoke together. At the end of the day, when the visitors were finally gone, we had a chance for an interview. She preferred that our interview not be taped and stressed her present activities rather than her past artistic life.[2] The enormous meeting room in which she received her many daily visitors—dressed in completely white clothes, which, as she explained, suit her name Yasmin and her conviction that Islam means beauty, cheerfulness, and lightness—contained many significant mementos of her life. The walls were full of photographs of her late father with important religious and nonreligious personalities such as the presidents Nasser and Sadat, and important colleague sheikhs and scholars such as Muhammad al-Ghazali. The wall was also adorned with her own certificates: her visit to Bosnia and a picture of her *'umrah* trip together with "her son" 'Amr Khalid. Together with the gifts I received, a book by her late father[3] and a tape with her own songs,[4] these details form a compelling ambience for a complex story.

Yasmin al-Khiyyam was born as Ifrag al-Hosari, daughter of the famous sheikh and Qur'an reciter, Mahmud Khalil al-Hosari (1917–1980). This fact has been one of the most influential facets of her life to the present day. Her father was born near Tanta and established himself as a reciter in the well-known Ahmadi mosque in Tanta at the age of twenty-five. Ten years later, he moved to Cairo and became the reciter at the Hussein mosque in 1955. He studied at al-Azhar University and became a well-known religious scholar, as well as author of many books on aspects of the Qur'an. He held the title Shayk al-Maqari', an official title as head of the reciters, and was one of the top four reciters in Egypt. He became involved in radio and was the first to record and broadcast in several styles of recitation (Nelson 2001, 193). Also, Ifrag was taught the Qur'an, enjoyed a religious education, and memorized the Qur'an at a young age. She inherited her father's talent and had a beautiful voice in reciting the Qur'an (Abu al-'Aynayn 1999, 51).

After finishing secondary school, she wanted to continue her education at Cairo University in the department of philosophy. However, her father opposed her wish, stressing that, for a girl, secondary education was sufficient. She could only fulfill her ambitions under the guardianship of her husband and on the condition that her home came first. Ifrag pursued her education and eventually worked for the Maglis al-Sha'b, the parliament (Abu al-'Aynayn 1999, 53).

During an official occasion she was asked to inaugurate the party for the women's delegation with a Qur'an recital. Jihan Sadat, who was present, was apparently impressed by her voice. President Sadat invited Ifrag, together with her father, and asked her to sing for him. She sang several songs of Umm Kulthum and impressed Sadat with her voice. He insisted that she should perform on the first memorial of Umm Kulthum's death in January 1976. Sadat tried to convince Sheikh al-Hosari to allow his daughter to sing, but he refused. Ifrag herself intervened and pointed out that her husband allowed her to sing. Sadat, reasoning that Ifrag's husband was responsible and that Sheikh al-Hosari would receive no blame for his daughter's singing, closed the matter. The next day Sheikh al-Hosari asked his daughter to join him on a visit to the sheikh of al-Azhar University, Sheikh 'Abd al-Halim Mahmud, to ask his opinion. He told Ifrag's father that singing is *halal* if it does not provoke *fitna*, disorder, and does not "incite the instincts," or keep people away from performing their religious duties. Thus began the singing career of Ifrag al-Hosari on Umm Kulthum's memorial (Abu al-'Aynayn 1999, 56–61).

While initially she intended to limit herself to the genres of religious and national songs, she felt challenged by people who said that she was not able to sing beyond these genres. She felt provoked to prove otherwise and expanded her repertoire. Her father, despite his love for the recitation of the Qur'an and acceptance of melodic reciting—holding the opinion that reciting with melody is permissible if it is performed in a way that does not distract the listeners from the religious meaning (Nelson 2001, 165)—strongly opposed Ifrag's new career. She was also heavily opposed by many of her father's colleagues, among them Sheikh al-Sha'arawi. He was particularly concerned about Sheikh al-Hosari's reputation. According to the account of Nasif and Khodayr, "extremists" told her father to pray in front of the *ka'ba* and ask God to take his daughter away, or at least her voice. They also threatened to throw acid in her face (n.d., 98). Yet she persevered, convinced that singing is not *haram*. For her father's sake, she decided to change her name to Yasmin al-Khiyyam (Abu al-'Aynayn 1999, 62–63).[5]

For Yasmin, the most important turn in her life was the decision to veil. As a young girl she strongly disliked the long clothes she was obliged to wear by her father. Amidst the Westernized schoolgirls, who were wearing short clothes and short hair, she felt embarrassed with her two braids, long skirt, and sleeves. She mentioned that she wore the type of clothes now common due to the Islamic Awakening, but rather strange during her childhood. She hid her embarrassment, though, behind a mask of assertiveness and claimed that her manner of dressing was her own choice. She developed a complex relationship with veiling. On the one hand, nonveiling symbolized freedom; on the other, she was fully aware of "the religious obligation to veil." She mentioned an interesting detail: the first picture her father took of her was while she was memorizing *sura* al-Nur. This *sura*, she explained, contains all the wisdom with regard to the position of Muslim women, including the veil. The picture reveals her intimate knowledge about her "duties" from a young age. Not being able to abide by them gave her a feeling of guilt and unrest (Nasif and Khodayr n.d., 99). Whereas Shams al-Barudi and Hala al-Safi claimed that they were not fully aware of their religious duties due to a lack of religious education, Yasmin had this knowledge through her father. He regularly advised her to veil, and while she covered in her father's presence, she unveiled in his absence. She had always been conscious about her appearance. She mentioned, for instance, her fondness of earrings. She even went to her favorite sheikh, scholar and friend of her father Muhammad al-Ghazali, to consult his opinion on earrings. Knowing she had to cover her body except for the face and the hands, she asked him whether the earlobes belong to the face or not. He replied that in the ablutions before prayer you have to wash the ears and the face, which means they are two separate body parts (Nasif and Khodayr n.d., 106).

After the death of her father in 1980, she visited Sheikh al-Sha'arawi to discuss her father's inheritance. She felt a strong bond with him due to her father's death. She expressed her wish to veil, but did not keep her promise (Abu al-'Aynayn 1999, 66). She also discussed her hesitance with regard to veiling with al-Ghazali and stated that she was convinced she should veil, but strongly disliked it. He told her that it was a sign of weakness in her personality. She herself also perceived nonveiling as her major flaw with regard to religion. She traveled to France in 1989 and was impressed by a fourteen-year-old Moroccan girl who fought for her right to veil in school despite the threat of being expelled. It strengthened Yasmin's desire to show a similar courage. When she returned for the ninth commemoration of her father's death in November 1989, she covered her hair out of respect for him, as she usually did, but now remained veiled.

As a child she had a discussion with her mother's intimate friend Zeinab al-Ghazali, preacher and influential leader of the Muslim Women's Association, who also wrote the foreword in Shams al-Barudi's autobiography. Zeinab al-Ghazali asked Yasmin why she was not veiled. She answered that belief is in the heart and not in the appearance. After veiling also, she stuck to the opinion that the veil is a beautiful, pure manifestation, although it can also be used to hide disastrous behavior (Nasif and Khodayr n.d., 104). During the interview I had with her, she likened the veil to a beautifying frame, similar to that which highlights a beautiful picture. Veiling reminds women of their religious obligations and the importance of modest comportment, but is not the most crucial facet of faith. She considered the relationship with God and the performance of good deeds of utmost importance. God knows the real intentions and character of people and judges their deeds. Unveiled women can perform good deeds, while, conversely, veiled people can engage in un-Islamic behavior. One should not judge people on outward signs such as veiling, I was told. Despite her deemphasizing the importance of veiling, in *Ruz al-Yusif* magazine her efforts to promote 'Amr Khalid, the champion of veiling in middle- and upper-class milieus, are mentioned. Also noted is Yasmin's delight about the twenty-seven students from the American University who veiled after a meeting with 'Amr Khalid (*Ruz al-Yusif*, April 22–28, 2000, pp. 25–27). Veiling is in her view important, but should not be given exclusive attention at the expense of inner conviction and good works.

In an interview in January 1990, she stated that veiling did not mean leaving art, because singing is not *haram*. Yet later the same year, she sang her last song. What, exactly, prompted her to stop is not totally clear. Abu al-

'Aynayn described the influence of al-Sha'arawi in the process of retirement. Al-Sha'arawi asked her to stop singing for the sake of her father's memory. He told her that he would pray in front of the *ka'ba* and the grave of the Prophet during his *'umrah* and ask God to let her stop singing. Al-Sha'arawi told her that if she preferred to keep on singing while veiled she belonged to the "school of al-Ghazali." However, if she veiled and quit the field of art, she belonged to his school. Yasmin mentioned during the interviews I conducted with her that she admired al-Sha'arawi for his *tafsir*, exegesis of the Qur'an, but preferred al-Ghazali as an Islamic thinker. With regard to religion and art, in particular, she made it clear that she preferred the views of Muhammad al-Ghazali (see Chapter 6). According to al-Ghazali, singing can be meaningful and honorable. Also, from a dedication in a book he gave her to "Yasmin al-Hosari," combining her artist name and birth name, his acceptance of her religious commitment and career as a singer can be inferred (Abu al-'Aynayn 1999, 63).

The "sheikh of the stars," Dr. 'Umar 'Abd al-Kafi, might also have exerted influence on her decision to step down. Journalist Abdo mentioned that Yasmin al-Khiyyam had become his unofficial spokeswoman in the early 1990s (2000, 143). Researcher Wise called her "his most famous convert" (2003, 49–50).[6] During the interview I conducted with Yasmin al-Khiyyam, though, she did not mention him among the many preachers and sheikhs she liked. Abdo met her in 1997, and wrote that due to constant hassles and attacks in the press, Yasmin had become unwilling to discuss her close association with sheikhs such as 'Umar 'Abd al-Kafi. Abdo visited one of the religious lessons Yasmin organized, in which the conservative sheikh Yahya Ismail from al-Azhar was addressing the public. After trying to tape-record the lesson, Abdo was driven from the mosque, and Yasmin refused to meet her, assuming she was an Israeli spy. 'Umar 'Abd al-Kafi, a modern-looking sheikh from the well-to-do classes, but conservative in his religious views and style, was banned from preaching by the government. During an interview with Abdo he related that he was instructed by the authorities to halt all contact with movie stars or any other type of public personalities (Abdo 2000, 155). This warning might explain Yasmin's unwillingness to mention his name. On the other hand, she openly mentioned 'Amr Khalid as "her son." She is known to have helped him in his career as a preacher, and although he is banned and was chased from the country as well, she still supports him (Holtrop 2004, 10; Haenni 2002, 3). Therefore it is difficult to assess the extent of 'Umar 'Abd al-Kafi's influence on her decision to retire (see also Chapter 6).

In the interview I conducted with her, she framed her decision to retire as a change from art to charity. She did not modify her conviction about art.

It is *halal*, or at least the genre she performed. It had been her ambition to bring this particular genre of *halal* songs — religious and national songs — to a high level. Whereas in the past this genre was only sung at saints' day celebrations, she intended to have them performed in the opera. After accomplishing this mission, she felt she could quit. In the meantime, her duties with regard to her father's legacy became time-absorbing. She was no longer able to combine these two responsibilities. She thus simply moved her attention from singing to charity. Veiling and charity became her new avenues to proximity with God.

The Hosari Association started in ʿAguza and dedicated itself to the support of orphans and to running a health-care clinic. In 1996, several religious and social services were offered, such as literacy classes and religious lessons. Yasmin al-Khiyyam invited ʿAbd al-Kafi and ʿAmr Khalid to lecture. Both preachers started out in the Shooting Club in the upscale neighborhood of Muhandisin. When they were banned from the Shooting Club, they were offered space to preach in the mosque of Yasmin's father. These preachers were so popular that on the days of their lectures they caused a traffic jam. The attention they drew from the middle and upper-middle classes was, in particular, a nuisance to the authorities, who used the "traffic jam" excuse to ban their preaching from ʿAguza. A journalist described one of the overcrowded Hosari mosque lectures, with more than a thousand attendees, given by ʿAmr Khalid in 2000. It was organized by Yasmin al-Khiyyam, and she decided to ban the older women from attending in order to give room to the young generation. The older women were enraged, but Yasmin responded, "we know it already," and argued that the well-to-do students from the American University and the Shooting Club should be targeted particularly (*Ruz al-Yusif*, April 22–28, 2000, pp. 61–62).

The Hosari Association kept on growing, thanks to donations, and was relocated to the spacious 6th of October City, thirty kilometers to the northwest of Cairo. It was opened there in 2001 and continued, up to the present, to expand its activities and services. Besides religious and literacy classes, vocational training is now also offered. There are about 320 orphans cared for by the association. Children from outside the capital or of poor families can also join the kindergarten and classes. The association helps the poor, particularly during special occasions such as religious holidays and Ramadan, and organizes distribution of clothes. The Hosari Association also provides a place to celebrate weddings and assists poor couples in preparing the weddings. A medical center is under construction, as well as an enormous mosque.

Yasmin al-Khiyyam has been influential in spreading charity and *daʿwah* among women of the higher strata. Middle- and higher-class women's involvement in Islamic charity has expanded due to Yasmin al-Khiyyam's ex-ample.[7] *Da'wah* was disseminated among the higher classes by Yasmin al-Khiyyam's personal preaching and particularly by other *da'iyat* selected and facilitated by her. Yasmin al-Khiyyam also engaged in activities of a more explicitly political character. She participated in delegations of Egyptian art-ists and intellectuals in support of Muslim nations under siege, as when she visited Bosnia. She also traveled on the first Egyptian flight to break the 1990 air embargo imposed on Iraq and was described in a commentary as a "singer-turned-veiled-preacher Yasmin al-Khiyyam."[8] Also, the publication in 2006 by the Danish newspaper *Jyllands-Posten* of cartoons caricaturing the Prophet Muhammad led to meetings about the image of Islam. 'Amr Kha-lid's idea to go to Denmark and organize a huge conference to explain to the Danish people the importance of the Prophet sparked criticism. At the en-suing conference of journalists about the issue, Yasmin al-Khiyyam was one of the speakers, alternately labeled as the director of the Hosari Association or "*da'iyya islamiyya*," Islamic preacher.[9] She has thus retained a high pub-lic profile and still exerts extensive social, religious, and political influence.

VEILING

Veiling by women is the most noted aspect of the Islamic Awakening since the 1970s. It is a rich topic that has been debated since the beginning of the last century, when the first Egyptian women removed the face veil. Most scholars agree that the veil of the 1970s is not a reappearance of the veil that elite women used to wear until the beginning of the twentieth century. It is a new phenomenon with new meanings. The historic and social contextual-ization of veiling and its diversity in meanings across time, place, and social class are an important starting point for the analysis of the time period with which I am concerned—that is, from the 1980s onward.

In 1983, I lived at the campus of Cairo University for ten months to do research for my master's thesis and had lengthy discussion with many stu-dents, among others, on veiling. Half of them were veiled, in various shapes. Many unveiled students intended to veil at a later point in their lives. Mac-Leod mentioned a consistent growth of veiling among lower-middle-class working women from about one-third of her informants in 1983 to three-quarters in 1988 (1991, 105). Sherifa Zuhur's research took place in 1988, and two-thirds of her informants were veiled, either with a *higab* or *niqab*, the face veil (1992, 59). At present, most estimates are that about 80 to 90 per-cent of Muslim women in Cairo are veiled. Whether or not the statistics are completely accurate, they convey the idea that an overwhelming majority of Muslim women are veiled. Nonveiled women are often assumed to be Copts.

There are many different styles of veiling, and we cannot assume that they all have the same meaning. Different styles of veiling were in vogue in the beginning of the 1980s. Most of the students I spoke with first started to wear ankle-length skirts or robes, often worn with a belt and thus showing the waist, with long sleeves and a high neckline. The decision to add a headscarf—either tied in the neck or wrapped around to hide the neck—was not easy, because most of them felt a heavy responsibility that once the decision was taken, it could not be undone. Others opted—sometimes immediately, sometimes gradually—for a full *higab* consisting of an ankle-length robe flowing from the shoulder and hiding the bodily contours, with a wimple-like head covering concealing every trace of hair. Several varieties existed, but this Islamic garb was mainly in single, subdued colors. This style of covering is also referred to as the "*khema*," because of its tentlike shape. A common joke among the students was made by changing the commercial about the soft drink Schweppes—"*shwayya shwayya Schweppes gayya*," "bit by bit Schweppes will come"—into "*shwayya shwayya il-khema gayya*," "bit by bit the '*khema*' veil will come." Some of the students opted for a full face covering, the *niqab*, but in the university this was forbidden.

At present, some analysts note a trend toward "downveiling," which "refers to a subtle and seemingly growing tendency among certain circles of urban Egyptian women toward less concealing and less conservative forms of Islamic dress" (Herrera 2001, 16). Also the development of fashionable styles of veiling is an interesting trend. Veiled artists, particularly those who have kept up public visibility as media personalities, have played and still play a prominent role in making veiling fashionable, a topic to which I will return. Besides a trend toward downveiling, however, there presently seems to be a trend toward "upveiling" as well. I have the impression that the *niqab* also attracts a growing number of adherents in the urban landscape. With most women wearing a more or less stylish form of veiling, the veil as such lost its clear message of piety and modesty. With many "*muhajababes*" (Stratton 2006; LeVine 2008, 247) around, several of my pious informants felt the veil had fallen victim to "inflation" and tried to distinguish themselves by wearing the *niqab*. So many styles of veiling, signifying different degrees of modesty and piety, are available to express one's individuality. That also means that despite the fact that most women wear a form of veiling, it still is a major topic for religious lectures and discussion.

There are several theoretical frames for understanding veiling that have changed over time. In the late 1970s, scholars mostly focused on its sociopolitical aspects and conceptualized veiling as a form of protest or activism (El-Guindi 1981, 1983; Marsot 1984; Hoffman-Ladd 1987; Macleod 1991). Veiling, perceived as the symbol of Islamic authenticity, was theorized as a form of protest whether against the secular regime or against cultural dominance by the West. The frame of "identity politics" has also been applied to veiled women in the West. In the 1980s, several authors understood veiling as the symbol of tradition and submission. It was analyzed as the public evidence that women had internalized and accepted control over their bodies and sexuality. An interesting analytical mixture of submission and protest, in which veiling is perceived as "accommodating protest," was developed by MacLeod (1991). From the late 1990s onward, a focus on the religious meaning of the veil as a sign of piety has surfaced as a main frame to understand veiling (Mahmood 2001a, 2005; Deeb 2006). Presently, some studies pay attention to the commoditization of the veil and the trend of fashionable veiling (Stratton 2006; Gwilliam 2010; Sandikci and Ger 2010; Kılıçbay and Binark 2002). It will be clear that I work within the theoretical frame of piety. However, although I mainly draw attention to the value of the piety frame for my interlocutors, I do not intend to deny the importance of alternative theoretical approaches for other social groups and periods. Below, I will elaborate on the different frames of the different periods, as well as the importance of the piety frame for the "repentant" artists. I will also show the influence of the artists on the development of fashionable forms of veiling.

The first studies on veiling as activism mainly focused on the female students of university campuses in the late 1970s. Notably El-Guindi held that the students had two options: "either looking secular, modern, feminine and passive (hence very vulnerable to indignities), or becoming a *religieuse* (a Muslim sister), hence formidable, untouchable and silently threatening. The young women who are now in public and because of social change will remain there, made the choice to carve legitimate public space for themselves" (1983, 87). Particularly the students of the Jamaʿat Islamiyya at several universities were engaged in veiled activism.

In my discussions with students in the early 1980s, the main reason they gave was related to the religious motivation "to obey God." They did not use an elaborate pious discourse, but mentioned religion as an obvious and natural reason for veiling. Whereas religiosity was a prime motivator, the most elaborate discursive argumentation was linked to the protection veiling could provide them on their way to the university in crowded buses and on the streets. Their religious aura protected them against harassment by men and gave them respect. One of them remarked at the time, without irony, that in a Western outfit she was harassed six times a day, whereas as a *muhagaba* she was only bothered six times a month. Veiling, in the view of the students, also protected men from committing the sin of lustful looking. The students were mainly from provincial towns and were looking for ways to feel more comfortable with their feminine presence among strangers in the streets and marriageable colleagues at the university. They felt more secure, physically safe as well as morally upright, in an Islamic outfit. Few of them were active in the Islamic Students Association, so that may account for the difference with El-Guindi's observation on veiled activism. I remember one student who claimed that, particularly as a *muhagaba*, she could work in any field, even as a policewoman directing traffic. Most students, however, did not see veiling as a strategy to carve out space, but as a defensive shield, given the situation that they were already in that public space. Yet it seems likely that some female activists might have used veiling as a way to gain entrance into domains that were previously male-dominated, such as, for instance, religious education, preaching, and activism. Even if they did not consciously use veiling as a strategy, it enabled them to enter these fields.

The motives of the students I interviewed mostly concurred with those of the working women among whom MacLeod (1991) conducted her research in the mid-1980s. About 40 percent of her informants maintained that the *higab* functioned as a form of protection, warning men that the wearer was a virtuous person (1991, 112). For the women of her research, however, the *higab* was a form of symbolic action by which they expressed their feelings of conflict and confusion about combining work outside the home with marriage and motherhood (1991, 97). Although these lower-middle-class women were out in public, according to MacLeod, they actually felt that their main place should be in the house. By veiling they signaled to neighbors, colleagues, and strangers in the street that their primary role was that of a "traditional wife and mother" (1991, 121). By using the veil as a symbol, these working women also opted for a particular style of struggle: that is, an ambivalent mixture of resistance and acquiescence, protest and accommodation. MacLeod thus analyzed the veil as a bridge between "traditional and modern" values and behavior. The veil was used as a vehicle of protest, but carried a double-edged message of accommodating to the existing relations of power. Several researchers have criticized the equation of the veil with tradition and submission, pointing at the underlying assumption about religion as non-modern and piety as a form of submission (Deeb 2006; Mahmood 2001a). For the students of my research, veiling was a form neither of protest nor of accommodation. The veil was symbolizing neither tradition nor submission, but was a safeguard through the religious force it carried. They felt protected through moral-religious symbolism rather than "traditional" imagery. They perceived veiling both as a means, that is, "protection," and as an end in itself, that is, "to please or obey God."

In the 1980s, the role and extent of religious motives for veiling were under debate among scholars. Researchers studying the veil in the late 1990s criticized previous studies for their lack of attention to religious aspects in the choice for veiling (Deeb 2006; Mahmood 2001a, 2005). MacLeod noticed that few women in her research attended meetings for women in the mosque, prayed regularly, or read the Qur'an for themselves. She concluded that few of them turned to religion "in a genuine way" (1991, 110). Zuhur maintained, in evaluating the claims of the young women in her research, that "rather than the newfound piety[,] . . . it may be that their socioeconomic and political insecurities" provide the strongest reason for their acceptance "of the new image of women by Islamists" (1992, 83). Rugh, however, warned against underestimating the strength of piety as a moving force behind veiling (1986, 156). The students of my previous research had a religious-moral discourse with practical overtones. Yet the religious discourse was far less extensive than what one can overhear nowadays in Cairo from many women, including the "repentant" artists.

In the theoretical frames for analyzing veiling in the late 1990s, the religious aspects became more prominent. Mahmood (2001a, 2005), in particular, has studied the role of veiling in creating a pious self. According to the instructors of the piety movement she interviewed, veiling should not be seen as a custom, but as a religious duty. Veiling must lead to true modest behavior, "a challenge that far exceeds the simple act of donning the veil" (2005, 51). Veiling is a critical marker of piety, but also the "means by which one trains oneself to be pious" (2005, 158). Veiling is a "necessary component of the virtue of modesty because the veil both expresses 'true modesty' and is the means through which modesty is acquired." Participants in the mosque movement "draw [. . .] an ineluctable relationship between the norm (modesty) and the bodily form it takes (the veil) such that the veiled body becomes the necessary means through which the virtue of modesty is both created *and* expressed" (2005, 23). In this sense, veiling can be compared to praying, doing *du ʿa*, performing repentance, or engaging in charity. It is one of the means to construct a pious self that simultaneously expresses and harbors that feeling of piety.

I would argue that it may be not merely that the religious meaning and motivations of veiling have spread more widely since the late 1990s, but that the pious discourse on veiling in particular has become more elaborate among larger groups of women. With the growth of the piety movement, many women have taken lessons in the mosque and familiarized themselves with religious discourse. Accordingly, religious knowledge and pious discourse have permeated daily life and ways of speaking. Whereas women of Mac-Leod's study hardly attended religious instruction, many women from all classes did so in the 1990s. This circumstance draws our attention to the less overt pietization of everyday life in the early and mid-1980s as compared to present-day Cairo. Pietization not only takes shape in the form of behavior and outward comportment, but is also manifest and audible in everyday language, particularly among women following religious classes, listening to tapes of religious sermons, or watching religious TV programs. I was amazed by the change in knowledge and ways of speaking of several of my former acquaintances of Muhammad 'Ali Street, among them Ibtisam and the family of my assistant (see Introduction, this volume, and Van Nieuwkerk 1995). Not only did piety inform their behavior, but they had also familiarized themselves with an extensive pious repertoire of speech. For instance, my assistant's wife, who stopped dancing upon marriage a long time ago, had followed religious lessons. She explained her initial decision to veil and to wear *niqab* in terms of piety. Yet also her decision to "downveil" around the age of fifty from *niqab* to stylish *higab* was explicated by quoting the arguments she had heard in the lessons about beauty and the age of women, reiterating the argument that older women no longer need to fully cover. This example points at both the ubiquity and variations in religious discourses on veiling available to women.

The pietization of everyday speech also became clear to me when I tried to find the right expression to offer my condolences for the death of a relative of my assistant. I came up with the colloquial expression I had learned from them in the 1980s—"*il-ba'i fi hiyatak*"—but was corrected by my assistant's wife that they had learned that the religiously correct expression nowadays is "*al-baqa lillah.*" Instead of wishing that the remainder of the life of the deceased would be added to the life of the living relatives, the expression now wishes the deceased the remainder of life in the company of God. It illustrates the extensiveness of the pious discourse that has become available through religious instruction. As Deeb also observed for Lebanon, religion permeates speech beyond such conventional expressions as "*al-hamdulillah*" and "*insha Allah*," "thanks be to God" and "God willing." Piety is not only embodied in praying, veiling, religious study, and charity, but also inscribed in pious discourse. This discourse is spread, debated, authenticated, and reinterpreted during lessons and social gatherings (2006, 119). The "discursive piety" (Deeb 2006, 118) might thus account for foregrounding the pious dimension of veiling among scholars and veiled women themselves.

For the "repentant" artists or veiled actresses, the main motivation for veiling is clearly expressed in terms of piety. For most artists, veiling was a personal pious choice occasionally instigated by direct spiritual interference, as we have seen in the story of Shams al-Barudi and Hala al-Safi. Others were confronted with the death of a relative, as befell Mona 'Abd al-Ghani and 'Afaf Sho'ib. They felt an immediate urge to veil before they would be confronted on the Day of Judgment with the "enormous sin" of having revealed themselves. This was the case with Hana' Tharwat, who had strong feelings of relief and blessing that God had given her the length of life to veil. They felt an acute sense of " *khashiya*," anxiety, and " *khauf*," fear. In the knowledge that the veil was an important, missing part in their devotion, taking this last step resulted in a strong sense of rest and calmness, " *sakina*." Besides expressing the feeling of being "God fearing," they also explained their motivation in terms of " *hubb*," or "love," for God. Actress Miyar al-Bablawi said, of her decision to veil, that she had a nightmare and was afraid to die and be sent to hell because she "did not wear what God had commanded." She felt very near to God and perceived the veil as his greatest gift. She veiled for four years despite her husband's strong dislike of it. She then removed the veil for five months, but felt extremely uncomfortable. "I could no longer do without the veil. I felt naked without. . . . I did not want to unveil; I simply could not do without. I had to veil again."[10] As the instructors at the mosques in Mahmood's research also explained: Initially the decision to veil is perhaps taken because it is felt to be God's command. Yet over time, one also learns to feel shy and uncomfortable without the veil. It increasingly becomes part of one's inward pious disposition (Mahmood 2005, 157).

Although veiled (retired) artists I talked to agreed that veiling was important, they also stressed that it should only be done out of inner conviction. As we have seen, Yasmin al-Khiyyam compared the veil to a beautifying frame that reminds women of their religious obligations and modest behavior. As an empty outward bodily form, the veil is not an essential aspect of religion. The most important thing is the content of one's relationship with God and one's deeds, which are then expressed and framed by the outward form. Veiling is only a sign of true devotion when the two come together. Deeb's Lebanese interlocutors also discussed whether the veil always represents an inner state of piety (2006, 115). Not all pious women in her research wore Islamic dresses, although most stated that they intended to do so if they were totally convinced about and completely prepared for veiling. Piety is thus a constant personal effort, practice, and struggle to strive for complete *iltizam* that can be reached by several means.

Veiling not only is a form of personal piety, but also has a clear public aspect. It can be perceived as the most visible embodied form of piety and as a public declaration of the choice to uphold morality (Deeb 2006, 111). For that reason the veil also leads to a heavy responsibility and is very difficult to remove. Unveiling and immoral behavior by veiled women are extremely sensitive matters when they become public knowledge. For that reason the importance attached to real inner conviction is understandable. The public visibility of piety in the form of veiling highlights another aspect of the relationship between piety and publicness. Most researchers have argued that veiling enabled women's appearance in public. As the working women in MacLeod's study argued—which is in accordance with the students I talked to—intentionally or unintentionally, the veil legitimized women's presence in public spaces. Yet, as I will discuss in Chapter 9 in more detail, veiling also restricted the kind of presence of women in public spaces. The moral responsibility of veiled women to keep up the "right image of Muslim womanhood" also circumscribed women's conduct, for instance in artistic productions.

Recently, fashionable forms of veiling have drawn attention from scholars and sparked debates in Egypt (Gwilliam 2010; Sandikci and Ger 2010; Kılıçbay and Binark 2002). The growing religiosity among the higher classes and the "lighter" religious discourse of trendy preachers (see Chapters 6 and 7) are among the factors that encouraged the development of veiling as a fashion item. The veiled artists, in particular, have been very keen on developing elegant styles of veiling. Veiling, as we have also seen in the story of Yasmin al-Khiyyam, is an extremely difficult decision, which is not taken lightly. This holds generally true, but perhaps even more for artists for whom physical appearance is an important pillar of fame. Some of them, as Shams al-Barudi narrated, might be bothered by the attention arising from their attractiveness. Yet it goes without saying that beauty is a key to their success. Hiding beauty is thus a concept that is at odds with mainstream ideas about female artists and the artists' own self-conception. So whereas they agree that "hiding beauty" is a religious commandment, they understand this to refer to the hair and attractiveness of their bodies. It does not necessarily mean they should become "ugly." The black "*abaya*," worn by some of the first retired artists such as Shams al-Barudi, Hana' Tharwat, and Hala al-Safi, was considered unnecessary and overdone by several other artists. They reasoned that the veil can and should be beautiful. "The veil is a beautifying frame," as Yasmin al-Khiyyam explained, for which reason she also preferred white clothes instead of black or somber colors. Miyar al-Bablawi exclaimed, "How strange would it be to be prominent while I was dressed in the wrong way and hide while I am wearing a correct outfit!" She felt she should return to the screen and display—with a good-looking small veil and elegant clothes—that Islam means beauty.

Several artists thus developed stylish forms of Islamic outfits combining variously colored chic shawls to fit their elegant ensembles, often with makeup and trendy accessories. Soheir al-Babli (see Chapter 5), after her retirement from acting in 1992, opened a company making Islamic clothing. Miyar al-Bablawi (see Chapter 7 and illustration 7.1) showed me her photo album with fashionable styles of veiling she wore as a mannequin for various fashion magazines. Several other artists have become veiled fashion models, notably Hanan Turk. Magazines such as *Hijab Fashion*, featuring veiled stars and fashion models, have appeared, and recently a trade union of veiled fashion models has been founded by the famous model Yasmin Muhsin.[11] The veiled stars have thus helped to establish veiling as a new "*moda*." They came to feel that it was part of their mission to promote veiling, which could be made to appeal to upper- and upper-middle-class women as well by the development of chic *higabs*. As we have seen in Yasmin al-Khiyyam's story, the well-to-do young women from the American University and the posh Shooting Club in particular should be targeted. The media attention the artists received as celebrities, their positioning among the well-to-do, and the elegant, expensive styles of dressing they embodied created an Islamic message and image that was well received by upper-class women. In this way, the artists have helped to create a chic moral alternative to Western styles that was diffused among the upper classes.

Veiling can thus be analyzed as a contested issue, with personal and public aspects of piety, as well as other dimensions, that influence the decision to veil. Women can choose to veil for a wide range of reasons, such as piety, practical circumstances, or religious or peer pressure. Veiling can be politically motivated or become a fashion statement. Choices can also change over time, or differ according to context and social backgrounds. Veiling among the artists can be interpreted as a personal and public form of piety. Because of their visibility, the artists have had a huge impact on fans and the well-to-do classes.

CHARITY AND MORAL POLITICS

The "repentant" artists were not only important in spreading Islamic salons and (fashionable) veiling among the upper classes, they were also persuasive in spreading Islamic charity as a morally upright pastime for elite women. In this section, I will first discuss the development of Islamic charity and the involvement of elite women. Second, I will go into the perception of social activities such as charity as "apolitical," a perception shared by scholars, political advocates, and Islamic activists. It is also partly shared by the regime, enabling the Islamic welfare sector's further expansion in society. Third, I will go into the related debate over whether the piety movement and its moral engagements can be analyzed as a form of empowerment for women. This section will thus provide insight into the extent of the piety movement's political aims and impact more generally.

Charity and voluntarism have a long history in Egypt. Islamic welfare organizations were founded in the nineteenth century. In the beginning of the twentieth century, the Muslim Brothers were particularly active in Islamic charity. Under Nasser, the government tried to control private initiatives. The state, however, was not able to replace the services of these private voluntary organizations (PVOS), and they cropped up during the reign of Sadat and Mubarak (Sullivan 1994, 66). Nongovernmental organizations are not independent of the government. They are registered and regulated by the Ministry of Social Affairs. After the establishment of Law 32 in 1964, the Ministry was entitled to refuse to give permission for the formation of associations, prevent them from receiving money from abroad, and deny permission to raise funds through donations. The Ministry could also appoint a temporary board of directors, dissolve an association, or merge two of them. Involvement of political groups in charity is curbed due to this law, but there are also unregistered organizations (Sullivan and Abed-Kotob 1999, 24–35). Despite the regulation by the Ministry, the Islamic welfare sector had, according to Wickham (2002), a substantial degree of autonomy at least in the first decade of Mubarak's rule. This had to do with several factors, among them the right to dispose of voluntary donations to mosques. The latter provided mosque-based forms of charity a way to circumvent the restrictions of Law 32. Besides, the vast numbers and decentralized character of mosques and welfare organizations made it difficult for the regime to effectively control the sector (2002, 104–105). Yet, from 1992 onward, the government tried to tighten its control over mosques and Islamic charity.

During the 1980s, the parallel Islamic sector expanded vastly, not only in number of organizations, but also in the efficiency and scale of its services. The government's development programs had fallen into crisis, particularly after the *infitah*'s adoption of liberal economic policies. In the 1980s, one-third of Egypt's private voluntary organizations were Islamic in character, while in the late 1990s an estimated 6,327, or 50 percent of all welfare organizations, were considered to provide Islamic services and charity. The number of beneficiaries from Islamic charity is estimated to have increased from 4.5 million in 1980 to 15 million in 1992 (Bayat 2002a, 12). The Islamic nongovernmental organizations are generally considered to outdo the nonconfessional ones and to function better than others (Bayat 1998, 156). The perception of many people is that, for instance, patients receive better care from Islamic hospitals than from those of the national government, although the same doctors might work in both sectors (Sullivan 1994, 79). A clear example of the inefficiency of government services was provided during the earthquake of 1992. The government was not able to provide any tangible services even within a week after the quake, whereas Islamic welfare organizations provided food, clothing, and temporary housing within hours (Sullivan 1994, xiii). Islamic charity organizations thus also helped to alleviate the crisis and were for that reason not curbed by the regime.

This new mosque-based form of Islamic charity did not seem to have had many elite women involved in the early 1980s. At that time, Islamic activism and charity were mainly a lower-middle-class phenomenon (Hafez 2003, 59). Hafez described a development in the 1990s toward cross-class-based welfare organizations. Upper-class women have always been involved in welfare activities, but now they also became active in Islamic charity. I guess that the involvement of upper-middle-class women in Islamic charity led to an increase in both elite and cross-class forms of Islamic charity. The Islamic salons functioned as an important recruiting base for donations and volunteers, and these are mainly upper-middle-class settings. Shams al-Barudi organized the first Islamic association for upper- and middle-class women in Muhandisin in the mosque of Mustafa Mahmud. Yasmin al-Khiyyam's welfare activities, in particular, are mentioned as inspiring other wealthy women to become involved in Islamic charity. Her influence as a role model, as well as her social network, pulled many elite women into Islamic charity.[12] Madiha Hamdi is another veiled actress heading a huge charity organization.[13] Women involved in religious charity stress the difference between the Rotary Club style of welfare and Islamic charity by using materialism as a distinguishing factor (Hafez 2003, 58). Distinctions based on socioeconomic difference and material wealth were replaced by the religious morals of the participants. The charity workers hold that instead of showing off wealth and the amount of charity work one has done, the only thing that counts is "who is the better Muslim" (Hafez 2003, 58).

According to an article written on the Islamic website Islam Online, "politics is thrown out of the window," whereas "charity came in by the door" since the middle of 1990s.[14] Islamic activism was more and more taking shape in the form of charity, welfare, and piety. The mosque movement as a whole was criticized by Islamic activists, in that its objective was directed at "quietist morality" instead of "radical reform." This view on the apolitical character of the piety movement is shared by several observers and political analysts (Baker 2003; Bayat 2005b; see also Mahmood 2005). Piety and politics are

analyzed as mutually exclusive categories, and accordingly the piety movement as being in contradistinction to political Islam (see also Chapter 1).
Therefore also women's engagement in piety, their veiling, and their moral
engagements are often described as nonpolitical. The extent to which the
pious public engagement of women in charity should be seen as an empowering form of politics or merely as quietist nonpolitical activities is accordingly
under debate among feminist scholars as well.

An example of analyzing the moral engagement by pious intellectuals
and elite charity workers as mainly politically neutral is provided by the study
of Salvatore (2000) on Mustafa Mahmud. Mustafa Mahmud, who converted
from Marxism to Islamism,[15] founded the mosque that also housed the first
association frequented by the "repentant" artists. Mustafa Mahmud was a TV
personality and media star like them. He blended religion, science, and common sense in his successful TV program *Science and Faith*. Mustafa Mahmud
was also a scientist and a cardiologist. In 1975, he founded a charitable organization, the Mustafa Mahmud Society. He started with a library for the study
of Islam, a geological museum, a seminar hall, and a health center and hospital. The hospital has sixty beds, of which half are for charitable purposes and
low-cost. However, it also has first-class single rooms with air-conditioning
and television. In 1979, he extended his activities to social services as well,
and ten years later around eight thousand families received financial aid and
medical services annually (Sullivan 1994, 70–71). Salvatore stated that Mustafa Mahmud emerged as a "normative entrepreneur" who was able to "invest the moral view of individual responsibility, social obligation, and impera-
tives of progress into the new conditions of the cultural and media markets
and the religious fields allowed by the *infitah*" (Salvatore 2000, 14). Mustafa
Mahmud was also a well-known intellectual who ventured as a lay personality into the religious field, a field that was at the time completely dominated
by religious scholars and preachers. His approach is characterized as neither
theorizing nor preaching, but as simply explaining the relationship between
God and nature with visual examples. In addition, he is conveying a "politically neutral message," taking sides neither with the regime nor the "militants" (Salvatore 2000, 15).

The piety movement of the 1980s rarely engaged the institutions that are
associated with the political fields, as in making claims on the state, participating in the electoral process, or using the judicial system to further its cause.
For that reason it is easy to ignore the political character of the piety movement or moral reform movements more generally (Mahmood 2005, 35). As I
argued in Chapter 1, the lines between the political and apolitical are difficult
to draw, and I will not make a clear-cut break between them. It is important

to understand both the activist components of the Islamic trend and the more inwardly turned pious trends. First, even if the quietist pious turn is dominant in the piety movement and it does not aim at direct political change or reform, its political consequences for Egypt are tremendous. As Singerman (1997) has also argued, the political is visible not only in the intention of individuals and movements, but also in the consequences of their actions. The sociopolitical change in Egypt in the 1980s as a result of the changing religious landscape is due to both Islamist activists and the pious turn of so many individuals. The transformative power of the piety movement has been tremendous and could be said to transcend that of conventional political groups (Mahmood 2005, 35). In addition, as Mahmood argues, the political efficacy of the piety movement is particularly realized through the work it performs in the ethical realm. It influences the public sensibilities that are essential to any state. The Egyptian state is engaged in a liberal-secular project, whereas the piety movement directs sensibilities away from the state-endorsed forms. The notion of politics should thus be widened to acknowledge the importance of ethical practices for political projects (Asad 2003; Mahmood 2005, 34–35, 74–75). The crafting of moral or ethical sensibilities is an essential aspect of politics. Moreover, although the piety movement is mostly aimed at correcting the self, many of those involved have eventually taken on a more activist stance and are involved in Islamic activism and outreach. We thus need a longitudinally dynamic view of politics. Finally, the Egyptian state eventually changed its laissez-faire attitude toward the quietist mosque movement in the 1990s due to its vast impact. The state could thus no longer close its eyes to the sociopolitical consequences. This undergirds the importance of locating politics not only in overt aims, but also in (unintentional) consequences.

A similar discussion about the (a)political character of piety takes place with regard to whether women's pious involvement in the piety movement is a form of "empowerment" or of "passive submission." Paralleling the debate on veiling, we can discern three types of analysis. First, women's pious turn and the piety movement are interpreted as an illiberal movement engaging in nonpolitical activities. Other feminist scholars have interpreted veiling, piety, and charity as a form of empowerment and resistance. By stressing the empowering aspects they criticize approaches that interpret such activities as a form of submission to male-dominated discourse and practice. A third group of scholars, among them Sherine Hafez (2003), holds that whereas these activities are empowering, such a feminist concern is not what drove these women activists. "Theirs was a preoccupation with self-perfection to attain a proximity to God. To these women, activism as a service to others lies at the heart of this process of perfecting the self. Contesting male authority, resistance, and [. . .] empowerment [. . .] are but unintended after-effects of the pursuit of higher religious attainment" (Hafez 2003, 2).

I think this latter observation most closely represents the ideas of the women I have interviewed and the effects of their pursuits. They were engaged in forms of personal and public piety and strove for proximity to God. Charity was felt to be a moral obligation that created a space for individual self-enhancement that they also considered socially beneficial. Charity was a public moral engagement backed by a personal pious discourse. We have seen that for many "repentant" artists the process of repentance inspired them to become active in performing good deeds. There is not only an inward element to *tawba*, but also an active and outward aspect. Piety is located not only in the *ʿibadat*, acts of worship, but also in the *muʿamalat*, social practices or transactions. So the personal and public aspects of piety were closely connected. As also Deeb observed for her interlocutors, mainly volunteers and charity workers affiliated with Hezbollah, "piety, humanitarian sentiment, and political awareness fuse into a perfect braid" (2006, 202).

Personal piety has induced several "repentant" artists to become active in Islamic welfare. Among them are Yasmin al-Khiyyam, Madiha Hamdi, and Kamilia al-ʿArabi, who opened an orphanage. Also, singer Hanan and actress ʿAfaf Shoʿib have become active in charity and relief work. Charity can be a personal way to make up for sins committed in the past, and also a spiritually rewarding form of public engagement. Although the main aim of involvement by the artists—and women more generally—was related to devotion, this does not mean that it was apolitical or without political consequences. As a side effect of their pious activities, they enlarged women's scope in the religious and political domains, whether in preaching, instruction, or charity. Besides locating empowerment or politics in results rather than intentions (Singerman 1997), we need a redefinition of agency and empowerment. Hafez (2003) and Mahmood (2005) try to find an alternative for analyses that explain Islamic activism as either submissive or empowering activities. They try to do so by revisiting the concept of power and agency. They thus deconstruct the tacit underlying assumption that piety and politics are mutually exclusive.

Mahmood tries to bring the perspective of the women of the mosque movement into the discussion on power and agency. According to Foucault's theory on power, power is not only repressive but also productive—that is, a subject is not only dominated in relations of power but also formed by power. Instead of pointing out that the emphasis on female piety by the mosque movement legitimates women's subordination, Mahmood tries to understand the significance of piety for the women themselves. By using the argument, familiar to anthropologists, that the terms by which people organize their lives are not universally shared, she emphasizes the historically and culturally specific conditions that inform forms of disciplinary power and agency. Following, among others, Foucault and Butler's reworking of Foucault's notion of power, Mahmood argues that agency should not be seen as synonymous to resisting domination, but as a "capacity for action that historically specific relations of subordination enable and create" (2001a, 203). In most feminist studies, agency is understood as "the capacity to realize one's own interests against the weight of custom, tradition, transcendental will, or other obstacles" (2001a, 206). Women's agency is positioned in forms of resistance against structures of male domination and located in acts directed at freedom from constraints. Yet, as Mahmood argues, agency can also be analyzed as the "capacity for action that specific relations of *subordination* create and enable" (2001a, 210). Drawing on Butler's notion of subjectivization—that is, the process by which a subject becomes a self-conscious identity and agent—Mahmood argues that agency is not outside the workings of power, but a product of these operations. She thus argues that agency should be analyzed in terms of capacities and skills required to undertake certain kinds of acts, of which resistance is merely one kind. More important, the agent is inevitably positioned within historically and culturally specific conditions of subject formation (2001a, 210).

In the case of the women of the piety movement in general, we deal with a historically and culturally embedded form of agency which we can describe as "moral agency" (see also Mahmood 2001a, 203). Within the context of the present discursive piety and the growing pietization of everyday life and lifestyles, agency has taken a pious form as well. Instead of dichotomizing piety and politics, or dislocating pietization and empowerment, we should analyze the specific conditions and forms of pious agency women have created and dispose of. Pious forms of empowerment have taken the shape of moral agency. By using a moral-religious discourse and a pious repertoire of action, women have enlarged their scope of activities. Piety in speech and action makes women invulnerable to and untouchable by moral criticism. Although not necessarily intentionally used as an instrument, pious activities can thus be empowering on a private and public level. Moral agency is a form of pious self-transformation and sense of moral worth that extends beyond the individual. It is extended toward other women in social and religious exchange or moral guiding. It is expanded to the social environment and public sphere through attending mosques lectures and Islamic salons, and involvement with welfare organizations. It is widened to the religious sphere by entering the male-dominated field of religious instruction and preaching. The moral agency of the "repentant" artists has had a great impact because of their celebrity power. They affected upper- and middle-class ways of living, fashion, and ideas about religion, culture, and art. Their pious way of life has become a modern, stylish alternative to Western styles of living and secular sensibilities. The pious lifestyle encouraged by "repentant" artists and the piety movement more generally has a potentially huge transformative power through altering public sensibilities.

In the chapters of Part One, it became clear that "repentant" artists' involvement in the piety movement, whether in veiling, preaching, or charity, was part of a wider current. They have, however, also helped to spread pious lifestyles among their own circles. In this process, pious lifestyles have been transformed into chic, new forms of religiosity. Veiling, visiting Islamic salons and lectures, and charity became an important form of ethical self-making for women, including upper-class women. These pious activities, whether in the form of religious instruction, preaching, veiling, or charity, have personal and public, as well as political, aspects. The political impact of the piety movement became more pronounced in the 1990s, which resulted in clashes with the government, developments to which I will turn in Part Two.

PART TWO

The 1990s

DEBATING RELIGION, GENDER, AND THE
PERFORMING ARTS IN THE PUBLIC SPHERE

The early 1990s, and particularly 1992, were a turbulent period in Egyptian history. Egypt was targeted by a series of terrorist attacks on Copts, policemen, and foreign tourists. The writer Farag Fuda was assassinated in 1992. The moderate Muslim Brotherhood moved from the periphery to the center and enhanced its influence through electoral victories in professional groups such as the Lawyers Association, over which the Brothers won control in 1992. The Mubarak regime began to hunt down "Islamists," "extremists," and "terrorists" and blurred distinctions among them. The government's tolerance of the public activities of the Brotherhood came to an end (Wickham 2002, 200). In October 1992, Egypt was struck by an earthquake. It struck greater Cairo, an immensely populated area. An estimated 560 people lost their lives, many thousands were injured, and innumerable people became homeless due to faulty structures and the corruption of construction companies (Badawi and Mourad 1994; Farag 2002). The expanding Islamist service sector was the first to arrive and assist the Cairene poor, further emphasizing the state's inefficiency and negligence. The earthquake was interpreted by Islamists and many other believers as a sign of God's wrath at the corrupted condition of Egypt (Sullivan and Abed-Kotob 1999, 91). Egypt was also struck by an incessant stream of "repentant" artists. In the 1990s—with a peak in 1992—the "caravan" of retiring artists increased at a staggering speed: Shahira, 'Afaf Sho'ib, and Madiha Hamdi veiled and retired, soon to be followed by Soheir al-Babli, Soheir Ramzi, Sawsan Badr, Farida Saif al-Nasr, Mona 'Abd al-Ghani, Hanan, 'Abir Sabri, 'Abir Sharqawi, and several others. As we will see in the coming chapters, to suggest a relationship between the "repentance" of artists and "extremism," as well as the earthquake and "repentance," is to take part in a heated debate about the reasons behind the retirement and veiling of so many famous performers during a short period of time.

The battle between the regime and the "extremists" was no longer limited to the military, political, and social field. In the cultural arena confrontations were taking place as well, including the destruction by militant Islamists of billboards advertising theater plays, and attacks on theatrical groups, performers, and video shops (Ramzi 1994). As Zubaida noted, conservative Islamists attempted to impose religious authority on culture and society, which meant a quest for "the moralization of the public space, the imposition of ritual observance, and the censorship of cultural and entertainment products" (2002, 19). Whereas the militant attacks could be discounted as "terrorist extremism," the general Islamic revivalist campaign for morality in society and art was less easily dismissed by opponents and the government. "Street censorship"—that is, the interventions of nonstate actors in the cultural field—became a common practice. Religious authorities, journalists, and lawyers tried to constrain cultural products and imposed conservative religious values (Mehrez 2008, 7). They were accorded ample space by the state, since it was trying to profile itself as more religious than the "extremists" (Tadros 1994). The government was at the same time opposing and accommodating various strands of Islamists, depending on shifting evaluations of the danger they were perceived to pose to the regime (Hirschkind 2006, 61–62). Yet the regime also used the cultural field to present a modern image of Egypt (Mehrez 2001).

Within this tense climate the "repentance" and veiling of many actresses, singers, and dancers proved to be a complex and sensitive issue. The "repentant" artists accordingly became objects of intense media debates. Conservative Muslims and Islamists capitalized on the "repentance" and veiling of artists to promote their views on morality for Egyptian society. These views were contested by secularists and liberals, and were met with ambiguous responses by the regime. The artists also increasingly used the media to counter the attacks on them by liberals and secularists.[1] They partly aligned themselves with the Islamists, but were also somewhat uncomfortable with certain strict views on art and gender, views that became more diversified and liberal among strands of Islamists in the second half of the 1990s. Initially pious role models, they increasingly became objects and subjects of great national concern. The fierceness of the disputes indicates that issues of central importance were at stake. The veiled actresses became icons around which to debate national, religious, and cultural identity.

Gender, the family, and "the position of women" are generally ways to discuss national and religious identity. As Baron (2005) has shown, nationalists everywhere have used family metaphors and gender rhetoric in their imagery of the nation. In Egypt, the nation was almost invariably presented as a woman. Although artists and intellectuals agreed that Egypt should be represented as a woman, they had different ideas about her visual imagery. There was a multiplicity of images that reflected the struggle for power and contestations over Egyptian culture and the construction of the nation. The images were in particular tied to debates on veiling. In visual representation, the fact that most elite women until the early 1920s did not expose their faces in public constituted an artistic obstacle. Initially, unveiled pharaonic and peasant woman—who do not always cover while working the fields—were most feasible as representations. The famous sculpture *The Awakening of Egypt*, made by Mahmud Mukhtar in 1920, shows a peasant women unveiling, symbolizing the liberation of the modern nation. From the 1920s onward, coinciding with the lifting of the veil among urban women and the growing public visibility of women, the "new woman" became exemplary. The image of the "new woman" was based on educated, young elite women who unveiled. Unveiling became a metaphor for national independence, a metaphor that was contested (Baron 2005, 57–82). In debating the issue of the veil, contestants of both sides had come to see veiled women as symbols of the nation, either of its backwardness or its purity. Religious nationalists supported veiling as a sign of moral virtue, and women became markers of cultural purity. The more secular-oriented nationalists preferred the "new woman" and adopted the veil as a sign of backwardness.

The veil of female artists, debated in the mid-1990s, ties in with recurrent nationalist debates over gender and family imagery and rhetoric. In debating the veiled artists, Islamists strongly argued for the importance of women as the pillar of the Islamic family that supports the Islamic society and community, whereas their opponents argued for the liberation of women from these confines. The veil again became the symbol of these competing views of the national and religious identity of Egypt. The fact that these women were artists, though, added a new and important dimension to this continual debate. We have to take into account the great importance of the cultural field for the making of the national identity of Egypt. Art has for a long time been used by the regime for building nationhood and is a field of great national importance (Abu Lughod 2005). Art had remained a last stronghold for secularist projects of nation building, which was crumbling down and permeated by Islamists. Gender, art, and religion—all of these, fused together, were at stake in the veiling and retirement of female artists, making them an explosive phenomenon.

THE PUBLIC SPHERE AND THE COUNTERPUBLIC

The fierceness and multiplicity of voices in public debates in the media about such key issues as the religious versus secular political and cultural identity of the Egyptian nation can be analyzed as indicating the emergence of a "public sphere" in Egypt. The idea of a public sphere—as introduced by Habermas—designates an arena in which political participation is enacted by rational and open debate. It is the space where people deliberate about their common affairs and develop a consensus about the "common good." This space is distinct from the state and the economy. It is an arena of discursive relationships that can be critical of the state (Fraser 1990). Habermas's ideas have been applied and criticized by many scholars (Fraser 1990; Calhoun 1992; Gestrich 2006), treatments I will not review here. I will deal in particular with the relevance of the Habermasian notion of the public sphere as elaborated and criticized by scholars working on the Middle East (Eickelman and Anderson 1999; Salvatore and Eickelman 2004; Salvatore and LeVine 2005). The concept "public sphere" has become an important framework for analyzing the political dimensions and extent of democratic development in the region, as well as for studying the emergence of "public Islam" (Salvatore and LeVine 2005). In particular, the role of new media as facilitating debates in the public sphere about crucial public issues has received wide attention (Eickelman and Anderson 1999). New communications media have enabled an extension of the number of participants debating issues related to the "common good" (Salvatore and Eickelman 2004, xi). The critical discussions on the public sphere in the Middle East have focused on four main points: the gendered nature of the public sphere; the separation of the public and private spheres; the relegation of religion to the private sphere; and finally the character and form of the (counter)public.

First, following Fraser (1990), critical investigation has been carried out on the implicitly gendered notions of the public sphere. Fraser criticizes Habermas's liberal model of the bourgeois public sphere, which excluded women. She argues that the rational public sphere was deliberately constructed in opposition to a more woman-friendly salon culture in nineteenth-century France. Ryan has documented the various ways in which nineteenth-century North American women accessed public political life, despite their exclusion from the official public sphere, by building women-only voluntary associations and moral reform societies. They used the idioms of domesticity and motherhood to participate in public activities (in Fraser 1990, 61). Fraser thus points at the existence of various publics and indicates that the analysis of women as excluded from the public sphere rests on an ideological "class- and gender-biased notion of publicity" that takes the male bourgeois public as *the* public (Fraser 1990, 61). The Islamic salons that became a noticeable trend in the 1990s in Egypt (see also Chapter 2) are a clear example of women's participation in the public sphere based on notions of domesticity and aiming at moral reform of society.

The fact that these female voluntary associations and woman-only salons are barred from the public sphere is related to a sharp distinction between the "private" and the "public" realms. Feminist scholars have long criticized the distinction between private and public and the relegation of women to private spheres (Rosaldo 1974). In the juxtaposition between private and public realms, two notions can be discerned. First, a spatial conception of private and public spheres locates politics and rational deliberation in the public domains and institutions. In this spatial notion the private is usually conflated with the domestic sphere. Second, a topical approach can be distinguished in which public stands for themes dealing with issues of general interest that are accessible and a concern to everybody, as opposed to private concerns (Fraser 1990). Scholars have criticized both conceptions and shown the intertwining of private and public spheres in practical politics (Singerman 1997), and demonstrated that what counts as common or private concern is a contested matter. For instance, feminists have made clear that domestic violence, although initially viewed by many as a private concern in the domestic sphere, should be considered a legitimate topic of public discourse and concern. What counts as a common concern is accordingly decided through discursive contestation (Fraser 1990, 71). The distinction between private and public is a cultural classification and often deployed in political rhetoric to delegitimize some views and valorize others (Fraser 1990, 73).

Connected to the private/public distinction is a third debate regarding the specificities of the public sphere in the Middle East. Religion has increasingly been relegated to the private sphere in Western societies, a contested development and positioning as well. Most conceptions of the public sphere view "secularly oriented rationality to be the normative terrain on which public life thrives" (Salvatore and LeVine 2005, 7). Scholars working on the Middle East have pointed to the continuous and growing importance of religion in the public sphere in the region concerned. As Salvatore and Eickelman hold, the role of religion changed and developed in Muslim-majority societies but never receded (2004, xiv). They analyze the fragmentation of religious and political authorities and the emergent new voices debating Islam, from self-described religious authorities, secular intellectuals, and members of Sufi orders to mothers, students, and many others. In this process, which they describe as the "publicization of Islam," there is a para-

dox in modern Muslim societies in that, although there is no singular public, but rather a multiplicity of overlapping publics, the "common good" is
increasingly defined within the parameters of Islam. Salvatore and LeVine
even hold that in Muslim-majority societies secularity seems to clash with
the "common sense," because in such societies there is often no conception
of the possibility of a secular "good sense" and secularity is perceived as alien
(2005, 12). Although religion undeniably defines the parameters of debate in
Egypt, competing ideas on secular versus religious normativity exist side by
side, at least in the cultural field.

This brings us to the last issue debated with regard to the public sphere in
the Middle East, the character and form of the (counter)public. Within this
debate four issues are important. First, as Fraser has pointed out, the public
is not homogenous, but consists of multiple publics. As we have seen with
regard to gender, the view that women are absent from the public sphere is
biased and reproduces the male conception of the public sphere. There is a
plurality of competing publics. We need to analyze the multiplicity of competing and sometimes overlapping publics and their different views on key
social, moral, and political issues. Second, the existence of multiple publics
should not disguise the fact that groups are unequally positioned with regard
to access and means to participate in debates. Some groups are marginalized
and do not have equal access to the public sphere. We also need to study the
"techniques of hegemony" deployed and the way certain views and discourses
become dominant (Salvatore and LeVine 2005, 1). In addition, the public
sphere is often conceptualized as independent from the state and the economy. The public sphere is not the state, it is the "informally mobilized body
of nongovernmental discursive opinion that can serve as a counterweight to
the state" (Fraser 1990, 75). A sharp separation between associational, or civil,
society and the state is, however, difficult to hold for Egypt. On the one hand,
an independent oppositional (counter)public appears difficult to maintain in
Egypt due to the encompassing authoritarian character of the state. Yet this
does not necessarily foreclose contesting movements and ideas. On the other
hand, the state itself is fragmented and not a single entity. The Egyptian state
is not a monolithic bloc, but comprises numerous agents, institutions, and
individuals influenced by the Islamic trend.

Finally, Hirschkind's idea of counterpublic merits attention (2006). He
analyzes the piety movement, or *da'wah* movement, as a counterpublic. He
does not use the notion of Fraser (1990) in the sense that the (counter)pub-
lic is autonomous and sovereign with respect to the state. In his study of
the Islamic cassette media, Hirschkind shows that this Islamic soundscape
combines ethical exercise, political debate, and popular entertainment. It is

a form of political contestation and cultivation of religious sensibilities and affect that creates a separate moral space. Building on the insights of Talal Asad (2003) that the public sphere is not an empty space, but is constituted by the distinctive sensibilities and moralities of its participants, Hirschkind analyzes the role of audition in crafting public sensibilities. He thus shifts the attention from Habermas's ideas of political deliberation as a rational, disembodied form of reasoning to the ethical values and religious sensibilities and affect informing social and political life (2006, 30–31). In Part One of this book, we have come across the importance of moulding public sensibilities for political projects. The power of the piety movements is particularly directed at inculcating in its members moral sensibilities that oppose or undermine secular liberal sensibilities (Mahmood 2005). Hirschkind also emphasizes the different sensorium and moral dispositions underlying the discursive practices of the oppositional *da'wah* movement. The Islamist counterpublic aims at the formation of an ethical counterworld that buttresses and goes beyond the content of political deliberations (Hirschkind 2006, 105–143).[2]

Taking into account the specificities of the public sphere in the Middle East, counterpublic can be a useful concept to examine the actors in the heated debates in the media that will be central in this section. Due to new communication technologies such as cassettes, video, (satellite) TV, and the Internet, new players have entered the debate. Focusing on media debates causes the distinction between "public" and "private" to vaporize, both in its spatial and thematic conceptualization. As Eickelman and Anderson (1999) hold, large numbers of people, and not just the elite, can have a say in political and religious issues in this emergent media sphere. New leaders and spokespeople claim the right to speak in the political and religious arenas and disseminate their ideas through various media. Also, women and minorities find their way into the fields of political and religious discourse. However, access is unequal, with regard to groups as well as media. Whereas some media such as cassettes and the Internet are relatively accessible, other media such as TV are more heavily controlled. With the introduction of satellite TV and private companies, though, the extent of state control has lessened. New media seem to open possibilities for new people to express their views in new ways. Yet, as we will see, not only the state, but also "the street"—including oppositional Islamists—censors cultural products (Mehrez 2008). State and "street" censorship exist side by side with forms of self-censorship by actors in the cultural field. Whether the "new voices" produce new ways of thinking, as Eickelman and Anderson (1999) suggest, needs to be investigated. Yet for all of the actors, whether elite, marginalized, hegemonic, or oppositional, old or new, Islam appears to form an inescapable parameter of debate. This does not necessarily mean a disregard for some participants' secular notions of the "common good," but indicates a strong influence of public Islam on the debate.

I will thus show that the debates about and by the "repentant" artists are good examples of the emergent public sphere. First, art and gender became issues par excellence for debating notions of the "common good" and the "good Muslim." Second, the debates on the "repentant" artists highlight the intense use of media. Because of the "dangerous" mediatized publicizing of the Islamist version of Islam, it is fiercely countered in official media and supported in other media. Third, there is a divergence of voices consisting foremost of secularists, conservative Muslims, Islamists, the regime, and "repentant" artists. For all the voices concerned, religion becomes the way of framing the discussions on art and gender. Finally, conservative voices dominate the discourses of the early 1990s. These conservatives are given media space by the government. Sami Zubaida generally argues that the conservative Islamic attempts at imposing morality fit in well with the aim of authoritarian rulers. They have a common quest for "cultural nationalism" that seeks the restoration of authenticity and the eradication of inauthentic cultures or products of "Western corruption." This quest reinforces social control and authoritarian rule, which is much favored by the regimes in the region (2002, 19). The emergence of new voices in the public sphere does not automatically lead to the proliferation of liberal and democratic ideas. All kinds of views, including conservative, antidemocratic, and authoritarian ones, can be spread. Whereas the conservative voices are probably not to be analyzed as a counterpublic independent of the government, the case of the "repentant" artists is more ambiguous. They clearly belong to the "new people" who find their way into the arenas of political and religious discourse, profoundly using the media due to their status as celebrities. What ideas about the "good Muslim" and particularly the "good Muslim woman" do they disseminate?

In the following chapters, I will focus on the debates about Islam, art, and gender during the 1990s. I will trace the developments throughout the decade by reconstructing the life stories of several famous performers; show the different voices in the debate (that is, the secular cultural field, the state, different strands of Islamists, and the "repentant" artists); and follow up with descriptions of the general sociopolitical, religious, and artistic developments ongoing in the 1990s. We will meet a multiplicity of publics, and voices promoting their view of the "common good," the "right Islam," and particularly the "good Muslim woman." Thus, this media debate about the "repentant" artists highlights key moral, religious, and political issues, as well as various imaginings of the Egyptian nation.

4.1. *Actress 'Afaf Sho'ib (gift of 'Afaf Sho'ib to the author)*

(FOUR)

The Islamist (Counter)public

In this chapter, I will open with the spiritual journey of actress 'Afaf Sho'ib. Her story and those of other "repentant" artists became part of the Islamist press campaign against "the enemies of Islam." The Islamist debates about art, gender, and religion will be the focus of the second part. In the third part, I will describe the relationship of Islamist actors and movements with the state in the early 1990s.

THE SPIRITUAL BIOGRAPHY OF ACTRESS 'AFAF SHO'IB

"Your decision to step down has shaken the earth." In this manner Sha-hira, a former actress who retired and veiled in 1991, congratulated her friend, actress 'Afaf Sho'ib.[1] The earthquake, which had just struck Egypt, had an enormous impact on the socioreligious and political landscape of Egypt. 'Afaf Sho'ib veiled three days before the earthquake of October 12, 1992, a fact she proudly stressed several times during the interviews I conducted with her in 2005.[2] Whereas many actresses retired after the earthquake, leading to accusations that they retired out of spontaneous fear generated by the earthquake rather than strong experiences of piety, 'Afaf Sho'ib felt like a special case, because she could not be accused of being motivated by panic. It gave her the feeling that she was preferred by God, because he had "guided" her before he struck the nation with his wrath. The earthquake features in several forms in her story, as we will see.

The two interviews were conducted in her spacious apartment, richly decorated with verses of the Qur'an in gold leaf, which was located in the well-to-do neighborhood of Muhandisin. She recounted her story, detailing several key spiritual moments. One of her brothers was home and occasionally translated a few words. He tried to calm her down when she became overambitious in her missionary efforts toward me.

> My eldest brother died in 1988. I had a lot of work at the time, but when my brother suddenly died I asked myself, "What is this world (*dunya*)? In just a second he died!" He had phoned me at 10 p.m. and told me, "Afaf, I am going to die." I asked him, "Are you calling me just to tell me you are going to die?!" "Yes," he replied, "I am going to die, *ma'a salama*." Three hours later my other brother phoned and told me he had passed away. I told him, "That is impossible; we have just talked over the phone." So in just a few seconds he died without being sick. He was like jasmine! He came home, took a shower, prayed, and read Qur'an. He kept on crying and then his soul went to God. It was such a strange story. I am from a religious family, *al-hamdulillah*, my father prays, my mother prays as do my brothers and sisters, but I did not pray regularly. There was no *iltizam*, commitment. At my brother's funeral, I asked myself, "What is this *dunya*; it is just a second and gone!"
>
> I had a good name, was asked to act in many productions, and earned a lot of money, but I got the feeling that God wanted something of me. I then went with my mother, who was mentally tired due to my brother's death, to America and considered plastic surgery for myself. My mother and brothers were against it and told me it was *haram*. I said I will do *istikhara* and see whether I should have the surgery or not. I then had a vision in which I saw my brother. He told me, "The *dunya* is trivial and just a big theater in which people cheat on each other. The real world is the Hereafter. There is life after death. People think there is no life after death but there is; there is hell and paradise." I told my mother about the vision, and she told me not to do this surgery. So, I returned to Egypt and continued shooting for the serials in which I was acting. I love art and the people I was working with, and a country without art is backward and lacking in civilization, but I did not want the fuss. I wanted to do something which would make God very satisfied about me. I had followed several religious lessons with the veiled actresses and it was Friday, the 9th of October 1992. I prayed, read Qur'an, and thanked God with the prayer beads in my hands. I asked, "God, if the veil is the right dress, let me wear it quickly; if not, leave me like I am." I prayed *salat il-'asr*, and then as if hypnotized I walked over to my cupboard and took out a headscarf. I told myself, "I now wear the veil and will not act again."[3]

Other sources more or less confirm this story or add details.[4] An interview headlined "A Verse from the Qur'an Quaked My Soul" in the religious magazine *al-Nur* was conducted a few days after her veiling (October 12, 1992). 'Afaf Sho'ib mentioned that some veiled actresses gathering at the al-Hosari mosque had made supplicatory prayers in which they asked for 'Afaf's spiritual guidance. On Friday, 'Afaf Sho'ib did *istikhara* and opened the Qur'an at arbitrary pages. The Qur'an opened at a verse stressing the importance of obedience to God and his messenger. She repeated the *istikhara* prayer and opened the Qur'an again. It now opened at a verse about guidance and illumination: "My lords, open my heart and guide me to the right path. Untie my tongue so that people can understand my words." She repeated the ritual for a third time, and this time it opened at the verse "Time has verily come." This latter verse indicated so clearly to her that she had to act instantly that it felt like "an earthquake that struck her being and shook her soul" (*al-Nur*, October 12, 1992).

During her interview with me, she stressed her intense spirituality and closeness to God, even to the extent that it frightened her. She had several visions and could predict what would happen. "At that time if you would have come to visit me, ya Karin, I would have known you were coming even before you knocked on the door." One of these visions concerned the earthquake, which she foresaw a few days before it actually happened. This vision is detailed—together with the one about her brother—in an interesting and contested video serial produced in Saudi Arabia about the "guided artists."[5] The serial was censored, and the dreams and visions featuring in it were called contradictory to rational belief (*iman 'aqil*).[6] 'Afaf Sho'ib tells the interviewer, the Islamist poetess 'Aliya Go'ar:

> I retired three days before the great earthquake. [. . .] Thursday evening I had a strange dream. Near our house, close to the university bridge, I saw many people. They looked very weird, their hair ruffled, and they were naked. I was standing near the bridge and screamed, "What happens to our beautiful Egypt?!" I screamed and screamed, and woke myself up. What is this, people leaving behind their children and running?! It was exactly the image I witnessed during the earthquake a few days later.

The earthquake, her vision of it, and, more important, her being guided by God before the disaster gave her the feeling that she was called by God to spread his message.

'Afaf Sho'ib involved herself immediately in charity for the victims of the earthquake, a duty she shared with many volunteers, among them several of the retired artists. She felt God wanted something special of her and that she was chosen to become his *mubaligha*, spokesperson. One of her key messages was her deeply felt conviction and sudden insight, which dominated both the vision of her brother and of the earthquake, that the *dunya* is just "a second" compared to the afterlife. She told me:

> There is no refuge except in God. What is this world? Today you have visited me and tomorrow you will say I have visited ʿAfaf Shoʿib. It will be past time. Our whole life is past time. This world [*al-dunya*] robs us, but the important thing is our scales with God. Are they filled or not [with good deeds]? One day in the *dunya* is as a thousand days in the company of God. With this time reckoning we are only two minutes on earth, and God will say, "Oh human creatures, could you not even worship me for these two minutes?" On the Day of Judgment [*yom al-hisab*] everyone will be gathered and asked what we have done in this world and with our lives. Everyone will cry, and everything that was will be gone. We either go to heaven or to hell. When you contemplate about these things you are overwhelmed by a feeling of fear [*khauf*]. I want to go to heaven. This world is the prison for the pious believer [*muʾmin*] and paradise for the unbeliever [*kafir*].[7]

Her other important message was connected to the importance of veiling. She had established close contacts with some of the veiled actresses and took religious classes with Hanaʾ Tharwat, whose preaching on paradise, hell, and the "agony of the grave" influenced ʿAfaf. ʿAfaf was especially frightened by the knowledge that women are accountable for every hair they have left uncovered and every inappropriate word coming from their tongues.[8] During the interview with me, she also mentioned the scary punishment for unveiled women, who will be "hung from their hair in hell." She has perhaps for that reason become such an ardent missionary in spreading the veil. She had not only succeeded in converting several Christians, but also in convincing several Muslim women to don the veil. She wished me the same good fate. After the first interview, when I had just arrived home, she called me to say that she had forgotten to tell me something very important. I immediately took out a paper and pencil to take notes. ʿAfaf then lectured that Miriam/Mary, Jesus' mother, was veiled as well! While I was initially somewhat bewildered by this bit of information, it later dawned on me that she implied that there was no need for me to convert to Islam before taking on the veil. This shows the extreme importance ʿAfaf Shoʿib accorded to veiling for women's spiritual well-being and afterlife. As with the other veiled ex-actresses we have met in previous chapters, she perceived veiling and praying as equally important religious duties.

After seven years, 'Afaf Sho'ib decided to come back and act veiled roles. She claimed that she had never asserted that art was *haram*. Yet according to the interview in *al-Nur* (October 12, 1992), she initially considered the field of art *haram* for women. After consultation in the Mustafa Mahmud mosque, she argued that acting is forbidden for women, because her hair is visible and she wears makeup. This will invoke desire in the audience, who will thus commit sinful acts. However, she left open the possibility that acting with a veil could be religiously permissible. During the interview with me in 2005, she had returned and stressed her responsibilities as a veiled actress: acting in proper roles, not using improper language, dealing with religiously or morally relevant topics, and sticking to Islamic dress codes. In the beginning, she had been afraid she would stray from the right path, because she was used to constantly changing her acting roles. But in the meantime, she had become unwavering in her veiled path. Besides, there were hardly any roles for veiled actresses during the early 1990s, because the government banned all veils from the screen. "Producers are afraid as well," she explained, "afraid that I will spread my religious messages. We want to teach people the morally right conduct, this is *haram* and this is right, we want to invite them to the faith. Art has a mission. Art, that is, the TV for many people, this small box is the central spot where many people gather around." So her returning to acting was also an extension of her self-image as a religious messenger.

Despite her religious zeal, certain aspects of the *dunya*, such as her well-to-do background, were not irrelevant for her life story. In an interview with the magazine *al-Mawed* (November 1992, 24–28), 'Afaf Sho'ib mentions that her mother was of Moroccan origin and her father an army engineer who supervised important infrastructural projects. Detailing the educational and professional background of her four brothers and the husbands of her four sisters, including their titles, she conveys the picture of a well-established family. 'Afaf Sho'ib was allowed to graduate from the Drama Institute on the condition that she would abide by her family's conservative values. During the eighteen years of her career, she had featured in many TV serials and films and built up a considerable reputation and wealthy lifestyle. Also, during one of the interviews with me, she frankly stated that she was accustomed all her life to a comfortable style of living, a huge apartment, and a servant, and that she had an electricity bill of five hundred Egyptian pounds a month.[9] Since her mother's death, she could live off her parents' inheritance, but before that she felt insecure without her own source of income. She married and divorced twice, first with a producer and afterward with a friend of her brother who stayed in Canada. She married him on the condition that she could stay and work in Egypt. One of her fears with regard to leaving the field of art was related to living without her main source of income. This is also alluded to in the reconstruction of her story written by Abu al-ʿAynayn (1999). ʿAfaf Shoʿib and Shahira visited Sheikh Mitwalli al-Shaʿarawi together with their friend Yasmin al-Khiyyam. ʿAfaf Shoʿib had consulted him about her fear of what could happen if her marriage with her absent husband would fail: how could she provide for herself except by working as an actress? The sheikh answered that provision is from God, "a truth that made her cry" (1999, 131–140). Her family's financial position initially enabled her to live a comfortable and spiritual life without a husband and without a profession. Her diminishing income, though, is probably one of the reasons for her eventual return.[10]

One of the recurrent themes I discussed with several of the retired artists, including ʿAfaf Shoʿib, is the alleged payment to step down and veil by "Islamic groups." In most of my interviews with the veiled artists this theme came up, and they expressed anger about these accusations (see also Chapter 5). During one interview with me, she denied the accusation by pointing out its illogical character: "For all those years I am veiled now, that would have cost them millions!" ʿAfaf Shoʿib confirmed that the rumors about payment circulated even to the extent that some artists actually stepped down, but returned to acting when they did not find the money they were expecting waiting for them. Dancer Hala al-Safi snapped during the interview I conducted with her that no one would ever pay for veiling, only for revealing. Other veiled actresses reversed the argument and mentioned that they were offered money for resuming acting and unveiling. The rumors of payment for veiling and retiring became such an issue that some of the veiled actresses felt impelled to react in the media.

Just one and a half months before ʿAfaf Shoʿib stepped down in 1992 several of the retired artists[11] signed a letter written by Hanaʾ Tharwat. It was sent to many newspapers and magazines, but published in only a few, among them *Kolenas* (October 9, 1992, p. 15). The retired artists complained about the false campaign that was launched against them in the press by authors who apparently had nothing else to write about other than topics "emerging from the depth of their sick imagination." The letter continued by stressing the initial patience of the retired artists with regard to the false accusation, awaiting their recompense from their Creator. When it became clear, though, that this ignited even worse allegations, they were left with no choice but to reply. The most villainous accusation was that they had taken recompense for their obedience to God and received thousands of pounds in return for "their refusal to unveil and use makeup" any longer. On the contrary, as the ex-performers argued, they had turned away from the opportunity to make thousands and millions of pounds while they were still in their youth. They left the life of beauty and cheap enjoyments to devote themselves to obeying God, because "all obedient servants are promised paradise." They concluded their missive by warning the malicious press that God detests hypocrisy and wishing its reporters the same divine guidance as had befallen them.

However, the campaign against the retired artists continued. They were particularly stung by actress Nagwa Ibrahim's story of groups paying large amounts of money. She claimed to have been offered seven million pounds for veiling. This time the famous retired singer Shadia took the initiative to write an open letter to several newspapers. Twelve retired artists, among whom was now ʿAfaf Shoʿib,[12] wrote a statement that if it was really true that groups secretly paid money, it was a dangerous development for the nation. It was therefore Nagwa Ibrahim's duty as a citizen to protect the country and to bring forth the names of those who offered payment. They also requested their former colleague Nagwa Ibrahim to carefully look out of the window while she was driving around Cairo, or to look out of the television building where she was working, and take note of all the veiled women around her. "Who pays for all those veils?" they asked rhetorically. They implied that it could only be defamation and slander (reprinted in Kamil 1993, 31–32). They concluded that only what was written in the religious press was reliable (*Kolenas*, October 9, 1992, p. 15). The stories of the divine guidance of ʿAfaf Shoʿib and her colleagues, as well as the defamation of their spiritual journeys in the secular media, became important ingredients in the Islamist press campaign against "the enemies of Islam."

THE ISLAMIST PRESS

The Islamist press readily came to the aid of the "repentant" artists. This was partly due to the ex-performers themselves. They chose the Islamist press to tell their stories. Shams al-Barudi narrated her "journey from darkness to the light" to the Islamic newspaper *al-Nur* (February 10, 1988). Also, ʿAfaf Shoʿib preferred to tell her story to *al-Nur* because she trusted this Islamic magazine (October 12, 1992). Islamist authors, though, also capitalized on the stories of the artists and used them to further their own aims. Islamist authors challenged the secular nationalist discourse by formulating their own conservative Islamist ideas. They thus formed a counterpublic, although, as we will see in Chapter 5, there is an ambiguous overlap with some state actors. As Ismail (1998) analyzed also, the conservative Islamist discourse shows recurrent themes, which are clearly visible in the Islamist books I will analyze below. First, the narrative of confrontation with the Other, and the threat of a cultural attack on Islam, is articulated. Second, the confrontation with the Other is described as a corrupting influence and analyzed as a conspiracy against Islam. Finally, the cultural assaults are constructed as a danger of destruction of Islam (1998, 204–205). The genre of repentance literature, particularly the more sociopolitical examples, is thus part of a broader conservative Islamist counterdiscourse.

Most stories about and interviews with the "repentant" artists were published by the Islamist publishing companies, which emerged and blossomed during this period. That emergence led to a considerable number of books in which the "repentant" artists feature. A first group of books stress the religious dimension of the stories and carry titles such as *Tears of the Repenters* ('Abdallah 2004), *People Returning to God* (al-Sangri 1999), *Women Returning to God* (al-Sayyid n.d.), and *From the World of Fame to the Acceptance of Faith* (al-Juhayni 1989; see Figure 4.2). A second group of books put the phenomenon in a broader context and have more sensational titles, such as *Artists behind the Veil* (Kamil 1993, 1994) and *The Campaign against the Veil: Secrets behind the Paid Veil* (Farhat 1993). Nasif and Khodayr changed the title *Repentant Artists: Unpublished Testimonies* (2nd ed., n.d.) into the juicer *Repentant Artists and the Sex Stars* (8th ed., 1991). Most authors introduce the reason for publishing the artists' stories in terms of the defense and promotion of Islam. In accordance with the difference in titles, the two groups of books have different purposes. The first group of authors aim to enhance sincere repentance in believers and deem the stories of the artists of great value in instilling moral and religious values. The second group of Islamist authors have a broader religious-political goal.

Of the first groups of books, some only concentrate on the "repentant" artists. Others are collections of repentance stories of men and women of different walks of life: burglars, scholars, football players, etc. Some mix the stories of men and women; others concentrate on pious role models for women as a means to call all women to return from unbelief and sins to obedience to God (al-Sayyid n.d.). Booklets with titles such as "those who return to God" occasionally combine stories of (Western) converts with those of penitents. Both groups are perceived as comparable with regard to their journey from unbelief, sin, or—put more generally—their distance from the divine, to God's presence. In these books, the "repentant" artists are given special attention as pious role models. Their fame adds to the usefulness of their stories for devotional and missionary purposes, because they have resisted all kinds of temptations. Or, as Sheikh al-Sha'arawi holds, the "repen-

4.2. *Book cover,* Min 'Alam al-Shuhra ila Rihab al-Iman / From the World of Fame to the Acceptance of Faith, *by Abu Bakr al-Juhayni*

tant" artists are preferred by God because they were used to sinful activities. If one is able—despite the habituation to sin—to turn to God in sincere repentance, God will change every sin into a *hasana*, a good deed (in Nasif and Khodayr n.d., 149). Al-Juhayni (1989) also focused on the stars, because being able to make the step from stardom to devotion bears witness to strong faith. They are accordingly considered an exemplary "torch" for other Muslims. The authors dedicated their books to all Muslims (al-Sayyid n.d., 4) or to Muslim women and all "girls who longed for fame and stardom at the expense of religious knowledge" (Siraj al-Din 1993, 2). Some of these stories are also available on audiotapes (*Ruz al-Yusif*, November 1, 1996, pp. 49–52)[13] and videotapes. They circulate widely on the Internet as well. About forty websites disseminated the interviews of Amal Khodayr with ten "repentant" artists under the title "My Journey to the World of Faith."[14] Several repentance stories were told on ʿAmr Khalid's live talk show *Kalam min al-Qalb / Words from the Heart* and evoked strong emotional responses from the audiences.[15]

The repentance literature encourages people to leave all kinds of sin. The stories stress the fact that God is merciful, listing the sins from which one has to repent and the conditions for repentance (see Chapter 2). They also detail the subjects' visions, dreams, and illuminations to show the extent of God's guidance. They highlight the strong sense of calmness (*sakina*), rest, and peace of mind that descended upon the penitents after their repentance. These authors use the repentance stories to enhance religious commitment and piety, and are engaged in a religiously edifying project. They try to strengthen the religious sensibilities of believers by providing them with a rich, tangible vocabulary of "the sweetness" of faith and the "taste" of belief. The Islamic *daʿiyya* Zeinab al-Ghazali described in the foreword to Shams al-Barudi's *Dossier* the different cups from which Shams al-Barudi had drunk to finally take up "the cup of those who love to be on their way to God" (Siraj al-Din 1993, 3). These narratives present to the believer role models with which they can identify and which can evoke the desire to repent and to become one of the "lovers on the way to God" as well. The stories, whether in written, aural, or visual representations, thus provide means for ethical self-making. These media circulations of repentance stories constitute a counterworld, or counterpublic, in the sense Hirschkind meant. These stories—reading, watching, or listening to them—constitute a moral universe in which the audiences can cultivate their religious sensibilities.

The second group of authors focusing on the stories of the "repentant" artists also intend to promote and defend Islam. They do so by sociopolitical analyses that aim to explain the attacks on the veiled ex-performers by the "enemies of Islam." They write in a less sweet-voiced prose and frequently use exclamation marks and rhetorical questions to strengthen their arguments. Magdi Kamil (1993, 1994), for instance, compared the impact the repentance and veiling of artists had on the "foes" to a "bomb." The danger was, in his view, not related to their decision to retire—that was totally welcomed by him—but to the "war" launched at the artists by those in art and media who profited from the "degeneration in art." The limits of "obscenity and debasement" were reached, for Kamil, when the accusation of money paid for veiling and retirement was launched in the secular press. He felt the need to defend the artists from this "immoral campaign," which cast their true belief in Islam into doubt. He rhetorically investigated the assumed "crimes" committed by them: "Is it wrong to state that not everything in the field of art is satisfactory?! Is it a crime to describe their retirement as repentance?! Is it an offence to invite their colleagues, after being guided by God and blessed with piety, to join the Caravan of Light?! Did not God [. . .] tell us: 'Call to the faith with wisdom and good admonition,' and did not the Prophet [. . .] tell us: 'Who witnesses forbidden acts, should change them'?!" (Kamil 1993, 17). He considered it his religious duty—and that of the veiled artists—to speak out. The author Yasir Farhat, working for the international association for *da'wah* and media, aimed "to throw the truth in the face of the attackers and support the firm believer in his way to God" (1993, 16).

In the analyses of the second group of authors, the example of the "repentant" artists is not simply used for moral guidance and spiritual edification, but foremost to launch a counterattack on the "enemies of Islam" and to oppose misrepresentations of Islam. These authors do so along three lines: first, by attacking the field of art for its "corruption"; second, by offsetting the false representations of Islam, particularly the position of women in Islam; and finally, by promoting the importance of veiling. They outline the great importance of art, women, and veiling for the Muslim community and make clear that these three topics are crucial areas, defining the national, cultural, and sociopolitical identity of Egypt. The topics of religion, gender, and art are intertwined and condensed symbolically in the veiling and retirement of female artists. By using the case of the veiled artists, they thus promote their views on religion, gender, and art and engage in public debate with secularists (for the views of the secularists, see Chapter 5). They thus deliberate in the public sphere—in the Habermasian sense—and disseminate their views about "the common good" and the "good Muslim," or in this case particularly the "good Muslim woman." I will first discuss Islamist views on the contemporary world of art, then the misrepresentation of the position of Muslim women, and finally the importance of veiling.[16]

The authors point at the great importance of art in building society and particularly point at the influence of art on the new generation. For that reason they attach great value to the field of art. Artists are important role models for their fans, whether in "shameless fashion" or Islamic *higab* (Farhat 1993, 13). The authors do not argue that art is generally *haram* and should be banished, but are alarmed by the present state of art in Egypt. Nasif and Khodayr mention that they are not against art, but against the "*maskhara,*" "shamelessness," in art (n.d., 16). "We don't say that art is *haram* and belongs to the devil, but we argue against the present state of art that does not set an example and does not show moral demeanour" (Kamil 1993, 15). On the contrary, it "incites the instincts," shows "uncurbed, heavy-breathing" women in "tight-fitting revealing fashion," "promotes prostitution," shows the drinking of alcohol and drugs under the cover of showing the danger of this poison, while in fact encouraging this behavior, and, last but not least, imitates the West with its stress on violence and crime (Kamil 1993, 45–47). The way religion is represented in films also disturbs the authors, who blame the field of art for negatively portraying religion instead of fighting serious problems such as religious extremism. Art in its current state thus plays a dangerous role in society. It deforms youth instead of building an upright new generation (Nasif and Khodayr n.d., 16). So according to them, the danger is not—as "the secularists" claim—that veiling and retirement of the stars are an attack on a crucial national source of income—that is, the film industry—but the danger is that art itself spreads corruption. The Islamist press thus uses the smear campaign against "repentant" artists to slander the scene of art.

The Islamist authors defame the art scene as a particularly harmful field for women. Art is deemed to debase women's virtue. The artists' return to the home is presented as bliss (Kamil 1993, 21). Kamil and Farhat point to the crucial importance of women for the Muslim family, on which the future of the whole *ummah* relies. To corrupt women is to corrupt the Muslim family, which will lead to the fall of the Muslim community. This is exactly the intention of the "enemies of Islam," Farhat argues. They know the importance of women, their virtue, and the stability of the family for the Islamic faith. If this pillar is destroyed, Islam would be ruined. They want the Muslim woman, "a vulnerable, easily influenced creature," to leave the home, reveal herself, and work in such disreputable fields as art (Farhat 1993, 11). In order to convince women to leave the home and to unveil, the adversaries of Islam tell them that Islam keeps women in a state of bondage. The opponents of Islam argue, therefore, that veiling and retirement by artists represent a return to "the ages of oppression" (Kamil 1993, 21). The "enemies" urge women to leave the house and work outside the home as a way to liberate themselves. If women would answer this call and leave the house and their duties as caretakers, they would eventually cause the destruction of the Muslim family (Farhat 1993, 11).

These Islamist authors thus expend efforts and go on for pages describing the elevated position of women in Islam. Reiterating familiar arguments about the elevation of women during the advent of Islam, their advanced position in comparison with women among the ancient Greeks and Romans and among the British, who did not accord women the right to possession of property until 1933, Kamil disputes the opponents' views about the status of women in Islam. The author argues that we have regrettably entered the era of the "new *jahiliya*," which, like the era before the advent of Islam, is characterized by a lack of obedience to God. In this "new *jahiliya*," women are threatened by many "devils" that seduce them. Women, "the pillar that either elevates or destroys the community," have been influenced by "the campaign to further moral regression." Most problems of the "new *jahiliya*" era, according to Kamil, can be related to women abandoning the home, and neglecting their duties as caretakers of the husband, home, and children. A crucial "treatment" for these social ills and preventive measure against moral regression are provided by the veil (Kamil 1993, 171).

Farhat (1993) particularly focuses on the attack against the veil and tries to untangle why this "conspiracy" against veiling exists worldwide. How is it that wearing a bikini is defended as a matter of personal freedom, while wearing the veil is attacked as a crime against freedom, Farah rhetorically asks. Starting from the case of the veiled artists in Egypt, he continues by detailing the ban on veiling for schoolgirls in France, the UK, Turkey, and Egypt. Farhat argues that clothing intimately relates to and marks a personality. The *hijab* ensures women's piety and moral standards. Islam is the only remaining religion that prohibits revealing the body, whereas other religions have discarded this original prohibition. Removing the veil will melt down the Islamic personality (1993, 25). The battle against the veil—that is, representing it as the symbol of oppression and backwardness—is a campaign to detach women from their faith, to disperse the Muslim family, and eventually to ruin Islam.

Who are those "enemies of Islam" attacking the veil? Most Islamist authors attack those who attacked the veiled actresses (see Chapter 5), but Kamil and Farhat, particularly the latter, hint at a broader "conspiracy" against Islam. In his book *The Campaign against the Veil: Secrets behind the Paid Veil*, Farhat tries to reveal the "huge campaign" going on to destabilize the Muslim family. It is not simply the secular press of Egypt, but a larger alignment of the West and Zionists, who constitute the "crusaders" against Islam. His question is not who is paying for veiling, but who is paying for the campaign against the veil. He points at the governments in the West and

4.3. *Book cover*, Ma'raka al-Hijab: Asrar wara' al-hijab al-madfu' / The Campaign against the Veil: Secrets behind the Paid Veil, *by Yasir Farhat*

"secular" governments such as those in Turkey and Egypt. He also indicates "the Jews" as having an interest in the fall of Islam and accuses them of paying for conferences on "the backward position of women in Islam" and the veil as the epitome of this "backwardness." Farhat quotes Henry Ford's book *The International Jew* (1920) in support of his argument.[17] According to Ford's theory, Jews dominate three fields: banks, the cinema, and fashion. Banks, cinema, and fashion are precisely the fields involved in the case of the payment and veiling of actresses. The "Jews" and other enemies earn money by "killing morality," "spreading lust," and "short skirts." They thus annihilate "girls' purity" and "destroy the family" (Farhat 1993, 10). The cover of his book tries to illustrate his theory in a somewhat mysterious way (see Figure 4.3). It shows women wearing veils that are imprinted with pictures of dollar notes, giving the reader initially the impression that "the West" and its allies pay for veiling. Eventually it turns out to mean that dollars are paid for slandering the veil. In countering this "smearing campaign," the veil of the artists is a tremendously symbolic and valuable icon. Despite the "attacks on the veil" and the "mischievous campaigns" against the veiled artists, they insisted on veiling and have chosen the "virtuous path for women." The veil of female artists thus carries the symbolic message of the final victory of Islam over the "enemies of Islam."

The former artists, however, are also a somewhat ambivalent agent or symbol for embodying the Islamist ideals for women. They are still identified as artists, whether former artists, veiled artists, retired artists, or repentant artists. Their fame and the great religious transformation they have experienced enhanced their symbolic value. Yet they are also a somewhat unstable icon that needs to be pinned down in the present blissful state. All ties with the field of art need to be completely severed—symbolically and materially. First, symbolically, the abandonment of art resulted in the artists' present lives being contrasted sharply with, and represented as a critique of, their former lives. Kamil severely contrasted the former "dissolute lifestyle" with the "total harmony and devotion" of the ex-performers' present lives. The former performers were harshly judged as "sinners" and even "sex stars," while their artistic accomplishments were disregarded. Materially, the artists had to dispose of the wealth accumulated from their former profession. The Islamist press debated what artists should do with the money they had amassed from working in art. If the artists were to happily live off their "*haram*" money, this would greatly diminish their value as icons of piety. Kamil discussed this issue with several religious scholars, concluding that the scholars agreed on the sinfulness of this money, but disagreed on what should be done with it (1993, 147–151). The former artists could neither use it to support themselves nor use it for charity purposes, because the money was generated from an unlawful source. They first had to purify the money. Sheikh al-Shaʿarawi advised the artists to invest the money into a new, religiously permissible project. If this project generated capital, the money would be *halal* and could be spent on the living expenses and charity. As we have seen, Hala al-Safi opened a religious school due to his advice. Also, other artists invested in Islamic businesses that were expanding in the parallel Islamic sector.

These were sensitive topics for the artists, and not all of them agreed with the Islamist representation of their former lives and the way the Islamists appropriated their stories. Even if they admitted mistakes or sins in their previous careers and emphasized the blessings of their present lives, they also perceived themselves as respectable and talented actresses or singers. As we will see in Chapter 5, other participants in the debate also appropriated the stories of the "repentant" artists to disseminate their views on gender, art, and religion. We thus see the immense importance accorded to the veiling of artists. From a personal choice it was transformed into a matter of great national concern. The personal preference of pious individuals became a central topic by which the national, religious, and cultural identity of the nation was debated. This central concern fused in the act of veiling by female artists, turning them into a powerful symbol for Islamists and a growing nuisance to secularists and the state. The presence of the Islamist voice and the number of Islamist publications on the topic bear witness to the growing presence and strength of Islamists more generally, a presence that was increasingly perceived as a threat by the Egyptian regime. The state and secular press promoted their secular nationalist discourse through attacking the veil of the artists. The veiled artists were depicted as "fundamentalists" and put into the same category as "extremists." The blurring of distinctions pointed to the general confrontational atmosphere in Egypt during the tense period of the early 1990s.

THE ISLAMIST LANDSCAPE AND THE CRACKDOWN BY THE REGIME

The relationship between the regime and Islamists changed from a period of relatively peaceful accommodation and tolerance in the 1980s into one of confrontation and repression in the 1990s. During the period 1990–1995 in particular, the conflicts increased dramatically (al-Awadi 2004). From "selective repression," the government turned its policy into general repression of all Islamist activities, including those undertaken by the moderate Muslim Brothers. Several reasons related to developments both on the side of Islamist groups and that of the government account for this change in policy. On the one hand, the power and visibility of the parallel Islamic sector were increasingly translated into political demands. In combination with militant Islamist confrontations, Islamists of all sorts were perceived as a threat by the state. On the other hand, the state's strategy of accommodation and co-optation of moderate Islamists and its "Islamization policy" had failed to contain the Islamist movement. Confronted with an economic crisis, a crisis of legitimacy, and a security crisis, the state was prompted to confront the Islamist opposition en masse.

In Part One, we have seen already the immense growth in the number of mosques and charitable associations run by Islamists. These continued to grow in the 1990s and were provided with several occasions to show their effectiveness vis-à-vis the state. The earthquake of 1992 was such an occasion, which made visible that Islamist charitable organizations arrived ahead of the government in rendering aid. The well-organized character of the Muslim Brothers became clear through an efficient transfer of resources to the victims that surpassed the performance of the state. The Doctors' Association volunteers were the first to set up tents and to distribute food, blankets, and medical care to the victims. This outstanding performance of the Islamists was not only noted by the state, but also by Western media. The Egyptian government is reported to have complained about "the state within the state," and the Western media inferred from the failure of the state and the success of the Muslim Brothers a possible Islamist takeover of Egypt (Sullivan and Abed-Kotob 1999, 91; al-Awadi 2004, 149–153; Wickham 2002, 203). As Sullivan and Abed-Kotob remarked with regard to the civil institutions that inhabited the public arena in Egypt during the 1990s, these became "vital [. . .] not *despite* the increasing number of Islamic activists and institutions but *because* of them" (1999, 12). Also, in the fields of economics, media, and politics, the physical infrastructure of the Islamists was growing at a staggering speed.

In the period of economic crisis, particularly due to the fall in international oil prices since the mid-1980s—combined with the fact that the other main sources of revenue for Egypt, tourism, the Suez Canal, and workers' remittances, were uncontrollable and unpredictable as well—it was difficult for the government to sustain the "social contract." Violent acts by Islamic militants harmed the revenues from tourism. Egypt was rewarded for backing the Gulf War, but these gains were outweighed by the loss of remittances due to the return of many migrants who had been working in Iraq. The crisis also pressured the state, albeit reluctantly, to conform to the restructuring plans of the International Monetary Fund (IMF) and World Bank. It led to an agreement in 1991 to reduce budgetary imbalances by cutting, among others, subsidies for basic food (see Chapter 8). Between 1990–1991 and 1995–1996, the poverty rate in urban and rural areas increased from 20.7 to 44.3 percent and unemployment rose from 8.6 to 11.3 percent (al-Awadi 2004, 158, 161). This resulted in growing social unrest.

The Islamists, however, had gained legitimacy by providing social and economic services. This was supported by the wealth amassed by private companies of Islamists and Islamic investment companies (see also Chapter 1). An estimated 40 percent of Islamic investment companies were owned by members of the Muslim Brothers or those sympathetic to their ideals (al-Awadi 2004, 133). Many people had withdrawn their money from public-sector banks—an estimated 8 billion Egyptian pounds between 1983 and 1986—and transferred it to Islamic banks and investment companies. Another important source of income was the monthly subscription fee, equal to 5 percent of their income, paid by the members of the Muslim Brotherhood to the organization. The Muslim Brotherhood also encouraged its wealthy members, including well-to-do entrepreneurs working in the Gulf, to voluntarily donate substantial sums of money (al-Awadi 2004, 103).

In addition to the Islamist presence in the socioeconomic field, Islamist voices also became important in the media. As we have seen above, they debated "true Islam" and "the good Muslim woman" and formulated a conservative Islamist counterdiscourse that challenged the state-supported national secular discourse. They disseminated their ideas through religious schools and mosque lessons, cassettes, radio and TV programs, and the growing Islamist publishing industry. How many Islamic books and journals were published and sold is hard to determine. We also have to take into account that some journals were published by the government. In an attempt to outwit the Islamists and publish their version of "true Islam," the state increased religious programs on television and radio, and published Islamic journals such as *al-Liwa al-Islami* and *al-Aqidati* (Starrett 1995b, 55; Bayat 1998, 156; al-Awadi 2004, 120). With regard to the Islamist press, Wickham mentions that the circulation of *Liwa' al-Islam*, the successor of the popular Brotherhood journal *al-Da'wah*, grew from 35,000 in 1987 to about 95,000 in 1991. Over half of the copies were sold in Egypt. They probably circulated among a much larger number of readers, because not all people could afford to buy the journal (Wickham 2002, 101). Dozens of Islamic daily newspapers, weeklies, and monthlies had high circulation rates.[18] In 1994, over one-quarter of all books published were religious, a 25 percent rise since 1985. An estimated 85 percent of books sold during the 1995 book fair in Cairo were Islamic (Bayat 1998, 155–156). The tapes of religious preachers such as Sheikh Kishk, numbering over a thousand, sold in the millions. Hours allocated by the state to religious programs on national television and radio increased, reaching 14,500 hours annually, compared with the 8,000 for entertainment programs (al-Awadi 2004, 120). Radio Quran, a channel devoted entirely to religious matters, was highly popular during this period (Bayat 1998, 156).

The Islamists had not only become competitors in providing socioeconomic services and at the level of cultural and moral-religious values, but also in the political field. The Muslim Brotherhood was not a legal party, but demanded legal status to increase its legitimacy. Due to this lack of legal status, it had concentrated on gaining strong organizational positions in the university campuses, teachers' clubs, and professional organizations. According to al-Awadi (2004), the Brotherhood's attempt to acquire political legitimacy from syndicates and universities had been a way to compensate for the movement's failure to secure recognition as a legal political party. They were also the power base from which further demands for legal status were launched. The group thus moved from the periphery to a more visible political center stage (Wickham 2002, 176–204). The Brotherhood became the most powerful force on university campuses from 1984 onward. Despite security surveillance, it gained control in elections in universities in Cairo, Alexandria, and Zagazig in 1987 and 1988. In 1989, it extended its control over al-Azhar University and the University of al-Mansura (al-Awadi 2004, 93, 122–123). It provided students with cheap study materials, as well as medical treatment. It also gained access to the teachers' faculty clubs in major universities by promising an increase in salary, organizing housing for young teachers, and improving health care.

The Islamist candidates also won elections in the professional syndicates, consisting of middle-class employees of the public and private sectors. As al-Awadi mentions, the presence of the Muslim Brothers in the professional syndicates was a logical outcome of the fact that they had been students in the 1970s, had graduated in the meantime, and were employed in these professional fields (2004, 95). Whereas professionals are often described as the vanguard or elite of Egypt, Wickham warns that—despite their continued status—there was also an underclass, or "lumpen elite," within their ranks. This was due to the mass entrance into the job market of holders of university degrees, whether employed in their field of study or unemployed (2002, 182). The Muslim Brothers were elected to the council of the engineers' syndicate in 1986, and the pharmacists' syndicate in 1988. In 1986, they introduced subsidized health insurance in the medical syndicate. The beneficiaries of the health scheme included more than 17,600 doctors and their 43,960 dependents. The coverage was extended to the engineers' syndicate and benefited 72,000 individuals (al-Awadi 2004, 126–127). The Brothers also held annual sales of consumer durables, the first of which was organized in 1986 at the Cairo University faculty club and yielded about a million Egyptian pounds (al-Awadi 2004, 125). In 1992, the "Islamic Trend," as the Muslim Brotherhood faction was known, also won the election of the Lawyers Association. This had been the last remaining stronghold of liberals and leftists and thus shocked secular politicians and intellectuals. Together with the victories of the Islamic Trend in other professional associations—of doctors, scientists, and engineers—this indicated an increasing alienation of the professional educated middle classes from established politics and the emergence of the Islamic Trend as the only remaining alternative (Wickham 2002, 178). These associations became important sites of the "Islamic counter elite" that promoted a "new Islamic subculture" (Wickham 2002, 179).

The Muslim Brothers had also been successful in the national elections. In 1984, they were allowed to participate in alliance with the New Wafd and won eight seats. In 1987, they allied themselves with Amal and the Ahrar party and won thirty-six seats (al-Awadi 2004, 113–114, 141–144). The list-based electoral system in use during the 1984 and 1987 elections was suddenly changed into a system of independent candidates—that is, the elections were based on individuals and not on parties. The Muslim Brothers doubted the intentions of the state and boycotted the 1990 elections. They thus openly contested the regime instead of abiding by its rules. They also warned against Egypt's negotiations with the IMF, which was pressing for structural reforms to combat the economic crisis, and publicly condemned the state's involvement in the Gulf War. They openly criticized Mubarak's policy to sanction the participation of the Egyptian army in the Western alliance against Saddam Hussein. The elections of 1995, in which the Brothers decided to participate with 170 candidates, made the regime very nervous. It prevented the opposition from succeeding by harassment, violence, and massive arrests of candidates and Muslim Brothers more generally.

Another important factor in the state's shift in policy from accommodation to repression was the growing religious violence and social unrest during the early 1990s. In 1988, there were nine violent incidents between Jamaʿat Islamiyya and the police and sixteen riots by Jamaʿat Islamiyya. In 1989, this had increased to fourteen bloody clashes and nineteen riots. According to a semi-official report in 1990, there were as many as fifty-one confrontations between Islamists and the security forces, with over 115 casualties (al-Awadi 2004, 117–119, 154). In 1992, the secular intellectual Farag Fuda was assassinated by Islamists (Wickham 2002, 156). In 1993, there were attacks on the minister of information and minister of interior, and during that year the confrontations between Islamists and the government forces left 1,106 killed or wounded, and 17,191 arrested (Bayat 1998, 155). In 1995, there was an attempt to assassinate Mubarak when he visited Ethiopia (al-Awadi 2004, 117–119, 154). Not only state officials, but also Western tourists, were targeted. Jama'at Islamiyya in particular was connected with the violent attacks on the tourism industry. It carried out a grenade attack in Luxor in 1992 and shot at tour boats on the Nile. Russian tourists were stabbed in Port Said. In 1993, it urged tourists in its communiqués to leave the country. In the same year, the Cairo Museum was the target of a bomb attack, followed by a bomb attack near the Pyramids, and eight tourists in a bus in Cairo were wounded. In 1997, one of the most deadly attacks on tourists took place in Luxor, killing sixty-six people, of whom fifty-seven were foreigners. In the same year, a tour bus was bombed in Cairo, killing nine tourists and their driver (Sullivan and Abed-Kotob 1999, 86). The state tried to crack down on these Islamist groups with every method available. The government was angered by the Brotherhood's reluctance to support its campaigns against Islamist terrorism.

The mid-1990s, and the year 1995 in particular, saw a peak in the confrontation between the state and Islamists of different shades. The government had undertaken several strategies to contain and accommodate the Islamic Trend. Generally, neither of the state's strategies, control and co-optation—that is, its "Islamization policy"—was very successful. As we have seen in Part One, the government had attempted to gain control over the mosques and the NGOs during the 1980s. In 1992, it announced a plan to control private mosques and to incorporate ten thousand of them each year under the authority of the Ministry of Religious Endowment (Al-Awqaf), a plan that failed due to budgetary constraints (Wickham 2002, 106). The regime also appointed its own religious teachers and imams. The number of imams working for the Ministry of Al-Awqaf increased more than threefold, from 6,000 in 1982 to 22,000 by 1996 (Bayat 1998, 167). In 1993, the government launched the program "Caravans of Light," which sent Azhar graduates throughout the country to spread its message of Islam. According to Bayat, al-Azhar controlled in 1995 over ten thousand mosques, around six thousand educational institutions ranging from primary schools and Qur'an classes to branches of the University (Bayat 1998, 167). All NGOs were regulated by Law 32 of 1964, which outlawed political activism. Yet in general, Wickham argues, the regime found it difficult to reclaim the space it had given to Islamist groups and organizations in the parallel sector, because of its decentralized structure, the state's inefficiencies, and the alliances Islamist actors had made with members within the state apparatus itself (2002, 104).

This brings us to the ambiguous results of the state's "Islamization policies." The Islamization of the state took place from three sides: first, the penetration of Islamists into the state, second, the concession of influence to al-Azhar in many fields, and finally, the Islamization policies of the state itself. First, the Egyptian state bureaucracy was enormous and employed an estimated 5 million people in the early 1990s. The influence of Islamic ideas, institutions, and orientations also influenced those working in the state institutions. The piety movement had spread all over Egypt to almost all levels of the population, including state employees. There was little opportunity and effort to screen all civil servants (Wickham 2002, 108). Next, "the revolution by stealth," the growing influence of the conservative al-Azhar clergy within the judiciary, educational system, and state-run media, imported conservative Islamic thought into the state's own ranks (Wickham 2002, 211). As we will see in Chapter 5, al-Azhar was given increasing authority in censoring intellectual and artistic productions. Finally, the state began to offer its own brand of Islam through such Islamic weeklies as *al-Liwa al-Islami* (published by the ruling National Democratic Party) and *al-Aqidati* (a project of a Westernized publisher). They were established to "spread correct Islamic thought and culture among Egyptian youth" (in Bayat 1998, 167). As Bayat remarks, both publications exhibit "traditionalist and at times remarkably fundamentalist versions of Islam" (Bayat 1998, 167). The net result was the spread of conservative Islamic ideas by the state itself.

Confronted with its failed strategies, violent confrontations, and an increasingly effective, visible, and demanding Islamist opposition, the state transformed its strategy. It changed its policies into overt confrontation and repression of all sorts of Islamist actors and activities. The state embarked on a general crackdown against Islamists and started to obscure distinctions between Muslim Brothers and terrorists. The weak state economy had prompted the government already to take steps against the Islamic economic sector in order to reverse the movement of capital from Islamists to its own financial institutions (al-Awadi 2004, 132). From 1988 onward, the regime started an aggressive campaign against Islamic investment companies and put an end to them. The regime also used its role in the Gulf War to ask the Gulf countries to tighten their control on Islamic organizations with links to the Muslim Brothers in order to stop their financial donations from abroad (al-Awadi 2004, 188). In 1992, the regime also halted donations to the professional syndicates for the victims of the earthquake and obliged Egyptians to deposit their donations in government accounts. The government's clampdown on the Islamic investment companies constituted a huge blow to one of the most powerful sources of financing the Brothers. The state also accused Islamist syndicate boards of financial mismanagement, and some were placed under official custodianship (Wickham 2002, 201). The Brothers were removed from the boards of several professional syndicates, after which many of their services ended as well. As al-Awadi notes, the health care scheme of the engineers' syndicate, which was paid for by subscriptions of the Muslim Brotherhood constituencies and by the group's popular sales of consumer durables, ceased to exist (2004, 187). All these measures were taken in order to curb the Brothers' power and dry up their financial sources. The state justified these steps by claiming that the Islamic sector financially supported militant groups.

Beginning around 1992, Mubarak initiated attacks designed to uproot the underground militants. Security forces brutally raided Upper Egypt, rounding up thousands of Islamists, injuring and killing several of them. In 1994, the minister of interior, Hassan al-Alfi, mentioned that ten thousand detainees were held in prisons. Security forces raided assumed hideouts of Jama'at Islamiyya in different parts of Cairo, in Asyut, and near Aswan in 1994. Suspects were tried in quick military trials, and six militants were hanged in 1996 (Sullivan and Abed-Kotob 1999, 86–89). During the first ten months of 1995, 333 people were reportedly killed in acts of political violence in Upper Egypt (al-Awadi 2004, 179).

The line between militant Islamists and moderates became blurred, and also the Muslim Brothers and their power base were attacked. In 1993, the professional associations were confronted with a new law requiring a minimum attendance rate of 50 percent. The elections of the associations were supervised by appointed judges. In 1995 and 1996, the regime arrested and imprisoned many leaders of the Muslim Brotherhood. During the 1995 election campaign, ninety-five important Islamist figures, candidates and non-candidates, were arrested. They were tried in military courts and sentenced to three to five years of hard labor, which dealt a severe blow to the Muslim Brotherhood (al-Awadi 2004, 174). The Brotherhood was generally attacked as an illegal organization that allegedly aimed to overthrow the government. The Brotherhood and terrorist organizations were presented as "two faces of the same coin" (Wickham 2002, 153, 201).

It was particularly the blurring of distinctions between militant and moderate Islamists, and the deliberate conflation of "Islamists," "extremists," and "terrorists," that informed the reception of the veiled artists among secular intellectuals and the state. In Chapter 5, I will investigate the secular nationalist discourse and reaction to the "repentant" artists. The assumption of a conspiracy by "Islamist extremists" against the nation by way of the phenomenon of the veiled actresses is in line with the general attack on all brands of Islamists.

(FIVE)

The Secular Cultural Field

This chapter features the life story of actress-comedienne Soheir al-Babli. The second section will follow the debates on the
"repentant" artists, but now from the side of the secular press,
which articulated its secular nationalist discourse by attacking the veiled artists. In the third section, the relationship between the Egyptian state and
the secular cultural field, and the secularists' co-optation by the state in the
struggle against Islamists, will be discussed.

THE SPIRITUAL BIOGRAPHY OF ACTRESS SOHEIR AL-BABLI

The retirement of the famous comedienne Soheir al-Babli in 1993 appeared to be the final blow in the face of the secular cultural field (for a picture of her see book cover, Figure 6.2, and DVD cover, Figure 9.2). The famous
actor 'Adil Imam, her costar in many plays, asked her whether she had become
crazy. Soheir al-Babli quit while working in 'Atiyya, the Terrorist, a play the
director Galal Sharqawi had just rewritten to include allusions to the terrorist
attacks of the time. With so many artists stepping down, and Soheir al-Babli
on top of that, a limit was reached. When the play resumed its second season, the cream of the artists' world showed up. They wanted to demonstrate
their support for the play and their dismay at the "fundamentalist turn" of so
many artists (Brooks 1998, 241–242). Soheir al-Babli's veiling was felt as ex-
ceptionally shocking because she had become synonymous with the theater.
No one expected this decision from the star of comedy and political satire.
The reaction to her retirement, although in line with the attacks on other
veiled artists, was accordingly very fierce.

I received her telephone number from the head of the trade union, but my call was never answered. The next year, during my visit to actress Sha-hira, I was given Soheir al-Babli's number again. It was the same number, but I tried once more. Soheir al-Babli appeared to have many houses scattered over Egypt, Saudi Arabia, and Germany. She particularly liked spending many months in the Holy Land. Yet I was lucky this time: she was in Egypt, and the next day she would have a shooting in the studios of 6th of October City, to which she invited me.[1] Next day, after some back-and-forth talking and phoning at the gate of the film studio, I was allowed entrance and was driven through the large area with pharaonic temples and a street with stately mansions, and finally we arrived in the corner with a countryside village. The shooting took place in front of a slightly dilapidated house exuding a certain lost grandeur. After acquainting me with the director, producer, and some other actors, she had me seated near the house so that I could watch the shooting until the break half an hour later. During her break we had a lengthy talk, but she made it clear that there was not sufficient time to tell her whole story. We accordingly talked about the serial she was acting in, *Qalb Habiba*, which was to be released the following Ramadan (see Chapter 9), the reasons for her return to the screen, and the conditions she stipulated for signing a contract. After that we also discussed some stages in her life story, in reverse order.

There are quite a few interviews published in periodicals and broadcast on TV from which to reconstruct her biography. Of particular interest is a recorded meeting in Los Angeles where she is invited to speak about her trajectory toward veiling. She is given the floor for forty-five minutes—without any interruption—to tell her story in the way she prefers.[2] The story is literally staged. We see her sitting on a stage behind a table and only hear the responses from the audience. It is her first appearance back on stage after an absence of six years, she announces as she commences her talk, which immediately provokes vigorous applause from the audience. The story is told in a lighthearted tone and narrated as a comedy. She clearly intends to entertain her audience with her story, while also using it to edify her public. She uses drama techniques and presents her story as a scenario, describing the unfolding events in expressive detail. Whereas the joking way of narrating is part of her personality, as she mentions herself, she had also developed a certain ambiguity toward satire and tried to distance herself from her former work as a comedienne. Before telling her story to the Los Angeles audience, she states that comedy needs lies, exaggeration, sarcasm, and mockery. She used to feel powerful and would order people around. She now prefers to tell her story lightheartedly, but also with self-reflexive humility. The spectator feels like someone at a one-woman show, instead of someone listening to a speaker at an Annual Convention. Soheir al-Babli clearly manages to enrapture her audience, as becomes clear from its laughter and applause.

The first episode in her story is the lesser pilgrimage she habitually made:

> I did the *'umrah*, every year, me and my colleague Yusra, a great artist. For nine years in succession we did the *'umrah* and after that I took off my veil. I joked, danced, wept, and resumed my ordinary life. I completed my *'umrah* and I thought that this was Islam. [. . .] If people heard that I did the *'umrah* they asked, "Did you repent?" Then I responded, "Repent?! Repent from what? I am fine!" [. . .] And I asked them, "Did you repent?" Then they asked, "From what?" "That you watched me!" [Audience laughs]. [. . .] Until the last *'umrah*. I was fed up, two years the same text, it was political satire about politics in the Arab world. At the end of the year I went on *'umrah*. After the *maghrib* prayer, [. . .] I told "my sisters" Yusra and Yasmin [al-Khiyyam], "You can leave already, I want to pray." I knelt down. I found myself expressing *ya rabb ya rabb* [. . .] and a tab of water came down from my eyes; I never wept that way in my life before. [. . .] I said, "*Ya rabb*, I am fed up, I am tired, give me a sign that you are satisfied with me." I hated the theater and felt it was like a devil. I had given many interviews in which I told that I would die on stage. That would be a disaster because not only me but all those who watch me would be held accountable for this. [. . .] I said, "Provide me with a husband who is devout, he does not need to be rich." [. . .] I wept the whole time. [. . .] Yusra asked, "Did you do supplicatory prayer?" I told her, "Yes, I asked God to accept my repentance and make me leave the theater (*yitob 'alayya*)."[3] She almost screamed in my face, "Impossible! Is this Soheir al-Babli belonging to the stage, did you really ask this?!" [. . .] People around me asked, "Soheir, what's wrong?" [. . .] Someone said, "Take care that you do not veil." I replied, "No, no, far from me those things." But inside me I felt something was changing.

Soheir al-Babli concludes this first episode with some general considerations about the difficulty of veiling for any person. But particularly fame, stardom, and the audience made it very hard for her. Accordingly, she initially thought about leaving the stage, but had no intention to veil.

The desire to veil became more pronounced during the second episode, consisting of a six-months period in which she met her future husband and was slowly becoming more religiously involved. As she mentions in other sources,[4] her family is from the province of Dumyat, where she was born in 1935.[5] Her parents had taught her the do's and don'ts, but condemned certain behavior as *'eb*, shameful, rather than using religious idioms such as *haram* or *halal*. She was not used to praying or reading the Qur'an. The second episode is situated in Alexandria, where she was supervising the repairs of her "villa" before resuming the play in Cairo for the next season. She asked for a "*taqi*," devout, person who would carry out the work on her house, because she had been cheated before. She asked to meet the person before he commenced the job:

> I went in and said, "Hey!" [audience laughs]. He did not look at me at all. I felt a little bit embarrassed. I was wearing jeans and a T-shirt. So I told him I want this and that and he told me to register this with the manager. I wanted to give him money in advance. But he told me to keep the money. I went out to the manager and he did not look at me either [audience laughs]. I asked, "What's going on? Is there something wrong with me? I am a Muslim woman and want you to restore my house. I heard you are honest workers. Take the money!" They said without looking at me, "We'll take your money and come to your house at seven o'clock" [audience laughs because she acts out the way the manager approached her with his face averted]. I have never felt so shy in my life.
>
> Next morning at seven they were in the house. When I saw them I exclaimed, "*Ya lahwi!*" [exclamation of great dismay]. It was the time of terrorism and the scene I saw gave me palpitations. I told the man, his name is Mahmud, "*Ya* Hagg, I don't want you to pray in my house." It was the time of terrorism! [audience laughs]. Because what I witnessed was a row of praying men, he sat in front and the rest behind him. I said, "*Ya lahwi!*" and imagined the news that would be spread in magazines: "A group of terrorists praying in Soheir al-Babli's villa." He said, "We are not terrorists, we pray and work." [. . .] He said, "I beg you, *ya* Hagga, don't go to my workers while you are dressed in this way." I was angry and said, "I am not a Hagga" [audience laughs], I had a different understanding of this word at the time and thought he told me I was old, and said, "I am free to wear what I like." [. . .]
>
> Fifteen days later he sent me booklets and I started reading. What does this man want of me?! He really is a terrorist! [audience laughs]. We all had learnt that faith is terrorism and I was ignorant of my religion! [. . .] He sat with me and I told him, "Do you know who I am!" He answered, "A Muslim woman." "I am Soheir al-Babli!" "So what?" he said. "I am a great artist!" "I don't care," he said. Slowly I felt ashamed, I started to read, to put something over my hair. [. . .] I started to wear wide clothes. [. . .] I started to understand.

During the third episode, she should resume acting and rehearsals for the play *'Atiyya, the Terrorist*. She met with the director, Galal al-Sharqawi:

I had done supplicatory prayers to be removed from the theater and there came the great producer Galal al-Sharqawi and he said, "*Yalla*, come on, we'll start." All advertisements were made and the final rehearsal was to take place. I said, "*Hadir*! At your service!" Here was Mahmud [raising her right hand] and here Galal [raising her left hand] [audience laughs at the obvious symbolic use of right and left for the "good" and the "bad"]. I said, "I am leaving, *ya* Hagg, to work" [resume acting]. He said, "So it was to no avail?" I felt ashamed.

They had a lengthy discussion about what to do, and in confusion she left for Cairo together with her daughter, not knowing what and how to decide.

I prayed, I wept, I went to sleep and awoke for the *fajr* prayer [in the early morning]. I never ever woke up for *fajr* prayer [audience laughs], *Subhan Allah*. [. . .] I usually came home at that time! I performed *fajr* prayer and kept on weeping. I said, "God reassure me." [. . .] I slept as a baby while tears were watering down from my eyes—my daughter later on told me—I am never able to sleep except with sleeping pills. Money, art, the *dunya*, life . . . But now I slept as a baby and was happy. It was still not in my mind to veil. Next day, I went to a famous doctor.[6] I did not ask him about the veil, I only asked him to tell me whether my money was *halal* or *haram*, [. . .] He said, "Madam Soheir, should I be honest or make you compliments?" [. . .] He said, "It is *haram*!" I said, "Thank you!" and I left. [. . .]

I went home and was sitting on my bed. My daughter came in, she was wearing the veil. I said Nevin, show me your headscarf. [. . .] I had the feeling that the theater was a devil waiting for me. [. . .] I took the head-scarf and put it on my head. I looked at myself in the mirror. [. . .] At that time there was an artist, Shahira,[7] whom I did not see for two years. It was really like a scenario. She phoned me at that particular moment. I said I do not want to talk to anyone. Shahira told my daughter that she had had a beautiful dream: "Your mother was at the *ka'ba* and did the pilgrimage, the *higg*."[8] My daughter said, "Okay, I will tell her," and wanted to hang up the phone. Shahira is the person who brings the news to journalists; I took the receiver and said, "*al-salama 'alekum*." She said, "*alekum al-salam, ya hagga*!" I did not say, "I am not a *hagga*" this time. I said, "*ya rabb*, tell all newspapers that Soheir al-Babli has veiled!" And I immediately dropped the receiver in order not to retreat on my steps. Within ten minutes they all called: Shadia, Shams, Yasmin al-Khiyyam, Hana' Tharwat, they congratulated me and wept. Within half an hour, they all were on top of me [audience laughs and claps].

She took this decision on June 6, 1993, and the next day the news made the front pages (*al-Musawwar*, August 27, 1993).

During the fourth and final episode, doubts remain about her decision. She married Mahmud on June 15, 1993 (*al-Musawwar*, August 27, 1993), but changing her lifestyle was not easy.

It really looked like a theater play. [. . .] Next day the headlines in the newspaper read "Higab of Soheir al-Babli." 'Adil Imam asked me whether I had gone mad [. . .] and then Galal. He had heard the news from the newspaper. I came in with my headscarf deep over my eyes [audience laughs as she tears her scarf down] so that he would be convinced that I am a *muhagaba*. [. . .] Galal told me, "Write on a piece of paper that you renounce from this and that." I had money out with him. I said, "Give that paper," and I wrote down that I renounced all my rights. They had told me my money is *haram*! Inside I said to myself, "What have you done?! How can I live without a source of income?!" [. . .] Also, my previous husband had told me my money was *haram*![9] [. . .] [Sheikh] al-Sha'arawi told me, "Away with your money, start anew, clean. Start from zero but now in illumination!" [. . .] What I wanted to tell . . . I veiled and the Hagg called me. He really is a good man, immediately we married and we had our honeymoon. Where? At the *ka'ba*! [Mecca, audience laughs]. *Wallahi*, By God! [audience claps]. Before my honeymoon had been in Paris! [. . .]

I will tell you what was going on inside me. My husband was poor, rich in morals, but materially poor. I was used to the best hotels, huge apartment, enormous car that drove me from the airport. Suddenly I was sleeping in a hotel [. . .] for two riyal. Before, I slept for a thousand riyal, but of course this time my husband paid. He said, "I pay and you have to live in accordance with my [financial] standard." I argued with him. We went to pray [. . .] and suddenly the devil appeared [. . .] and he told me, "What have you done?! You were fine, you were an artist, you did not do anything wrong!" I started to talk to myself and asked God what should I do?! Should I return? [. . .] There is no other profession to eat from than acting! My husband took my hand but I pushed him away. I was disgusted. I returned to the hotel. At the reception they told me there is a letter for you. I went to my room. My husband came after me with the letter, with his eyes wide open. [. . .] He said, "Look, take it . . ." This is what happened: Downstairs I had asked God to send me a sign [. . .] and this letter read, "Dear sister, for the great artist, stay on your path, don't look back, we want Soheir al-Babli in the Islamic faith." [. . .] This shows the greatness of God. After that moment I never looked back.[10] They offered me a blank check if I would return, even with the veil, but no way. I have chosen my path!

At this moment, Soheir al-Babli is notified that her time is almost over. Of course, she could have added many episodes, some of which I will reconstruct from other sources and the interview I conducted with her.

The stories she related in interviews right after her retirement are not radically different from this reconstruction, although they focus more on religious learning. For instance, in an interview with *Kolenas* in 1993,[11] she mentioned that she had been thinking about retirement and veiling for two years and that it was not a hasty decision at all. She had been thoroughly studying the Qur'an and *tafsir* and *fiqh* books, and going to religious meetings and lectures by Muhammad al-Ghazali, Dr. Mustafa Mahmud, and Dr. 'Umar 'Abd al-Kafi. She bought videotapes with Qur'an interpretations by Sheikh al-Sha'arawi and the preacher Yasin Rushdi. She started to memorize many verses from the Qur'an and stories from the *hadith* and read through the Qur'an entirely four times. In an interview with *al-Musawwar*, she also stressed the religious reason for marrying "Hagg Mahmud." There are many nice men, she told the interviewer, "but I took him for his religious knowledge and education that will support me and complement my imperfect religious knowledge" (*al-Musawwar*, August 27, 1993, pp. 50–51).

In interviews conducted in 1993, she made public her new plans for the future. First of all, she started an Islamic business in fashion. She had, however, after Dr. 'Umar 'Abd al-Kafi's *fatwa* about the unlawfulness of her money, distributed most of her wealth (*Ruz al-Yusif*, November 14, 2005, pp. 82–83). She opened a small factory for the production of Islamic fashion for *muhagabat*. She intended to design the patterns herself and supervise the production process. She wanted to sell the product for a minimal price, because the factory was not meant for profit but to design elegant clothes for veiled women without straining their budget (*Kolenas*, 1993, pp. 19–20). In 1999, she still spoke about her business, no longer manufacturing but mainly trading between Saudi Arabia and Egypt in veils and clothes for women, which she sold from her houses in Jeddah and Egypt. She maintained that trading was in her blood (*Sabah al-Kher*, January 7, 1999, pp. 20–21). However, from later interviews it appeared that her business had failed. Also, in the interview with me she said: "I am an artist, not a businesswoman."[12]

She also announced her plans to launch a new journal for Muslim women and a new TV channel, dedicated to promoting "upright Islamic conduct for women and youth." It was meant, as well, as a venue for veiled presenters to keep on working. Compelled by recent cases of two TV presenters, Mona Gabr and 'Afaf 'Abd al-Raziq, who veiled and were for so doing fired by the state television, this had become a hot issue again. Soheir al-Babli announced her plan to ask the minister of information to open a special channel for religious artists. "I will ask for our rights as *multazima* artists. I will ask them: 'Why do you reject us? I beg you—may God guide you—don't destroy our right to wear the veil and appear on screen as a *muhagaba* and present our artistic message'" (*al-Sha'ab*, June 25, 1993). Together with others, she intended to develop an alternative, and to maintain their presence in the media from which they were blocked.

From her talk in Los Angeles, we could deduce that she did not intend to resume acting with a veil. Yet, in several other interviews, she was more outspoken in her ideas that art was not *haram*. In the newspaper *al-Sha'ab*, she even claimed that she was not going to retire, because art is not *haram* (*al-Sha'ab*, June 25, 1993). In some interviews around 2001, she was repeatedly asked to return to produce religiously committed art with a veil by her audiences. She explained that the conditions were not favorable and respectable art series or quality historical plays about Islam's glorious past needed a lot of capital. In a live interview aired by al-Jazeera (January 28, 2001), she explained to the audience that her advanced age had an effect, in the sense that it made her realize that her remaining time in the *dunya* was short. On the Day of Judgment, she would be asked about her "good works," and artistic productions would not be sufficient. She was also repeatedly asked to work in productions such as, for instance, those of the theater al-Ghad, which presented plays of the Islamist trade unions of the engineers.[13] Yet she explained that, for her, art was not a hobby and that she did not intend to act in nonprofessional productions. But if there were a great professional production, she would welcome it (Islam Online, January 30, 2001). Besides general changes in the field of art and the media that might facilitate her return, there could also be some personal circumstances. As it happened, her husband Mahmud disappeared from her talks, lectures, and interviews (*al-Ahram*, December 10, 2005). In an interview in 2010, she mentioned that she had been divorced five years before, which thus coincided with her return to the screen (*al-Malaf*, February 19, 2010).

Soheir al-Babli's first comeback, in 2002, occurred in a commercial on TV for household appliances. She argued that the commercial was like a small artistic film with a scenario. Besides, she appeared in Islamic dress, the commercial contained no words or scene that harmed Islam, and it promoted useful products (*al-'Alam al-Yawm*, November 24, 2002, p. 16; *al-Bayan*, January 11, 2003, p. 7). Her comeback led to disapproving reactions from some of her retired colleagues. The newspapers mentioned that Yasmin al-Khiyyam was highly surprised, Hana' Tharwat disapproved and maintained that women should stay at home and work only in case of urgency, while Shams al-Barudi was said to consider the return a shock to those retired artists who tried to keep out of the spotlights. Soheir Ramzi and 'Afaf Sho'ib, veiled actresses who both eventually returned to the screen themselves, saw no harm in Soheir's return (*al-'Alam al-Yawm*, November 24, 2002, p. 16; *al-Bayan*, January 11, 2003, p. 7). She thus had a gradual return to the screen, first through frequent interviews, talks, lectures, and chat sessions, then in a small TV commercial, and finally her full return to the screen with the shooting of *Qalb Habiba*, which I witnessed during the interview in 2005. She told me that she had needed the ten-year break for studying her religion, attaining closeness to God, and ordering her life in accordance with worship and devotion. Her return should not come as a complete surprise, though, as her retreat had been partly due to the lack of respectable options and good offers in accordance with her conditions. When her conditions to return were met, she took her chance. She told me about the conditions she stipulated in her contract, such as veiling and no embracing, touching, or kissing. In her role as elderly widowed mother, Habiba, her sons were only allowed to kiss her on her hand or forehead. She required that there would be no improper words and only respectable dialogues. In Part Three of the book, I will come back to the conditions that several artists stipulated and the productions in which they returned. I will now turn to the period of Soheir al-Babli's retirement and the shock this caused to the secular field.

THE SECULAR PRESS

We have seen the shock and disbelief Soheir al-Babli's veiling caused to her friends and colleagues, such as Yusra, 'Adil Imam, and Galal Sharqawi. This impact resonated outside the circle of artists through the whole secular field. Mirroring the Islamist press, which capitalized on the stories to promote its conservative Islamist discourses, the secular press used the stories to further its ideas about liberal secular progress for the nation. It felt the national project was greatly endangered by the Islamist encroachment in all ranks of society. Although the secular press could be critical of the state, the two entities converged in their anti-Islamist stance. The secular press charged that artists received money for veiling from outside "groups," caused the Sauditization of Egypt, and spread Wahhabi ideas on art and gender. The accusations of the secular cultural field regarding the artists' veiling was also formulated as a kind of "conspiracy theory," but the source of danger differed from that of the Islamist imagination. The *Ruz al-Yusif* journalist Ibrahim ʿIssa wrote the book *al-Harb bi al-Niqab / The War with the Face Veil* (1993), which makes an interesting diptych with the book by the Islamist author Farhat (see Chapter 4). The two authors' visions for the nation are diametrically opposed. Yet it is interesting to note that they concur in the central space allotted to gender and art. Accordingly, for the secular field also, the veiling and the retirement of female performers were an extremely sensitive issue, which formed a stark contrast with their ideas about the "common good." Below, I will examine the diverse forms of attacks in the secular press in order to highlight its vision of the nation.

First, the general public and the performers' adversaries reacted with jokes, harassment, and debunking remarks. Cynical jokes like the following were told among the Egyptian populace: Who are the second best-paid women in Egypt? Belly dancers, of course, because Saudi tourists throw banknotes of a hundred dollars on their feet while they are dancing. Who are the best-paid women in Egypt? The converted belly dancers, of course, because Saudi sheikhs transfer banknotes of a thousand dollars to their accounts if they stop dancing (in Brooks 1998, 242). The "repentant" artists were accused of being interested only in money, before and after veiling. It was added that the "repentant" stars were becoming older anyhow and this was the way to make a last big haul (Brooks 1998, 242–243). Shams al-Barudi was faced with repeated programming of her old seductive films, particularly the film produced in 1973 by Abu Saif, *Hamam al-Malatili / The Malatili Bath*, in which she appeared in a bathing suit. The films were said to be a greater success after the star's retirement than at the time of their first release (*Ruz al-Yusif*, March 7, 1988, pp. 52–53). The movie critic Kamal Ramzi (1994) wrote that it is easy to explain the phenomenon of retirement. Hala al-Safi had turned from a quick-moving dancer into a heavy and slow performer, and her colleague Sahar Hamdi had ever-mounting problems with the vice police. Soheir al-Babli should have retired long ago, as she was approaching sixty. The journalist Ibrahim ʿIssa commented that most of them were mediocre actresses and veiling was a clever way to remain in the spotlights despite lack of success as artists (1993, 86–90). These reactions confirmed the general image of artists as greedy for money and attention. It stressed their material desires and bypassed their spiritual accounts.

A second reaction by journalists, commentators, and performing artists emphasized personal circumstances and the earthquake as reasons behind their "repentance." The religious turn of Hala Fu'ad, Shahira, and Shadia was related to their sickness. The authors of *Repentant Artists and the Sex Stars*, who are sympathetic to the "repentance" of artists, claim that they were even offered money if they would write that veiling by artists was due only to illness (Nasif and Khodayr n.d., 170). The "repentance" of 'Afaf Sho'ib, Soheir al-Babli, Sahar Hamdi, Farida Saif al-Nasr, and Soheir Ramzi was related to the earthquake and their fear of the Day of Judgment. In these debates and reactions, the "repentant" artists were neither blamed, criticized, nor ridiculed, but their stories were treated as personal matters lacking wider social significance. The details of their visions might be questioned as very coincidental, but generally the personal freedom of anyone to retire, veil, or keep on working was stressed. Several performing artists I interviewed took this approach. What they detested, however, was the label "repentant" artist. Use of the term "repentance" amounted to a general claim that art is *haram*. This position was unacceptable to those working in the art scene. If there was a reason to repent, it might be because some of these actresses, singers, and dancers had lived a dissolute life, but not because working in the field of art in itself made "repentance" necessary, several actresses commented (in Nasif and Khodayr n.d., 131–144).

Third, the most common and enduring accusation or rumor was the outright payment of artists to retire and veil. The rumors were strengthened by TV presenters and actresses who maintained that they were actually offered money to quit, an offer that they, of course, refused. Fatin Hamama and Nagwa Ibrahim claimed payment, as well as Elham Shahin (*Ruz al-Yusif*, October 11, 1993). Fatin Hamama was allegedly offered seven million pounds (Kamil 1993, 21). Nagwa Ibrahim was promised $1 million and a monthly salary of $150,000 (Kamil 1993, 31). Elham Shahin was told in a phone call that she would be paid a million dollars for stepping down and veiling. This rich caller had his channels through the "repentant" artists, as well as journalists from the religious press, to check on her actual veiling and retirement. There was also the case of an Egyptian "art director," whose tale made the accusations more complex. He recorded his story of "repentance" on five tapes and turned into a preacher against art. He was later "exposed" as a failed student and a tool of "professional traders of extremism" who pay Egyptian actresses to "finish off" their careers (Ramzi 1994). These rumors and accusations were very difficult to refute by the retired actresses, who repeatedly stressed that the "sweetness of faith" has no price, an argument that did not sound very convincing to their adversaries.

More subtle were the allegations of rich oil sheikhs marrying the Egyptian actresses, forcing them to veil and retire, and shortly after divorcing one in order to marry the next. Soheir Ramzi was rumored to be such a case. Saudi sheikhs thus spread their Wahhabi version of Islam through the veiling and retirement of artists. Another alleged proof of this theory was the case of the videotapes *Those Who Are Guided* (see also Chapter 4). The fact that money was invested by a Saudi company in order to produce this serial and the willingness of the "repentant" artists to cooperate were perceived as evidence that their ideas concurred with the Wahhabi version of Islam. A million copies of the tapes were said to have been distributed, mainly in Saudi Arabia and also in Egypt. Through these popular videos, the Saudi understandings of Islam could thus be exported throughout the Middle East ('Issa 1993, 35). The tapes were censored and forbidden in Egypt. The Egyptian censor, Abu Shadi, considered them insulting to the performing artists (*al-Kawakib*, February 17, 1998, pp. 22–24). Shams al-Barudi allegedly received financial assistance to remove her old seductive films from circulation. Soheir Ramzi and Shams al-Barudi were invited to tell their stories of guidance in Jeddah and were said to have been amply remunerated (*Ruz al-Yusif*, May 3, 1993, p. 19). The veiled artists were thus accused of being actively used by outside forces, to wit Saudi Arabia, to spread the Saudi understanding of Islam ('Issa 1993, 77–79).

The "repentant" artists were accordingly perceived as dangerous due to their religious and political roles. The secularists attached such great significance to the case of the "repentant" artists because they perceived a strong relationship between the veiled artists and "extremism." The veiled artists were perceived either as victims of "extremists" or as vehicles for "fundamentalist" groups. First, some journalists perceived them as frightened victims of extremist attacks. In the early 1990s, a number of intellectuals and journalists were attacked, and artists could be the next targets. Farida Saif al-Nasr—who retired and later returned to show business—was attacked upon her return (*Ruz al-Yusif*, August 2, 1993, pp. 56–58). As described in Chapter 2, Hala al-Safi had a vision in which she passed a mosque and was frightened because she was not properly dressed. A man, who was later identified as the Prophet, appeared and covered her. The psychiatrist, novelist, and feminist Nawal al-Sa'adawi concluded that it didn't take a psychiatrist to interpret this vision as a reaction against pressure by religious extremists (in Brooks 1998, 244).

Second, some journalists perceived the "repentant" artists as direct instruments for and representatives of "extremist" and "fundamentalist" ideas.

In particular, the journalist 'Issa outlined the dangerous role the "repentant" artists played in spreading Wahhabi ideas. Ibrahim 'Issa worked until 1995 as a journalist for the weekly *Ruz al-Yusif,* where he rose to the position of managing editor. He had become particularly famous for his attacks on Islamists, including a fierce campaign against Dr. 'Umar 'Abd al-Kafi. At the age of thirty he became editor-in-chief of *al-Dustur,* which was closed down by the state in 1998. He was marginalized for a time, but made a remarkable comeback around 2005 and started to anchor several programs on Dream TV (Mehrez 2008, 59–71).[14] His book makes for an interesting comparison with the ideas of the Islamist author Farhat—although Farhat's work is certainly less thorough than 'Issa's book. While the authors' visions for the nation are diametrically opposed, both vindicate their ideals through the case of the veiled artists. Whereas the veiled actresses were the icons of the Islamist press, they were the anathema of the secular press.

'Issa starts his argument by sketching the general religious changes in Egypt. The migration of many Egyptians and their yearlong submergence in the Saudi way of life and thinking have brought about a situation in which "oil runs through the veins of Egyptians" and "covers everything" (1993, 21). The migrants were economically dependent under the sponsorship system and emulated the Saudi way of living and thinking. In light of the enormous Saudi wealth, this is to be expected, 'Issa argues, since migrants were used to the poverty and chaos of Egyptian saint's day celebrations, whereas they now experienced the air-conditioned, well-organized pilgrimage in Mecca. Many Egyptians eventually returned to Egypt with a strong attachment to Saudi Arabia, wearing "white *galabiyyas*" and spreading the "extremist ideas" that reign in the Kingdom. Whereas during the Iranian Revolution the cinema and theater were burnt down as "sites of corruption," there was no need for these measures in the Kingdom, because, basically, there was no art except for male singing. The Egyptian migrants were not able to watch artistic films and were fed with the idea that art is *haram.* The Egyptian films that were allowed entrance into the Saudi market focused only on religious themes and idealized "Bedouin life," while Saudi sheikhs financed media productions on *jihad* and Islamic *da'wah.* Radio and TV mainly broadcast religious programs. The migrants thus absorbed these ideas about art and were inculcated with these "Bedouin ideas about artistic inspiration." During the seasonal return to Egypt and the final return after the mid-1980s, they circulated the tapes and sermons from Saudi Arabia and the Gulf states dealing with the Day of Judgment and the corrupting influence of art and entertainment (1993, 21–49).

The migrants not only absorbed the "extremist" ideas on art, but also about women. The author describes his perception of the total lack of Saudi women's freedom of movement, the heavy veiling, the lack of civil rights, and total dependence on men. This treatment of women is related to the tribal culture of the desert, in the midst of which oil was suddenly discovered. In this desert culture the idea that women could study, work, and live as independent personalities is nonexistent. The working, learned woman, in the eyes of the Saudi men, is the "deputy of the devil," ʿIssa argues. The fear of female bodies and the idea that women cannot protect themselves produced the image of women's "immanent corruption." These "ignorant views" are consumed by migrants, who are offered booklets for free, and are flooded with sermons not only by Saudi preachers but also by Egyptian agents (ʿIssa 1993, 45–55).

Here we arrive at the role of the "repentant" artists and particularly the sheikhs backing them, such as sheikh al-Shaʿarawi and Dr. ʿUmar ʿAbd al-Kafi. The author quotes a characteristic example of Sheikh al-Shaʿarawi's admiration for Saudi views on women, taken from al-Shaʿarawi's book *Al-Marʾa fi al-Qurʾan al-Karim / Women in the Holy Qurʾan*. During his stay in Saudi Arabia, Sheikh al-Shaʿarawi once traveled with a fellow sheikh to his work. Suddenly the car stopped, one of the passengers got out, and went to the door of a house. In front of the house there was a wooden plate with bread dough covered by cloth, which he took with him into the car. When al-Shaʿarawi asked why he had taken the plate, he responded that if you find a plate with dough and a closed door, this means that the owner of the house is absent and there are only women present in the house. Passengers should take the dough to the bakery and bring it back afterward. Whereas for al-Shaʿarawi this anecdote exemplified the excellence of the Saudi pious community that helps women without relatives, for the author Ibrahim ʿIssa, it illustrates the community's complete backwardness: Even women without relatives are not allowed to work and would rather starve, if no one passes by, than earn a decent living (ʿIssa 1993, 59–60). Sheikh al-Shaʿarawi has been able to spread his idea about women as seductresses who should be hidden away, because he became the *mufti* of the veiled actresses. The veiled actresses were a golden chance to spread his influence. Sheikh al-Shaʿarawi could increase his media presence and thus promote his views on women, because his ideas would have a guaranteed newsworthiness if they were connected to the defense of famous veiled artists. Al-Shaʿarawi was also enabled to destroy Egypt's prime role in civilization and art, since he was given the media space to posit his views that art is corrupt and *haram*. While al-Shaʿarawi had maintained that art generally has two sides and could be *halal* as well as *haram*, his support for the veiling and retreat of female artists emphasized the idea of art's unlawfulness, 'Issa argued ('Issa 1993, 60–71).

'Issa also launched a massive campaign against Dr. 'Umar 'Abd al-Kafi in the weekly magazine *Ruz al-Yusif* in 1993, a campaign that is not detailed in his book. He had attacked 'Abd al-Kafi for dangerous sectarianism as a result of his *fatwa* that prohibited greeting Christians with the Muslim expression "*al-salam 'alekum*" and participating in Christian celebrations and funerals. 'Issa attacked his views on women, his *fatawa* that traveling by female students from Cairo to Tanta was *haram*, and that a female employee who traveled without her husband was a sinner. 'Abd al-Kafi had produced about ninety tapes, of which thirty-five addressed the Day of Judgment and "the horrors and suffering in the grave" (*'azab al-qabr*). According to 'Issa, 'Abd al-Kafi tried to emulate al-Sha'arawi's style of simple preaching, but he totally lacked the depth of the latter's knowledge and was good only at yelling at his audience and presenting heated sermons. Yet he was embraced by thousands, particularly in the well-to-do neighborhoods (*Ruz al-Yusif*, March 29, 1993, pp. 23–24). 'Issa maintained that again it was 'Abd al-Kafi's relationship with the veiled stars that had promoted his own religious stardom. Veiled actress Soheir Ramzi in particular is mentioned as having a close relationship with 'Abd al-Kafi. He was invited to her home to lecture with the other veiled artists in attendance. The most amazing thing, according to 'Issa, is that 'Abd al-Kafi is given the media space on the state channel to present his "extremist ideas." 'Issa particularly expressed his dismay at the talk show hosted by the only veiled presenter who is allowed space on the Egyptian state TV, Kariman Hamza, during Ramadan in 1993. She invited him as a daily guest and allowed him to spread his "extremist views" (*Ruz al-Yusif*, March 15, 1993, p. 63). 'Issa asked his readers: "If the Egyptian TV broadcast these ideas how come that the state does not understand why terrorism is so successful?!" (*Ruz al-Yusif*, March 29, 1993, p. 25). Although the author agreed with the veiled artists' anger at the state's firing of veiled presenters, he had serious reservations about what would happen if they were en masse allowed to disseminate their ideas on the screen.

Ibrahim 'Issa thus held that Saudi-influenced preachers such as Sheikh al-Sha'arawi and Dr. 'Umar 'Abd al-Kafi, the two most influential sheikhs on "repentant" artists, had risen to stardom through their mediatized appearances and their connections with artists. Their influence on artists had catapulted their own fame and enabled them to spread their Wahhabi ideology. He argued that the preaching of Sheikh al-Sha'arawi and Dr. 'Umar 'Abd al-Kafi destroyed Egyptian art production—the basis of Egypt's central position in the region and an important source of income. In addition, he accused them of preaching against the freedom of women (1993, 77–79). He feared the "fundamentalist," or "Saudi," campaigns to veil artists and make them stay at home as a way of sending women back to "ages of oppression."

Whereas the veil of artists was crucial in their defense by the Islamist press, the artists' veil is not directly attacked in the secular press. Although it is clear from the secular art productions, and the way these are entangled with the state project of nation building, that veiling is not the preferred national image, journalists such as 'Issa do not confront veiling as such. Many actors in the secular cultural field carefully stress the personal freedom of any artist to wear the veil. It would thus be too simple to posit the imagery of the veiled actress as icon for the Islamist press, as against the unveiled character for the secularist press. Although the statue *The Awakening of Egypt*, showing a peasant woman lifting the veil, is a strong symbol of the modern nation (Baron 2005), this is not directly evoked by the secular press or the secular cultural field. Veiling is treated as a matter of personal freedom and religious conscience that should not contradict full social participation. In cases where veiling implied "sending women back home," it was attacked. Preserving "autonomy" and liberating women from "ages of oppression" were considered more important than the veil per se. In the case of the veiled artists and the preachers backing them, however, veiling and a discourse on women's proper place in the house fused.

If we compare this discourse with the Islamist ideas analyzed in Chapter 4, we see the converging sensitivity of art and gender for deliberations about the nation and the great concern evoked by the veiling and seclusion of female performers. For both sides, women and art are crucial touchstones for imagining the nation. Instead of the Islamist ideal of the domestic woman, the socially engaged female is put forward by the secular press. The enemy is not the West and its allies paying for an antiveil campaign, but Saudis paying for veiling as a way to spread its extremist version of Islam. For both sides, Egypt and its national heritage should be safeguarded from foreign or false influences. The cultural nationalist discourse advanced by Ibrahim 'Issa and others warns against the inauthenticity of "petro-dollar" preachers and the veiled artists. They point to the danger of the Saudi-tization of Egypt and the loss of the cornerstones of Egypt's civilization, particularly its art.

Art has long been used by the state to promote its ideals about progress and the nation. The secular field has been closely tied to the state, and the state has used art to combat Islamists. Yet in the 1990s, it also became undeniable that the failed state policy of "Islamization" was leaving its footprints in the secular field of art. In the next section, I will elaborate on the state, its relationship with the secular cultural field, and the state-induced creeping "Islamization" within the field of art.

THE STATE AND THE ARTS

As we have seen in Chapter 4, the state—in the heat of the crackdown against Islamists in the mid-1990s—blurred distinctions among different shades of Islamists and turned its former policy of accommodation into repression. Not only the attacks by radical Islamists against the state, tourists, and secular intellectuals, but also the mounting clashes between the Christian Coptic population and Islamists, particularly in Upper Egypt, were perceived by the state as a great danger to national security and unity. In order to counter these tendencies, the state adopted a dual image: secular-modern and religious-nationalist (Mehrez 2001, 2008). The secular and modern image was particularly important for external consumption and with regard to the substantial Coptic minority. The secular cultural field played a crucial role in spreading this image. The religious-nationalist image was crucial for internal use toward the conservative Muslim majority. In order to reach the second goal, al-Azhar, the important religious institution that is largely controlled by the state, was given space to voice its conservative religious views. These views aimed at legitimizing the state's moral custodianship, however, sometimes closely resembled those of moderate Islamists. The state thus coupled a modernist image with that of moral guardian. As Mehrez holds: "[T]he Egyptian state has adopted contradictory strategies in its simultaneous attempts to recapture a modern secular image while aiming to establish itself, through its increasing investment in Islamic symbols, as the sole moral and religious authority" (2008, 3). These conflicting demands on the state informed its unclear course of action with regard to media and art, policies that will be central in this section.

In order to untangle these ambiguous policies, we have to analyze the triangle connecting the state, the secular cultural field, and al-Azhar. The reciprocal ties and interdependencies can be visualized as a pyramid with the state firmly on top. The state controlled the secular field by censorship, but also depended upon it for creating an aura of modernity. The secular cultural field was critical of the state, but was supported by state patronage and shared its anti-Islamist discourse. The state exerted control over al-Azhar, but needed the clerics for its image as moral guardian and its anti-militant-Islam campaign. This created some space for political maneuvering by al-Azhar authorities. Members of the al-Azhar establishment, as civil servants, were dependent on the state, but used the political space to criticize, among others, the secular cultural field. The strength of the state was not only augmented by its control over the secular and Islamist opposition, but also by the great ideological divide between the two potential oppositional forces. They formed antipodal poles, forces that were successfully manipulated by the divide-and-rule tactics of the state (Shehata 2010). The ideological divides between secularists and Islamists in the field of art have been amply demonstrated above. I will now discuss the interdependencies between the state and the secular cultural field and, next, those between the state and al-Azhar.

Several scholars have studied the importance of the cultural field for the production of Egyptian national culture, such as Armbrust (1996) for the film industry, Abu Lughod (2005) for television, and Winegar (2006) for visual arts. State control of the cultural field is particularly enforced via two instruments: censorship and patronage. Under Nasser were founded diverse cultural institutions and the Ministries of Culture and Information, which were to create and disseminate nationalist and populist culture (Mehrez 2008, 209). Radio and television were used by Nasser to promote national development and political mobilization (Abu Lughod 1993, 27). Television, in particular, became a key institution for producing national culture in Egypt (Abu Lughod 2005). Under Nasser, the state was the patron, promoter, and protector of cultural productions that were used to support the aims of the regime. Under Sadat, the role of the state in administering the cultural industry receded (Winegar 2006, 144–145). He closed down the Ministry of Culture in 1980, promoting "village ethics" over the modernist model, or the "developmental nationalist paradigm," that was valued under Nasser (Mehrez 2008; Abu Lughod 2005). Sadat also accorded more space to Islamist movements. After a period of marginalization of the cultural field, the Mubarak regime showed a renewed interest in the cultural field as a way of countering the influence of Islamist groups. The Nasserist cultural institutions were revived, and the cultural field was united under the "banner of enlightenment against obscurantism" (Mehrez 2008, 18). In order to recapture a modern secular image, the Egyptian state reinstated the Ministry of Culture to create a "national, modern and authentic Egyptian cultural sphere" (Mehrez 2008, 210).

The artists of Winegar's study spoke about the 1970s as a catastrophe, whereas they experienced the late 1980s and the 1990s as a renaissance of the Egyptian art world due to the increased state support (2006, 150–151).[15] It was not only a matter of financial support and protection, or dependency, though, that informed the close relationship between the art world and the state. The artists also shared the state's concern about the rising Islamization of the cultural sphere. The socialization in the state's higher education system had formed the artists' outlook and ambition to be productive and freethinking members of society. They were expected to make an important contribution toward national progress and the creation of secular-oriented national subjects. Most artists of Winegar's study were committed advocates of secularism, although they might be personally pious (see also Abu Lughod 1993, 28). They were especially concerned about the Islamist political opposition and saw their careers as threatened by Islamism (Winegar 2006, 77). For instance, the famous actor and comedian 'Adil Imam, who had asked Soheir al-Babli whether she had gone crazy, had toured with his play to the provinces—despite fierce opposition from Islamist groups—with the intention of driving "the forces of darkness and backwardness from Egypt" (Armbrust 1996, 173).

The state was, however, not only the artists' "patron," but also their "persecutor" (Mehrez 2008, 6). Radio and television were under almost complete state administration, although—since the early 1990s—the advent of satellite broadcasting has drastically transformed the mediascape (see Part Three). Censorship in its overt form and self-censorship were both essential instruments in controlling art productions. The most important taboo topics were religion, sex, and politics (Shafik 1998, 34). The 1976 censorship law stipulated that:

> Heavenly religions [i.e., Islam, Christianity, and Judaism] should not be criticized. Heresy and magic should not be positively portrayed. Immoral actions and vices are not to be justified and must be punished. Images of naked human bodies or the inordinate emphasis on individual erotic parts, the representation of sexually arousing scenes, and scenes of alcohol consumption or drug use are not allowed. Also prohibited is the use of obscene and indecent speech. The sanctity of marriage, family values, and one's parents must be respected. Beside the prohibition on the excessive use of horror and violence, or inciting their imitation, it is forbidden to represent social problems as hopeless, to upset the mind, or to divide religions, classes, and national unity. (Shafik 1998, 34)

This law illustrates well the ambiguity of the state media policy, showing particularly its role as moral guardian and protector of national unity rather than defender of "modern secularity." This role was related to the state's attempt to accommodate Islamist opposition. The censorship law, which was enacted under Sadat, was continued under Mubarak. Mubarak restored control over the cultural sphere as a way to counter the rising Islamist wave and recapture a modern secular image. Yet, confronted with continuing Islamist opposition, it was a particularly conservative morality that was furthered.

Players in the cultural field were not only restricted by state censorship, often internalized as a form of self-censorship, but also by street censorship. This concept is used by the cultural players themselves and coined by Jacquemond to refer to interventions by nonstate actors, such as journalists, independent religious figures, academics, and employees in publishing companies, etc., who tried to impose dominant religious values on the secular cultural field (in Mehrez 2008, 7, 210–211). Pressure from "street censors" was one of the reasons that the state maintained a firm image of moral surveillance over the cultural field despite its discourse about "freedom of thought and expression" (Mehrez 2008, 211). Therefore, in general, criticism of Islam was not allowed, but an attack on Islamism was encouraged. So disseminating treatments of Islam marking a clear division along the lines of "bad Islam" versus "good Islam" was particularly favored.[16] The positive representation of atheism was also not considered appropriate, but a "modern secularist" vision in which religion and politics are separated was advanced as the proper message of cultural producers. Taking into account the "conservative morality of the street," the state, however, banned several cultural productions based on religious justifications.

The state's policy to counter Islamists by way of media has changed over time. Initially there was a conspicuous silence on the topic and avoidance of overt signs of piety (Abu Lughod 1993, 28). In 1993–1994, a threefold media campaign was launched against "bad Islam" (Armbrust 2002; Abu Lughod 2005, 165–180). This included the television serial *The Family*, which was broadcast during Ramadan 1994, praised by the official press for its pedagogical value in protecting disadvantaged youth from becoming terrorists, and criticized by moderate Islamist thinkers for not distinguishing between extremism and religiosity. After the serial *The Family* had come to an end in March 1994, the *Confession by a Repentant Terrorist* was broadcast. The "repentant Islamist" 'Adel 'Abd al-Baqi told his story of how he had been initiated into an extremist group in which robbery and wife exchange were practiced (Abu Lughod 2005, 171). Shortly afterward there was another series of three broadcasts on television in which "repentant militants" discussed their "misguided views" with religious scholars of al-Azhar, "uncovering terrible practices" committed by Islamists. During 'Id al-Fitr, the holiday after Ramadan, the film *The Terrorist*, starring 'Adil Imam, was released. This film emphasized a stark contrast between modern enlightenment and Islamist backwardness (Armbrust 2002, 924). *The Terrorist* is again a repentance narrative, in which an Islamist assassin eventually converts to secularism, influenced by the secular middle-class family with whom he hides out. Thus, in the media campaign, a strong distinction was made between "the good, correct, and reasonable Islam of the people, the cultured and educated, al-Azhar, the state, and television [and] the bad, violent, misinformed, twisted Islam of the extremists" (Abu Lughod 2005, 172).

As Armbrust shows, the state's campaign had an "antisociological nature"; the Islamists were portrayed as weird, violent, antimodern characters, particularly in village settings, and never as the schoolteacher, cousin, or neighbor in cities engaged in daily activities to make a living (2002, 928). The same effect was produced by another kind of state-approved cultural production: historical costume dramas about the glorious religious past. An example of this was the Ramadan serial *Harun al-Rashid* of 1997, which dealt with the history of the Arabo-Islamic world. While its creators incorporated historic Islamic imagery in their production, any reference to Islam's contemporary social and political relevance was avoided. Islam was folklorized into bygone custom and tradition, a strategy also known in Syria (Salamandra 2008). Accordingly, there was a split into "bad" and "good" Islam and a specification of the proper, private or historical, place for religion, one not enmeshed in contemporary public daily life, let alone in politics. Another example of the "antisociological" nature of the state's campaign against Islamism was the ban on veils from television, a ban that hit hard on the retired actresses. Whereas an overwhelming majority of Egyptian women covered their hair, television presenters were fired if they donned the veil. Veiled actresses were also not allowed on state television.

The state, though, provided ample space for separate religious programs that were to teach the proper moderate Islam. This strategy did not in itself contradict the aim of separating religion and ordinary social life. It was kept segregated from popular serials and consisted of Qur'an recitation, the call to prayer interrupting programs, and Friday mosque prayers being televised. There were also religious serials, sometimes in classical Arabic that few people really understood (Abu Lughod 1993, 27). The state-approved al-Azhar sheikhs in particular were given television time to spread "moderate Islam." For instance, Sheikh al-Sha'arawi had a popular show in the 1990s featuring Qur'an exegesis, and the lay authority Mustafa Mahmud had a religious program entitled *Science and Faith*. Yet al-Azhar is not a monolithic institution, and some of its religious members also used the accorded space to air less moderate views. In order to understand this phenomenon, we need to have a closer look at the relationship between the state and al-Azhar.

Al-Azhar was radically reformed under Nasser in 1961. The reorganization was directed at the content of the knowledge that was transmitted by the institutes and university of al-Azhar. Secular topics such as natural sciences were added to the curriculum, and modern faculties such as medicine and engineering were opened. In addition, the administration of al-Azhar was subordinated entirely to the state, and its employees became civil servants. As Zeghal argues, the *'ulama'*, religious scholars, were granted a "'profession' whose function was to confer religious legitimacy on the regime's political decisions and policy implementations, and whose returns were government salaries and civil-servant status" (1999, 375). The reform opened al-Azhar students to modern systems of education. According to Zeghal, the "parallelism of conditions with modern universities" can partly explain why Islamist tendencies could emerge among its students (1999, 379). Most Islamists have been educated in modern institutions, and it is particularly the disparate and fragmentary mix of modern knowledge existing side by side with the religious and more homogeneous cognitive universe that led to the bricolage between modern and religious knowledge (Zeghal 1999, 379–380).

From the 1970s onward, during the rule of Sadat and Mubarak, the number of students and institutes increased rapidly. In 1962–1963 there were 212 institutes with 64,390 students; in 1992–1993 there were 3,161 institutes with 966,629 students (Zeghal 1999, 379). Sadat also assumed control of al-Azhar, but attached greater importance to the religious legitimacy of his regime. The sheikh of al-Azhar between 1973 and 1978, 'Abd al-Halim Mahmud, played a key role in the expansion of al-Azhar and strengthened its role in public debate. Sadat used 'Abd al-Halim Mahmud's *fatawa* against communists to launch his antileftist campaign in the media (Zeghal 1999, 381). The religious monopoly of al-Azhar, however, was broken by the emergence of Islamist activists. This led to a fragmentation of religious authority (Eickelman and Piscatori 1996). The official *'ulama'* countered Islamist activists, whereas members of Islamist groups denigrated the *'ulama'* of al-Azhar, among other reasons for their support of the regime. Al-Azhar and the regime were pushed together.

The strategy to use al-Azhar against religious militancy was strengthened under Mubarak. In 1982, he appointed Sheikh Gad al-Haqq, who was considered a quietist sheikh and kept this office until his death in 1996. With the help of the *'ulama'*, the Islamic weekly *al-Liwa al-Islami* was launched to disseminate the preferred "good" interpretation of Islam. Several al-Azhar sheikhs appeared on television to counter the Islamist activists' viewpoints. The al-Azhar establishment used this situation to push Mubarak into accepting an increasing Islamization of society. Thus, from political submission in the 1960s, and political emergence in the 1970s, al-Azhar moved to a major role in the public sphere in the 1980s and 1990s (Zeghal 1999, 372).

As a result of the fact that the religious field became more competitive and fragmented, and that al-Azhar was used to legitimize state policies against Islamists, several "peripheral" religious scholars emerged who distanced themselves from the official line (Zeghal 1999, 372, 385). Some of them refused to participate in the state's anti-Islamism campaign. They had been educated in al-Azhar, but had built their popularity outside its institutions through teaching, preaching, and *da'wah*. They were peripheral to the institutions of al-Azhar but widely popular among the populace. Among them were the famous preachers Kishk and Sheikh Muhammad al-Ghazali. The "peripheral *'ulama'*" appeared in the 1980s and became active players in the media debate in the 1990s. They sometimes had affinity with moderate Islamists. Conservative sheikhs at the core of al-Azhar, such as Sheikh al-Sha'arawi, sometimes joined forces with the "peripheral sheikhs," and the head of al-Azhar tried to disconnect himself from the regime by allying himself to parts of the periphery of al-Azhar. Sheikh al-Sha'arawi, for instance, preached against violence by radicals, but also against the state's repression of Islamists. He allied with al-Ghazali on this issue (Zeghal 1999, 388). This internal diversification thus highlights the different colors of Islamism, or "conservative Islamists" (Ismail 1998), inside al-Azhar's establishment itself. Although I cannot go into great detail about these alliances, two general tendencies are important for the discussion: First, in general, the more the battle between militant Islamists and the state intensified, the more space was allowed to al-Azhar for political leverage and freedom of speech. Second, al-Azhar not only lost its monopoly on religious knowledge, but also became internally more fragmented. The result was that "peripheral preachers" and "conservative Islamist" members of al-Azhar became outspoken voices that were accorded state-sponsored media space.

"Conservative Islamists" belonging to al-Azhar, such as Sheikh al-Sha'arawi, and several peripheral preachers, such as Dr. 'Umar 'Abd al-Kafi—both important for the "repentance" of artists—became important forces in the Islamization of society. They focused on the themes of culture and morality (Ismail 1998, 202). The group of "conservative Islamists" also initiated censorship cases through the courts to impose their views of public morality and orthodoxy, which together with other acts of "street censorship," led to an increasing Islamization of the cultural field and attacks on secular intellectuals and artists. While the state used secular cultural productions and media to discredit Islamists, it also allowed ample space to al-Azhar, including al-Azhar's "conservative Islamists," to ban secular productions on religious-moral grounds. Farag Fuda, a secular intellectual, was murdered in 1992 after a committee of al-Azhar had decided that "everything he does is against Islam." His assassins cited this condemnation as a justification for their murder (Mostyn 2002, 148). In 1994, the Nobel laureate Naguib Mahfouz was stabbed by two militant Islamists. In 1993, the state's Islamic weekly fulminated against the "heretic" Abu Zayd. In 1996, he was forced into exile because of the accusations of apostasy (Mehrez 2008, 230–231). The "peripheral preacher" of al-Azhar, al-Ghazali, issued a *fatwa* stipulating that any Muslim arguing for the suspension of the Shari'a is an apostate and could be killed. If the state did not do so, it was the duty of any Muslim to execute the punishment. In 1993, the sheikh al-Azhar, Gad al-Haqq, asked for clarification on al-Azhar's role in "confronting artistic works, audio and audiovisual artifacts that deal with Islamic issues or that conflict with Islam [. . .] preventing them from publication, recording, printing and distributing" (in Mostyn 2002, 148–149, 156–157). In 1994, the ruling was issued that legitimized al-Azhar's role in censoring, stipulating that al-Azhar's opinion was "binding" on the Ministry of Culture. The Islamic Research Centre was given the right to examine publications and art productions that dealt with Islam, and the sheikh al-Azhar was made "the final arbiter in the assessment of the Islamic factor" (Mostyn 2002, 149). According to Mehrez, his role—albeit powerful—is rather that of an advisor to the Ministries of Culture and Interior, which finally impose the ban (Mehrez 2008, 305). The Islamic Research Centre was headed by the son of Sheikh al-Sha'arawi, and it proposed the banning of several books and plays. In 1997, the progovernment magazine *Ruz al-Yusif* claimed that it had uncovered a plot by al-Azhar to ban 196 Egyptian books (Mostyn 2002, 149). In 2002, after many articles expressing concern about the increased power of al-Azhar to execute cultural interventions, the minister of justice assured intellectuals that the "search and seizure power" of al-Azhar involved unlicensed religious publications only (Mehrez 2008, 305).

We thus see a penetration of different shades of Islamism into the state and the growing influence of al-Azhar on the cultural field. The state tried to produce its own brand of Islam both by using secular players in the cultural field against Islamism and by providing space to al-Azhar, including "conservative Islamists" who used this space to attack the secular cultural players. As Abu Lughod holds, "the moral authority of the religious establishment and pressure from below [. . .] sympathetic to the Islamist project in its more peaceful forms, have made it impossible for television, or the state, to stand either against religion or for secularism" (2005, 174). The overall effect is an increasing domination of the entire cultural field by Islamist discourses in public debate.

This dominance of Islamic discourse over all players does not negate the power of the state. The state maintained its firm position on top of the triangle. What the discussion above reveals is the porous boundaries between the different actors involved. The fragmentation of religious authority, the penetration of Islamism into the state, and the state's control over the cultural fields as well as al-Azhar point to the difficulty in dividing the players in the public debate in Egypt into neat oppositional blocs. Separating publics and counterpublics is a difficult analytic problem that perhaps hides more of the ambiguous relationships than it clarifies. In Chapter 6, I will go into more detail about the conservative religious discourse on art and gender by leading scholars from the core and periphery of al-Azhar. We will see the growing fragmentation of religious authority and the importance of new lay figures outside the establishment of al-Azhar who developed less conservative discourses on art and gender in the late 1990s. This eventually opened up the possibility for the return of pious actors and actresses to the screen and stage (see Part Three).

(SIX)

Changing Discourses on Art and Gender

I n this chapter, I will present the life story of actress ʿAbir Sharqawi. In the second section, the religiously committed artists' own views on gender, art, and religion will be central. In the final section, I will highlight the changing discourse on art within the Islamist movement more generally, which resulted from the fragmentation of religious authority and the emergence of young preachers.

THE SPIRITUAL BIOGRAPHY OF ʿABIR SHARQAWI

The artistic career of ʿAbir Sharqawi started where that of Soheir al-Babli had abruptly ended, in 1993. When Soheir al-Babli decided to veil and to quit the play *ʿAtiyya, the Terrorist*, the director, Galal al-Sharqawi, was in big trouble. The advertisements for the next season were out, and the play was expected to resume very soon. He then decided to offer the main role to his own daughter, who had just finished at the theater department of the American University in Cairo.

I interviewed ʿAbir in her father's home in Muhandisin in 2005,[1] six months after her return to the field of art. The huge room was decorated with blown-up images of ʿAbir with and without a veil, and of ʿAbir with her son. She apologized for the mess on the table and the many pictures of herself on the wall. She explained that she would never do this in her own house, but after her divorce she lived in her father's house. She took my recorder in her hand professionally and related her story in a self-confident way:

I am from a family of great artists. My father is a great producer, known throughout the Arab world. So from an early age, I was used to the theater. My vacations were spent on the stage of my father. They tried to keep me away from the stage and to make me choose something else, a doctor, an engineer, a teacher. My father is "*shar'i*," "Oriental." His son can work in art, but not his daughter. He told me to finish my studies at the university first, and then we would see. It annoyed me, because I wanted to be part of my father's world and be like the nice people I met through my father. [. . .] At the university I chose theater and a minor in psychology. I was serious, respected the theater, and was prepared to sacrifice a lot for my ambition. My father saw my efforts and acknowledged my talent, which would improve with further training. He became convinced of me.[2]

She then talks about her father's problem after the departure of Soheir al-Babli:

> Soheir al-Babli told him: "The things I have done are *haram*, I veiled and quit your *haram* activities (*il-haram bita'ak*)." My father was convinced that his work was not *haram*. All actresses were afraid to be compared with Soheir al-Babli because she was a great name. They feared it would cost them their careers. So he decided to bring a totally new face to the stage. Someone who was not afraid to be compared with Soheir al-Babli. People surrounding him told him I could be this person. I had just one week. I worked immensely hard. This was a golden opportunity. Of course I did it my way. Soheir was a comedienne and I am more the serious type.[3]

'Abir Sharqawi considered her first appearance on stage a great success. However, she felt unhappy outside the artistic endeavors of the university circles where she had previously worked with dedicated and serious students. When she started in "the real world," it appeared to be not about "conscience," but all about money. Even if the cast was bad and the script worse you did the job, she remarked. "You make people laugh, and take the money." She summarized the style of work as "no headache about the message." This was not the stage she had dreamed of and wanted to work on.

> It was commercial theater. [. . .] I was not convinced of the work I did. [. . .] Women had to be *midalla'* [spoiled]. She should wear revealing clothes in order to be successful on the market. She has to kiss, then she will be a star. That was more important than her talent. This was the situation at the time I started to work, ten years ago. Things have changed now. I stopped in 2000, but back then it was important for actresses to kiss and

show her body. I did not want that and for that reason I did not have a lot of work, perhaps two films.[4]

'Abir Sharqawi married and veiled, at the end of Ramadan 2000.[5] According to a newspaper interview she gave in January 2001, right after her veiling and retirement, she was still married at the time she made her decision. Her husband encouraged her and was convinced of her talents and trusted that she would never destroy his or her father's good name. She intended to spend more time with her family and take care of her son. It was particularly the "*tanazulat*," the "concessions," that frustrated her. She told the interviewer that she was not prepared to pay or to have relationships with producers in order to get main roles in productions. She also rejected seductive roles, a principle that thwarted her success.[6]

Her marriage did not last long, and she became depressed:

I started to think about why all these bad things happened to me. I married and gave birth to my son, but I was divorced after one and a half years. My marriage failed despite that I loved him and he loved me and we had a baby. I started to see my life in a black light. [. . .] Inside, I had the feeling that all these things could not happen without a reason. There is a message God wants to tell me. Maybe I fell short in my duties toward him. I did not veil and had convinced myself that the veil is external to belief: the foundation of religion is the heart, your comportment, and moral behavior. But sure I was negligent in veiling and also in praying. So I had many problems in my relationship with my Creator. So I decided to make a step in his direction by veiling. The veil is not the most important thing, religion is much bigger than the appearance, but it was a step in the direction toward worship. I showed him I am coming back to you. I will improve myself because I cannot bear all these troubles. I feared him and felt he was angry with me. When I returned to him I realized two things: That I loved him so much and that he is so great, so forgiving! I had not understood God's power. You know, artists are conceited and arrogant, they think the world turns around them. That made me blind to see other things in the world. I did not see other things, like the greatness of God.[7]

Like many retired actresses, 'Abir Sharqawi did the pilgrimage and started reading religious literature. She became quite critical, though, about some of the sheikhs who were popular among her "repentant" colleagues. She visited some of their lectures and "Islamic salons," but decided that studying sources herself was a better use of her time. She consulted several disparate sources, including some on the Internet. She is clearly from a younger generation that became accustomed to seeking advice from a multiplicity of sources and authorities.

> After veiling, I started to think about religion. It is natural, after such a period of ignorance and then delving into religion, that you first think that everything is *haram*. I told my parents this is *haram* and that is *haram*, this is not part of religion, stop it. [. . .] I stayed at home and the only thing that counted was reading Qur'an. I read only religious books, watched only religious channels, I fasted and prayed. I remained like this the first three years. It is so difficult to really change your behavior. The appearance, *higab* and way of clothing, these are external changes. [. . .] But it was difficult to reach the level of commitment and change myself the way my religion asks of me. It took me a lot of time. I wanted to change my way of dealing with people . . . But as I told you, I was spoiled. [. . .] So in the beginning, I also thought that acting was *haram*.[8]

She had this to say when I asked her about her religious sources of inspiration:

> At present, I like al-Qaradawi most. But in the beginning there was strictness [*tashaddud*]. I like al-Sha'arawi, he is beautiful and moderate, and 'Amr Khalid, he gathers young people and has a lot of charisma but he is not a real scholar. 'Umar 'Abd al-Kafi, I don't like him. I heard his cassettes, but he talks about women as if they are second-class citizens. I was annoyed by him, and did not want to listen to his tapes anymore. He also preaches a lot about the torments of the grave, about the devil who will frighten you, and hit you in the grave. He intended to frighten us with all the terrifying things happening in the grave but we do not know exactly what will happen in the grave. [. . .] Many people love his sermons, but I did not like him at all. [. . .]
>
> But al-Qaradawi understands the world, some *fatawa* [rulings], do not fit our time anymore. I particularly like him because he argues that nothing on earth is 100 percent *halal* or 100 percent *haram*. Something is *halal* if it is more *halal* than *haram*. If we do not think with this kind of logic we will all sit at home frightened to do anything wrong. Everything and every person have good things and bad things. I don't know whether you are religious, or whether you have the *hisab*, the final reckoning? [. . .] If your good points are more than your bad deeds you go to paradise, if the bad deeds are more numerous, you go to hell. It is the same in life. Even alcohol has good qualities and can be helpful in treatment. But in this case the

bad things—like what it does to your brains, and that it can cause you to make an accident—is larger. For that reason it is *haram*. This way of thinking makes sense. [. . .]

I went to religious lessons for women with other artists. But it takes a lot of time. Before people arrive . . . and a few hours after the lecture women stay and chat for another two hours, and then there is the invitation for dinner. You know, Egyptians go crazy for food. So, before you realize it, the lesson took you four or five hours. We could do the same amount of learning in an hour and a half. So, I decided that if I read for myself, I will gain more.[9]

Through her reading she gained a different understanding of art. She decided that with the right script, together with trustworthy people and productions with a good message, acting would be better than sitting idly at home and wasting her talents. Like her friends among the young generation of artists, such as Mona ʿAbd al-Ghani, she decided to reclaim the public space as a veiled actress and to represent the many veiled women of Egypt on the screen. The comeback of such veiled artists was made possible by a change not only in ideas about art, but also in taste and sensibility, among the Egyptian public. ʿAbir talked about the existence of "clean cinema" as one of the signs of this changed climate:

The period of the 1990s until 2000 was a period in art with a lot of sex, underwear, bras, kisses, sexual arousal. If you did not comply with that, there was no work. But then there rose the generation of Muhammad Heneidi and Muhammad Saʿad. The older generation of artists stayed at home. The trend had changed. The public still wants to have good fun and to laugh, but it does not need to take the form of sexual excitement. Also for the director and producer, the film is successful if it makes people laugh, but no longer by way of sexual jokes. That is the new trend of clean cinema [*sinima nidifa*]. This development is taking place from the side of the artists and the audience. Egyptians have become more religious, there is more religious commitment [*iltizam*]. I don't know why but that is the case . . . also among the artists. Every single artist has her own story: Sabrin, after her serial on Umm Kulthum, ʿAbir Sabri, and me as the daughter of Galal Sharqawi, but we all wanted to be good examples for other people. But definitely also on the side of the public; they turned toward religion and were annoyed by films with sexual arousal. Families were angry and embarrassed to watch them. There were also many decrees, *fatawa*, about certain films with excitement and they were declared *haram*.

So people were also afraid to watch them. This held true not only for specific films but for movies more generally.[10]

'Abir's decision to retreat from art was clearly a great shock to her father:

> My father had in mind that he could make me a big star; it would be only
> a matter of time in his conception. [. . .] He said, "I will not impose my
> views on you, but know that when you don the veil you cannot take it off."
> He knew how much I loved the theater. He said, "You can work in histori-
> cal or religious productions." It really was a great shock to him. First, he
> had the situation with Soheir al-Babli and me entering the field due to her
> veil. And seven years later, the same happened with me! [. . .] So, he was
> very happy when I decided to come back to art. I don't know. I hope it is
> because of my talent and not for another reason. For instance that by re-
> turning with the veil that I might take it off as well [. . .].[11]

In other sources she more clearly indicates the role of her father in her return
to the screen.[12] He offered her a role and told her first to consult religious
scholars on religion and art. She came to the conclusion that most scholars
agreed that those art productions that did a service to the religion and did
not exceed the limits of religious teachings and values, while avoiding any
kind of sexual excitement, were approved. 'Abir Sharqawi decided that she
could return while sticking to her *higab*, and act in purposeful productions in
roles that would provide young women with a worthy model. She stipulated
that she would not act in plays that contradict Islam, e.g., those in which the
swindler does not get his punishment, those portraying prostitutes, those in
which dance and revealing clothes appear, or those with "hot scenes."[13] She
played in several historical and religious serials, though it was not her wish to
remain located in the niche of religious serials only. On the contrary, if she
were offered a social drama it would be even better in her view. Looking back
at her former productions, she stressed the great responsibility she feels as an
actress to provide the right example:

> I don't like to watch my previous productions. They could have been
> better. I hope God will forgive me. There are two kinds of violations.
> Someone can make a mistake but it is hidden. You are perhaps used to it
> and can't stop doing it, but other people do not see it. The other type of
> mistake is not hidden. People see it and for that reason the effect is much
> greater. Therefore, there is a *hadith* that says that God can forgive the sins
> except of sinners who show their sins in front of the people. For that rea-

son your mistakes on the screen are grave sins. And I did not do much, no nightwear, bathing suit, bed scenes, or kisses, only scenes in which I played a spoiled character. But still, it annoys me.[14]

Also, in other interviews she expressed a feeling of greater comfort in her present roles with a veil and suitable clothes. She also feels more at ease with her colleagues who are likewise more religiously committed, and who, in contradistinction with the past, leave the studio to pray on time.[15]

In an interview she mentioned that a few of the retired artists were angry with her because of her return,[16] as we also saw in the case of Soheir al-Babli. When I asked her about her views on the old generation of "repentant" artists, she responded:

I don't know all of them very well. I don't talk about Soheir al-Babli, but I have met two others, without mentioning names. But I think they are quite strict in their views. That was the reason I was quite strict myself in the beginning and declared everything *haram*. But I am an independent personality, I read and think and decide for myself [. . .].[17]

A generation gap seemed to have emerged among the artists, the old ones following those sheikhs who disapproved of women working in the field of art and the younger ones following the sheiks who permit art—conditionally—as a proper field, for women as well as men. The image of the generation gap is not totally correct, though, because some of the older actresses returned also and changed their opinions in accordance with the new readings of art and gender that become more prominent in the late 1990s. The transformations are better analyzed against the background of the fragmentation of religious authority, which left space for new voices and different opinions on religious issues and led to a variety of opinions on art and gender by religious scholars and lay authorities. Audiences and artists could select among the available options those views corresponding to their own understandings and interests.

The divergent opinions among retired artists and religious scholars further crystallized during the late 1990s and will be central in the remainder of this chapter. In the next section I will discuss the different views on art and gender among the retired artists, and in the final section I will analyze the religious discourse of those scholars who were their sources of inspiration. I will neither reconstruct a general change in the discourse on art and gender, nor select the authoritative voices in the debate myself. I will follow the choice of the artists and provide more information on those religious scholars or laypersons who were mentioned by them.

FEMALE ARTISTS DEBATING ART AND GENDER

'Abir Sharqawi is one of several young actresses and singers who took the veil and retired in the second half of the 1990s, spurring another debate in the press. Other actresses such as Miyar al-Bablawi and 'Abir Sabri, whom we will meet in Chapters 7 and 9, and singers Hanan and Mona 'Abd al-Ghani, as well as actresses Mirna al-Muhandis, Mona Liza, and several others, veiled and quit.[18] Several of them had not been very big names before they were given the chance to come to a level of stardom as a result of the retirement of some famous stars. Several of them decided to don the veil after only a few years of working in the field of art. Yet, unlike the big stars who had previously retired, they returned after a short break. Their comebacks coincided with those of some of the celebrities who had been off screen for more than ten years.

In Chapter 4, we have seen how the Islamist press used the stories of the "repentant" artists and veiled actresses to promote their views on art and gender and to attack those of the "secularists." The "repentant" artists were at least willing partners in this endeavor and told their stories to Islamist newspapers and magazines. Yet the Islamist embrace was perhaps somewhat too eager and warm. Not all "repentant" artists liked the negative images of the field of art and the depiction of their former lives. We can thus not assume that they completely shared the Islamist discourse on art and gender or lived according to its decrees. Besides, the "repentant" artists did not comprise a homogenous group. Moreover, views on art shifted among some of the artists, a change—as we shall see in the next section—consonant with a more general trend.

The first group of "repentant" stars, such as Shams al-Barudi and Hana' Tharwat, most closely shared the Islamist discourse on art as outlined in Chapter 4. Particularly Shams al-Barudi elaborated in some detail her view that art is like the devil. This is evident not only from the "exorcist ritual" in Mecca, but also from her exclamation: "I will never return to art, I will never return to the devil who stole everything from me. I tasted the sweetness of the belief in God and the sweetness of the closeness to God, like I tasted the life of the devil" (in Nasif and Khodayr n.d., 57–58). She shaded her views, though, and stated that art is not generally *haram*, by which she meant drawing, artisan works, or poetry written within the framework of the Shari'a. But acting for women is, in her view, *haram*. She reasoned that the Qur'an is clear with regard to the obligation to veil and to lower the gaze and not to shake hands with men. What is forbidden in real life is forbidden in acting. It is not proper for a woman to raise her voice, to touch men, and to mix with them.

Working as a veiled actress is, according to her, also not in agreement with the Shariʿa. However, men and children are allowed to act and perform or make a film in the service of Islam (in Abu Dawud and Bayumi 1994, 38–40). Her view of the permissibility of art is thus clearly gendered.

In an interview in 1988, she elaborated her views on gender and motherhood (in Siraj al-Din 1993, 66–67). Shams al-Barudi considered motherhood a divine task that suits the female nature. Women are created to be mothers, not to be engineers or farmers. But if they fulfill the task of motherhood adequately, they are allowed to work within the confines of the religious teachings. Women should not work if this results in the neglect of children and only if it is a matter of sheer necessity. Women who leave their children in a kindergarten are not acting according to Islam. She expressed the view that:

> The Qurʾan and the Sunna of the Prophet describe the characteristics and limitations of the woman, her personality and her work. The man is responsible for the livelihood and is the guardian of the family in his ability as a father or a husband. . . . If the woman is forced to work this is not forbidden on the condition that the woman is God fearing, follows the rules of Islam and the Shariʿa with respect to the Islamic dress, and does not mix with men. The woman's dignity and freedom are that we do not burden her with matters she cannot carry. (Abu Dawud and Bayumi 1994, 30)

Women are created, according to Shams al-Barudi, for the home, the family, raising children, and creating a place of rest for the husband. She reasoned that the "Western concept of self-realisation through work" resulted in the destruction of the social and familial order. Freedom for women does not mean that they should free themselves from religious obligation. Veiled women have a great amount of freedom in their own domain, far from immorality (Abu Dawud and Bayumi 1994, 31).

Hanaʾ Tharwat expressed a similar discourse in her interview with Abu Dawud and Bayumi (1994). After visiting Sheikh al-Shaʿarawi, she was convinced by his assertion that married women are not allowed to go outside or to work except in case of sheer necessity, such as the death of her husband or poverty. If she is forced to leave the house, she should be veiled. Therefore, given these conditions, how can acting be *halal*? After hearing his words Hanaʾ Tharwat retired and veiled (in Abu Dawud and Bayumi 1994, 44). She mentioned that she was not aware of these "religious rules" before meeting the sheikh, but now realized how *haram* it was to work in art, a view that was shared by her husband, Muhammad al-ʿArabi. Acting is one of the most "contaminated" fields to work in for women, he maintained. Actresses mingle and talk freely with men, they are filmed by men and men touch them in order to place them well in front of the camera, foul language is uttered, and people drink in their presence (in Abu Dawud and Bayumi 1994, 46). Hana' Tharwat shared the Islamist discourse against the "secularists" who try to convince "the Muslim woman" that "progress" means discarding her main duties of motherhood and taking care of the household. The "secularists" try to convince women that veiling and religious commitment mean "oppression" and "curtailment of their freedom." However, working outside the home destroys their religion, their marriage, and their children. Real progress is obeying God and not the commandment of the "Jews and the Devil" (in Abu Dawud and Bayumi 1994, 55–59). We thus see the familiar Islamist arguments and discourse as we have analyzed in Chapter 4.

Hala al-Safi explained her ideas on gender and performing during an interview.[19] According to her, art is *haram* and a particularly improper field for women. It inevitably means mixing with men, meeting people, and facing potentially incriminating situations. Besides the late Sheikh Mitwalli al-Sha'arawi, she mentioned Dr. 'Umar 'Abd al-Kafi as a source of inspiration for her retirement and views on art and religion. Kamilia al-'Arabi, although belonging to the first generation of retired artists, did not share this discourse on the sinfulness of art, and the importance of domesticity, for women. In the first years after being fired as a presenter because of her veil, she still hoped to be able to return. She spoke positively of media and art as important ways to provide people with the right information. She held that art is not *haram* (in *al-Nur*, April 1, 1992, p. 7) and that the view of Islam as against artistic creativity is erroneous (in *al-Sha'ab*, July 16, 1992). However, she contended that the media and art, presently, are tainted, since what is considered *haram* in real life should also be forbidden in art. Kamilia al-'Arabi deemed the refusal of "secularists" to allow the presence of veiled women on TV degrading, because of the important mission of art and the value of women. She fully endorsed the "*halal*" character of women appearing in the media while veiled. She also emphasized the importance of women's work in general (*al-Nur*, April 1, 1992, p. 7).

Sources of inspiration and the interpretation of those sources are not stable, even among the first generation of retired artists. In this respect it is interesting to have a closer look at Yasmin al-Khiyyam's views on art and gender. Al-Sha'arawi had told her that if she preferred to keep on singing while veiled, she belonged "to the school of al-Ghazali," while if she would veil and quit, she would belong to al-Sha'arawi's school (see next section). With regard to religion and art, Yasmin clearly preferred the views of Muhammad al-Ghazali (Abu al-'Aynayn 1999, 63).[20] Yasmin al-Khiyyam in the early

1990s—that is, during the period of her decision to retire—might have been influenced by ʿAbd al-Kafi;[21] later on, she provided a forum to ʿAmr Khalid. During the interview I conducted with Yasmin al-Khiyyam, she clearly stated that she intended to promote a new vision of Islam, which can be summarized in her words by "Islam is love, not war and terrorism." She stressed Islam's merciful nature and explained that the previous generation had received a wrongheaded education. She deemed it of utmost importance to educate the young generation in the "right Islam," its peaceful character, and its similarity with other monotheistic religions.[22]

Former dancer Amira also highlighted her career among the sheikhs and *daʿiyat* she liked.[23] She started with ʿUmar ʿAbd al-Kafi and "learned real *iltizam*" from him. She used to watch al-Shaʿarawi and had always wished for herself "a father like him." She praised his beautiful sermons, and lately she found ʿAmr Khalid and other new preachers such as Khalid al-Guindi inspirational. ʿAfaf Shoʿib admired Sheikh al-Shaʿarawi—"even after a hundred years there will be no one like him"—but also Muhammad al-Ghazali, ʿAbd al-Kafi, and presently ʿAmr Khalid, whom she met and who had spoken positively about her return to the field of art. She was one of the few who mentioned Mustafa Mahmud as a source of inspiration. Several of the younger generation mentioned, besides ʿAmr Khalid, other lay preachers such as Khalid al-Guindi, and the Yemeni sheikh Habib ʿAli, but also the scholar Yusuf al-Qaradawi. For some of them these sources are equally inspirational; for others, as we have seen in the case of ʿAbir Sharqawi, it is a development from a certain view toward a different stance on art and gender. In particular, for those who returned to or stayed in the field of art as a veiled actress, the views of al-Qaradawi and ʿAmr Khalid were important. One of my interlocutors, who works at Islamic weddings as a singer and bandleader, considered al-Qaradawi the ultimate authoritative source on music, singing, and forms of relaxation.[24] He also presented me with ʿAmr Khalid's tape on art to illuminate the new spirit among religious artists about coming back and producing pious art.

Thus, the first group of "repentant" artists was initially influenced by Sheikh al-Shaʿarawi,[25] Muhammad al-Ghazali, and Zeinab al-Ghazali. The latter wrote a foreword to Shams al-Barudi's book and has been a source of inspiration to some others as well. For instance, the actress Madiha Hamdi mentioned her name besides those of al-Shaʿarawi and Muhammad al-Ghazali.[26] In the early 1990s, the retired artists were particularly influenced by ʿUmar ʿAbd al-Kafi, and from the mid-1990s onward, al-Qaradawi and ʿAmr Khalid became sources of inspiration. Even the younger generation, who preferred al-Qaradawi and ʿAmr Khalid, still liked al-Shaʿarawi: "We have grown up with him," Mona ʿAbd al-Ghani said affectionately. "He is moderate and we are so used to him."[27] In addition, several artists admired the older generation of retired artists, among them Hanaʾ Tharwat and Kamilia al-ʿArabi, for their sermons in Islamic salons. Although older authorities such as al-Shaʿarawi linger on, new faces and voices appear, and particularly at the lessons held in houses, many new authorities sprout and wither. And with numerous cassettes and TV channels also presenting sheikhs and religious opinion leaders, the choice has become extremely rich. Yet their effect can be quite diffuse. The artists might be strongly affected by their speeches on art but less by those on gender, or they might be inspired by them for their strong evocative discourse or eloquence in general. Although I will concentrate on the ideas on art and gender of the selected authorities, their influence on artists might stem from their power to evoke pious feelings in the audience rather than their views on art and gender. They might not even have a very elaborate discourse on art at all. Most have clear opinions, though, on gender and particularly on veiling.

The interesting thing, although perhaps not really surprising, is that consulting the same source can lead to different interpretations. Madiha Hamdi, who veiled in 1992, mentioned the same sources as her colleagues who "repented" and retired, but she drew the conclusion from these preachers' views that she could keep on working with a veil.

> They [al-Shaʿarawi, Muhammad al-Ghazali, and Zeinab al-Ghazali] told me its [acting's] *haram* is *haram* and its *halal* is *halal*. It is like a cup. You can drink something sweet from a cup or you can use it to drink alcohol. It depends on the content and form of your art. As long as you abide by the Islamic dress (*zayy islami*), and you are religiously committed (*multazima*), you don't use your voice in a sensuous way, lower your eyes and play purposeful roles, then it is *halal*. In my view God is beauty and loves beauty. He created the sea in blue colors, the trees in green, and sand in yellow. We all have one nose and two eyes, but we all look different. He is the greatest Creator or Artist (*fannan kibir*). The whistle of the bird is like music, the sound of the waves is like music, the rustling of leaves is like music. Even the rain has a voice. Everything he created is created with beauty. He is the greatest Artist.[28]

She used a vocabulary that became particularly widespread after the turn of the century when several artists returned to the screen and stage.

The power of preachers disseminating their messages through diverse media—cassettes, television channels, and lectures at Islamic salons—is nicely illustrated in the story of ʿAbir Sabri, who will be profiled more fully in Chapter 9. Three days after her veiling in 2002, she was interviewed on Dream TV. She said that she went to the theater and found some tapes of ʿAmr Khalid that her sister had put in her bag. She put one of them in the recorder and listened to it while driving. It addressed the topic of the importance of praying and particularly of praying on time. After work she listened to the remainder of the tape and was moved to the extent that she decided that she would never again let the duty of prayer pass. She performed a supplicatory prayer and asked God to give her enough time to make up for all the prayers that she had omitted. At home she prayed "really from her heart." Later that evening, ʿAbir Sabri listened on Dream TV to preacher Habib ʿAli, who delivered "a wonderful lesson." The next morning she decided to veil and told her husband about her decision. He was surprised and asked whether this was simply the effect of yesterday's lesson. She went to work and informed her colleagues about her decision to veil. She received an invitation to an Islamic salon that same evening, where Hanaʾ Tharwat was giving a lecture. ʿAbir Sabri was moved and impressed by her knowledge and veiled on the spot. Her journey among the preachers particularly points to the wide availability of religious discourse through diverse avenues at any time of the day.

We can discern a certain development in the discourse of artists, despite its fragmented nature, that coincides with a development in discourse and artistic practice more generally. Whereas most of the retired artists of the 1980s, such as Shams al-Barudi, Hanaʾ Tharwat, and Hala al-Safi, strongly argued for art's unlawful nature, particularly for women, most artists who retired in the early 1990s were more ambivalent in their views or changed their ideas on art in the course of time. After an initial stage of conservative views, they turned toward a more moderate discourse on art. The artists thus generally moved along with the developing ideas among Islamist thinkers on art. They selected, from among the diverse voices and authorities available, those views that supported their own—changing—artistic preferences and practices. We can thus conclude that the artists generally side with Islamist ideas on art, particularly since these views became more diversified and appreciative of art.

The artists also strongly converged with the Islamists in the discourse on veiling. All religiously committed artists advocate and publicize the veil. Women's veiling is seen as of primary importance for taking the final step to *iltizam*—that is, becoming observant, pious Muslim women. Preachers like al-Shaʿarawi and ʿUmar ʿAbd al-Kafi had made them aware that veiling is "obligatory" and a "commandment from God" just like fasting and praying. They were not aware of its "obligatory character" and centrality for pious Muslims. Doing charity, praying, fasting, and going to Mecca were in their view the quintessential conditions for piety. Yet through these preachers, they became aware that veiling is a condition just as important for pious woman-hood as the uncontested pillars of Islam. Putting the veil on the same foot-ing as the recognized pillars of Islam is, according to secular and moderate Muslim critics, a clear indication of the Saudi-tization of their Islam. Even though some artists, like ʿAbir Sharqawi, criticized the extreme emphasis put on veiling, they all deemed the veil obligatory.

Although most artists took the veil for religious reasons and shared the Islamist discourse on veiling, they kept up a high public profile. Many of them continued their media presence despite veiling, or perhaps even due to their renovated status as veiled stars. By veiling, they religiously legitimized their public presence and activities. These public activities by the veiled celeb-rities, though, were not envisaged by most conservative Islamists. Whereas the artists shared the Islamists' discourse on veiling, in its effect, veiling pro-vided them alternative space to stay in the public domain as veiled preachers, presenters, singers, and actresses.

Hence, whereas all retired artists advocate the veil, not all of them share the preachers' ideals of womanhood and domesticity, and even if they did so, they did not behave accordingly. As we saw, some of the retired artists voiced clear opinions of women's primary role as caretakers who were allowed work only if sheer necessity forced them to take it. However, even the first group of retired performers have remained active in public life through preaching in homes and mosques. The younger generation, among them ʿAbir Shar-qawi, disliked the views on women of conservative Islamist preachers such as Dr. ʿUmar ʿAbd al-Kafi. Whether they shared the opinions on the domes-ticity of women or not, most retired artists kept up a high public profile. They dedicated themselves to their husbands and children, but also became active in *daʿwah*, preaching, and charity. Most of the veiled actresses retiring in the early 1990s eventually returned to the screen, and some of them, such as Shahira, Mona ʿAbd al-Ghani, and Miyar al-Bablawi, presented religious programs. They all sought ways to combine an active public presence with piety and use their (mediatized) presence to publicize their ideas of pious womanhood. For all of them it holds true that they have remained influen-tial public figures and influenced the concepts of piety for women. They are working out new models for active pious womanhood in which they com-bine veiling with public influence and visibility/audibility. Their public role especially—although in service to piety—was not in accordance with Islamist ideals for womanhood.

The "repentant" artists can thus be positioned close to the Islamist (counter)public. However, they keep a critical distance in some respects. As we have seen, the veiled artists were an important icon for the Islamists, but also a slightly ambiguous one as a result of their fame as former artists. For that reason, in the Islamist discourse it was deemed important for them to sever all ties with their former profession and public presence. Most retired or veiled artists did not live up to this expectation. The artists were not passive pawns in the Islamists' agenda. They were willing partakers of at least a part of the Islamists' notions of the pious woman. Particularly with regard to the importance of veiling, the religious discourse of the veiled artists and Islamists collide. Their role was ambiguous, though, because on the one hand, the artists actively promoted veiling among women, but on the other, they did so through their public prominence. With regard to art and gender, a mixed picture emerged as well. In the early 1990s, conservative views on art and gender prevailed. Many, but not all, former performers shared this view. Even if they upheld ideas on the centrality of women's domesticity and the Muslim family, though, they did not totally live up to this ideal in their personal lives. Whereas they all agreed on the primacy of women's role in the family, most of them combined these tasks with public roles. They have remained important public personalities, as preachers, as businesswomen in Islamic businesses, or in charity. With regard to art there is ambivalence, too: not all of them distanced themselves from their art productions, and several of them eventually returned. Yet this was during the late 1990s and particularly after the turn of the century, as we will see in the next part. In these years, part of the Islamist movement had changed its ideas on art toward a more accommodating view. In that sense the artists stayed close to the—developing—Islamist discourse.

FROM SHEIKH AL-SHAʿARAWI TO *USTAZ* ʿAMR KHALID

In this section, I will analyze the discourses of those sheikhs and preachers who were most influential on the artists' decision to veil and retire and later on to return to the screen with a veil. As I have mentioned before, we should be careful not to posit any direct relationship between the sheikhs' discourses and the artists' decision. They were one of the elements, along with several others, that informed the artists' choices. We can discern a transformation, from a discourse that was rather restrictive for women, urging them to leave performance, in the 1980s, through a centrist discourse declaring art generally permissible within certain confines, toward a relatively open view that encouraged artists to return with pious productions in the late 1990s. However, not all female artists returned, despite the new discourses, and some women had tried to stay despite the former views that rejected the field

6.1. *Book cover,* al-Shaʿarawi . . . wa al-Fannanat / al-Shaʿarawi . . . and the Female Artists, *by Saʿid Abu al-ʿAynayn*

of art as being improper for women. I will trace the fragmentation of voices, which spawned different views on art and gender from which the artists could choose the ones that suited them best. I will particularly elaborate on the emergence of the centrist views of the "new Islamist school" (Baker 2003, 2005). The *wasatiyya* trend partly developed out of the peripheral preachers of al-Azhar. Both Muhammad al-Ghazali and al-Qaradawi were prominent intellectuals of the *wasatiyya* group. They were Azharis and had—at times—close relationships with the Muslim Brothers, yet remained largely independent. This section will thus illustrate the fragmentation of authority and the relationship among different shades of Islamists, as analyzed in Chapter 5, by going into the discourse on gender and art of those sheikhs central for the "repentance" and comeback of artists.

Sheikh al-Sha'arawi, Zeinab al-Ghazali, and Dr. 'Umar 'Abd al-Kafi, who can be considered "conservative Islamists" (see Chapter 5), do not have an elaborate discourse on art. They have been particularly influential in creating the new ideal for Islamist women (Hatem 1998; Abu Lughod 1998). Sheikh al-Sha'arawi (1911–1998) was venerated by many and died with an almost saintly aura. He was an Azhari cleric, critical of the state and sympathetic to the Muslim Brothers. As we have seen in Chapter 5, he had a huge media presence in state television despite his orthodox views. He did not extensively tackle the topic of art in his sermons, but generally held that art is like a glass or knife. It can be used for good purposes or for bad ends, a quote that was repeated in several variants by the artists I interviewed. If art reveals what should remain concealed and transgresses the limits of God's teachings, it is *haram*. However, if it conveys social values and moral principles, it is an important civilizing source (in Kamil 1993, 37–40). He considered singing by women to be "itching the sexual instincts": "God made the sexual instinct that itches. Do not then excite it more! As much as possible, do not excite it since it is made already to itch" (in Tadros 1994). Noting that God preferred a woman's prayer to be in her house rather than in the mosque, in her room rather than elsewhere in her house, and in her bedroom rather than in her living room, he concludes that working or acting with a veil is not an option for artists (in Abu al-'Aynayn 1999, 110). He is generally unfavorable toward work for women (in Fawzi 1993). Islam does not forbid women to work, but only allows it if this is motivated by necessity. Devout women should accept their husband's income.[29] Working in order to better the financial situation is thus not in accordance with Islamic teaching. If women work outside the home, they should not abandon their most important tasks as wives and mothers. Women have gender-specific skills and tasks. Their concerns should be, first, the well-being of their husband and, second, that of the children.

They should work within the framework of Islamic principles and veil. Veiling protects men from temptation and thus protects the wife at home from her husband being seduced by a younger woman (in Hatem 1998, 96).

Dr. ʿUmar ʿAbd al-Kafi (b. 1951) expresses similar views. He received his doctoral degree from the al-Azhar University in the Faculty of Agriculture and master's degree in Islamic and Arabic studies (Fawzi n.d.). ʿAbd al-Kafi is considered one of the first modern-looking sheikhs without the customary *imam* head covering and caftan. He is a student of both Sheikh al-Shaʿarawi and Muhammad al-Ghazali. He worked as a media consultant for the Islamic World Alliance, an international Saudi organization (Tadros 1994). ʿAbd al-Kafi has preached in several mosques in middle-class neighborhoods and in the elitist Shooting Club. Although he is convinced that women can be modern and Islamic at the same time, he called upon them to return to the role of wife and mother (Abu Lughod 1998, 251). Like al-Shaʿarawi, his view is that the best place for women is to be protected at home. Women should work only if necessary and should preferably limit themselves to work as a physician, nurse, or teacher. He also agrees with al-Shaʿarawi on the necessity of loose clothing that shows no form of the body, leaving bare only hands and face without the use of makeup. He recognized the importance of education for women. With regard to art, he mentioned that art is "creativity whose right is right and wrong is wrong. What we see in the movies and plays that provoke the sexual instincts is not art." He called the cinema "devil homes" (in Tadros 1994). According to ʿAbd al-Kafi, there are three conditions for the permissibility of singing: First, a man should not sing in front of a woman or a woman in front of men. Second, there should not be accompanying musical instruments. Finally, the words of the song "should not speak except of morals and belonging to religion and the State" (in Tadros 1994). Art, in all its forms, should "lift morals and values and principles, according to God's Book and the Prophet's Sunna" (in Tadros 1994).

Zeinab al-Ghazali (b. 1918) shared several ideas with the previous preachers, but left more room for women's public engagements. She was closely related to the Muslim Brothers, but her own organization, the Muslim Women's Association, remained independent (Ahmed 1992, 197). Zeinab al-Ghazali believed that Islam provided women with all rights. Since these rights were not granted in society, women should study Islam. Like al-Shaʿarawi, she stressed the husband-wife relationship and outlined the behavior required of women to build a happy home. She advised women not to express feelings of tiredness and always to comfort their husbands. They should select their friends carefully, and neither share problems and secrets with them nor complain about in-laws. Motherhood was also important for Zeinab al-Ghazali.

She particularly stressed the importance of education and training in Islamic teachings for women as a prerequisite for raising good Muslim children (in Hatem 1998, 96). Although women's primary role is in the family, they are entitled to work and to fully participate in political life (in Ahmed 1992, 198). She particularly emphasized the vital role for women in the Islamic call: "Islam does not forbid women to actively participate in public life. It does not prevent her from working, entering into politics, and expressing her opinion, or from being anything, as long as that does not interfere with her first duty as a mother, the one who first trains her children in the Islamic call" (in Ahmed 1992, 199).

The conservative Islamist view on art and the stress on domesticity expressed by al-Sha'arawi and 'Abd al-Kafi are clearly echoed in the first group of retired artists such as Shams al-Barudi and Hana' Tharwat. The Islamist ideals of religious education and engaging in *da'wah* voiced by Zeinab al-Ghazali particularly resonate with the aspirations of Shams al-Barudi, Hala al-Safi, Yasmin al-Khiyyam, and others. Her views combine conservative Islamist ideas on veiling and motherhood with advocacy of opportunities for a public presence in pious engagements. Despite their influence on artists, these preachers' discourse on art itself was not very detailed or sophisticated. The discourse on art was more elaborate among the emergent trend of "centrist," or "*wasatiyya*," thinkers such as peripheral al-Azhar scholars Muhammad al-Ghazali and Yusuf al-Qaradawi (1997a; 1997b; 1998; 2001).

The *wasatiyya* group, or "New Islamist Trend," consists of a group of centrist Islamist intellectuals. They can better be characterized as a school or loose network than as a movement or an organization (Baker 2005). The term *wasatiyya* was probably coined by al-Qaradawi (Gräf 2009, 181; Stowasser 2009, 213). As Gräf shows, the term *wasatiyya* (meaning "center," "mainstream," "middle ground") has become a buzzword with strategic application. Tracing the genealogy of the term in al-Qaradawi's prolific oeuvre, she shows that in the 1970s he used the term to offer a political alternative between capitalism and socialism. In the late 1970s, he used it to distinguish between "traditionalists and those who accept new ways." The middle position he favored combines the useful things of the old and the good things of the new way. From the 1980s onward, *wasatiyya* received the connotation of the middle ground between "secular" tendencies and "extremism." The content of the middle ground is thus defined by the "extremes" and can mean different things depending on whether it is applied to social questions or to political issues (Gräf and Skovgaard-Petersen 2009, 8). At present the term—in combination with the word "moderation" (*i'tidal*)—has developed into a notion for propagating a positive image of Islam, as a form of global *da'wah* (Gräf 2009, 204).

Baker (2003, 2005) situates the *wasatiyya*, or New Islamist Trend, between the "quietist pietistic" current, which focuses on individual belief and ritual, and "extremists," who seek to remake society by means of violence. They emerged from the mainstream Muslim Brotherhood, but have become an independent trend. Besides Yusuf al-Qaradawi and Muhammad al-Ghazali, several scholars, journalists, and intellectuals, such as Muhammad ʿImara, Kamal Abul Magd, Fahmy Huwaidy, Muhammad Selim al-ʿAwa, and Tariq al-Bishri, are important thinkers of the *wasatiyya*. After the death of Muhammad al-Ghazali, al-Qaradawi became the most influential representative. They formulated their ideas at the beginning of the 1980s. Their manifesto, "A Contemporary Islamic Vision," was published in 1991 and sparked debate in the mid-1990s (Baker 2003, 1). They pleaded for a new interpretation and method of *fiqh* making use of rational thinking and reasoning that is consistent with and applicable to modern times. Both al-Qaradawi and al-Ghazali argued that the Qurʾan is the ultimate and most reliable source. The Sunna came later and should be used to elaborate on and understand the Qurʾan. So the Sunna cannot contradict what it should explain. The Qurʾan and Sunna should be taken together, but if the Sunna contradicts the Qurʾan, the Qurʾan takes precedence. In addition, the Qurʾan and the Sunna are texts that can have contextual meanings that literal interpreters fail to capture. Differences of interpretation are unavoidable and should be cherished. Finally, the flexibility of *ijtihad* enables Islam to meet human needs in all times and places (Baker 2003, 92, 105). The *wasatiyya* intellectuals have reformulated Islamist positions on many social, cultural, and political issues. Gender and art, though, are prime topics with which they demarcate their "moderate" ideas from those of "hard-core Islamists." Instead of reviling art, they made it a focal theme to position their centrist views.

Muhammad al-Ghazali (1917–1996), the "sheikh of the Muslim Brothers," as al-Qaradawi calls him (Skovgaard-Petersen 2009, 32), was one of the early Azharite scholars who joined the Brothers and was one of their most important sheikhs prior to the 1952 revolution. In 1954, he clashed with the Muslim Brotherhood leadership and was dismissed from the organization. He criticized the Brotherhood's ideas and leadership. Yet he remained one of the most important symbols of the Muslim Brotherhood's thought and a central figure in the Islamic Awakening of the 1970s (Tammam 2009, 77). Muhammad al-Ghazali has written both on art and gender issues. He is said to have transformed his ideas on gender from a more traditional to a more liberationist stance (Tadros 1994; Stowasser 2009, 183). He argued for a rational, rather than a literalist, understanding of the Islamic texts, including those pertaining to women. He contended, with regard to the position of women in Islamic communities, that the "extremists" rely on misunderstandings of *hadiths* or on unreliable ones. The "extremist" views hold that women are second to men in reasoning and religion, and women cannot rule. He stipulated that the Qur'an prescribes "absolute equality between men and women with only those explicit exceptions, few in number, that God set" (in Baker 2003, 93). These exceptions respect the "natural differences" between the sexes and the consequent responsibilities delegated to each of them. Caring for the family is the first duty of women. In his book entitled *The Legal Condition of Woman between Stagnant and Recent Traditions* (1994), he points out that the Qur'an specifies the right of women to work and full political participation (Marsot 1991, 1431). He strongly opposed the "followers of Bedouin *fiqh*" (Tammam 2009, 82–83). He, for instance, resisted "extremist" views or prescribing the face veil for women, holding that this practice derived from traditions of the Arabian Peninsula and had no basis in Islam (Baker 2003, 97). He declared, with regard to all the attention to veiling, "I am less concerned with the veil to cover the face than with the one placed over the mind!" (in Baker 2003, 98). Like al-Qaradawi, however, he clearly favored the veil and regarded it as a religious duty.

Muhammad al-Ghazali also resisted "extremist" views forbidding music and singing as an absolute. He argued that neither women nor their voices are ʿawra (taboo) (Marsot 1991, 1431). Al-Ghazali called the 1994 assassination attempt against Nobel laureate Naguib Mahfouz "a crime against Islam," despite his censoring of Mahfouz's novel *The Children of Gebelawi* (in Baker 2003, 53). According to him only a "sick person" can reject the cultivation of beauty in Islamic civilization and the splendor in God's creation (Baker 2003, 59). Islam respects serious art that encourages noble values, but rejects art that arouses the instincts (in Farhat 1993, 122). About singing, he is quoted as saying: "[It needs] [m]ale singers. By male I do not mean a man, but I mean the male qualities of strength of character and solid strength, and fierceness of fighting till the last drop. [. . .] If sung by a serious woman whose heart has been torn apart because of her people's misfortunes and defeat then that is all right. But is there such a woman fit for such work, or do we only find women crying for the desertion of a lover and pained at his rejection of her?" The artistic field in the Arab world, according to him, was "on very vile and imbalanced soil" (in Tadros 1994), and he characterized the state of art of his time as "*haram, haram, haram!*" He condemned the famous song by ʿAbd al-Wahhab "Min Gher Leh" for its "blasphemous" sentence "we do not know where we come from and where we are going to" (in Kamil 1993, 43). However, he leaves room for certain forms of art, a view that is more pronounced in al-Qaradawi's thought.

Dr. Yusuf al-Qaradawi (b. 1926) considered Muhammad al-Ghazali his second teacher after Hassan al-Banna. He has also been a student of Sheikh al-Sha'arawi, who had been his teacher in rhetoric at al-Azhar (Tammam 2009, 77). Al-Qaradawi self-identified as Azhari (Skovgaard-Petersen 2009, 29). He was the leader of the Muslim Brothers among the students at al-Azhar. He worked briefly at al-Azhar, but in 1961 he moved to Qatar. He has been able to develop a special relationship with the Muslim Brothers, close but independent (Skovgaard-Petersen 2009; Tammam 2009). Al-Qaradawi is perhaps the most prolific writer on art. His most famous book, *The Lawful and the Prohibited in Islam*—first published in 1960—devoted a section to recreation and play. Several pious musicians I interviewed considered his views on art authoritative and final.

Al-Qaradawi states that there is no conflict between piety and moderate entertainment. He refutes both the people who excessively indulge in art and diversion and those totally ignoring art because they are of the opinion that Muslim society should sanctify only worship. Some hard-liners, he argues, always have solemn, melancholic faces and equate their ominous countenances with religious virtue. While religion allows individuals to impose such restrictions upon themselves, it forbids them to propagate "their extreme ideas on a large scale forcing them on society" (al-Qaradawi, 1998, 1). Al-Qaradawi advocates the middle course and contends that the Islamic approach to life is realistic, because it urges man to fulfill the needs of his body, soul, intellect, and emotions in moderation. He considers art a source of emotional fulfillment. Aesthetic and utilitarian elements coexist in everything God has created, but "He does not love the excessive" (1998, 5). The *hadith* "Allah is beautiful and He loves beauty" is further quoted to stress art's general permissibility. Besides, the Qur'an itself is a miracle of beauty. Diversion is essential to re-create, but one should find a balance between religious obligation and recreation.

With regard to music al-Qaradawi states that, despite huge controversies, Muslim scholars agreed on two things: Any statement that includes an unlawful word is *haram*. From this opinion it follows that every song that includes forbidden words is "altogether unlawful particularly when rhyme, rhythm and side effects work together to make the evil meaning attractive" (1998, 16). Thus, the powerful effect of music on the senses, leading to distorted conceptions of right and wrong, is feared. Second, al-Qaradawi argues that scholars also agreed that songs that do not play on sexual arousal and are not accompanied by musical instruments are *halal*, provided that they are not sung by a woman in the presence of men who are strangers to her. On other issues, fierce dispute ensued among scholars. The general rule is that everything is permissible except if it is clearly stated in the Qur'an or Sunna that it is *haram* or if there exists a consensus among scholars that something is *haram*. Singing can be "purposeful" or "useless." The permissibility of singing ultimately depends on the good intention of the singer. Good intention turns diversion into a rapprochement with God. Listening to "useless songs" is not forbidden, provided that the time does not interfere with religious obligation or duties. Like al-Ghazali, he refuted as weak the *hadith* that the voice of women is taboo. Also, listening to music played with conventional musical instruments is allowed (1998, 44). Yet there are conditions governing singing and listening to music: First, with regard to the content, he stipulates that it should conform to the moral code of Islam. This means that it should not encourage drinking alcohol, "flatter the oppressor," or "glorify handsome men and pretty women." Second, with regard to the performance, the way the singer transmits meaning through the presentation, costumes, lights, and location, if aimed at seduction and sexual arousal, music is *haram*. Third, with regard to the context, the singing should not be accompanied by unlawful activities such as drinking alcohol or displaying bodies. Finally, again, a balance must be found between religious obligation and need for diversion. Islam forbids excessiveness, even in worship itself (1998, 50–51). The present state of art, however, is in his view totally corrupt and needs immediate repentance: "[W]hoever works in show business theatre, cinema or TV is plagued by this devastating atmosphere. Therefore, each time Allah bestows His guidance and remorses on someone who works in this corrupt field of art, he opts for immediate retirement and flees in search for salvation" (1998, 57).

Al-Qaradawi's gender discourse is not encouraging for female performers. He considers the home their "great kingdom." Anyone attempting to remove women from their kingdom in the name of freedom, work, or art is the "enemy of women" and is rejected by Islam (1997b, 2001). Stowasser (2009) analyzed his gender views and typified his ideas with regard to women as largely "traditionalist": "One the one hand, there are the old and still ongoing themes of women's domestic duties and rights, issues concerning 'Islamic dress,' and the problem of women's access to public space, all defined in largely traditional terms. Of more recent (and radical-liberationist) vintage are issues of women's political rights and obligations, such as the right to vote and stand for election" (2009, 183). Stowasser argues that while he is more to the traditional side of the middle range, he is, at the same time, pragmatic and stresses the need for women's participation in *da'wah* and politics to oppose the secularist dominance.

Despite the importance of *da'wah* among the *wasatiyya* intellectuals, they did not develop the notion that art could be used for a religious-moral mission. Despite their positive ideas on art in general, *wasatiyya* intellectuals fulminated against the current state of art. The discourse stopped at the point of general claims that art is not *haram*, given certain conditions and stipulations. However, it did not extend into a clear missionary discourse that art was needed for the Islamic Awakening. Their gender discourse allowed space for women's work as long as her primary and natural role was properly executed. Veiling was a cornerstone for female public activities. Art, though, was not deemed an appropriate field for women. In order to understand the discourse that supported the comeback of the veiled actresses, we have to look at the youngest category of preachers. These lay preachers without al-Azhar training became an important voice in the debates about gender and art, among others, by using new media.

The trend of new preachers extensively using new media was already foreshadowed by al-Sha'arawi and particularly by al-Qaradawi. Al-Qaradawi had become very influential through new media such as satellite TV and the Internet. He had hosted his own program on Qatar TV since 1970, but extended his influence by shifting his activities from national TV to new transnational media (Galal 2009). His weekly program *Shari'a and Life* started in 1996 on al-Jazeera, and his involvement with the portal Islam Online turned him into a "global *mufti*" (Gräf and Skovgaard-Petersen 2009). He is probably the first *'alim*, religious scholar, with a personal website (Gräf 2009, 224). Due to the use of transnational media, national censorship could be circumvented, traditional authorities could be challenged, and a transnational Muslim public could be reached (Galal 2009). It created opportunities for media stardom through stressing religious features. In these new Muslim media the law-based way of reasoning was increasingly replaced by an experience-grounded manner of reasoning (Eickelman and Anderson 1999). Young media stars such as 'Amr Khalid, Habib 'Ali, Khalid al-Guindi, and, recently, Mo'ez Mas'ud could compete with traditional authorities by the way they reached out to transnational and primarily young Muslim publics, "using the media in an experience-based and entertaining manner" (Galal 2009, 163). It is no longer the rationality of the message or the interpretation of the text that is important, but the intensity of belief and the effect on the audience (Galal 2009, 163). We thus see a shift from national TV and interpretation of texts by al-Sha'arawi to *fatwa* programs for a transnational audience by al-Qaradawi and finally to global "emotion" TV by young lay preachers.

As several authors have indicated (Wise 2003; Moll 2010), religious authority became not only fragmented, but also drawn from a different source. Instead of drawing on traditional channels of learning and power, the new preachers' authority is based on charisma, youthful looks, communication skills, and charm, the ability "to be identified with, rather than merely looked up to in awe" (Wise 2005). As Moll also argues, the new preachers' authority derives not from a mastery of the authoritative textual canon of the Islamic tradition, but rather from their status as "ordinary Muslims." For instance, ʿAmr Khalid has authority "not because he is different from the audience he preaches to, but because he is one of them" (Moll 2010). This "ordinary" basis of authority was contested by traditional authorities. Al-Qaradawi, for instance, stressed in an interview that ʿAmr Khalid "does not hold any qualifications to preach. He is a business school graduate who acquired what he knows from reading and who got his start by way of conversations with friends about things that do not really involve any particular thought or judgment" (in Wise 2003).

The most important preacher of these new religious media stars with regard to the veiled actresses is probably ʿAmr Khalid. He has become one of the most popular media preachers since the death of al-Shaʿarawi (Wise 2003). There is a huge difference between al-Shaʿarawi's and ʿAmr Khalid's preaching with regard to the message, style, and setting of the lessons: *fiqh* and *fatawa* versus personal piety; paternalistic-authoritative versus participatory; and the formal gender-segregated environment of the mosque versus mixed-gender audiences in a studio setting. In 1995, he entered the religious arena without religious education. This new participatory concept of preaching and lecturing was not immediately successful, as the producer of *Words from the Heart*, Ahmad Abu Haiba, related.[30] It was only after *Words* was available on videotapes that it became successful and Iqra started to be interested. ʿAmr Khalid was prohibited from preaching in the neighborhood of al-ʿAguza, but through his connection with Yasmin al-Khiyyam, he started preaching in her mosque in 6th of October City. After he faced another prohibition in 2002, he left Egypt and now works for Dream TV, and the Iqra satellite channel. Wise (2003) argues that despite his rather apolitical, socially conservative Islamic discourse, he is perceived as dangerous by the government. This is due to the fact that he provides an alternative Islamic discourse that is more popular and better marketed than al-Azhar's official version, and also destabilizes the state's attempt to portray all Islamists as backward, dangerous fundamentalists. Khalid presents himself as a moderate, modern Islamist and brings a pleasurable message that combines Islam and a comfortable lifestyle.[31]

The importance of culture, art, and media is addressed in an episode of his program *Life Makers*, a lecture that was also sold on tape.[32] Culture is crucial, ʿAmr Khalid argues, because it distinguishes every community or nation. If one would like to know the features of a people, one has to look at its art and culture. Just as a person can be recognized by the features of his face, so

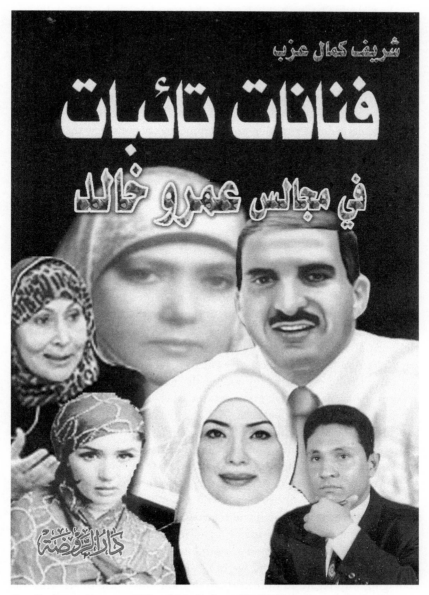

6.2. *Book cover*, Fannanat Ta'ibat fi Maglis Amru Khalid / Repentant Artists in the Presence of 'Amr Khalid, *by Sherif Kamal 'Azab (from left to right, upper row, Soheir al-Babli, Shams al-Barudi, 'Amr Khalid, and in the middle below, 'Abir Sabri)*

can the features of a people be recognized in its culture and art, Khalid maintains. He continues: "Imagine that you look at the mirror one morning and do not see any feature on your face! What will happen? You will go mad and ask yourself, 'Where am I?' Do you get the great significance of art and culture?!" 'Amr Khalid points out the great responsibility of artists for the community: they can spoil the people, import characteristics that do not suit the nation, or edify the *ummah* with art that befits the stage of its renaissance. He particularly draws attention to the erroneous religious view that art is *haram*, a view that dissuades committed artists from engaging with art. Religion is innocent of the charge that it repudiates art, a thesis Khalid underpins by stating that beauty is essential in Islam. The Prophet enjoyed beauty and art, and did not reject the art present at his time. On the contrary, he turned it into a tool for building and vitalizing the new community. This is, according to 'Amr Khalid, exactly what needs to be repeated at present. Yet the current state of art does not fulfill that role at all; it drives society toward collapse and consists of imported cultural forms from the West. The main problem with imported culture, according to Khalid, is not merely that it is obscene, but more important, that it is inauthentic and misrepresents the *ummah*. "It is like a mask on the face," he explains. He thus has a clear message for artists in general: create art that suits the stage of the revival of the *ummah*, uplifts the spirit of the people, and is authentic, and for the "repentant" artists in particular: "come back and use your talents for the renaissance of our land."

'Amr Khalid explicitly calls upon male and female artists to return and support the Islamic Revival. He rejects the label "repentant" artists, because repentance is something between God and the artist-penitent and not between God and art. He also rejects the label *i'tizal*, or retirement, and discourages retirement from art for religious reasons. He urges the retired artists to return to produce purposeful art. 'Amr Khalid strongly favors veiling for women, but is not against women's participation in work, including the field of art. He is one of the first preachers who not only outspokenly defends art's importance in general terms, like al-Qaradawi or Muhammad al-Ghazali, but actively calls upon artists to use art as an instrument to rectify the nation. This discourse, labeled as "*fann al-hadif*," became quite articulate after the turn of the century, as we will see in Chapter 7. He was also the most encouraging with regard to women's participation in the field of art. This was an important voice for those retired artists who wanted to come back and try to produce "committed art," or "art with a mission." He was particularly popular among the veiled actresses, who saw their ambition to return to the screen religiously sanctioned.

As we have read in the life story of 'Abir Sharqawi, the fragmentation of authority and the possibility to choose from moderate voices on art and gender were important factors in the return of religious artists to the screen and stage. Yet the changed sensibilities among large parts of the Egyptian audience also created a market for pious productions. People were demanding a moral alternative to mainstream productions. This is particularly related to the Islamization of the middle and upper classes. Preachers like 'Amr Khalid also reached these well-to-do classes with their moderate messages. They stimulated what has been labeled a "new religiosity" or "pleasant religiosity" (*al-din al-laziz*) in Egypt. This new religiosity also left ample room for fun and recreation within the confines of the Islamic teachings. With the availability of satellite channels such as Iqra, Dream TV, and al-Risala, the mediascape also provided opportunities for religious-moral productions outside the censorship of the Egyptian state. This eventually developed into a lively scene of religious-moral productions, such as religious wedding bands, *halal* soaps and songs, and clean cinema. In Part Three, I will follow the development of the new religiosity and religious sensibilities among the higher classes, and the emergent religious market for art and creation. I will also trace the development of the discourse on art with a mission and the Islamic aesthetics of the artistic productions catering to these new markets and sensibilities, a development that became particularly salient after the turn of the century.

(PART THREE)

The New Millennium
PERFORMING PIETY

In Part Two, we have seen the immense debates that ensued in the public sphere about art and gender in the 1990s. It became a crucial way to discuss the imagined direction for the Egyptian nation. Also, Islamists realized the enormous power of art in transforming society and individuals. They reformulated ideas on art and started to use it as a mobilizing tool to reach out to people, particularly youth. In the process of instrumentalizing art, they formulated specific ideas about what would count as suitable art forms. It should be different in message and format from "lowbrow" art. It should enhance pious conduct and cater to religious sensibilities. This process of developing art in accordance with moral-religious ethics was influenced by global forces, both from the East—mainly Saudi Arabia—and the West. In order to follow the development into the new millennium, I will first go into the "power–performing arts nexus," borrowing and extending Nooshin's notion of the "power-music nexus" (2009)—that is, the power of art and the power through art. What makes performing arts so powerful and sensitive? How can art create pious subjectivities? In which ways are Islamic ethics translated into aesthetic forms? What are the limits of religiously framed aesthetics, and how have they changed due to market forces?[1]

CULTURAL POLITICS

Artistic performances play a critical role in the construction and maintenance of group identities—whether along religious lines or other markers vital for the identity construction of individuals and communities. Art is thus generally an instrument for cultural politics. The power of performing arts to sustain, reproduce, challenge, subvert, or critique ideologies and regimes of power is accordingly a critical field of inquiry (Schechner 2002, 19). In addition, popular culture, entertainment, and performing arts are specific targets for the cultural politics of competing groups because they are very influential in people's day-to-day lives and lifestyles. They permeate daily life and people's imaginations through fan and celebrity culture. Moreover, issues of embodiment, the body, and sensory experience are central to performing arts, and this field is accordingly intricately linked to body politics (Kirshenblatt-Gimblett 2004). The body, the pious body included, is highly gendered and an important matter of concern to (religious) authorities. Because of the important role played by popular and performing arts in cultural politics, as well as in body politics and day-to-day processes of identification and imagining, they are crucial arenas of contest.

First, it is important to examine the possible intrinsic power of art itself. We can distinguish two kinds of views regarding the inherent power of performing arts, a theme that is particularly elaborated with regard to music. As Nooshin discusses, according to some, there seems to be something intrinsic to music that lends itself to the expression, circulation, and negotiation of power (2009, 9). The ability of music to inspire and to heal, as well as its close connection to the supernatural, conjures up associations of power. Racy (2003) discusses the strong link in the Arab world between music and emotional transformation, epitomized by the concept of *tarab*, enchantment or aesthetic emotion evoked in musicians and listeners. Both Hirschkind (2006) and Frishkopf (2011) point to the ability of music to bypass rational faculties and directly affect the senses. As Frishkopf argues, "sonic forms are powerful forces in naturalizing embodied, affective social identities — [. . .] despite their nondiscursivity — indeed all the more powerful for lying outside of the discursive realm" (2011, 118).

According to others, power is not a quality of music itself, but is more a matter of the uses to which music is put (Randall 2005). In accordance with an understanding of power as fluid and relational, power is not viewed as an inherent quality of music itself. Although it seems convincing that power is not an innate quality of music or art itself, it remains intriguing why they are such good channels for cultural politics. After reviewing different stances on the power-music nexus, Nooshin argues that "if one cannot claim for music that it *possesses* power," it can be claimed that "it possesses qualities which make it a particularly suitable channel for power" (Nooshin 2009, 15). According to Nooshin, this is related to the intensity of music and the immediacy with which music evokes emotions and memory. These powerful effects, though, always depend on the multiple meanings conveyed through and attached to music and performing arts.

Second, the power of performing arts is usually substantiated by the uses to which music and art are put. Several studies deal with the extent to which performing arts can subvert power relations (Fabian 1990, 1998; Carlson 2004). Fabian (1990) warns against the political naïveté of some approaches toward performance as resistance and points at the possibility that colonial rulers encourage performances as entertainment—that is, as a way to co-opt or channel social protest (1990, 17). In *Moments of Freedom*, Fabian (1998) examines popular culture for the spaces of freedom and creativity it might provide. Popular culture is often understood in opposition to (high) culture. Popular culture can create sites for individual or collective freedom, but is not in itself liberating (1998, 19–21). "If freedom is conceived not just as free will plus the absence of domination and constraints, but as the potential to transform one's thoughts, emotions, and experiences into creations that can be communicated and shared [. . .] then it follows that there can never be freedom as a state of grace, permanent and continuous. [. . .] Freedom [. . .] comes in moments" (1998, 20–21).

To perceive the relationship between dominant power and popular culture and art in terms of conformity versus resistance is thus far too simple. As Fabian holds: "The issue of power and resistance in studies of popular culture [. . .] cannot be reduced to determining whether or not, or when and where, expressions of popular culture qualify as acts of resistance; what we need to understand is how popular culture creates power to resist power" (1998, 69). He also draws attention to the "power from within"—that is, the possibility that processes and forms of domination that popular culture opposes also work within popular culture. Power is constantly established, negated, and reestablished. "It is not its being power-free that distinguishes popular culture [. . .] but its working against the accumulation and concentration of power, which, when institutionalized, cannot do without victims" (Fabian 1998, 133). Fabian's theory sensitizes us to oversimplified approaches of conformity versus resistance and opens our eyes to power structures within popular art.

The power–performing arts nexus has until now particularly been applied to anticolonial struggle or to art forms from the margins, such as hip-hop and rap, resisting dominant forms of power. Several studies have pointed to the use by young Muslims of music—for instance, rai, rap, hip-hop, and heavy metal—as a way to protest against forms of discrimination and stigmatization of Muslims in Europe (Solomon 2011; Swedenburg 2001; Gazzah 2008; LeVine 2008). Yet to what extent can we regard the pious productions as subversive? I think the notion of "counterpublic" as used by Hirschkind (2006) is important in analyzing the possible subversive power of the pious productions. Whereas in Part Two I have discussed and illustrated the Habermasian notion of public and counterpublic in the sense of debates in the public sphere, in Part Three I will look at counterpublic as the alternative aesthetics developed by Islamists through their artistic productions. Hirschkind particularly emphasizes the different sensorium and moral dispositions underlying the practices of the oppositional piety movement. The Islamist counterpublic aims at the formation of an ethical counterworld (Hirschkind 2006, 105–143). Also, Mahmood (2005) has shown that the power of the piety movements is particularly directed at inculcating in its members moral sensibilities that oppose or undermine secular liberal sensibilities (Mahmood 2005). Do pious productions form a counterworld through their aesthetics based on religious ethics and sensibilities?

PERFORMING BODIES AND RELIGIOUS SENSIBILITIES

As we will see, the positioning of the body is a crucial contested matter among holders of different (religious) sensibilities. The focality of the body in performing arts makes them a critical tool for cultural politics. Notions of the body and embodiment have seen an increase in attention among scholars recently (Blackman 2008). Within anthropology, the body already has a long career, which can be divided into four stages (Csordas 1999). Mauss introduced the notions of practice and habitus in his essay "Body Techniques" (1979).[2] The concept of habitus has afterward been developed by Bourdieu (1977). In later decades, interest in the body was subordinated to communication as a cultural process. Douglas's model of the physical body as a microcosm of society is a famous example of approaches that see the body as a medium of expression. The third stage is characterized by Csordas as a shift from "the body as a topic" to "the body as a theoretical problem" (1999, 178). Foucault, Bourdieu, and Butler are but a few of the scholars who called into question the mind-body distinction and transformed the body from a natural, stable substrate or passive lump upon which society inscribes its codes into a source of agency. At present, the body is no longer a background or perceived as a text, but has become key to understanding culture and self "from the standpoint of embodiment as an existential condition in which the body is the subjective source or intersubjective ground of experience" (Csordas 1999, 181). Csordas proposed the concept of embodiment to bridge the mind-body distinction. There are multiple modes of embodiment, and the body can be understood both as a source of representation and a source of experience and subjectivity.

In the field of performance studies, the work of Merleau-Ponty has received attention for understanding the critical importance of the body and the embodied nature of lived experience (Auslander 2008; Verrips 2008). Merleau-Ponty criticized body-mind dualism and argued that people are not disembodied thinking minds, but rather bodies and concrete entities through which perception occurs and subjectivity is formed (Auslander 2008, 137). Our access to the world is through the body and not primarily through the mind. Perception occurs in the world of lived experience and is directly connected to the lived body. Subjects are embodied, and this embodiment is the connection to the experienced world. In introducing the concept of embodiment, Merleau-Ponty explains that the body plays a central role in how the world is experienced. As Auslander holds: "Merleau-Ponty's concept of embodiment speaks potentially to all aspects of performance: the performer's embodied experience of performing as much as the spectator's embodied perception of the performance" (2008, 139).

In Part Three, I will primarily deal with the performing body and the moving body in connection with pious performances. For that reason, I will look at some of the studies on the body and embodiment in the field of Islam and Islamic piety that theorize the pious body at a religious-experiential level. This will give insights into the way religious sensibilities among large audiences have created a receptive climate for pious productions. The moving body in performance as embodying Islamic ideologies, and the translation of these discourses into performing bodies, will be dealt with as well.

Within the study of Islam and the Middle East, Bourdieu's elaborations of the concept of habitus have been taken up and criticized by Starrett (1995a) and Mahmood (2005). Bourdieu's notion of bodily hexis is also considered a promising field for further study (Abu Lughod 1989; Starrett 1995a). Bourdieu is interested in understanding how individuals contribute to the reproduction of social restrictions, a problem for which the concept of habitus offers an important tool. Habitus is defined as "systems of durable, transposable dispositions, structured structures" that structure and generate human practice, yet are not felt as enforcing and typically go unnoticed (Bourdieu 1977, 72; Auslander 2008, 67–72). Once internalized, habitus dispositions are taken for granted and appear as natural. Bodily hexis refers to the way individuals come to live as natural through their bodily movements, which are "*em-bodied*, turned into a permanent disposition, a durable manner of standing, speaking, and thereby of *feeling* and *thinking*. [. . .] [P]rinciples em-bodied [. . .] are placed beyond the grasp of consciousness [. . .] achieved by the hidden persuasion of an implicit pedagogy" (1977, 93–94). Although inspiring, this approach has also been criticized for its emphasis on the unconscious character of the habitus and body hexis, whereas Mahmood shows the intentional and pedagogical training of the body as a site of moral virtue among the members of the Egyptian piety movement she studied (2005, 139).

Besides his lack of attention to the conscious pedagogical process of instilling disposition, Bourdieu is also criticized for lack of attention to the relationship between bodily hexis and the ideology or public discourse about hexis (Starrett 1995a). Instead of an unconscious transmission of bodily habits, the embodiment of ideology in hexis is "a set of processes through which individuals and groups consciously ascribe meaning to—or learn to perceive meaning in—bodily disposition, and to establish, maintain, and contest publicly its political valence" (Starrett 1995a, 954). Starrett analyzed the relationship between body hexis and discourse as it pertains to prayer and showed the difference between the colonial discourse, in which the rocking body in prayer is perceived as irrational, and the discourse of Egyptian educators, who advocated a modern version of prayer as related to cleanliness and discipline. Embodying an ideology, in this case pertaining to prayer, is thus not an unconscious process, but an explicit and discursive practice. This brings agency back into processes of embodiment and bodily habits, and underlines its learned, conscious, and contentious character.

The work of Foucault has been another source of inspiration for scholars working on Islam and piety, particularly Mahmood (2001a, 2005). Foucault explored the issue of the ethics of self and identified sexual, political, and religious "Technologies of the Self" (2003) that are constitutive of a sense of oneself (Foucault 2003, 146). The technologies are practices that discipline the body and mind. "Individuals can resist power and transform their own subjectivity by applying techniques of the self. Techniques of the self are about discipline, they are not simply about discipline as domination of the self; they also entail positive transformations of the self" (Auslander 2008, 101).

Mahmood (2005) has given an in-depth analysis of the piety movement in Egypt and the way the devotees train pious dispositions and work on the body to cultivate an ethical self. Participants in the mosque movement regard religious practices such as prayer, styles of comportment, dress, and the movement of the body as ineluctable means for training, cultivating, and realizing a virtuous self (2005, 27–31). Prayer is not simply the expression of piety, but also the means to develop piety. It is a positive way of discipline and ethical self-making. As Hirschkind (2001, 2006) has shown, one of the ethical practices of self-discipline can be to listen to tape-recorded sermons. By extension, listening to religious songs is not only an expression of the devoutness of listeners, but also a form of ethical self-improvement. Pious performances can thus help to inculcate pious dispositions and sensibilities into audiences.

Sensibility is a concept used by Strathern and Stewart to point at "the moral and the aesthetic dimension of choice in action" (2008, 70). Sensibility mediates between the mental and the sensory. It encompasses conscious thoughts and actions and also includes the senses that are focal in the context of performances. It incorporates the idea of culturally appropriate or habitual behavior as well (Stewart and Strathern 2002, 5–6). Pious productions do not simply cater to religious sensibilities, but also instill piety into the body and senses of the devout. This enables the realization of the virtuous self in an embodied way within the discursive field of the "appropriate." Pious art is thus for both producers and consumers a sensory means for ethical self-making in accordance with religious ideologies.

Accordingly, in short, how can we theoretically link ethics with aesthetics? The use of art and music to instill moral values comes close to the ancient Greek philosophy of "ethos," the belief "that music possessed moral qualities and could affect character and behavior" (Sprout and Palisca in Nooshin 2009, 9; see also Racy 2003, 4). Aesthetics is usually understood in reference to the beautiful in the sphere of arts. Following Meyer (2006) and Verrips (2008), who link aesthetics up with Aristotle's notion of aistheses,[3] I would also like to foreground the sensorial character of experiencing the world and this sensing knowledge of it as kernel for the aesthetic understanding. Therefore, it is the sensory experience—in our case, of the art world and its ethical-moral values—that will be examined in this section.

This brings us back to several questions: what counts as ethical or morally appropriate in specific cultural or religious contexts? What ideologies or discourses are embodied in pious productions and how? Which norms or scripts do pious productions in diverse cultural settings enact, embody, and perform? How are ethics transformed into aesthetics? There are various ways in which Islamic ethics are embodied in aesthetics, depending on the mission of the different brands of Islamists. In this section I will particularly follow the moderate Egyptian Islamists and their *fann al-hadif* project to produce moral-ethical art. This project, though, is influenced by global forces.

RELIGIOUS MARKETS AND GLOBALIZATION

Globalization is often understood as a Western force—mostly perceived as secular—influencing, among other things, art and entertainment. The development of the Western formats of pop and soaps are indeed very influential in Egypt and have affected the religious field of art production. Yet globalization can also pertain to Islamic international forces influencing local art productions. This holds true for the financial structure of the entertainment industries. Not only American dollars, but also petrodollars, go global and influence the mediascape. Censorship and funding from the Arabian Peninsula are important factors in the shaping of Egyptian media and art productions as well. In Egypt, the Gulf states are the main customers of drama productions and can enforce their censorship regulations. And with the petrodollars, Islamic morality and prudishness moved in (Shafik 2001).

Forms of global Saudi influence on the soundscape in Egypt have been analyzed by Frishkopf (2009). He described the development of new ideological distinctions between Egyptian and Saudi styles of Qur'anic recitation. With the growth of the Islamic trend in the 1980s, a Saudi style of recitation gained ground and turned the traditional Egyptian style into an oppositional style. The return of the migrant workers from Saudi Arabia not only brought specific religious ideologies, but also wealth, back into Egypt. The mix of wealth and Islamist consumerism led to a conservative climate whose material interest was safeguarded by maintaining political stability. Islamic media production companies were founded and capitalized on the new Islamic trend. They produced, among other things, Saudi-style recitation and songs, expressing "a direct relationship to God, affectively coloured with fear" and produced with an "artificial reverb," indicating a mosque recording, as well as album covers, not showing the reciters' photograph but abstract symbols and graphics (Frishkopf 2009, 101–102). Even the places where the cassettes were sold changed from music kiosks to religious stands selling Islamic booklets and religious paraphernalia. Thus, the aesthetic forms are formidably affected and colored by both Saudi and Western global forces. This "double foreign colonisation of Egypt's sonic media space" (Frishkopf 2009, 98) — and, I would argue, media space including films and soaps more generally — will be detailed in the following chapters.

The artistic productions are not only influenced by diverse global forces, but also go global themselves. Not only Western music and art, but also Islamic artistic productions, are exported. In this process the pious art productions can change as well. In Part Three, I will accordingly also analyze the development of religious markets and the impact of market forces on pious productions. The changing formats and aesthetics demanded by, among other things, market forces also created pressure for adaptation of pious images and the ideals of the artists themselves. Such adaptation tested the limits of piety in performances and the self-realization of artists. This final part of the book thus provides insight into the extent to which the project of the ethical counterworld stays firm in the face of global forces, both at the level of pious productions and the level of individual artists' choices. In doing so, it will also provide a glimpse behind the image of pious perfection of the veiled — and now occasionally unveiling — stars.

7.1. *Miyar al-Bablawi (from website alazma.com)*

(SEVEN)

Art with a Mission and Post-Islamism

I n this chapter, the story of actress Miyar al-Bablawi will be portrayed. In the second section, the new discourse that developed around the turn of the century on "art with a mission," which opened up the possibility of returning to art, will be detailed. In the last section, the transformation of the piety movement into "post-Islamism" and the emergence of new forms of religiosity among the upper middle class will be central.

THE SPIRITUAL BIOGRAPHY OF ACTRESS MIYAR AL-BABLAWI

When I visited Miyar al-Bablawi in February 2006 for a second time,[1] we watched the announcement for the opening of a new TV channel, al-Risala, which was to begin broadcasting on the 1st of March. To my great astonishment, I saw several of the retired artists whom I had interviewed or who were still on my list parading across the screen: Mona 'Abd al-Ghani, 'Abir Sabri, Yasmin al-Khiyyam, 'Afaf Sho'ib, and Sabrin. We discussed the profile of the new channel, owned by Saudi multimillionaire al-Walid bin Talal, who also owned the Rotana channel. Actually, al-Risala was initially meant to be an open-minded religious channel—at least according to the managing director, Ahmad Abu Haiba—featuring music and talk shows next to preachers. Within several years it was transformed into a regular religious channel with one Saudi preacher after another, much to the dismay of the director, who left the channel.[2] Miyar al-Bablawi considered al-Risala, right from the start, to be too "parochial," because it catered to an already religious audience. She preferred to work instead at Mehwar, where she presented her own religious talk show, because it aimed at a mixed audience with a variety of programs.

Miyar al-Bablawi talked candidly and in great detail about her career and private life, even giving insights into aspects of her personal life that she preferred to be off the record. Her openness surprised me a bit, and not only because she was used to dealing with journalists who would take down gossipy bits and pieces of information whenever they had a chance. But she was also very conscious about her image as a veiled public personality judged by invisible audiences on the potential harmfulness of her conduct to Islam. She gave insight into the fact that she regularly experienced this expectation of exemplary conduct as a burden. During the first interview I conducted with her in 2005, she related her story of how she had changed from an actress into a veiled housewife and then returned to the screen again as a veiled presenter.

Miyar al-Bablawi was born in 1971 as Manal Muhammad Tawfiq, in a family she described as "normal," probably meaning middle class: her father was an army officer and her mother was a housewife. She has two sisters. She studied classical languages (Greek and Latin) at the university and was a good student, a "queen in memorization" as she described herself. She was inclined to art and poetry and waited for a door to open itself into a different life: she had decided she did not want to become an "ordinary person." During her time at university she was chosen to work in some commercials. She was considered very pretty ("*amura awi*") because she has an atypical appearance, with a "light complexion and green eyes." For that reason she was chosen by directors. Her family is "upper Egyptian," as she explained, which made working in this field quite difficult: "They always compare an actress to a dancer." She worked for a year without her family knowing it, until they saw her on TV. "My father wanted to slaughter me." She thus had a hard time convincing her father to allow her to continue working, but keeping a low profile. On the condition that she would not neglect her studies, she was allowed to work in minor roles. She was offered minor roles, but her studies and acting were difficult to combine. She declined offers for major roles and repeated a year at university, but after six years she managed to graduate.

She already had met a director who proposed to her, but her father did not want her to marry before graduation. Her suitor was from Saudi Arabia, his father was the minister of information, and he was extremely rich. After graduation they married, but the marriage lasted only one month. This was a great shock to her and her family and triggered a lot of stories in the tabloids. "It was extremely difficult. I was considered beautiful, famous, well-educated and yet divorced after a month! It was a shock, but it also brought me something else: fame! Everyone was talking about me. It harmed me a lot and helped me a lot. It was annoying, although it also brought repute. It is normal that a dog bites a human being, but not that a human being bites a dog: it was normal that Miyar would marry and live a happy life, but not normal that she was divorced after a month."[3] As with other stars, Miyar occasionally talked about herself in the third person, as if she was reading about herself in a newspaper. Reflecting on herself through the mirror of her audiences and fans was a constant theme in her story.

Indeed, the affair did not do her any harm: she was offered a lot of work and earned much money. Especially the period between 1996 and 1999 was a golden time: "My work was my life during that period. I watched what I ate in order not to become fat. I watched how I dressed, I wanted to wear jeans, but you can't. I especially wear red clothes, because red suits my light skin. So even the colors I wore were related to my work. My whole life was work: I slept, I ate, and I went to the theater and studio, national and more and more international. I went to the film festival in your country, in Rotterdam. It was a great moment in my life."[4]

And then—as the reader might have expected—she met her "Prince Charming." "I loved him at first sight." However, he required her to leave the business.

> He was Oriental, an Oriental man, he did not want anyone to see his wife. He did not like the field of art. He did not ask me to veil or to do the pilgrimage, but merely to stay at home.[5] It took me five to six months to decide. I was weary. I had reached all I wanted and to leave this all? . . . but I was in love! I was twenty-five and here in Egypt no one is so late in marrying. Besides, I had already a failed attempt. And I loved madly to be a mother. All those years I did not have any private life. If I kept on like this I would never become or have time to be a mother. I witnessed some actresses who were pregnant and tightened their bellies in order to keep on working till the eighth month. I felt sorry for them. I wanted to enjoy my pregnancy, to feel my belly grow, to sleep and be pampered. He offered me this on the condition that I would leave art. I decided to stop working for a time and try to convince him that I should return later on.[6]

She married and stayed at home. He turned out to be very jealous and denied her access to her former friends. It was, however, an ambiguous refusal. According to Miyar's understanding, he wanted to be married to the star Miyar al-Bablawi, who was famous and the talk of the town; yet, at the same time, he wanted to keep her at home for himself. She started to wear more modest clothing as a compromise with his jealousy. She became pregnant. Although she was far from happy, she decided that she did not want another rushed divorce. In this period her religious turn slowly took place.

She started reading the Qur'an. It made her much more at ease and accepting of her situation. She started thinking about veiling as something God had ordered.

> I became very near to God, there was *raha*, calmness, and I felt the problems less. They existed, but if you are close to God there is a feeling of rest, which is very comforting. There was a strange feeling. Before, when I went to sleep I had nightmares: that I was about to die and was going to hell. I did not wear what God had ordered. All of a sudden you have a beautiful house, a husband whom you should love, and a baby of which you have dreamed all your life. This all is a gift from God. You have to be thankful to God for all this. I felt I was able to thank God and was coming very close to him. I started wearing the veil. Instead of experiencing it as a sacrifice, I felt it was the most beautiful thing that had happened in my life: I left art and looked at the field of art as a stranger. I now was Miyar the Egyptian housewife who wanted to cook, to clean the house, and to raise her baby. She knows her religion and is educated. She knows of the world but is not "of this world" or of the people; she is only for her husband.[7]

Miyar al-Bablawi lived for three or four years in this state until the problems mounted.

Religion had helped her to deal with her problems, but her closeness to God and her veiling were not what her husband envisaged for her. "He wanted me to dress up again like before. He had changed. He perceived me as an ordinary housewife. He loved me when I was a star. But after some time I was less known. He felt I had changed. I was not special anymore: a wife like any wife." Miyar explained that something similar had happened with his previous wife, who was a former singer. He turned her into a housewife, but despite his own insistence on this course he lost interest in her and divorced her. He told Miyar: "You are a Taurus and will take off the veil again." And so it happened: "I donned the veil and took it off. I felt that my husband was looking at other women and I became jealous. So I unveiled for five months. But I couldn't anymore. I felt so naked! So I veiled again."[8] Her husband then forced her to choose between her marriage and the veil, and she eventually chose the veil: "He actually asked me to choose between God and him. I told him: 'I have left the world for you, but the afterlife I will not leave for anyone.'"[9] She took her son and left his house.

Miyar al-Bablawi went to the apartment in which I interviewed her, in Faysal Street near the Pyramids, which she still owned. It had been aban-

doned for five years, and she had no money to furnish it. She was not from a
rich family and had to start working again. However, she was not a name in
the business anymore, she had gained weight, she was thirty by now, and—
most significant—she was veiled. She was friends with the former presenter
Kamilia al-ʿArabi (see Chapter 2). The latter had a huge Islamic school and
orphanage:

> I started to work for her as a teacher. But the money was so little and I am
> not used to money being scarce. I worked in kindergarten and taught Ara-
> bic, Qurʾan, and English. I was happy but I just could not manage the lack
> of money. Besides, I felt there was something wrong with the situation.
> When I was dressed improperly I was famous and now that I dress in the
> correct way I cannot work as a veiled star. Why should I hide while I dress
> rightly and reveal myself when I dress immodestly?! I should regain my
> name while working in an appropriate way. Besides, the veil is abundant
> in the street, and the screen should reflect this reality.[10]

She preferred not to return as an actress, but rather as a presenter. This
choice was made by several returnees because they considered it a less compromising field. By presenting a religious program, they felt more in control
of the issues dealt with in the program and less in direct contact with the
field of actors and actresses. Miyar al-Bablawi took a training course to work
as a presenter. She also took religious courses at a *daʿwah* institute and set her
sights on presenting a program on the Iqra channel. However, the management there decided not to let her work as a presenter. She was desperate and
had still not been able to refurnish the flat she inhabited with her son and her
mother. Then, she became acquainted with a producer who was looking for
a young veiled presenter for a religious program at Mehwar, a mixed variety
channel. Most veiled actresses and presenters like ʿAfaf Shoʿib, Shahira, Soheir
al-Babli, and Soheir Ramzi were much older. The idea of a veiled presenter at
such a mixed channel was not easily received. However, the initiators had a
clear mission, as Miyar explained:

> On Iqra everyone is religiously committed and pious [*multazim* and *mu-
> tadayin*] [. . .]. If you are a religious person you watch a religious channel.
> If you like pop music you open a pop channel. But we wanted to dissemi-
> nate a principle. *Daʿwah* should not be performed from the mosque. Who-
> ever is going to the mosque will pray. We wanted to reach people who are
> in the disco, but want to pray. For that reason we went to a channel like
> Mehwar. They have video clips, films, songs, and advertisements and have

youngsters as their audience. Despite the opposition, we managed to carry out our idea for a religious program at Mehwar. God guided us inside the channel.[11]

After that, Miyar al-Bablawi presented a talk show on various topics related to religion and social issues to which she invited, as guests, sheikhs and scholars. People were invited to call and join the discussion or ask the invited guests questions. At the time I was watching Mehwar in Egypt, the Danish boycott over the *Jyllands-Posten* cartoons was raised, as well as topics such as "the mothers of martyrs." When I visited her again in 2006, she had made thirty episodes during Ramadan related mainly to the position of women in Islam or other matters of importance to women. Miyar al-Bablawi also worked as a model, wearing a beautiful orange veil, for some fashion magazines. She is very conscious about the importance of wearing beautiful forms of veiling and discussed this as a form of calling to Islam. It should be within religious confines, but tasteful. "I look beautiful; I wear chic dresses and a beautiful *higab*. I dress as God has commanded. This is the point we want to transmit to the veiled women. It is so easy to wear a black *tarha*, shawl, and a black *abaya*, coat, no makeup. But this is not Islam. So I started with a small *higab* in a beautiful color and people liked it. They liked my new look."[12]

Miyar al-Bablawi also worked in some religious series like *Imam al-Nisa'i*, *al-Mar'a fi al-Islam | Women in Islam*, and *Imam al-Du'a*, about Sheikh al-Sha'arawi. She preferred presenting talk shows, but due to financial circumstances she accepted some offers for series. Most religious series are historical plays, a tendency she does not like. They are usually in standard Arabic and do not relate to contemporary issues and problems. She would rather play the role of an ordinary — veiled — mother, student, or professional, of which there are many in the Egyptian streets. "In the past if someone wore the veil that meant *khalas*, she is no longer of this world. But nowadays if someone is not veiled you wonder whether she is perhaps a Copt [Christian]. At all levels of society, poor and rich, they wear it. Everyone can dress in a fashionable way within the limit of the religious teaching, for example, jeans with a long blouse and a shawl."[13] At the time of the interview, she expressed the wish to play a veiled role in a social drama that would stimulate the trend of fashionable veiling. Recently she started to work in social drama (see Chapter 9).

Miyar al-Bablawi experienced veiling as a serious responsibility. As a public veiled star, she felt any mistake on her part would harm Islam. A clear example of this was her strategy with regard to divorce and marriage. The first divorce was in full daylight and widely publicized in the media. The second time, however, she left in silence:

I left everything behind so that people do not have this image of a *hagga* and *muhagaba* and she has a case in court! People will say, "You see . . . all *muhagabat* are like this." If I make a mistake they say, "the *muhagabat*," not Miyar; in the past they said Miyar, but now it is "you see what those *muhagabat* do!" . . . I was in a plane lately and there was turbulence, people took my hand and asked me to read Qur'an for them. I have become something like a holy figure for the public, *muhagaba, muqadisa.*[14]

Recently she met a man in whom she was interested. However, she could not show her interest.

In my heart I wanted to talk with him, but I could not. I wanted to give him a short blink, but people would watch what the *hagga* was doing. I begged God not to let this man leave without noticing me. He finally addressed me in a polite way. I felt like talking with him. I am only thirty-two and a woman needs a man . . . I replied in a soft voice. You can't address him warmly like "Hey, how are you?!" People are watching: is she smiling? Is she giving him something?[15]

It shows the great care she has to take, not only as a woman, but as a veiled public figure, to deal with her reputation and the reputation of all *muhagabat*. It greatly structures the minute details of her comportment: how to talk, to walk, to dress; her facial expression; the tone of her voice, etc. "The veiled artist is put under unusually strict limitations," Miyar al-Bablawi remarked. What these limitations meant for the veiled actresses in their enactment of professional roles was to become a lively debate when four soaps of the veiled actresses were launched during Ramadan 2006. The "appropriate conduct for a veiled actress" proved to be a limiting force provoking some actresses to take off the veil and others to put on a wig. Miyar al-Bablawi also has experimented with a wig in her recent work on *Ayam al-Sarab*, a huge soap opera from the Gulf, a step for which she has reportedly "repented." These issues will be discussed in Chapter 9.

ART WITH A MISSION

When I returned to Egypt in 2008, I planned to concentrate my research on the return of the actresses, their art productions, and the new discourse that had become prevalent under the umbrella term "art with a mission," "*al-fann al-hadif*," which I had discussed in a more haphazard way in 2005 and

2006. I went to the annual book fair to see if any new books on the "repentant" artists, religion and art more generally, or perhaps even more specifically on "art with a mission" had been published. I walked into several stands of an obviously religious character, discussed my research topic, and asked the sellers if they had any new stuff for me. I was also looking for an issue of a certain Islamic journal for women and children, *al-Zuhur*, because one of the female leaders of a wedding band, whom I had interviewed, had given the magazine a lengthy interview with pictures (see Chapter 8). I stumbled by accident on the shop of the publishing house of *al-Zuhur*, and it had all issues except for the January issue I was looking for. There was, however, an issue that contained a notice of an annual conference the staff had organized on the topic "*al-fann al-hadif*" on April 7, 2007. After I had a lengthy talk with the saleswoman, she arranged for me to come back the next day, because the conference on *al-fann al-hadif* had been taped and she could perhaps bring me a copy on CD. She had to go back to the office first and ask permission from her boss. I returned the next day and was given a free copy of the January issue and the CD, and I was invited to the office to talk to the director-in-chief of the magazine, Mrs. Nur al-Huda Saʿad, who had organized the gathering on *al-fann al-hadif*. I had an interesting interview with her the next week. She provided me with a list of people who might be willing to be interviewed and had been guests at her conference. I managed to make appointments with a few of them, and the CD itself proved very interesting. Artists as well as young preachers and scholars gave their views on "purposeful art." The speakers were introduced by Miyar al-Bablawi.

For this section on "art with a mission," I will thus draw on the material of the CD, consisting of ten invited speakers and some small interviews by Miyar al-Bablawi with invited guests.[16] I also discussed the notion and productions of purposeful art with many others active in the field of art, particularly the veiled actresses themselves and producers. In addition, I spoke to several fans of the religious art productions.[17] Moreover, in order to locate the *fann al-hadif* project within the larger field of art, I talked to eight journalists who critically follow developments in the art scene in Egypt, several from Islam Online, *al-Fajr*, *Migallit al-Zuhur*, and *Masry al-Yawm*. Finally, I also interviewed twelve producers and artists, among them directors Dawud ʿAbd al-Sayyid, ʿImad al-Bahad, and Attiyat al-Abnudi, who are critical of pious art productions and experienced the negative consequences of the present conservative climate for their own work.[18]

The idea of *fann al-hadif* is not totally new in the Islamist movement. Hassan al-Banna, who founded the Muslim Brotherhood in 1928, already considered art an important field that could be useful for Islam. Al-Banna strove for a new form of art, which he labeled *al-fann al-hadif* (Tammam and Haenni 2005). Tammam (2004) also labeled al-Banna's art project *al-fann al-hadif al-mufid*, "useful purposeful art," strongly emphasizing that art should have a message and is not a purpose in itself. *Anashid*, first of a religious and later of a more political nature, and sketches—particularly by Masrah al-Ikhwan al-Muslimin / Theatre of the Muslim Brothers—were performed at their associations. It was a rather open form of art in which entertainment and participation by women were allowed (Tammam 2004). Due to the revolution of 1952 and the collision with the Free Officers in 1954, many Brothers were imprisoned and their cultural activities stopped. As a result of the growing influence of Wahhabi thinking, especially from the 1970s onward, the idea that art was (close to) *haram* gained ground (Tammam 2004).

However, outside Islamist circles the idea also existed that art could or should have a mission. I discussed the term "art with a mission" with the film director Dawud 'Abd al-Sayyid.[19] It was interesting to hear his reconstruction of the term. According to him this label was also used to denote the new realist genre during Nasser's reign. Realist productions at the time had the goal of raising people's consciousness and reforming society. The nationalist and Islamist projects are often understood in a contrasting and competitive light.[20] Yet the Islamist and nationalist projects regarding art and entertainment converge in their claim that artistic expression and diversion should have a purpose. Art with a mission can serve nationalist and Islamist purposes. In both cases the underlying idea is that art should have a mission. The crucial difference between new realist films and the current pious project is that the former aimed at national or social reform and the latter aim at moral reform. The Islamist ideas mainly differ in that their goal for art and entertainment is the moral improvement and the pietization of the believers' lifestyle (see also Schielke 2008).

The generally positive views on art among new preachers and *wasatiyya* thinkers, as outlined in Chapter 6, paved the way for the discourse on *fann al-hadif*. Moderate Islamist thinkers, such as al-Qaradawi and Muhammad 'Imara, laid the foundations for a generally positive attitude toward art. However, before art could be used as a source for spreading a moral-religious message, another step had to be taken. Preachers such as 'Amr Khalid transformed art into a project: a mission aimed at moulding society and individuals in line with the Islamic message. Religiously committed artists found in this discourse a source of inspiration to work out actual formats of art production in accordance with this project. As a result, from a discourse and an ideology, *fann al-hadif* was turned into a project, and finally into an artistic practice. For that reason, the people involved in the art-with-a-mission project are an interesting mix of thinkers, ideologues, preachers, and artists.

Fann al-hadif is not the only term used to convey the ideas behind "art with a mission" or "purposeful art." Also *fann al-nadif* (clean art), *fann al-multazim* (pious art), *fann raqi'* (uplifting art), *fann al-mabadi'* (art based on principles), *fann al-badil* (alternative art), and finally *al-fann al-islami* are current. The concept, however expressed, is in clear opposition with *fann al-habit* (lowbrow art). *Al-fann al-islami* as a label is becoming obsolete. It was used to denote the first generation of Islamists pioneering the field of pious art, among whom was the group around Masrah al-Qima / Theatre of Values, which started in 1991.[21] Many committed artists at present either avoid the term or stress that by Islam they mean a nonexclusive notion pertaining to Muslim civilization, including religious minorities.[22] In order to avoid misunderstanding, most people I spoke to refrained from using the adjective "Islamic" and emphasized the overarching morals and values of religious traditions that should be represented in art. Purposeful art is not necessarily Islamic and Islamic art can be without a purpose, the editor-in-chief of *al-Zuhur* magazine explained.[23]

Ahmad Mursi Abu Haiba, the playwright of the trilogy *Isha Ya Basha / Wake Up*, *Vietnam 2*, and *al-Shifra / The Code*, which was performed by Masrah al-Qima, claimed that troupe members never used the term Islamic for their theater. On the contrary, he had always opposed calling his plays "Islamic theater," although the label was attached to them nonetheless:

> We named it *"masrah al-hadif*," purposeful theater, *"masrah multazim,"* religiously committed theater, *"masrah raqi',"* uplifting theater, and values theater, *"masrah al-qima."* We never said Islamic theater. [. . .] There is nothing like Islamic theater. It is nonsense. There is Islamic economy because there are scripts in the Qur'an and Sunna that speak about it. But there is nothing specific about arts, just general verses about poetry or about the poets themselves, what is good and bad. [. . .] I believe art in every society should respect the standards of the society.[24]

The renowned actor Wagdi al-'Arabi—also connected to Theatre of Values— rejected all labels. In his view, art should always be based on principles, values, and beauty. To include these qualifications in the label would mark the art production as exceptional, and this would be counterproductive. He prefers to call the plays "comedy" in order not to frighten the audience. The public could associate "Islamic" theater with being boring, austere, and in contradistinction to fun.[25] Most informants considered "purposeful art" a neutral and more attractive label, because it avoids association with "overpoliticized" or "extremist" Islamists. Several artists use the label *fann al-hadif* to avoid the image of the pulpit, while still being able to express their moral stance.

The reasons why its advocates deem art with a mission important are various. First, they realize the extreme importance of art as a tool in fashioning society and individuals. They see art as a powerful channel for spreading moral-ethical messages. Not only can music captivate the hearts of its listeners, but also the little screen that has entered into every Egyptian home can be an influential medium for reform. Second, the field of art is much too critical to leave it to the present players of the cultural field. If art is left in their hands, the art scene will go on destroying the "moral fiber of society," "sell[ing] the souls of youth," and "corrupt[ing]" women and the family.[26] Third, the pressing need to develop an alternative is not only in critical opposition to the reigning *fann al-habit*, with its indecencies and obscenities, *fawahish*, but also to combat misguided views on Islam. Just as much effort as is expended to combat secular artists, who "cherish absolute freedom of expression," is directed at "religious bigots" who distort Islamic views on beauty and art. Religious scholars who "blast art without distinguishing between *fann al-habit* and *fann al-hadif*" are regarded as equally dangerous.[27] "Backward thinking," which contends that Islam and Muslims have nothing to do with beauty, should be uprooted.[28] They thus spend much energy in explaining the positive relationship among Islam, creativity, and art in order to combat strict views within the religious field.

In order to distinguish their views from Salafi ideas, they firmly base their ideas upon the *wasatiyya* discourse of moderate Islam. Yet the *fann al-hadif* missionaries argue beyond simply refuting the notion that Islam and art are incompatible, noting instead that Islam and art are organically linked. Several examples highlight this argument. First, they point at the imperative to beautify the mosque by which devotion is directly connected to beauty. Muhammad 'Imara explained: "I would like to highlight some features, which characterize our civilization, which is, in turn, informed by our Muslim religion. We are a community of believers (*ummah*), whereby its religion taught us the organic link between art and the mosque and devotion. It is said: 'Let people ornament every mosque.'"[29] Second, the Qur'an is the clearest example of beauty, which makes appreciating beauty a religious practice. As 'Imara lectured: "From its beginning to its end, [the Qur'an] expresses deep meanings by recourse to its verses, the apex of beauty. It is a Book that teaches people beauty."[30] Third, it is argued that God knows the basic constituents of man and that nothing beneficial to the human being is prohibited in Islam. Creativity nurtures human feelings, and for that reason it cannot be forbidden in Islam. Or, in the words of preacher Muhammad Hamid:

> Truthfully, one of the salient features that distinguish Islamic Shariʿa is that it is propagated by God who created man and knows what is good for him (*yuslihuhu*) and what is bad for him (*yufsiduhu*); God who knows the basic constituents of man: reason, body, feeling, and conscience. That is why the injunctions of Islamic Law address all of these [. . .]. Do not think that Islam or the Qurʾan prohibits creativity (*al-ibdaʿ*) or beauty, because, as we all know, creativity and beauty are the things that nurture feeling and conscience. That is why all the proofs employed by those who fault creativity are speculative proofs.[31]

Finally, the *hadith* "God is beauty and He loves beauty" is another indication of enjoying beauty as devotional practice. The idea is that God created beauty and in order to thank God for this blessing it is incumbent upon men to enjoy this beauty.[32] A person cannot be devoted to God and at the same time be incapable of sensing the beauty in this universe. Art and enjoying God's beauty are a devotional practice, and *fann al-hadif* is a means to implant pious dispositions into people, particularly the new generations.

The perceived organic link between Islam and art, going beyond the idea that they are merely compatible, was crucial for turning art into a mobilizational tool. The discourse of *fann al-hadif* transformed art into a (religious) pedagogical project. Most speakers and interviewees pointed to the power of art to rectify, uplift, and reform individuals and society. Purposeful art is a "source of noble values" that supports "the didactic role of the family," "enhances people's morality," "inculcates good values in youth and society at large," and rectifies the image of Islam.[33] All creative persons are influenced by the epistemological paradigm surrounding them. If this paradigm is Islamic, cherishing values and morals in accordance with the Shariʿa, the creative person will never create anything that contradicts Shariʿa or its ethics.[34] If the field of art is left to nonreligious people, all existing creativity will violate the Shariʿa. When artists use the power of art to Islamize society, all individuals will develop pious dispositions. *Fann al-hadif* thus encourages devotion, raises pious individuals, and helps to realize an alternative to the art currently fashionable. This pedagogical view of *fann al-hadif* explains its importance and makes it into a critical project. Or in the words of playwright and actor Ahmad Mursi: "Participating in the work of *al-fann al-hadif* is a vital choice for our community. If *al-fann al-hadif* does not prevail in our community, then it will be lost."[35] *Fann al-hadif* is crucial for creating pious subjects.

Several speakers at the *al-Zuhur* conference emphasized the religious aspect of *fann al-hadif* by defining it as "art that makes the human being thank God for his blessings of beauty in this universe"[36] or as "virtuous art that makes the believer God-fearing (*yitaqi bi Allah*)."[37] Actor Samih al-Sariti gave an example from the *hadith* of how art was already used at the time of the Prophet to instruct people in a subtle and nice way. He described how Hassan and Hussein witnessed a recent convert to Islam doing the ritual ablution in the wrong way. Instead of directly approaching the man and correcting his mistake, they staged their ablution as a performance to be witnessed and followed without offending the man.[38] Despite the religious emphasis, pleasure and enjoyment are not totally neglected. Art should provide "high pleasure," that is, it should motivate people to perform good deeds. Actor ʿAbd al-ʿAziz Makhyun maintained: "*Al-fann al-hadif* is neither depressing nor somber. Art should be cheerful; *al-fann al-hadif* should motivate people to excel and use their positive energy in a good way rather than wasting it on sensual pleasures that are evoked by *al-fann al-habit*."[39] Also, actor Wagdi al-ʿArabi's labeling of his plays as "comedy" suggests the wish to combine entertainment and morals.

The aim of the art-with-a-mission project—that is, the inculcation of pious dispositions, in contradistinction to liberal-secular sensibilities—was largely shared among Islamists. However, less unity existed within the Islamist movements regarding the translation of religious ethics into artistic practices. Whereas the secular field particularly criticized the *fann al-hadif* for using art to spread its moral-ethical project, the *fann al-hadif* missionaries particularly debated the appropriate aesthetic forms. Several artists felt uncomfortable with forms that remained too close to the moral or religious pedagogical message without taking the artistic format seriously. They felt they would not reach new audiences such as youth and the well-to-do if they did not fully explore the range of artistic opportunities. However, several forces, such as conservative censorship by Saudi sponsors, limited the creative development of the field. Accordingly, there was a tension between the ethical and aesthetic dimensions of the project. But before continuing with the debates among members of the *fann al-hadif* scene, I will first briefly turn to the critical views of directors outside the field of art with a mission.

According to secular producers and their secular artistic sensibilities, art should be totally disengaged from morality or religion. Producer Dawud ʿAbd al-Sayyid perceived art neither as a tool to promote morality nor as an instrument against morality. It should be located outside the scope of morals entirely. The *fann al-hadif* project is according to him "*tablighi*," "missionizing," whereas art's purpose should be to provide enjoyment because of its high creative quality. There should be total freedom of creativity and no limiting frame.[40] Most secular artists and producers agreed with this point of view. For instance, *al-Fajr* journalist Muhammad al-Baz argued that art is neither related to morals nor to preaching, so purposeful art is bound to fail.[41] Like several other secular art directors, Dawud ʿAbd al-Sayyid mentioned that there is only one measure in evaluating art: its quality. In short, they strongly criticized the present forms of art produced under the banner of "art with a mission" for a lack of creativity and for poor quality. They also attacked *fann al-hadif* productions for being imitative and in need of refinement and professionalism. Their emphasis, therefore, was on aesthetic quality, and they dismissed art in which ethics prescribe the aesthetic forms.

Several artists working within the field of art with a mission also felt the need to develop the *fann al-hadif* project from a strictly moralizing project into a professional form of art that balances ethics and aesthetics. Not only secular producers, but also several journalists who generally favor the development of art with a mission—including, for instance, contributors to Islam Online—criticized the current state of *fann al-hadif* as lacking in quality and creativity. The playwright, actor, and media man Ahmad Abu Haiba strongly expressed the need to move toward professional art with a mission. Although he himself started performing his plays within the circles of Islamist students in the early 1990s and selected the "actors" for their "right" religious views rather than for their acting skills, he has drastically changed his views and ardently pleads for an Islamic message expressed in a contemporary and artistic format. However, large professional productions and media need big money, which is invested neither by the Egyptian state nor private Egyptian investors, and thus he had to turn to Saudis for funding. Ahmad Abu Haiba has in the meantime repeatedly experienced the limits set by these sponsors whenever he produced contemporary forms of religious art. Abu Haiba not only left al-Risala because his ambitions were thwarted, but also his youngest endeavor, the Islamic pop channel 4Shbab, featuring "music and women" (see Afterword), has been turned into a conservative channel by the Saudi funders.[42] Despite the difficulties, the *fann al-hadif* productions in both music and visual media moved toward greater professionalization. The creation of contemporary Islamic formats such as moral-religious soaps and pop songs catering to audiences of primarily women and youth continued and crystallized, particularly in the second half of the 2010s.

In the next section, I will examine the emergence of a market for the pious productions among larger audiences. I will sketch the developments in Egyptian society that form the background for the *fann al-hadif* project: the growing religious sensibilities among the middle and upper classes and the move toward what perhaps could be labeled as a "post-Islamist" understanding of Islam among parts of the Islamist movement.

NEW RELIGIOSITY AND POST-ISLAMISM

From the second half of the 1990s onward, the piety movement has spread among large segments of society and has also become influential among the upper middle classes. After a period of violent clashes with the state and the severe repression that followed, the militant Islamists were largely silenced. The murder of tourists in Luxor in 1997 was a turning point. Many Egyptians were repelled by the continuation of violence in the name of Islam. Also, a group of younger-generation Islamists adopted principles of democracy and liberalism and founded parties such as al-Wasat (The Centre) and al-Islah (Reform). The broad pious current in its various guises has come to the surface more prominently—a development that is also reflected in academic research. I have described the development of a large parallel Islamic sector: the growing number of mosques and religious classes, religious charities, and Islamic schools; and the sale of commercial products such as religious booklets, taped sermons, and decorations. The landscape and soundscape of Cairo have taken on a more and more religious hue. Not only are prayer rooms more visible, but many shops currently carry religious names: al-Nur (the Light) for a pharmacy, al-Iman (Belief) for a grocery store, and Tawhid (Oneness or Monotheism) for a department store. Taxi drivers play Qur'an recitation in the car, sellers of religious booklets or random preachers hop on and off buses and metros, and during Friday noon prayers, streets are blocked by prayer mats. A large majority of women don the veil. Stickers on walls urge the unveiled to take this step, and specialized shops provide "*hijab* fashion." The possibilities of spending leisure time in a religiously appropriate way have increased as well: religious lessons, religious voluntarism, and Islamic charity, not to mention the growing number of TV outlets, both satellite channels from the Gulf and national Egyptian channels, providing sermons and religious talk shows. The Islamization did not only accrue from the Islamist sector, but also from the state. Bayat denotes the state "seculareligious" because it provides a conservative religious alternative to the appeal of Islamism to an increasing extent (2007b, 48). I have indicated already many instances of this in the 1990s, and this phenomenon continued after the turn of the century. For instance, in 2002 the holiday for the Feast of Sacrifice was extended, and the call to prayer was broadcast from Cairo's metro. The vice squad monitored the Internet for moral crimes and arrested 150 people in 2003 (Bayat

2007b, 168). The combined Islamization by the state and Islamists resulted in the spread of a conservative religiosity among large sectors of the population. This had been going on for at least two decades and was perhaps no longer remarkable, except that it had also started to influence the well-to-do.

The spread of the piety movement into the affluent classes of society is also captured by the notion "new religiosity." Many factors contributing to this development are not particularly novel. They are for the most part in line with the general pietization of everyday life among large segments of society, as has been described in the previous chapters and is illustrated by the life stories of the "repentant" artists. The novel development was not the pietization as such, but the class component. As Bayat also observed, what seems to be novel since the late 1990s is that "affluent families, the youth and women in particular, have begun to exhibit an *active* search for religious devotion, exhibiting an extraordinary quest for religious ideas and identity" (2002b, 23). I would like to look more closely into some aspects that might have contributed to the combination of religiosity and wealth, such as the return of wealthy migrants from Saudi Arabia, the role of the "veiled stars," and finally the messages of the new preachers such as ʿAmr Khalid that were specifically targeted at the well-to-do. The emergence of the "new religiosity" is particularly linked to this latter development. Upon reaching the upper classes, the form and content of religiosity transformed into a less austere and more comfortable style of religious conduct, also known as "*al-din al-laziz*," a nice or pleasant religiosity. I will begin the examination of religiosity and wealth with the migrants.

The returning migrants from the Gulf are particularly noted for the conservative lifestyle and mindset with which they presumably came back. Immersed in a Saudi way of life—a Salafi interpretation of Islam, lack of frivolous entertainment, and strict segregation of the sexes—the migrants became used to this lifestyle and its religious legitimization (see also Chapter 5). I heard this kind of reasoning quite often, particularly among those interviewees who strongly opposed the "creeping Islamization," and I became intrigued by it. In checking the *al-Ahram* archives for debates about the veiling of the stars, I was assisted by an Egyptian student who happened to have lived her youth in Saudi Arabia and discussed this theory with her. She indeed affirmed that returning to Egypt had been a great shock to her. She had to learn to talk to men—for instance, her university professors and male colleagues—without being embarrassed and shy to a degree that she did not dare to open her mouth or lift her gaze. Because she had been raised with sermons that declared most leisure activities *haram*, she had to learn to listen to music without feeling sinful, and to watch Egyptian films without embarrassment.

It took her several years to arrive at the person she had become when I met her: a lively, outspoken, and inquisitive student looking for possibilities to do her master's research. She was now a proponent of an open-minded interpretation of Islam, wore a fashionable veil with jeans, and was active in cultural circles—particularly the literary meetings of young writers that were, according to her, a new trend among youth. Whereas she confirmed the possible validity of the theory about the returnees, her own transformation partly negated it. I asked her to introduce me to other (young) people who had been raised in Saudi Arabia to discuss their youth in the Kingdom, their adaptation to Egypt, and particularly their views of and experiences with leisure activities in Saudi Arabia and upon returning to Egypt. I interviewed ten people in all, which of course is not a large or representative sample. I will for that reason use what they told me only as anecdotal evidence.

The picture I got from these interviews was rather mixed. They all stressed the big difference between the two countries regarding religion, family life, *ikhtilat* (mixing of the sexes), and the extent of entertainment. Entertainment was mostly restricted to shopping-mall visits, family venues, and listening to religious *anashid* at home. Yet some of the interviewees visited Egypt regularly in the summer and were accordingly acquainted with the latest songs and films. Public life in Saudi Arabia was more overtly dominated by religion, but according to some it was ascribable to local customs and not necessarily based on religious conviction. For instance, a veiled Saudi woman was not necessary a *muhagaba*, but perhaps instead *muhtashima*: not veiled out of conviction, but shy due to cultural expectations. The veil could be discarded outside of Saudi Arabia. The idea that the return migrants brought a Salafi influence into Egypt, in particular, was criticized as lacking in nuance by most of my interlocutors who had been raised in Saudi Arabia. They especially drew attention to the duality of trends inside Saudi Arabia, as well as among the returnees. They mentioned the fact that as a result of the strict climate, people could also try to "breathe more freely" and party or drink alcohol in private or abroad. The image of Saudi male tourists in Egyptian nightclubs is a favorite theme among Egyptians (see also Wynn 2007). Return migrants could, despite having been immersed in the Saudi religious lifestyle, break out of its confines at the earliest opportunity as well. As one of the interviewees expressed it: tendencies in Saudi society are extreme to both sides, that is, toward "religious fanaticism" and toward "corruption." The same could be said about the migrants who returned, several of them argued.

Thus, the conservative Saudi style of religiosity and views on leisure could be affirmed and practiced, or, on the contrary, denounced and rebelled against. However, all informants were used to a combination of affluent lifestyles with observance of religious practices. They were all rather well-to-do and middle-class and had experienced religiosity in a comfortable or even luxurious setting. The association of strict religiosity with slums like the Cairo quarter of Embaba was not familiar to them. Many return migrants settled in relatively well-to-do neighborhoods like New Cairo (Bayat 2007b) and mingled with the more secularized or passively religious Egyptian upper and upper middle classes. Return migrants have introduced religious classes and preachers into elite clubs such as the Shooting Club, have opened businesses with a religious flavor, and were important in the creation of the trend of large shopping malls (*mollat*), which sprang up in Cairo and provided spaces of air-conditioned luxury in the middle of the crowded city.

Another phenomenon that highlights the combination of religiosity and wealth and has exerted influence on the affluent classes is the veiled celebrities and pious stars themselves. Again, the argument is not merely that the pious stars inflected Egypt with a conservative morality that was imitated by their admirers. It is very difficult to investigate the concrete influence of the pious stars on fans (and critics). It has become clear, though, that they have received a lot of media attention from Islamist and secular media and have become touchstones for discussing different imaginings of the nation, piety, and femininity. Thus, they might have directly influenced the religious turn of their fans, although this is hard to verify in an exact way from my material. Whether and how people modulate themselves with regard to these examples is open to investigation. What the veiled stars did exemplify, however, is, again, the combination of wealth and religiosity that was a rather novel blending. What had initially amazed a lot of people and was stressed in the media was the fact that they were rich and became pious. It was reiterated often that "they left behind wealth for a pious lifestyle," thus reinforcing the disconnection between wealth and piety. Yet most stars remained rather well-to-do after their artistic careers, whether through marriage or by making a career in a religious niche or a comeback through Islamic media. They were well connected to the upper middle classes, and, as we have seen from the life stories of several of them, they were influential in spreading Islamic charity, as well as religious salons, among the well-to-do neighborhoods.

The "Islamic salon" is a clear example of upper-class religiosity. Whereas religious instruction already existed in the form of lessons in the mosques, in the late 1990s it was supplemented by lectures at the homes of the affluent classes. These lessons and religious gatherings were not only paths to individual ethical self-making. They also provided venues for religious ways of social distinction: the salons were forms of competition with regard to the fame of the preacher to be invited to the salon, the number of guests to be hosted and fed, and the religious knowledge and devotion in evidence there. It became fashionable among the middle and upper classes to host a weekly or biweekly salon. Also, going to Mecca—whether for the *hajj* or the lesser pilgrimage (*'umrah*)—could bring esteem to one making the journey, with respect to not only the number of times she was able to perform the pilgrimage and the luxurious circumstances of traveling and accommodation, but also with whom she went. Many artists went together and stayed in comfortable places, to the extent, even, that Miyar al-Bablawi told me during our second interview that she doubted whether the *hajj* from which she had just returned was valid due to the high level of comfort: they even had a sheltered place to stone the devil instead of doing this amid the crowded mass, which occasionally caused accidents. Religion thus became fashionable, "pleasant," and a measure of social distinction among the middle and upper classes.

The new preachers have been of particular importance in this blending of wealth and faith. In particular, 'Amr Khalid has become one of the most popular preachers among the well-to-do. As several authors have mentioned (Tammam and Haenni 2003; Murphy 2002; Abdo 2000; Wise 2003; Bayat 2002b, 2005b, 2007b; Holtrop 2004), 'Amr Khalid was liked for his clean and shaven modern looks, his accessible style of preaching in colloquial Arabic, and the content of his message, which catered particularly to well-to-do youth and women. One of his lessons addressed the topic "Youth and the Summer" (al-Shabab wa al-Saif), explaining to young people how to behave while enjoying their holidays on the Mediterranean beaches. He is also described as the "sheikh of the *rawshana*," referring to "cool," "hip," or "fashionable" groups of middle- and upper-class youth, or as a representative of the "Islamic chic" (Bayat 2002b, 23). It was rumored that he even influenced Mubarak's daughter-in-law (Wise 2003, 92–93). His ability to recruit followers from the ranks of the powerful and the elite made him dangerous in the eyes of the regime. This was one of the reasons behind the ban against his preaching. The same probably holds true for 'Abd al-Kafi, Khalid al-Guindi, and Yemeni preacher Habib 'Ali, the latter deported from Egypt in 2002 because he concentrated on preaching to the upper class, businessmen, and artists (Shahine 2002).

One of the main reasons 'Amr Khalid managed to create a following among the affluent classes had to do with the content of his message. 'Amr Khalid held that piety and prestige can go hand in hand and that wealth is no obstacle to reaching paradise. On the contrary, wealth is a sign of being chosen by God. It is incumbent upon wealthy Muslims to use their money to further the religious cause and to execute moral and religious responsibilities. Being productive and ambitious is a divine quality, and fortune is God-given

(Holtrop 2004). Patrick Haenni compares the success of messages such as that of 'Amr Khalid to a "Protestant ethic" or "theology of prosperity" (2005, 10), a comparison also made during an interview I held with director Da-wud 'Abd al-Sayyid.[43] Haenni, accordingly, labeled these kind of messages as "market Islam" (2005).

Another label mockingly attached to 'Amr Khalid's message is "air-conditioned Islam" (Tammam and Haenni 2003). The authors assert that the message by which the affluent classes are reached and which the well-to-do adapt to in their search for pious lifestyles has departed substantially from former Islamist understandings of piety. They summarize the background of the "lite preachers" as follows. Almost all come from secular parts of the educational establishment, they are young and from privileged backgrounds, they try to combine the "teachings of different cultural models with Islam, which then loses its centrality; and they claim to have broken both with official and political Islam. But the values of this trend are far from revolutionary. Instead they are the disenchanted, here-now gone-tomorrow yuppie values: hedonism, individual ease and consumption. We are moving away from the era of politics" (2003). Also Wise points at 'Amr Khalid's ability to stand with one foot in the "modern world of consumerism and globalization and the other rooted in the 'traditional' sphere of religious piety and rituals" (Wise 2003, 88).

This new form of religiosity—whether it is called "air-conditioned Islam," "Islam lite," "market Islam," or, as I came across in Egypt several times, "*al-din al-laziz*," pleasant religiosity—is perceived as an expression of the transformation of Islamism into "post-Islamism." As Bayat holds, 'Amr Khalid "exemplifies a transformation of Islamism into a post-Islamist piety— an active piety which is thick in rituals and scriptures and thin in politics" (2002b, 23). The term post-Islamism was introduced in a 1996 essay by Ba-yat to describe the shift in realities within the Islamic Republic of Iran. The notion was taken up by other scholars primarily to indicate a shift in attitudes and strategies of Islamist militants in various Muslim countries and among Muslim minorities in Europe (Bayat 2005b, 5). Post-Islamism is a term now used by Roy (2004), Bayat (2002b, 2005b, 2007b), Kepel (2000), and others (Stacher 2002; Tibi 2008) to denote slightly different but interlinked developments in the Islamist movement. Roy links post-Islamism to the individualization and privatization of Islam (2004, 97–99). Post-Islamism is not directed at reconstructing the state but at the re-Islamization of individual practices. This view stresses the turn from "religion" into "religiosity" and focuses on the development of new forms of piety and religiosity in countries such as Egypt. This take on post-Islamism is related to a fragmentation of religious identity and authority and a blossoming of new and different forms of religiosity and religious movements (2004, 3). In Roy's description of post-Islamism, religious lifestyle rather than political aspirations are emphasized. These changing religious sensibilities in Egypt and the development of post-Islamist religious taste cultures have been described above and were crucial for the development of pious art markets.

Bayat and Kepel primarily relate post-Islamism to political transformations—that is, the moderate turn of Islamist movements away from violence or rigid doctrinal views toward a fusion of religion with democracy. Post-Islamism does not mean the end of Islamism, but a reformulation of Islamist discourse from within the Islamist movement. Bayat describes post-Islamism as a condition and a project. Among the social and political conditions that gave rise to post-Islamism was a period of trial and error that induced Islamists to reformulate their views. As a project, it aims to reconcile "religiosity and rights, faith and freedom" (2005b, 5). Post-Islamist movements acknowledge "ambiguity, inclusion, and compromise in principles and practice" (2005b, 5), which is a departure from religious and political discourse emphasizing exclusivism, universalism, and monopoly regarding rights of religious minorities and women.

Bayat (2007b) evaluates the Egyptian post-Islamist movements—in comparison to Iran's—as rather weak. By the late 1990s, Iran experienced a post-Islamist turn, while in Egypt Islamism witnessed a "growing fragmentation, accelerated economic and cultural globalization, and a 'secularreligious' state pushing for a 'passive revolution'" (2007b, 48). Islamism particularly changed from a political project challenging the state "to one concerned with personal piety, ethical concerns, and global malaise" (2007b, 146). Accordingly, the trend of conservative religiosity and piety, engagement with personal salvation, ethical enhancement, and self-actualization appeared to be the chief heir of political Islam. The establishment of the political party al-Wasat in 1996, though, signaled the emergence of a "post-Islamist" tendency, albeit weak and marginal compared to conservative forces (2007b, 174). Al-Wasat did not get official recognition, and the Muslim Brothers distanced themselves from the project. Yet some of the founders of al-Wasat continued by establishing a nongovernmental organization, the Egyptian Society for Culture and Dialogue, which was officially registered with the Ministry of Social Affairs. The society's declared purpose was "to promote greater freedom of expression, a culture of pluralism, national pride, and civilizational identity through conferences, publishing activities and development work" (Utvik 2005, 293–294). Intellectual movements such as the *wasatiyya* trend (see Chapter 6), which had influenced the outlook of al-Wasat's founders, were also a clear departure from Islamist thinking, yet, according to Bayat, their social impact remained negligible (2007b, 178). Egypt's intellectual life of the period could, for the most part, be classified as one of "deep stagnation" (2007b, 178).

The nonexistence of a pluralistic political landscape and the dominance of a conservative passive Islamization were due not only to the developments within the Islamist movement—or more accurately, its lack of evolution toward a lively post-Islamist discourse of democracy, rights, and pluralism. They were due also to the state's policies. In addition to the state's having its own Islamization project, the regime severely repressed all kinds of political activism, whether from the direction of Islamists, liberals, human rights activists, or bloggers. The policy of neoliberalism led to the privatization of significant sectors of the economy. The material, social, and economic conditions in Egypt worsened, leading to demonstrations and social unrest against rampant inflation and severe human rights violations. The call for democratic reform started to surface around 2004 with the movement for change, Kifaya ("Enough"), and the establishment of the Ghad Party. The oppositional Kifaya movement triggered demonstrations in 2004 that broke the people's fear of protesting against the government (Abaza 2010, 33; Bayat 2007b, 183).

We have thus seen two different understandings of post-Islamism. Post-Islamism, understood in the meaning of Roy as a new form of religiosity, clearly came to the fore in the late 1990s in Egypt. With regard to Bayat's notion of post-Islamism as a political project, I partly concur with Bayat's depiction of the marginality of its political influence in Egypt. Yet I think his analysis better reflects the realities of the first half of the new decade than the second half. Besides, while the impact of the *wasatiyya* discourse within the political field might be rather weak, in the field of art I think it had a significant bearing. "Post-Islamist thinking" within the art scene is not only related to the *wasatiyya* discourse. The emergence of post-Islamist thinking, and particularly the lifestyle that it entailed, should also be understood against the background of global market forces. The development of the new religiosity among the upper classes created a demand for pleasant religious art. The development of market forces, neoliberal state policies, and globalization more generally all affected the post-Islamist pious taste cultures. The development of market forces within the field of pious art will be sketched in Chapter 8.

(EIGHT)

Halal *Weddings and Religious Markets*

I n this chapter, I will focus on the trajectory of male artists by presenting the story of singer Mustafa Mahmud. In the second section, I will present one of the ways the artists have come back to the field of religious art by examining the development of religious wedding bands and religious songs. In the final section, I will discuss the emergence of religious markets and the influence of globalization in Egypt in the first decade of the twenty-first century.

THE (SPIRITUAL) BIOGRAPHY OF SINGER MUSTAFA MAHMUD

When I did my research about popular weddings in the late 1980s, there were some incidents of *"sunniyyin,"* breaking the musicians' instruments or chasing the dancers off the stage. Some neighborhoods known as Islamist strongholds, such as Embaba, were avoided by the popular entertainers of Muhammad 'Ali Street. When I returned in 2005, I went with my former assistant Sayyid to visit some old acquaintances in the Muhammad 'Ali Street to hear the latest news. I was particularly interested to know if some of the musicians had become involved in the "Islamic alternative" — that is, the Islamic wedding (*farah islami*) or Islamic wedding procession (*zaffa islamiyya*) — which proved hardly to be the case. We went to a tiny office for wedding processions with many colorful tambourines piled up on both sides and talked with a former bagpipe player, now the owner of the office.[1] He claimed that the religious weddings also existed at the time I did my research, but that the demand had increased considerably. He was now asked to perform the religious procession once every ten days, although the regular processions, such as the Nubian style, were still in favor. I asked him whether it was possible to witness a few of the religious processions, but he was not very eager. He instead wanted to organize an Islamic *zaffa* for me personally that I could film, of course paying the full amount of money for this staged event. It showed the extent of commercialization that had inflected the scene. This was not a new phenomenon, because competitive market forces became increasingly important since the 1980s, when the open-door policy of Sadat started to influence Muhammad ʿAli Street (Van Nieuwkerk 1995).

Sayyid took me to Bab al-Shaʿriah, one of the favorite spots for musicians to gather and chat before work. On the way we tried, without success, to contact the person in charge of the *"salit al-munasabat,"* annex to the mosque, because "the venue for special occasions" was potentially a location for Islamic weddings. Sayyid introduced me to one of the musicians, Muhsin, praising his religiosity by pointing at his *"zibib,"* literally raisin, a black spot on the forehead from frequent prayer and a widely acclaimed sign of piety among men. Muhsin explained that generally people who are very religious try to retire, because in the trade of popular music and weddings,

> people *yitaqi* [are devoted] to money. There is degeneration, but after all what counts is how to survive. There is a huge inflation so how can you feed your family? Everything is so expensive, food, school, everything. So I keep on working although the trade is *haram*. Well not everything is *haram*, part of it is *halal*. It is *sharʿi* [in accordance with the Shariʿa] to work at weddings because it is stated that you have to publicly announce a marriage, but I try to keep as far removed from the trade as possible.[2]

As with most men who are religiously committed and had doubts about the religious permissibility of their work, he decided to keep on working, albeit steering clear of some "sinful" aspects of the job, such as dancers, drugs, and alcohol.

Until now I have mainly presented the life stories of female artists who retired or returned with a veil to produce pious art, yet there are many men involved as well. Their stories are somewhat dissimilar to those of female artists. The rupture in the male artists' lives appears to be less profound, and their religious turn appears to have had fewer consequences for their careers. They have accordingly received less media attention. Most of them continued working and simply avoided the less appropriate fields of art or their questionable aspects, as musician Muhsin explained above. The necessity to provide for families also made the decision to keep on working acceptable even if the field was not totally "clean."[3] Some men, though, also decided to quit completely, such as actor Muhammad al-ʿArabi, husband of actress Hanaʾ

Tharwat, and actor Muhsin Muhiy al-Din, husband of actress Nisrin (Abu Dawud and Bayumi 1994). Hassan Yusif, husband of Shams al-Barudi, returned after a short while to produce religious productions (Abu Dawud and Bayumi 1994). I interviewed several well-known male artists who experienced a religious turn or worked in religious art productions: actor Wagdi al-ʿArabi;[4] playwright, actor, and producer Ahmad Abu Haiba;[5] Ahmad al-Kahlawi, son of the famous religious singer Muhammad al-Kahlawi and a singer himself, who after a period of singing in a variety of styles also turned to the religious genre;[6] singer Adham al-Saʿid, who had a personal crisis and decided to stop singing for religious reasons, but since then has returned to his band Wust al-Balad, a band popular outside the religious field of art production but with young *muhagabat* as fans;[7] and several lesser-known singers, producers, and actors. One of the rising stars in the field of religious wedding bands is Mustafa Mahmud.[8]

I interviewed Mustafa Mahmud in his office near Giza Square, next to the shop in which Islamic tapes with *anashid* and their popularized versions were sold. The interview was regularly interrupted by phone calls, as was often the case with other artists as well. It became an interesting exposé reflecting changes in the scene of Islamic weddings rather than a detailed life story. He briefly explained that from a young age he used to play several instruments, among which was the *urg*, electric organ. He performed at school parties, as well as at university. His father did not mind his musical performances, but discouraged him from becoming a professional musician and accordingly thwarted his ambition to enter the Music Institute. During his second year at university, Mustafa Mahmud became acquainted with Islamic groups. Mustafa was not very religiously committed, although he prayed, but after meeting with those groups he started to take religious lessons. He initially felt attracted to them; however, when he started to attend their parties he disliked them for their lack of artistic quality. "But the important thing was that I discovered that there was something like 'Islamic art' (*fann al-islami*)," he stated. After finishing a phone call, he explained:

> The *anashid* at that time were all from Afghanistan, and al-Sham, particularly Jordan, Syria, and Palestine. When an Islamic song from Palestine discusses from the beginning till the end the *jihad*, death, martyrdom, and all aspects of the struggle, it is natural. The same for Afghanistan, but Egypt is different! The songs that came to Egypt—and there were many because lots of Egyptian believers listened to them—did not correspond to our lives. Our problems are different, the form of our struggle differs; even the shape of our religiosity is different. It strengthened our commitment

to the Palestinian cause and I think it might even have helped to create movements that went into the direction of violence. All those songs talk about religious zeal, *jihad* and death. In Palestine, OK, they have the right to defend their land. But in Egypt . . . ! In the beginning I went along with these songs, unfortunately, but when I started to think what I really wanted to make myself, I realized this was not what I aspired for at all.[9]

After another phone call Mustafa explained how difficult it initially was to develop his own style. Even using his own name as a singer instead of the imported practice of using "Abu Kaza" (or "Abu whoever") — the habit of naming persons as "father of" that is common in Jordan, Palestine, and Syria — was difficult.[10] "So I had to develop my own style, religious but with topics that addressed Egypt and Egyptian youth." Mustafa Mahmud thus tried to develop his own religious style, about local problems and themes, in colloquial Arabic. He also chose to sing under his own name instead of "Abu Whoever" and put his image on the cover instead of an abstract deperson-alized picture.[11] The songs were thus vernacularized with regard to the lan-guage, locally connected with respect to themes, and personalized by using the singer's own name and image.

An alternative to the politicized *anashid* were the religious wedding songs. He started to work at Islamic weddings at the beginning of the 1990s, the time when the first Islamic wedding bands such as al-Nur and al-Shuru' devel-oped. Mustafa Mahmud explicated that "everything with regard to Islam is political in Egypt because of the relationship with the security police," a rela-tionship that is "partly pleasant and partly not so pleasant," as he put it mildly. Further, he said, "the weddings were a breathing space for the religious people [*mutadayinin*], an outlet for those who wanted to perform Islamic art. For a long time it was the only place where you could perform that. Religious persons are also allowed to celebrate their wedding the way they like and the security cannot prohibit this. On the one hand there are a lot of security police, but on the other hand it is a wedding party [*farah*]. [. . .] So what can they do?! [. . .] I started to make songs for the weddings and became famous for the Islamic flavor of my work."[12]

Mustafa Mahmud worked as a singer from the early 1990s till the begin-ning of "the satellite and 'Amr Khalid," as he put it, when the Islamic genre received an impetus and he founded his own band al-Wa'd / Promise, around 1997. An article on the website Islam Online in 2004[13] mentioned that by that time he had performed at a thousand religious processions with his band. I witnessed the performance of his band at a very expensive venue in the gated city outside Cairo, Dreamland. Whereas the women were entertained in a separate *sala* by the female band Sondos (see below), the male guests had their own venue with the large band al-Waʿd. Mustafa Mahmud has grown into the lead singer of one of the few prestigious Islamic wedding bands in demand by the upper middle classes. He has in the meantime also produced several tapes, among them *Medinit Salam / City of Peace* and *Baʿd al-Samt / After the Silence*.

Reflecting on the changes in the scene of Islamic weddings, he nicely illustrated the social and religious transformations toward post-Islamist sensibilities in Egypt, as outlined in Chapter 7, by saying:

> The last ten years the phenomenon of Islamic weddings began to increase. It is related to the form of religiosity in Egypt. Every period has its own modalities of religiosity. Twenty or twenty-five years ago there were forms of violence, and religious people were segregated from society. This was mirrored in the style of art they produced. Islamic art—or whatever you would like to call it—was very different from mainstream art. When I began, it started to approach the arts a bit. I personally have been influenced by different genres of music my whole life. When I became religiously committed [*iltizamt*], I did not listen to *anashid*, or whenever I listened to them, I did not enjoy them. I myself was one of the first to make this rapprochement between art and Islam. What is the problem if we use instruments? What is the problem if we discuss several topics? Why should we only address religious topics, or the Prophet? My art caused a shock among believers because it was not what they had become accustomed to. But as I explained to you, twenty-five years ago the religious people were very segregated from ordinary people. Lately they are more close to society through new preachers such as ʿAmr Khalid. And naturally if believers approach society and ordinary people, they become lighter [*akhaf*]. It simply does not work if you like to become friends with society, with its habits and thoughts, to keep a strict religiosity! So they came very close to society, became lighter, and were accepted by people. And the people who were not religious also became religious, but a moderate, light, pleasant—or whatever you would like to call it—type of religiosity. This in turn affected the religious people, who became less and less strict. They as well lightened up.[14]

The development of *fann al-hadif* was according to him related to this development of the nice and light religiosity (*al-tadayyun al-khafifa al-gamila*):

> In my view the matter is not to produce overtly religious art. For me everything I do is Islamic art as long as it is good and beautiful. I can explain

this without reference to any philosophy: my art accords with Islam a hundred percent, but others unfortunately insist that Islamic art only addresses Islam, God, and the Prophet. I know a hundred songs that have no mention of Allah and are in my view a hundred percent Islamic. I insist on that. I don't know who coined the term "art with a mission," but I think it is related to the opening up [*infitaha*] of religion. Everyone will say they make *fann al-hadif.* No one admits doing "*fann al-commercial.*" There is competition; everyone wants to present respectable art. So art with a mission is an expression of the increased openness of believers.[15]

Art with a mission is a neutral term and in line with the nice and pleasant religiosity, catering to diverse audiences including the well-to-do classes that would, perhaps, react adversely if it was called Islamic art. In that sense it is directly related to the development of (religious) markets, particularly among the middle and upper middle classes.

Mustafa Mahmud illustrated the fragmentation within the religious market between those who insist on strict religious art and those who prefer the lighter variant, as well as the bands' solution to this issue. The debates mainly focused on the permissibility of the female voice and the use of instruments, except for the *duff,* the tambourine, which is generally held as permissible in Islam. Al-Waʿd is an all-male band. Therefore, the issue of the female voice was not a practical issue the band members had to deal with:

> The debates about the voice of women and the use of instruments show the different forms of religion in society. As I told you in the beginning, Islamic songs should only be in standard Arabic, but I prefer the Egyptian dialect. Let alone the use of instruments. How can you make Islamic songs while using instruments?! But I developed them with instruments and with a quicker rhythm. Well, he believes he is right and so do I. With the development of the lighter religiosity, however, this issue has become less important. [. . .] But if someone comes and demands, "We want a wedding, but we do not want any musical instrument," then I perform without any instruments. I ask him to respect my vision, so I respect his view. It is my work, he is paying me, and I deliver in exchange what he demands. Of course I am free to say yes or no, but I feel I am more sincere if I respect him.[16]

The solution of performing on demand with or without instruments is a common solution among bands and producers of tapes. This nicely illustrates the existence of Islamist and "post-Islamist" taste cultures among audiences that are catered to, "on demand," by the same musical band.

The opening up by religious audiences not only caused a split between Islamist and post-Islamist taste cultures, it also dissolved the lines demarcating the religious and nonreligious markets. Mustafa Mahmud reflected on the latest development in the scene of religious weddings and explained:

> The huge gap that existed between religious weddings and normal weddings also decreased. Now there are believers who organize a wedding but do not organize an Islamic wedding. They can ask a respectable singer. With ʿAmr Khalid there are now also many artists who have become influenced and they are "*nidif*," clean, like in clean cinema [see Chapter 9]. Or among sportsmen there is now a climate of nice religiosity. So there still are very religious weddings, but many have become lighter. A religious person can ask normal singers who are respectable: those who do not bring a dancer or those who have become religious themselves and sing some religious songs. It now happens that singers of whom it is not known that they are religious or respectable perform a religious song! They sing in Ramadan [. . .] Saʿd al-Sughayyar, Hakim, ʿAmr Diyab, Tamir Hosni, almost all singers have a religious song and they are considered slightly religious. Because they are religious they can be invited. So the segregation in our branch has disappeared and that exerts influence on us. [. . .] There is a public that has opened up to the extent that they might no longer ask religious wedding bands. But people who go in the direction of religiosity also go in the direction of Islamic weddings: The new people who become religious come to us! So Islamic bands or at least Islamic songs at weddings still have a strong presence. We thus lose a part and we win a share of our customers, to use commercial language.[17]

At present there is thus a wide range of customers, within and outside the Islamist circles, looking for "clean," "appropriate," or "Islamic" forms of entertainment at weddings.

ISLAMIC WEDDING BANDS

Mustafa Mahmud related his personal experiences and observations with regard to the developments in the scene of religious weddings from its beginnings until the onset of the latest market pressures. I will now try to reconstruct the transformations in the scene of religious wedding bands using interviews with other players in the field and my own observations of Islamic weddings. I interviewed four male bandleaders or lead singers, two female bandleaders, a manager of a club that also hosts religious weddings, an impresario, a producer of religious wedding song cassettes, and two producers of (religious) video clips. Besides that, I visited eight religious weddings and talked with the band members other than the leader, as well as with the wedding guests and the couple. I also discussed Islamic weddings with several young Egyptians, among whom ten were raised in Saudi Arabia. In addition, the website Islam Online had an interesting dossier on Islam and art containing several articles on the development of Islamic songs and wedding bands.[18] Since I had witnessed many nonreligious weddings in the late 1980s (Van Nieuwkerk 1995), I could easily observe the difference in style and corresponding matters of etiquette.

As Mustafa Mahmud explained, there were two genres of *anashid*, the political-religious *anashid* and the wedding songs. The early political-religious *anashid* date back to the early days of the Muslim Brothers. The *anashid* accompanied demonstrations, meetings, religious occasions, and celebrations like the birthday of the Prophet and Islamic New Year. Although *anashid* have Sufi origins, these *anashid* were different in style regarding rhythm and instruments, as well as content, particularly the political character of the lyrics. As happened to the early *fann al-hadif* of the Brothers in general, the *anashid* also were almost silenced in the period of repression between 1954 and 1973, except for some lyrics describing the suffering in prison (Tammam and Haenni 2005). The *anashid* reemerged under the student unions, which were initially dominated by restrictive interpretations on Islam and art, but eventually moved toward a more receptive attitude toward music. Since 1987, several music festivals were organized to support the Palestinian cause, resulting in the revolutionary-military genre Mustafa Mahmud described. Since 1992, the *anashid* groups that had been founded around 1989 freed themselves from "the ideological dominance of the Brothers" (Tammam and Haenni 2005). The influence of market forces became more important in the further development of the *anashid* than the relationship with the Muslim Brothers and the state. This provided the condition for the development of the wedding *anashid*. In this section I will only discuss the transformations in the Islamic wedding songs and not the religious-political *anashid* outside the wedding context (see Sa'id 2001; al-Kafawin 2001; Tammam 2004; Tammam and Haenni 2005).

I asked several people, both performers and members of the public, what made a wedding "Islamic." This provoked different answers by my interlocutors. First, the Islamic label had to do with the level of commitment of the wedding couple and their guests. For instance, the bride and female guests are usually veiled — wearing either *higab* or *niqab*. However, not all veiled brides opt for Islamic weddings. Therefore, other features are important in creating an Islamic ambience as well. Second, there is a whole range of etiquette and implicit rules that distinguish (popular) weddings from religious weddings with regard to behavior, time, and money. Obviously, there is no alcohol or hash, and there is no mixed dancing or forms of "sexually suggestive dancing" resembling belly dance. Dancing at Islamic weddings does exist: men might take the groom on their shoulder, or clap while circling around him. At all-women parties, women can dance among themselves or with the bride performing a communal row dance. Yet forms of improvised solo dance — "*raqs sharqi*," "Oriental dance" — characteristic of nonreligious weddings, are largely absent. Religious weddings end relatively early and are not celebrated until the hours after midnight, because the guests should have the opportunity to pray the morning prayer. All-female wedding parties stop around ten p.m. There is also no system of *nu'ta*, tips given by the guests to the "owner of the wedding." The competition among men in tip-giving, the amount of which was shown and publicized, often resulted in quarrels (see Van Nieuwkerk 1995). This habit was frowned upon and abstained from at nonreligious middle- and upper-class weddings and is nonexistent at Islamic weddings.

In addition, an important defining feature of religious weddings is a degree of gender segregation between the male and female guests. Gender segregation can take many forms. The most obvious is two separate parties. For instance, I visited a lower-middle-class segregated wedding where the male guests were entertained with a band and the female guests — separated by a brightly colored cloth — had a DJ installation and danced among themselves. At a (lower)-middle-class wedding in the venue for special occasions of a mosque, I witnessed the female band Basmit Andalus for an all-female group of guests. At one segregated upper-class party I visited in the luxurious suburban Dreamland, the male and female guests had separate venues (*sala's*), and both parties had bands of entertainers with extensive shows, al-Waʿd for the men and Sondos for the women. The female guests could remove their veils, exhibit their fancy dresses, and dance freely among themselves. In the same venue, I witnessed another wedding where the women were entertained by Sondos and the men had a famous preacher who could be followed by the women as well on a large screen. Sondos also performed in a hotel for a small group of women attending a middle-class wedding. At the segregated weddings the female band members usually stop their performance when the groom enters the room to greet the bride or sign the wedding contract, causing disturbance and nervousness among the female guests, who have to recover themselves. Not all "Islamic" weddings are celebrated in two physically separated spaces. Several religiously committed young people I interviewed did not like segregated Islamic weddings, because in their view it should be an inclusive, mixed family affair. Mixed weddings can still be labeled "Islamic" if the female guests are veiled and share the table with their male and female relatives and avoid mixing with unrelated men. At mixed parties women usually refrain from dancing, although I witnessed an "Islamic wedding" where women danced. I was told, though, that it was uncommon and only older women directly related to the bride and groom were allowed to dance at mixed parties.[19]

However, even forms of gender segregation are in themselves not defining features of religious weddings, because popular weddings of the 1980s could also enact forms of segregation, whether separate rows for women or the custom of women leaving the party, after midnight, to male guests. Yet this was often the signal for the party to be heated up and for (more) dancers to appear on stage. Therefore, the form of entertainment and propriety of the style of entertainment are a crucial defining feature in labeling the weddings as Islamic: no belly dancers, female singers, or the common "indecencies" going on at popular weddings, but respectable artists who stay within the religious confines with regard to the style of music and songs they perform, the instruments they use, and the wordings of their songs. Mixed parties of an Islamic character were accordingly primarily defined by the style of entertainment that is performed. If the songs are "proper" and performed by an "Islamic" band that plays "suitable" music or performs "decent" shows, it is defined as *zaffa islamiyya* (Islamic wedding procession) or *farah islami* (Islamic wedding party). As I will elaborate now, what counted as "decent" and "Islamic," though, has changed over time.

Islamic weddings started probably around the 1980s as sober parties consisting of a short religious ceremony attended by male guests, after which the male and female guests divided into two separate venues to celebrate. They sang religious *anashid* or other lyrics praising the Prophet and played the *duff* among themselves. After they ate some snacks or had dinner, the party was over. The present elaborate form with entertainment and festivity is a more recent phenomenon of the early 1990s. The embellishment is due to several factors. First, the general opening up of the Islamist discourse toward art, particularly the views of al-Qaradawi as well as 'Imara (1991; see Chapter 6), was mentioned several times as a turning point (see also Sa'id 2001). One of the bandleaders called al-Qaradawi the ultimate authority who settled the debates on music, making it possible for devoted Muslims to practice music professionally.[20] Mustafa Mahmud also related that most members of the

Islamist movement used to consider music *haram* and situated the turning point around 1993—that is, the time that important religious scholars declared listening to music permissible (in Zayn 2001). Second, the rapprochement of parts of the Islamist movement with society, as Mustafa Mahmud described, was also an element, which is emphasized in the analysis of Hussam Tammam (2004), a journalist and expert on the Muslim Brothers. He argues that the overture of the Muslim Brothers to the Egyptian population necessitated approaching the taste and mentality of the Egyptian streets. This made leaving behind "Wahhabi" ideas on art and entertainment imperative. Third, the growing number of well-to-do believers eventually created favorable conditions for the flourishing of Islamic wedding bands, songs, and tapes. It stimulated the creation of an extensive religious market. Segregated parties also created a demand for female bands. Separate entertainment for women increased the costs of weddings, and the Islamization of the upper middle classes has accordingly been important in the further development of the female bands. Finally, there was a turnaround in the general security situation. Until the mid-1990s, the regime suppressed Islamist expressions, which hindered investment by professional production companies in Islamic songs (see also Zayn 2001). Therefore initially, the change in attitude and discourse among the Islamists did not easily translate into a flourishing practice of Islamic songs. The investment climate became more favorable after 1995.

There are thus several stages in the development of Islamic wedding songs. In the first stage, from 1989 onward, when the first bands were founded, they stayed close to the religious lyrics. In the second stage at the end of the 1990s, the genre diversified and professionalized. Finally, at present, a process of globalization and rapprochement between general popular styles and Islamic songs can be discerned. The initial stage developed in the Islamist student unions. Most bands I know of started at the universities at the end of the 1980s and beginning of the 1990s. The bandleaders I interviewed related that they started as students at the university. They were more or less involved in the Islamist student movement, the Jama'at Islamiyya. They performed sketches, sang, and played music for their colleagues at their wedding ceremonies. They felt, as was the case in Egypt generally, that weddings were such important occasions that they needed more attention and festivity than were customary in Islamist circles. However, the usual way with musicians, singers, and dancers from the wedding scene of Muhammad 'Ali Street was considered "vulgar" (Van Nieuwkerk 1995). Accordingly, they performed among themselves. This wedding style was very much appreciated by the guests. The student-artists were thus asked to perform at the weddings of the guests of their colleagues (see also Sa'fan 2004).

In 1989, the first Islamic wedding bands, al-Hada, Firqit al-Fath, and Fir-qit al-Nadi, started (Tammam and Haenni 2005). Al-Hada began in support of the Palestinian *intifada* and broadened their scope to include weddings, producing one of the first wedding tapes, *Afrah al-Hada | al-Hada Weddings.* They were followed by many others, including Basmit Andalus in 1994[21] and al-Waʿd around 1997. The all-female band Sondos started in 1995[22] and was one of the first female bands, followed by, among others, Banat Basmit Anda-lus, led by the wife of the bandleader of Basmit Andalus.[23] The female bands also started as groups of students at the university. They performed at the weddings of their colleagues in order "to bring happiness" to the couple.[24] In 2005, it was estimated that there were around fifty professional groups, among them five female bands, and dozens of nonprofessional bands (Tammam and Haenni 2005). The bandleader of Basmit Andalus, Muhammad al-Naggar, calculated that in 1994 and 1995 he had about 30 or 40 weddings a year. In 2005, he had 150 weddings. He estimated that in 2004 there were probably about 100 to 150 Islamic bands performing at weddings. Each of them had around 100 weddings — which in his opinion was a conservative estimate. He thus calculated that about 2 percent of all weddings — in 2004, 500,000 mar-riage contracts were registered — were performed in Islamic fashion.[25]

At the end of the 1990s, the demand increased, and the bands became more professionalized. The bands, starting as small groups with only "*halal*" instruments, began to experiment with other instruments and a more exten-sive repertoire. Which musical instruments are permitted is still under dis-cussion. Most bands added drums to the *duff*, and some also *urg*, synthesizer, and violins. Most bandleaders I interviewed took a practical stance toward this matter. It was up to the "owner of the wedding" to decide the range of musical instruments. The flute, however, was rarely added because this was considered *haram*.[26] The bandleader of Sondos decided to produce two ver-sions of their first cassette, one with only drum and one with other musical instruments added. The one with all instruments was more in demand (Saʿfan 2004). During the interview I held at a producer of Islamic tapes, al-Hayah Company, I was informed that it produced three varieties of wedding tapes according to market demand: voice only, with *duff* added, and with the full complement of instruments added. The "moderate" version, that is, voice and *duff*, was the most popular.[27] There had emerged also a religious market for songs in honor of *subuʿ*, the celebration for a seven-day-old baby; he also produced three varieties of these. The permissibility of the female voice is also under debate. As far as live performances are concerned, this is not an issue, because women only perform in front of women. At mixed parties there are only male performers. This discussion is thus directed at the cassettes that are produced by several Islamic wedding bands. Sometimes the female voice is replaced by those of very young children to accommodate religious markets (Tammam and Haenni 2005).

The repertoire evolved as well. From the religious genre of *anashid* it developed into "suitable songs," specifically catering to the occasion. As Mustafa Mahmud mentioned, several singers of wedding *anashid* looked for a vernacular form of songs that suited the happy occasion of a wedding. This developed into what is sometimes called the "*halal* song movement"—a label Mustafa Mahmud disliked, because it is not up to him to decide what is *halal* or *haram*. Islamic wedding bands, looking for songs to entertain the guests without offending them with "indecent" texts, initially started to rework existing songs. They took songs of famous singers and well-known melodies and restyled them to the Islamic context. Making songs *halal* could mean adding a few words or cutting out sentences that were not deemed proper, but also writing a new song to suit the occasion. Instead of singing about separation from a beloved girlfriend, the theme became love for the parents or husband. The importance of marriage was favored over lamenting divorce. "Going to the *mulid*," literally, a saint's day celebration, but also used to mean a chaotic place, was rephrased into going to paradise. The band Sondos restyled Sayyid Darwish's song in which improvident spending was encouraged into one praising generosity. They also adjusted a song for children of Sabaah and a song of Fayruz, which were already *halal*, to specifically address the topic of marriage and the bride. ʿAli Hamida's hit "Law Laki / Without You" was changed into "Islami / My Islam" (Saʿid 2001) and ʿAmr Diyab's lyric "*Min kam sana wa ana mayal mayal*," "For how many years have I been inclined (toward you)," into "*min kam sana wa ana dini al-Islam*," "For how many years has my religion been Islam" (Tammam 2004). The special song for the party for newborns, "Baba feen / Where Is Daddy," was transformed into "al-Muslim feen / Where Are the Muslims" (Tammam and Haenni 2005). These songs were liked among the guests because they were entertaining, well known, beloved, and now guaranteed *halal*. Many people I interviewed, though, also criticized this initial stage for lack of creativity and free-riding on the success of other artists. In the meantime, the bands have become more professionalized and create their own songs. They earn enough money to ask renowned songwriters to write suitable songs, or they compose their own lyrics. Several bands started to record their songs, and Sondos, Basmit Andalus, and al-Waʿd produced several cassettes.

The bands did not restrict themselves to music and songs only. They also added sketches and folkloric dance to their repertoire. They were looking for new forms of diversion in order to satisfy their publics. They had to refresh

8.1. *Islamic wedding: male folklore dance (photograph by author)*

their shows and keep on developing their repertoire, because the guests demanded constant change in style and appearance. Weddings are important occasions for social distinction and showing off. Therefore, the bands entertaining the upper classes have to restyle their show and outfits to cater to the demands of customers who want to provide their guests with something new. For instance, the band Basmit Andalus provides extensive male folklore dance repertoires similar to those of the regular folklore dance companies such as the National Troupe for Folklore, presenting the Upper Egyptian stick dance, the Suez fishermen dance (see Figure 8.1), Nubian dance, and the whirling dance called *tannura* (see Figure 8.2). These male folklore dancers are professional dancers hired by the band for the wedding. The bandleader can arrange for the dancers to perform, but can also perform without such a show. The female band members of Sondos and Banat Basmit Andalus also provide dances for female guests, with nice costumes and fitting veils, and do comedy sketches. These acts are performed by the regular band members and not by professional dancers and actresses. Sondos can provide wedding entertainment, for between 500 and 2,500 pounds, ranging from only a few young women with *duff* to extensive processions, dances, shows, and sketches. They can perform with a small group of young women doing simple forms of entertainment to keep the cost low or do the complete repertoire.

8.2. *Islamic wedding: male folklore dance (photograph by author)*

The professionalization raised the price of entertainment. However, Islam as (profitable) business was a sensitive issue among wedding bands. Monetary compensation can result in tensions between sincere pious intentions and the desire to be appropriately remunerated. Some of the religious wedding bands, particularly Sondos, have been under attack for asking a high fee, which was considered "un-Islamic."[28] The bandleader, though, intending to increase the degree of the band's professionalism, could see nothing wrong in investing in her business and earning a decent living from this work. She rhetorically asked why whenever something is "Islamic" it should be for free. "Is Islam against money?"[29] According to her, performing religious *da'wah* and earning money are not incompatible. She considered facilitating people in celebrating their wedding in an appropriate way a religious duty. It thus brings religious credit (*ajr*) and worldly money. Yet it clearly was a sensitive issue for several of her female band members. A few of them were slightly insulted when I talked about their performance as "work." They objected to the label "work," because they performed these "activities" for spiritual *ajr*, recompense, not for material gain. This was an important foundation of the respectability and religious status of their "work." Also, the families of the women performing at the wedding processions as *duff* players were uncomfortable with their daughters "working" at weddings, whereas they did not mind their daughters being engaged in "Islamic calling." Although it is perhaps tempting to analyze the religious scene as merely a profitable market, and religious performers as looking for material gain, for the artists involved the religious elements can be highly important. When I went with the young women of Banat Basmit Andalus to a distant wedding, it was interesting to see how—while still on the road—singing religious songs among themselves put them in the right pious mood for performing. Also, on the way back home, the *duff* player energetically kept on playing the instrument while the others sang the religious songs along with her, creating an atmosphere of enjoyment, relaxation, and spirituality in the microbus.

Yet, undeniably, whether individual performers are motivated by material or spiritual rewards, Islamic weddings have at present increasingly become a successful market. The religious market is no longer solely restricted to weddings, but increasingly includes other familial occasions as well, such as the *subu*ʿ, the "*higab* party" (Saʿfan 2004), people returning from *hajj*, and graduation parties. The profitable religious market has also attracted people from outside the religious realm. As we have seen above, Mustafa Mahmud experienced the entrance into the market of a host of singers who added a religious song to their repertoire. It was already fashionable, due to the growing pietization also among artists, to sing a religious song during Ramadan. Now many singers who perform at weddings, whether pious or otherwise, sing religious songs. Mahmud described the two-sided encroachment upon the Islamic wedding bands, from other performers and the customers. Several singers who usually sang nonreligious songs or even "vulgar" songs started to perform a few religious songs. The public became less strict with regard to the style of entertainment at their "Islamic" weddings. People feel that they can invite famous singers who have gained respectability and a religious image through an occasional Ramadan song.

As with all successful hype, *halal* songs and Islamic weddings invited imitation leading to a version of the songs and weddings diluted in their religious character or to a hybrid type of entertainment. The mixture of religious and ordinary can result from the preferences of either the performers or the wedding guests. To be a *multazim* wedding host, one does not necessarily have to invite an Islamic band. And if a religious or "appropriate" band is invited, the expectations of the guests can be different from those of the performers. I witnessed an interesting case of this where the band was stricter than most of the guests. At an all-female wedding party in a hotel, the first incident of embarrassment occurred when the groom delivered his bride to the venue and some of the female band members—including two *munaqa-*

bat—refused to raise their voices, that is, to perform, as long as the men were present. The band also refused to be filmed by the video crew when the bride was having her procession into the wedding *sala* and literally turned their backs to the camera. Filming is a sensitive issue at female Islamic weddings, and I was rarely allowed to take pictures. There are now female wedding photographers (*musawwaratiyya*) to make sure that the wedding is being filmed without causing any embarrassment to the female guests. Ensuring propriety also necessitated the development of the films by the *musawwaratiyya*. At this particular party, though, the photographer was male. After the photo incident, the female band members performed their repertoire of religious songs, which was appreciated, but some of the guests demanded regular wedding songs to dance to among themselves. Although it is not uncommon to dance at Islamic weddings, it usually is a communal stylized dance. At this wedding, some of the guests started to dance "*sharqi*," belly dance, which is not part of the Islamic etiquette. Some of the guests also started to sing some regular love songs. One of the female band members hesitated between laughter and disbelief about so much "ignorance on how to celebrate properly." Another protocol of the Islamic wedding was violated: the proper time. The bride arrived much too late—which is quite common at regular weddings—but the pious performers wanted to go home at a suitable time. They had arranged to work until 10:15 p.m. and had only worked for an hour upon reaching the arranged time. When they stopped, the guests were dissatisfied and asked for more songs. The band members felt ambivalent and hesitated between continuing their duty "to bring happiness" and the religious etiquette for the wedding—as well as for them personally—not to perform "late at night." They decided to perform another song. However, when one of the guests started to perform belly dance to the sound of the drum, the band decided that the party was over. The guests arranged a cassette recorder to play their own music and continued the party.

In this case, the guests demanded a "light" version of religious entertainment, with which the band members refused to comply, but other performers adapt their style. The style of entertainment increasingly in demand is of a pleasant and "post-Islamist" form. This type of entertainment can also be performed by people at the margins of or outside the *fann al-hadif* project: regular wedding performers singing religious songs on demand. However, religious singers also can try to come as close as possible to the regular wedding songs. One of the last interviews I held was with two young musicians of a religious wedding band.[30] They increasingly perform for a not overtly religious audience and have to inform the guests of proper conduct, such as no dancing by women at mixed parties. I asked if "even the mother of the bride," the one who is commonly understood to have an irresistible desire to express her happiness in dancing (see Van Nieuwkerk 1995), was not allowed to dance. He laughed, but insisted that if this happened they briefly allow her dancing, thank her, and then kindly seat her again. Still, they intend to cater to the "lighter" taste of their audience. After the interview, they made me listen to their latest song, which was still in the process of production. It made me laugh when I recognized the style of wedding songs I had heard so often in the late 1980s at popular weddings (*afrah baladi*). The composer clearly belonged to the regular nonreligious wedding scene. The young musicians still had to adapt some of the lyrics to norms of religious propriety, but the rhythm, style, and instrumentation apparently needed no adjustment according to the new post-Islamist religious taste culture.

RELIGIOUS MARKETS AND GLOBALIZATION

The religious lifestyle is still often understood as belonging to a culture of lower- or lower-middle-class taste. Accordingly, one of the remarks I often heard from those who do not favor Islamic weddings was that people opt for Islamic weddings for economic reasons rather than religious motives: they simply are more affordable than full-blown weddings and evaluated less for their conspicuous-consumption value.[31] While this could have been the case for the early simple style of wedding processions and parties, in the meantime the religious weddings have developed into expensive affairs — particularly those parties celebrated in two separate venues such as I witnessed in the gated community Dreamland, with two bands or a star preacher (live at the men's section and on a huge screen at the women's) and two crews of photographers, in addition to luxurious banquets for the male and female guests. The bands can adapt the number of musicians, scale of the shows, and length of their performance to the financial means of the customer. Religious weddings can thus be celebrated according to standards ranging from low-budget to high-class. Whereas, in conventional thinking, signs of religiosity are generally still associated with the (lower) middle classes, this no longer reflects social realities. For instance, upper-middle class professionals of De Koning's research remarked that certain leisure spaces are "very middle class, lots of *muhaggabaat*," although in fact many of their friends and family members are veiled, albeit in an expensive designer style of fashionable veiling (2009, 103).[32] It is therefore important to take class into account in the analysis of religious lifestyles, leisure, and consumption patterns.

The affluent religious-taste culture especially merits attention in understanding the Islamization of art and entertainment. First, as I mentioned in the volume Introduction, the phenomenon of the "repentant" artists is very much an (upper)-middle-class trend. It is not mirrored by the lower-class artists of Muhammad 'Ali Street, because they cannot afford the luxury of leaving "the trade" (Van Nieuwkerk 1995). Second, the affluent artists have also been instrumental in moving the new religiosity up into the higher circles. The pious example among class members invited emulation. Third, it has particularly been the Islamization of the middle and upper-middle classes that has resulted in a blossoming of upscale religious markets for art and entertainment. However, to characterize the new religious culture tailored to post-Islamist taste as simply the result of Islamization of the upper classes would miss an important part of the socioeconomic dynamics of Egypt at the turn of the century. The affluent classes were influenced by diverse sources of taste cultures and global flows of consumption and commoditization. In this section, I will sketch the political economy and development of the religious and global markets and their influence on the field of leisure and consumption. I will—in line with the topic of this chapter—particularly go into the upper segment of the (religious) market, although it goes without saying that this is a small, albeit wealthy, portion of the total market.

Egypt has witnessed a process of economic liberalization accompanied by political deliberalization during the last two decades (Denis 2006; see also Shehata 2010; Mitchell 1999; Singerman and Amar 2006). Economic liberalization had started already in the 1970s under Sadat, who opened the country to foreign and private investment. Sadat maintained an extensive public sector in order to appease the population by providing a range of social services and subsidies. Mubarak followed this dual strategy during the 1980s, but in the 1990s the economic situation worsened. Egypt was forced to accept loans from the IMF and the World Bank, and their accompanying structural adjustment program. The open-door policy had particularly encouraged the import of luxury consumption goods, paid for by revenues from tourism, the Suez Canal, remittances from abroad, and foreign loans, whereas productive investments lagged behind. In the 1980s, the drop in oil prices, combined with the return of labor migrants from the Gulf as a result of the Gulf War of 1990, led to high foreign debts. In 1991, Egypt had to implement the structural adjustment policies, entailing the state's withdrawal from social welfare, large-scale privatization, and further integration into the global market (Shehata 2010; Denis 2006; Mitchell 1999). Over the next fifteen years, the Mubarak government implemented important changes in the structure of the Egyptian economy, although gradually and often reluctantly, such as between 1999 and 2003 when economic reforms were suspended. Yet the process was speeded up after 2005 (Shehata 2010, 44). In 2006, 212 of Egypt's 314 public companies were privatized (Shehata 2010, 45) including those providing electricity, telecommunications, waste treatment, subways, and hospital services (Dennis 2006, 58–59). Also, in the field of print media and audio-visual media privatization took place. A large number of privately owned newspapers began to appear, and businessmen established their own TV networks, such as Mehwar, Orbit, and Dream TV (Shehata 2010, 40–41; Sadek 2006, 165). The army went private as well and penetrated the business and financial world: retired army officers became successful businesspeople (Abaza 2006b, 203). State subsidies for basic food had shrunk to four items: oil, sugar, flour, and bread. The soup kitchen and charitable tables were re-invented and flourished (Denis 2006, 57). According to Bayat, state subsidies for sugar and cooking oil have in the meantime been removed, as well as sub-sidies for fuel, electrical power, and transportation (2009, 67). As Mitchell (1999) observed, neoliberalism — in Egypt as elsewhere — has been facilitated by a harsh restriction of political rights.

The Mubarak regime began to rely more heavily on repression and divide-and-rule strategies, particularly driving wedges between Islamists and secularists (see Chapter 5; Shehata 2010, 33). A limited political pluralism was institutionalized, but the state of emergency, in force since the assassination of Sadat in 1981, enabled the government to override the political opportu-nities of political parties and the judiciary whenever this was deemed neces-sary. The number of legally recognized parties increased, but led to a further fragmentation and undermined the potential for effective opposition against the National Democratic Party. Those groups that were considered threaten-ing, such as the Muslim Brothers, al-Wasat, and the leftist party al-Karama, were denied formal recognition, although they could participate de facto (Shehata 2010, 36). After the success of the Muslim Brothers in the 2005 elec-tions, another crackdown by the regime followed. The leftist opposition was fragmented, but during the period 2000–2005, it assumed greater visibility. Movements such as Kifaya were largely informal, decentralized, and non-hierarchical. They succeeded, however, in organizing large demonstrations on issue such as support for Palestine and Iraq, or against globalization, and at the time of my research the April 6th Youth Movement of 2008 was estab-lished (Bayat 2009, 10; Shehata 2010, 68). Human rights organizations were formalized, but the government tried to co-opt their activists (Shehata 2010, 39). Human rights violations were rampant. The state of emergency placed any opposition party or individual under threat of persecution. As Abaza documents: "The golden age of Egyptian liberal tycoons is paired with the regime's record for the worst human rights violations, especially after the Taba

Hilton bombing in October 2005, which led to the detaining of twenty-four hundred people under inhumane conditions and torture. Egyptian security forces have been identified by Human Rights Watch as committing mass human rights abuses. For the first time in Egypt's history, women were violently sexually harassed" (2010, 38). In anticipation of potential unrest among those who suffered the consequences of the structural adjustment policies, measures were taken to constrain the autonomy of professional syndicates and trade unions. The new labor code of 2003 granted workers the nominal right to strike, but all strikes had to be approved by the trade union federation that was controlled by the regime (Shehata 2010, 42, 45–46). Yet in 2006, 2007, and 2008, there were massive strikes in the public and private sectors, particularly among textile workers of Mahalla al-Kubra, described as the most effective organized activism since the Second World War (Bayat 2009, 9).

In the analysis of several observers, Egypt's neoliberalism and integration into the global market resulted in a sharp social and economic polarization among the different strata of society, a segmentation in educational and job opportunities, and a bifurcation of consumption patterns and lifestyles (Abaza 2005, 2006b; Denis 2006; Vignal and Denis 2006; De Koning 2006, 2009). The educational system had, increasingly, a dual, class-based structure, and those who could afford them opted for private schools and language institutes. This duality accelerated in the 1990s, with the establishment of forty-five private universities, various private institutions of higher education, and high schools offering American and British diplomas (De Koning 2009, 50–51). The students were educated to work in the internationally oriented companies or international NGOs. The open-door policy had already given rise to a stratum of new rich. Labor migration created additional divisions within the middle class between those who worked abroad and were able to improve the economic situation of their families and those who stayed in Egypt. Tangible divisions have been created between a privileged upper-middle class working in the new segments of international professional and managerial jobs and other, less fortunate middle-class families. This upper-middle class is estimated to be 15 to 20 percent of the total professional middle class and comprises 5–7 percent of all Cairenes (De Koning 2009, 74, 169). A shift in the image of the middle class also indicates the present preponderance of the global market, a shift reflected in popular culture as well. The icon of the Nasserist urban professional was the doctor or the engineer. Sadat's period was famous for the portrayal of the nouveaux riches. This has given way to the image of the young upper-middle-class professional in a hypermodern international office (De Koning 2009, 37–38).[33] There are several ways to reach this fortunate class position. It is through access not only to the global European/American economies, but also to the Gulf countries (Armbrust 2006, 416). As De Koning maintains, Egypt is witnessing a division between "those with and those without a language," indicating a command of English as a prerequisite to working in the upper echelons of the labor market. These language skills, however, could also be acquired in a British school in the Gulf.

The class polarization is also clearly visible in the landscape and cityscape, particularly in the form of the gated communities and shopping malls in the affluent neighborhoods (Mitchell 1999; Denis 2006; Vignal and Denis 2006; Elsheshtawy 2006; De Koning 2006, 2009; Abaza 2005, 2006a, 2006b). From 1994 onward, the Ministry of Housing began to sell lots on the margins of the Cairene desert, and luxury construction projects mushroomed. In the first five years of the boom, around eighty gated city projects were developed, with names such as Utopia, Beverly Hills, Palm Hills, Belle Ville, and the aforementioned Dreamland (Denis 2006, 52–53). Protected, walled enclaves with their own amusement parks and golf courses, these condominiums are a far cry from the crowded and polluted inner city. Expatriate workers in the Gulf could start payments for the desert compounds at agencies in Jeddah and Dubai, where they were advertised as having "no factories, no pollution, no problems" (Mitchell 1999, 28). Although the concept of the protected city is mainly an American invention, the influence of the Persian Gulf oil-rich extravagance and luxury is clearly visible (Denis 2006, 53). Several Gulf countries such as Dubai invest in developments such as, for example, the Smart Village Project (Elsheshtawy 2006). As Vignal and Denis also note, the Persian Gulf countries play a mediating role. They bring not only capital, but also transnational lifestyles such as gated cities. "The references at first glance seem American, but passing through the Gulf imprints them with specific moral and symbolic codes" (2006, 119–120). This holds true not only for the gated cities, but also for the shopping malls.

Most of the malls opened in the late 1990s. With eight malls, Nasr City had the largest number and became known by many Cairenes for "the smell of money"—that is, the variety of shops, restaurants, and coffee shops symbolizing "the tastes of the returning middle-class professionals who spent the last two decades, if not more, as migrant workers in the Gulf oil-producing countries" (Abaza 2006b, 204). According to sociologist Mona Abaza, one interpretation among her informants holds that the mall culture is imported to Cairo from the United States by way of the oil–producing countries; others view the mall as a consequence of Saudi influence on Egyptian culture and the new taste culture that former migrants have created in Egypt. These returning migrants were accustomed to spending their leisure time in air-conditioned, luxurious, and walled-off spaces (Abaza 2006b, 205). Whether mediating or directly imported, the influence of the Gulf is emphasized over the global American dimension. Armbrust observed of the new expensive theaters located in luxury hotels and in new shopping malls that they are to a large extent built by Gulf money and cater to returning migrants, as well as the substantial number of visitors from the Gulf (2006, 431). De Koning also mentioned that among her upper-middle-class professional respondents, Gulf locations, particularly Abu Dhabi and Dubai, were seen as first-class consumption opportunities and favorite destinations for shopping (2009, 128).

There is thus obviously a strong link to global markets through the Gulf: in the form of money, from investment in luxurious gated communities, shopping malls, and five-star hotels; people, whether migrants or returning migrants, visitors from the Gulf, or Cairenes visiting the Gulf for shopping; and lifestyle, as in the concept of the walled city, or "compound" as it is known in local parlance, and protected leisure such as shopping malls. The Gulf connection points at the need to broaden the concept of globalization. As Ghannam indicates—without denying the significance of flows from the United States and Europe—we also need to account for the multiplicity of flows that shape cultural identities and practices (Ghannam 2006, 252). This holds true for lifestyles as well as the financial structure of cultural industries. Not only American dollars, but also petrodollars, influence global leisure, consumption, and taste cultures (Van Nieuwkerk 2008a). Globalization does not pertain only to Western—mostly perceived as secular—influences on art and entertainment in the region, for instance, heavy metal, hip-hop, pop, and soaps, but also to Islamic genres going global. Not only Western music and art, but also Islamic lifestyles and consumption patterns, including artistic productions, are disseminated worldwide.

What do these global forces from the Gulf mean for the religious character of the market? As we have seen in the interviews with children of returning migrants, it would be fallacious to create a simple equation between the influence of the Gulf and a religious taste culture. This affluent taste culture of shopping malls and condominiums appears not to be necessarily related to religion, but more to the luxurious cosmopolitanism of a global upper class. Yet, as quoted above, the Gulf leaves "specific moral and symbolic codes" imprinted on the materialization of the global taste culture. This can be—and according to others should be—in accordance with religious prescriptions. This intersection of global and religious sensibilities takes specific forms. It is "*halal*" rather than religious in a strict sense. It is understood more as not contradicting religious proscriptions than as produced, consumed, or conceptualized with a religious purpose or motivation. It is "clean" in the double sense of the word—that is, first, spotless or hygienic, and second, morally respectable or orderly and appropriate. We will come across "clean cinema" in Chapter 9 as a genre of films and soaps catering to religious sensibilities without overtly religious references. In this chapter we have seen the development of religious songs, as well as the "halalification" of songs by cleansing the songs of inappropriate wordings. They are cleansed of impropriety and immorality. I would suggest, accordingly, that we can analyze the religiously inflected market as a broad spectrum of products and services. Congruent with the fragmentation of religious authorities, discourses, and practices, there is also a diversification of consumer markets. The religiously inflected market consists, first, of an explicitly religious market, second, of a segment that is Islamic in name and motivation, but not overtly so, and finally, of a market for clean, upscale forms. The goods and services in the third category have no religious references, but are in accordance with the "nice religiosity" of the upper-middle class and do not hinder their participation in an affluent consumerist culture.

The first section of the market, the emergence of religious leisure in the strict sense, such as Islamic weddings, religious songs, and religious wedding bands, has been illustrated in this chapter. In Chapter 9 I will discuss religious soaps. Here I would like to draw attention to the extent of the overtly religious consumer market that has appeared in Cairo more broadly (Starrett 1995b, Abdelrahman 2006). Besides religious books and pamphlets, there is a boundless number of religious paraphernalia, such as these items listed by Starrett (1995b, 53):

> Qur'ans, prayer beads, skullcaps, and rugs are only the beginning. Spend a day in Cairo and you can find bumper stickers, keychains, posters, board games, jigsaw puzzles, coloring books, fans, clocks, framed Qur'anic verses, banners, greeting cards, decorative items in ceramic, brass, wood, cloth, and paper, cassette tapes and videos, paper models of mosques, miniature plates in ceramic and plastic, apotropaic devices of various sorts, gigantic strings of prayer beads as big as your fist, and the ultimate in Egyptian syncretism: Qur'anic verses hand-painted on papyrus or fired in blue ceramic to resemble the ancient faience found in pharaonic tombs. What characterizes these diverse items as religious is either a direct association with acts of worship, as with prayer beads, or, more commonly, their bearing of sacred images or writing, often only the single word "Allah" or "Muhammad."

Maha Abdelrahman adds to this list a supply of goods and services—relating this market again to the Egyptian migrants who work in the Gulf states and brought back a religious lifestyle—such as Islamic swimming suits, Islamic designer garments, Islamic hairdressers, and also Islamic nail polish, Islamic elevators, Islamic foot cream, Islamic farmhouses, and Islamic agencies for domestic workers (2006, 69–70). Whereas in some cases the Islamic reference makes sense—the Islamic nail polish is easily peeled off in seconds and thus congruent with the prescribed ablution for prayer—other references are slightly far-fetched. The Islamic elevator plays Qur'anic verses as soon as the door is opened, and the doll Hend congratulates Muslims upon the arrival of the month Ramadan.

The second section of the market consists of several consumer products that are not related to religious purposes or references, but advertised or symbolically linked to Islam. The branding of a product as "Islamic" is viewed as convincing and attractive, but there is nothing intrinsically religious in the product or the process of production and marketing (Abdelrahman 2006, 71). An example of this is the Islamic farm, advertised in Egyptian newspapers, that consists of a large piece of agricultural land with luxurious modern-looking villas. These goods and services can be produced in non-Islamic countries according to global capitalist systems of production. As Navaro-Yashin observed for Turkey (2002), the processes of commoditization behind any market, secular or religious, are similar. Muslim businessmen may advertise themselves as morally different from their competitors, but are, after all, implicated in the same capitalist consumption market. Consumption habits between secularists and Islamists may differ, but the production of Islamist commodities bears witness to similar processes of commoditization. The Turkish "Tekbir" fashion company, named after the habit of calling "God is great" at public demonstrations, strives for worldwide prestige. Covered women began in time to discriminate among veils according to brands and qualities rather than simply for the modesty they afforded (Navaro-Yashin 2002). Abdelrahman observes the same for Egypt. "Religious" products form a market parallel and virtually identical to that for non-Islamic Westernized products, offering practicing Muslims the opportunity to express piety without abandoning their consumerist lifestyle. They are branded as religious commodities to convince consumers of their religious relevance, although the same profit principles and marketing strategies are involved: Islam sells.

Finally, at the other end of the spectrum of religiously inflected goods, are products or services not branded as Islamic, but still appropriate enough to cater to religious sensibilities. These products and services are what I have labeled above "clean"; they combine upper-class cosmopolitan values with moral-religious respectability. The coffee shops studied by De Koning (2006, 2009) are an interesting example of the clean, chic, and proper spaces I have in mind. The new leisure culture of coffee shops in Cairo gives visitors a "First World feel" and is part of "global flows of distinctive cultural consumption" (De Koning 2009, 108–109). Yet, at the same time, the shops are not associated with immorality like bars and nightclubs and do not serve alcohol. While the coffee shops are not marked as Islamic, they do "negotiate religious prescriptions and desires for conspicuous consumption" (De Koning 2009, 109). Particularly for women, they provide a mixed gender space that is respectable and classy. The high prices "protect" the place from entrance of the lower-middle classes and their potentially "impolite" manners. Women and men from the upper classes are assumed to know how to behave properly in mixed-gender interaction, because that is part of respectable upper-class manners (2009, 140). According to De Koning, this new coffee shop leisure culture must be situated in the "complex field of contestation over gendered norms of propriety, religiosity, and Western influence" (2009, 113).

Thus, the religious market, or religiously inflected market, caters to diverse classes and taste cultures, with products and services ranging from strictly religious, with an Islamic purpose, to clean and classy ones without a religious reference, but minimally in accordance with religious prescriptions. From *anashid* and strictly segregated Islamic weddings to *halal* songs and weddings made appropriate by an occasional religious song; from religious salons to clean coffee shops; and, as we will see in Chapter 9, from religious soaps featuring the life of Sheikh al-Shaʿarawi to clean comedies. An interesting question Abdelrahman (2006) raises with regard to this broad market of Islamic consumption is whether we should analyze it as a transformation in the nature of the Islamist project or as a co-optation of the Islamist movement by global capitalism (2006, 73–75). Related to this question: are Islamist ideas and aims furthered by the post-Islamist turn or has Islamism become an empty shell? Should we interpret the new "lite" trend in Islamism as an extension of the Islamist political project by, seemingly, nonpolitical means? Or does it indicate a change of direction away from political activism toward consumerism and individual pursuits? Or, put more mundanely and closer to the experiences of members of Islamic wedding bands such as Mustafa Mahmud, will Islamists extend their message to a larger market segment or will they be outwitted by the clean, religiously shallow alternative? In Chapter 9, I will illustrate similar developments with regard to Islamic visual culture and return to these questions in the Afterword.

9.1. ʿAbir Sabri (from magazine al-Mawed, October 23, 1999)

NINE

Ramadan Soaps and Islamic Aesthetics

In this final chapter, I will go into some of the ambivalences and contradictions in the field of moral artistic practices. In the first section, I will present the life story of actress 'Abir Sabri, who not only returned to art but eventually unveiled as well. In the second section, I will discuss the emergence of another genre of religious art production, that is, Islamic and "clean" soaps. In the final section, I will discuss the way religious ethics are translated into multifarious forms of Islamic aesthetics.

THE SPIRITUAL BIOGRAPHY OF ACTRESS 'ABIR SABRI

While the artists who feature in this chapter started the trajectory to "moral perfection," as did several of the other celebrities we have met in this book, on their way to *iltizam* these artists changed their course. They were faced with personal circumstances or financial hardship, or were burdened by the heavy responsibility of upholding the righteous image of a veiled actress or committed artist. They also changed their convictions due to the new realities and shifting discourses within the field of "morally upright" art. These artists do not simply represent a case of "moral relapse," but show the complexity of lived realities. They also illustrate the current ambiguous outcome of the art with a mission project, which has opened up its horizon to new formats and trends.

Until now we have mainly looked into the "success stories" of piety—at least as narrated in the self-presentation and religious discourses of the artists themselves. Yet a more realistic life story that shows an "ambivalent relation to religion" and highlights the "more profound contradictions of different urges and wishes which even the most pious are likely to experience" needs to be drawn as well (Schielke 2009, 36). As anthropologist Schielke argues, the current studies on the piety movement tend to present an image that is too coherent and idealized. Not only are the religiously committed individuals easily taken as "paradigmatic representatives," but scholars also tend to analyze the attempts to realize a pious self, rather than the actual outcome of the endeavors. Besides, by taking exceptional, committed activists rather than the majority of people as the basis of analysis, these studies tend to reproduce the bias of the specific group under study (Schielke 2009, 37).

The criticism that Schielke deservedly addresses at piety studies can be deemed applicable to the present study as well. However, it was my explicit intention to study my subjects as paradigmatic examples that inform lifestyles and sensibilities rather than as real-life ordinary individuals or as representatives of pious women in general. I deliberately chose to focus on selected celebrities for whom, due to their high media profile, their exemplary character is particularly forceful. Since they are famous stars, they themselves feel an urgent need to "celebritize" piety, to hide breaches and imperfection, as well as to uphold and carefully monitor their public images as pious exemplary personalities. Whether they are perfect pious role models or not, they feel a heavy responsibility to act as paradigmatic representatives of *iltizam* because of their influence on large groups of fans. Besides, I did not have a chance to go beyond their self-presentation or behind their carefully constructed facade. The type of fieldwork I conducted thoroughly diverged from my previous study among singers and dancers of Muhammad ʿAli Street. With them I traveled to distant places where they performed at village weddings or saint's day celebrations. I toured with them during the night to clubs or visited them at home to have small talk. While they also carefully managed their image of respectability, breaches were more easily observed. The stars were better able to control their image of morality, religiosity, and respectability by selecting the people and journals by which their stories were conveyed.[1] I had to rely on the interviews I conducted with them, or on archival sources, in which they carefully staged their stories, leaving scarce possibilities to observe breaches, ambiguities, inconsistencies, or imperfections. The danger of reproducing their biases and portraying their stories as exemplifying success was accordingly real. They felt they had a mission to accomplish and used the interviews with me as an outlet for this. Yet it was precisely this mission I wanted to study. As stressed repeatedly during this study, I have presented strivings and representations, ideas, ideals, and imaginings, rather than observed behavior, realistic outcomes, or lived realities. Finally, I have sketched the strivings of a small group of artists to be exemplary individuals. I have studied a specific group of star performers and did not, for instance, follow the singers and dancers of Muhammad ʿAli Street from my previous research in their attempts to combine their profession with a religious lifestyle. As stated in the Introduction, the pious lifestyle of the stars felt to them like a moral luxury that they simply could not afford. The lower-class artists were forced to keep on working in a trade that hindered—in their own experiences—the realization of religious perfection. So I have chosen to present a study of a group of exceptional, privileged individuals that strive to provide exemplary models of piety and have analyzed them as such for the powerful impact of their paradigm.

Yet also within this group of well-positioned and famous artists, we can discern some "breaches" and "ambiguities." We have met some artists who were wavering in their course to piety and unveiled several times before they finally veiled. Several of them have come back to the field of art to produce "appropriate" art, interpreted by others as a "relapse" in their religious commitment. Others returned to the field of art and either felt pressured to "downveil" or were convinced themselves of the legitimacy of doing so, thus providing them with a wider range of artistic options. Instead of donning the *higab*, wearing wide covering clothes, and abstaining from makeup, they opted for a small headscarf, fashionable tight clothing, accessories, and makeup. The opening up of "art with a mission" to less strict forms, combined with a trendy, "lite" version of Islamism, allowed for "clean art" with a less forceful missionary purpose. A few female artists unveiled and returned to the artistic styles they used to perform before their religious turn. In this section, I will present the story of ʿAbir Sabri, who veiled after ten years of stardom, but unveiled a few years later and to the present day still works as an "unveiled actress."

I interviewed ʿAbir Sabri in February 2005, three years after she left the scene, veiled and changed her career to become a presenter of religious programs at the Iqra channel (for picture of her with a veil, see book cover, Figure 6.2). In 2008, she returned to act unveiled roles (see Figure 9.1). Of course, I tried to interview her a second time and phoned her to this effect, but as soon as she noted my interest in her story of unveiling, she refused. She stated that this part of her life was private, "something between me and God." Whereas her veiling story was public and publicized, her unveiling story was felt to be a private matter. This presentation of self connects with the above-mentioned tendency to display "exemplary conduct" and under-report "less commendable" demeanor. It is a form of self-protection as well. The famous actress Sawsan Badr—whom I briefly met during the shooting of a film—also veiled for a short period at the beginning of the 1990s, but soon returned to high-quality productions as an unveiled actress. She, too, felt her religious views were a private matter.[2] Farida Saif al-Nasr was one of the first to return unveiled and mentioned the anonymous threats she had received because of her unveiled acting (*Ruz al-Yusif*, August 2, 1993, 56–58). She refused me an interview, and I suspect this was due to the negative reaction she had experienced. Several other young actresses, such as Hala al-Sheikha and Mirna al-Muhandis, were reported to have veiled and unveiled again, and I was not given their telephone numbers by the veiled actresses, because of their delicate position and the sensitivity of their choices.

There are a few short biographies of 'Abir Sabri available on the Internet. They also, as in this example, highlight her presumed reasons for retiring around 2002:

> Abir Sabri, celebrated for her alabaster skin, ebony hair, pouting lips and full figure, used to star in racy Egyptian TV shows and movies. Then, at the peak of her career a few years ago, she disappeared—at least her face did. She began performing on Saudi-owned religious TV channels, with her face covered, chanting verses from the Qur'an. Conservative Saudi Arabian financiers promised her plenty of work, she says, as long as she cleaned up her act. "It's the Wahhabi investors," she says, referring to the strict form of Sunni Islam prevalent in Saudi Arabia. "Before, they invested in terrorism—and now they put their money in culture and the arts."[3]

Also, on Danceanddance.com, one of several dance websites to devote attention to 'Abir Sabri, she is described as a "belly dancer who starred in Egyptian TV shows and movies. She suddenly started to cover herself up on religious channels due to the Sunni Islam ownership of the networks that promised her work. She is an example of the Saudization of Egyptian culture."[4] We see accusations similar to those levied against the veiled actresses in the 1990s directed at the younger generation of veiled stars—that is, they are after material gain and under the influence of Wahhabi Islam. Yet the descriptions also reflect the fact that the growing Saudi presence in the mediascape offered them space to work as veiled presenters and actresses.

In an interview on Dream TV, three days after she veiled, 'Abir Sabri described the influence of diverse preachers on her decision to veil. These were, however, not Wahhabi preachers, but rather the younger generation of post-Islamist lay preachers, notably 'Amr Khalid. I have used 'Abir's example already in Chapter 6 to illustrate the diffuse power of cassettes, preachers, and lectures at Islamic salons. She narrated that she listened to some tapes of

'Amr Khalid that addressed the topic of the importance of praying and particularly praying on time. Later that evening, she listened to preacher Habib 'Ali, who delivered "a wonderful lesson," and decided to veil. She received an invitation to an Islamic salon that same evening. A lecture given by Hana' Tharwat there greatly affected 'Abir Sabri, and she veiled on the spot. In my own interview with her, three years later, she repeatedly stressed the importance of reading religious literature for her decision to step down. No dreams, visions, or mystical experiences, but knowledge, was crucial in her gradual realization of the importance of veiling.

'Abir Sabri graduated from the faculty of law, but changed her field to art, which is not uncommon. During the eight years of her career in art, she became a relatively successful actress of the young generation. Yet, as we have seen with several artists, despite the success, she experienced a certain feeling of anxiety and unrest:

> Inside me there were always questions about religious matters, issues of *halal* and *haram*. Was God satisfied with what I did? Life does not end on earth, but has a completion in the Hereafter. I pondered about hell and paradise. I had all these kind of thoughts, but hardly any time to think about it seriously. I was always busy with my work. Despite my success, I felt I missed something. I was not convinced about what I was doing and felt that I perhaps should do something else. These were sleeping thoughts, which were activated. Life is like a mixer [*khallat*]. It is going on and on. I felt I had to take a rest to really think about what is important.[5]

In an interview in 2004, she also stressed the fact that her retreat and veiling were the result of reading and research into religious matters and not due to a specific reason or particular circumstances except for her state of "*al-nafs al-lawwama*," "the reproachful soul."[6] This indicates a state in which "the self" continually blames itself for its choices, yet is indecisive in its struggle to choose the right course of action. The right choice would result in the "*al-nafs al-mutma'inna*," the "serene" or "tranquil self." Many artists described the initial state of unrest before "repenting" and the state of rest and calmness, *sakina*, they found when they finally decided to veil and retire from art. I did not often come across the use of the term "*nafs al-lawwama*" in the narration of other artists, but the trope of unrest changing into rest was pertinent in most stories (see, e.g., Chapters 1 and 2).

I will briefly go into this notion of the wavering soul because I think it is crucial to gain a more profound understanding of the ongoing struggle for and trajectory toward ethical self-making, including the drawbacks and temptations. The different states of perfection of the soul are a common theme in Sufi literature. As we have seen in Part One, the piety movement and several Sufi ideas and conceptions are not as far apart as they are purported to be by Islamists. Particularly in the discourse pertaining to the states of the soul and techniques of disciplining the self—whether in the form of performance of ritual duties, weeping, or habitual repentance—the notions of Sufism and the piety movement have a strong resemblance. The three states of the soul or "self" on the way to perfection referred to in Sufi literature and among pious circles begin with the evil-inciting soul (*al-nafs al-'amara* or *al-nafs al-'amara bi al-su'*)—that is, the state in which the ego and carnal self reign and incite to evil. Their desires should be restrained and the self be made patient. For those who strive for perfection, it is important for the self to enter into the stage in which it blames itself for its own limitations, the state of the "*nafs al-lawwama*," the reproachful soul. The final stage of perfection is the obedient and "contented self," "*al-nafs al-mutma'inna*," in which the soul finds tranquillity.[7] These stages are not necessarily linear and final. The other states of the soul are continuously influencing the self and may gain dominance or not.

In his *Fourth Book on Repentance* (see also Chapter 2), the eleventh-century imam al-Ghazali discusses the extent to which people differ in their perseverance in repentance, distinguishing four categories: The first of al-Ghazali's categories consists of sinners who keep their penitence intact for all their remaining days. They do not revert to their sins except for those lapses of habit from which they cannot disengage themselves as long as they are not on the level of saints and prophets. This "sincere repentance" is that of the "calm soul," or the "serene self" (*al-nafs al-mutma'inna*). The second category is that of the penitents who abandon all mortal abominations, but are not free of sins. They are unconsciously gripped by sins without the intention to commit them, yet regret them, censure themselves, and renew the intention to avoid circumstances that expose them to such acts. This soul is the "reproachful soul" (*al-nafs al-lawwama*) and perceived by al-Ghazali as in a high-ranking stage, albeit inferior to the first. It is the most frequent state of penitents. The third category is that of the soul who repents and, for a while, persists in uprightness. Then the desires take over again, and the sins are committed with intent. Yet, along with that, the person persists in acts of obedience. This soul is called "the tempted soul" (*al-nafs al-masula*), that is, the soul that lets himself be seduced. The fourth category al-Ghazali distinguishes is that of the penitents who proceed, for a time, in uprightness, but

then revert to the temptation of sins without admonishing their souls to repent and without regret for their actions. Such a soul is the soul that incites
to evil and flees from good (*al-nafs al-'amara bi al-su'*).[8]

I did not attend many lessons in the Islamic salons of Egypt due to lack
of time. The different states of the soul, however, were a recurrent theme
among pious women's study circles I visited in the Netherlands over the
course of two years. My Dutch-Moroccan teacher had a flexible interpretation of the states of the soul. She explained that the different states of the
soul can be present during the same day. She added the negligent soul (*al-nafs
al-ghafila*) and illustrated how the different states of the self manifest themselves in the course of one day. During *fajr* prayer, her contented self reigns
as she starts the day full of devout intentions. Then her workday starts, which
makes her susceptible to different kinds of evil-inciting temptations. During
the afternoon, the self-blaming soul reigns as she chats with friends, possibly
gossips, but tries to correct her misdemeanor. In the evening, the negligent
soul dominates, as she is tired, has to cook, and must take care of the children,
and perhaps forgets to pray on time (see Van Nieuwkerk 2007, 2010). The
next day, the striving for perfection repeats itself. The state of perfection and
tranquillity is thus not a stable stage, but a continuous effort and endeavor.

I was not provided with the chance to discuss the self-understanding
and soul-searching of 'Abir Sabri, but the comments of Adham al-Sa'id, the
lead singer of the band Wust al-Balad, commenting on himself and several of
the younger-generation artists, point to an acceptance of human weaknesses
without undoing the pious trajectory as a whole. He narrated how he experienced a personal crisis and stopped singing, but after a while experienced the
"comeback of the self" (*rugu' al-nafs*).

> You have the desire and encouragement to overcome the crisis you are
> in. But inside, the artist is perhaps convinced that he is an artist after all.
> The psychological crisis weighs heavily on him, he knows he made mis-
> takes when he worked in art. [. . .] Without mentioning names, but an
> actress has perhaps retired because she did bad things and then she is in-
> flicted with an accident or she is caught in a compromising situation. [. . .]
> Then a few sheikhs sit down with her and she wants to return to God.
> She promises God that if he helps her out, she will stop working in art in
> return. It is like a vow (*nadr*) [starts laughing]. Like with slaughtering a
> sheep, you promise to slaughter a sheep, stop singing, or quit acting be-
> cause God helped you out . . . During the crisis your personal relation-
> ship with God is very strong, but as the crisis gradually subdues, the self

returns. The person and his character did not change. He returns to his human nature, the character he was born with. And then you visit some other sheikhs—what is your name? So I go to Sheikha Karin and ask, "Can I go back?" They tell you, "Yes you can go back," but for instance with a veil [. . .] and after a while you perhaps return to acting without a veil.[9]

Adham himself went to ʿAmr Khalid and was told that he could continue singing, but should stop some of his bad habits that were not intrinsically related to art. It is about the way you go back rather than the comeback itself, Adham claimed. He now chooses the topics and wordings of his songs more carefully. According to him, the same holds true for the returning actress: she has to decide whether she is simply acting or doing "other things" as well.

What I intend to highlight with this discussion on the soul and the perseverance of "repentance" is that the step to come back to art, with or without a veil, does not necessarily contradict the striving for piety. While taking on the veil can generally be considered an act of faith, removing the *higab* is not necessarily a statement indicating a lack of devotion. This choice does not inherently designate a case of "moral relapse," but is part of the complex lived reality in which the continuous striving toward self-perfection is embedded. This complex lived reality for actresses such as ʿAbir Sabri is that it has proved until now to be very difficult to continue working as a successful veiled actress. Most of them did not want to restrict their artistic careers to explicit religious genres and intended to return as veiled actresses in social drama. It was hardly possible to do this and remain a star. As we will see in the next section, the soaps through which several veiled stars tried to realize their comeback were not perceived as successful for various reasons. ʿAbir Sabri related, in the interview I had with her, that she decided to work as a TV presenter, because there was hardly any work as a veiled actress:

> Perhaps there is one good role a year. That is not what I deserve as a good professional actress. I was on stage for many years and made many series. This limited amount of work is not suitable for me. So I better quit. [. . .] I am offered work in historical productions. But I only cooperate in productions of which I know the producers and the quality of the production. Otherwise I should work with nonprofessionals, or actors and actresses who are amateurs. There are hardly any good producers in the religious field, they don't have the money. [. . .] Even in the clean cinema they rarely choose a leading role with a veil. So I thought *khalas*.[10]

When I asked her how she would wish to work in the future, she answered agitatedly and in frustration—whereas before she had been quite serene during the interview:

> That I can work! That there are more financial possibilities for high-quality productions! That there is no discrimination against veiled women! That there is no punishment against us: you are veiled so you are not allowed to work! You have to retire. *Fannana mu'tazila* [retired artist] they label us, we are forced to step down! You are religious so you are not allowed to work. [. . .] Religiosity is something of the inside and no one has anything to do with that. I can be very useful for people. Since I am closer to God, I have changed for the better: my behavior with people is better, my morality is high. I wish there is no punishment for the devout people (*mutadayinin*), that you can work and be successful as a religious person.[11]

She thus makes it clear that she felt forced to quit and would have preferred instead to keep on working as a professional veiled star. Although I was not granted a second interview, a journalist who spoke with her after her return mentioned that indeed the lack of roles, as well as the lack of income she needed to live up to a certain standard, made her change her mind.[12] The lack of options for veiled actresses was also one of the reasons 'Abir Sabri mentioned in other interviews, throwing back at the world of art the criticism she had endured: "I did not get any production during my period of veiling; it is not my fault or responsibility. It is the world of art that refuses to work with *muhagabat*" (*al-Arabiyya*, February 18, 2008). Maintaining that the old stars could more easily act, for instance, while pursuing the role of a mother, for her generation it was much more difficult to combine acting and veiling. Another reason 'Abir Sabri mentioned—which is also part of the complex realities of trying to be successful as a veiled star—is that she could not live up to the heavy expectations and responsibilities of the veil.[13] On a talk show, she related: "I could no longer carry the responsibility of this duty. My personal circumstances, psychologically and with regard to work, I was not able to carry on with this step. I could have stayed on with a veil and I would still have excited criticism of the people. So I preferred that my situation with the people was correct."[14] As we have also seen in the life story of Miyar al-Bablawi, the veil raises a host of expectations with regard to conduct and demeanor, which weigh heavily on public personalities. It also informs the way actresses can move, speak, and behave in their professional lives on screen or on the stage. This can be felt as a limitation in professional options and in artistic freedom. In the next section, I will discuss the various—albeit lim-ited—genres in which the veiled actresses can work, ranging from religious soaps to some of the "clean" productions. These discussions also shed light on the decision of some of the actresses to unveil or to look for more "freedom in artistic expression."

RAMADAN SOAPS AND CLEAN CINEMA

There have emerged different genres of religious art or purposeful art in the field of soap and film production. I will particularly concentrate on the Ramadan soaps by the veiled actresses. Soaps are an immensely popular genre, and Ramadan, in particular, is the season for new soap productions. These soaps are watched by a large audience, who follow the serials during the whole month. Soaps are therefore potentially a good medium to popularize values and ideas, and inculcate the desired or propagated lifestyles, whether of a nationalist, socialist, or religious kind (Abu Lughod 2005). Due to the soaps' influence in inculcating a pious lifestyle, it is not surprising that the *fann al-hadif* artists chose the Ramadan soaps for their comeback. Particu-larly Ramadan 2006 was a flourishing season for religious soaps, and four of the veiled actresses returned to the screen.

Within the genre of soaps of the religiously committed artists, we can distinguish different varieties. These varieties largely align themselves along the continuum I introduced in Chapter 8 with regard to the wedding songs, and the religious market more generally. First, there are productions that are explicitly religious in content and missionary in purpose. They center on historical or contemporary religious figures, such as the companions of the Prophet, imams, and sheikhs. These productions intend to edify the audience rather than entertain them. Second, there are "purposeful art" productions that try to balance a moral message with pleasurable entertainment. Reli-gious morals and family values are central and expressed by several means without turning the soap into a religious story. Not only the way of dress-ing and behaving, but also the abundant use of religious expressions and the positive representation of Islam, tend to Islamize the soap. The third type of soaps by the veiled actresses can be categorized—in line with the genre of "clean cinema"—as "clean soaps." Clean cinema cut out any acts that could insult moral sensibilities and replaced them with a light scene of jokes. There are no messages involved, let alone religious messages. Clean cinema is just meant as innocent and floating moments of laughter. Hardly any veils, or reli-gious expressions or imagery, are used in this genre. Not specifically meant for religious audiences, through their "clean" and "chaste" imagery, and by cutting out any "indecencies," the productions nevertheless conform to religious sensibilities.

Recent soaps of an explicitly religious nature are particularly those on leading religious figures, such as the soaps on Sheikh al-Shaʿarawi, *Imam al-Duʿah*, and *al-ʿArif bi Allah*, about the former sheikh al-Azhar, ʿAbd al-Halim Mahmud, produced by scriptwriter Beha Ibrahim and lead actor Hassan Yusif.[15] These soaps have an overtly and dominant religious theme through the portrayal of religious figures and their efforts for religious reform, education, and propagation. Yet, as is usual in the format of Egyptian soaps, the sheikhs are also portrayed within the context of their relatives and neighbors. The central characters are thus brought to life as ordinary humans with whom the spectator can identify as a son, neighbor, friend, husband, or father, and not only as a morally upright teacher, leader, or high-ranking religious official.

The leading characters in both soaps are played by the "repentant" or veiled artists. In both soaps, actor Hassan Yusif played the mature sheikh. In the soap about ʿAbd al-Halim Mahmud, the role of the sister is played by veiled actress Miyar al-Bablawi and the mature wife by ʿAfaf Shoʿib. The role of mother is played by Madiha Hamdi, who retired in 1992 and kept on acting in the historical religious genre.[16] The degree of the mother's religious devotion and patience is clear from the start as she proposes to help her husband out of a delicate matter. The father had committed himself to the family of a young woman in the village by agreeing to have her as the future bride for his son. The son and mother, however, had unknowingly become acquainted with another young lady, and, given the choice, the young ʿAbd al-Halim opted for the latter. The father felt embarrassment toward the family of the first prospective bride, and the mother proposes that he himself take her as a second wife. The father refuses, but the mother insists on having her as a cowife, and so it happens. The young ʿAbd al-Halim is depicted as an extraordinarily devout person who ardently aspires to know and to see God. He aspires to the knowledge that will enable him to prove the theories of Darwin and other secularists wrong. He is particularly interested in the human *"fitra,"* the innate kernel of faith present in every human, and becomes impressed by Sufi spirituality.

The soap about the late sheikh Mitwalli al-Shaʿarawi is particularly interesting, because he is one of the preachers most connected to the "repentance" of Egyptian artists. His influence on artists is represented in the soap through the character of Badriyya. Badriyya is a good-hearted poor girl from his natal village. As a child, she was fond of listening outside the *kuttab*, the religious village school, to hear the Qurʾan recitation of the pupils such as the young

Mitwalli al-Shaʿarawi. Despite her "good *fitra*," innate religious character, she has to work in a coffeehouse. She constantly feels remorse, but continues on the wrong path and becomes the rich owner of a nightclub. During her meetings with Sheikh al-Shaʿarawi, Badriyya expresses her sincere intention to veil, leave the sinful profession, and open an orphanage. Yet it takes many years and encounters with al-Shaʿarawi before she finally "repents." Badriyya is played by the actress Sawsan Badr, who retired and shortly after returned unveiled. The scene in which Badriyya, dressed in white clothes—symbolizing her state of purity after her "repentance"—meets the sheikh is noteworthy. The sheikh is chaperoned by his daughter and visits the humble hut of Badriyya. She is immersed in reading the Qurʾan. She mentions that in her new life she is completely committed to studying the Qurʾan and prayer. She no longer leaves the house, nor does she watch TV or listen to the radio, so as not to waste a single moment that should be used to compensate for her "sinful past." The sheikh kindly advises her to complement her religious practices with the performance of good deeds and to become involved in charity. She finally opens an orphanage.

After this clearly religious form of series comes the second variety of soaps—the main body of "art with a mission"—which is social-moral drama. These soaps do not represent explicit religious themes or figures; however, through the Islamic aesthetics and moral messages involved, the soaps get Islamized. *Qalb Habiba* / *Habiba's Heart*, starring Soheir al-Babli, *Habib al-Ruh* / *Sweetheart*, with veiled actress Soheir Ramzi, and *Awlad al-Shawariʿ* / *Children of the Street*, with Hanan Turk, are examples of these soaps, and they were all screened in Ramadan 2006.[17] The soap *Habiba's Heart* is about a widowed head of household, Habiba, living in an Upper Egyptian village. Habiba's well-to-do family, consisting of two sons and an adopted daughter, is supported by her lenient, moderate brother, who is the sheikh of the village. *Habiba's Heart* is cast in the image of most Egyptian soaps, and, intensified by its rural context, family relations and values are central: respect, honor, reliability, filial love, and the importance of marriage and having children. These values are threatened by materialist seductions induced by the economic "open-door policy" initiated under President Sadat. Habiba's dream of having a peaceful extended family with many grandchildren is endangered as well. The eldest son, Mawas, is a "hot-tempered upper-Egyptian" character, forming a contrast to his younger intellectual brother and pious nephew. Mawas is lured by material success and leaves behind traditional moral values. He marries a second wife, who flouts moral virtues such as humbleness, decency, and respect. The second wife aspires to conspicuous consumption and a comfortable material life in the city. He neglects his

9.2. *DVD cover, soap* Qalb Habiba, *starring Soheir al-Babli (screened Ramadan 2006)*

pious, virtuous first wife, who stays in the house of his mother. Habiba advises her daughter-in-law to be patient. Despite feelings of remorse, Mawas squanders the family inheritance, including that of his brother, and engages in risky endeavors eventually leading him, a "country bumpkin," to Cairo. A sophisticated urban lady seduces him into a secret, *urfi*, marriage and a blank check as a dowry. Mawas eventually repents and is granted forgiveness by Habiba, but in an exchange of gunshots with one of his rivals, he gets killed and finally dies in the arms of Habiba.

The soap *Habib al-Ruh / Sweetheart* has a somewhat similar story line, but this time the "bad" character is the husband rather than the son. It is situated in the urban upper class, thus giving rise to different aesthetics than those of the rural setting of *Habiba's Heart*. It is a complicated familial drama in which the son, from a former marriage, finally dies as well. Soheir Ramzi plays the character of Ruh, a doctor who enters a second marriage with an ambitious man. The son becomes involved in religious circles through his late — biological — father and gets estranged from his stepfather. Ruh's second husband becomes involved in various kinds of dubious transactions. He cheats on Ruh with his female secretary, with whom he engages in an *urfi* marriage. The secretary, who is a Christian of foreign descent, plays a double game and is also involved with "bad guys" who try to get hold of "her lover's" wealth. Ruh has been patient and tried to endure her husband's conduct and to show him

9.3. *DVD cover, soap* Habib al-Ruh, *starring Soheir Ramzi (screened Ramadan 2006)*

an alternative, uncorrupted lifestyle both at home and in the workplace. The secretary becomes pregnant and truly starts loving the father of her child. She finally "repents" and becomes Muslim. Due to the upper-class setting, the soap shows various forms of fashionable veiling. The moral message, the stark contrast between the good and the bad, and the positive depiction of moderate Islam make the soap clearly recognizable as purposeful art.

Another Ramadan soap screened in the same year, *Awlad Shawari' / Children of the Street*, is situated among the poor classes of Cairo. It addresses the topic of street children and all the abuses they are exposed to: rape, drugs, removal of organs for donor transplantation, etc. The veiled leading character, though, played by Hanan Turk, despite living in the street remains remarkably well on the right path. This soap was quite successful, and Hanan Turk has returned in Ramadan 2009 in the soap entitled *Hanim Bint Basha*. This soap also revolves around an "unprotected," but strong, female character who works in a lower-class neighborhood as a seller of coffee. She is responsible for the family, because her father is imprisoned and eventually dies. She fearlessly defends her family and her honor in the style of a *bint al-balad*, "daughter of the country" (al-Messiri 1978; Van Nieuwkerk 1995). *Bint al-balad* represents a female role model of a strong, assertive woman in a lower-class neighborhood who is accustomed to interacting with men and is prepared to draw a knife to defend her virtue. Hanan Turk has also returned in the successful soap *al-Qitta al-'Amiyya / The Blind Cat* in Ramadan 2010. In this soap she plays the leading character, who originates from a humble family background, but graduates from the faculty of law and starts working as an attorney. She is offered the chance by a powerful attorney to start an ambitious career in his famous legal office, and almost neglects her fiancé. Yet she becomes part of a conflict within the powerful attorney's family and is accused of murder. She has to flee and is on the run, "protected" only by a gentle, albeit simpleminded, taxi driver. When she finally surrenders and is interrogated by the police, she realizes that she has been blinded by ambition and errantly chased after fame, money, and cars. She "opens her eyes" and returns to the humble office she started working in, realizing that marriage and begetting many children are the utmost fulfillment in life. The soap has hardly any references to religion and falls into a genre akin to "clean" soaps. Hanan Turk is, however, veiled throughout the soap, and the end of the story line contains a clearly gendered moral message.

The third genre along the continuum described above is the "clean" soaps, a genre that we can understand as part of the broader current of the clean cinema, *sinima nidifa*. The trend started with the box-office hit *Ismaeliyya Rayih Gayy* in 1997 (Tartoussieh 2007). When the producers made the film they did not expect any success at all and were overwhelmed when the response from the public proved them wrong. The assistant director of the film explained that he and his colleagues started to be fed up with the ʿAdil Imam type of film with "hot kisses." He related the embarrassment he felt when he had to shoot a film with ʿAdil Imam and his female counterpart more or less "doing it" on the beach amidst a curious crowd.[18] Clean cinema erased hot scenes, kisses, embraces, and any scenes or gestures that could insult moral sensibilities. Hot scenes were replaced by jokes and satire. It could contain wordplays with a sexual overtone or other kinds of sexual jokes, but no direct depiction of sex. The light comical genre of clean cinema set off a whole trend of similar productions. As an example of the "clean" genre produced by the veiled actresses, we can take the 2009 Ramadan soap *al-ʿUmdah Hanim | Lady Mayor*, with veiled actress Sabrin.[19] She opts for a style of "downveiling," a small shawl tied at the neck, and also appears visually unveiled in those in-house scenes that "demand" an unveiled appearance (see below). In these cases she wears a wig to cover her hair or *higab* and is thus not clearly recognizable as a "veiled actress." She looks instead like a village woman with her small scarf and two long braids. She plays the wife of the village *ʿumdah*, mayor, who—like most men in the village—is quite lazy and laissez-faire. The village is "infected" with "globalization" by way of the "*dish*," the satellite, which introduces new lifestyles. It particularly shows alternative role models for women, and the soap plays out the comical frictions emerging from the enactment of these new roles. The wife eventually challenges and beats her husband in the elections and becomes the first female *ʿumdah* of Egypt. Although the women were quite successful in their new roles as mayor and police guards, "order" is eventually restored.

Despite the differences among the three genres produced by the committed artists, veiling in its different manifestations was a common and crucial element of the soaps and also was the major condition the veiled actresses imposed for their return. The veil, however, proved to be a contentious issue for the art producers, audiences, and—as we will see in the next section— the actresses themselves. I discussed the 2006 Ramadan soaps of the veiled actresses with several fans and critics.[20] The most obvious critics were artists and journalists belonging to the secularist fold. They stressed that there is no problem in veiling as such. Wearing the *higab* is an individual decision and belongs to the realm of personal freedom.[21] The problem emerges when the "rules" of the veil are enforced on art. My secular interlocutors clearly distinguished between a "veiled character" and a "veiled actress." The first is possible, the second is not. They pointed out the many unnatural scenes resulting from using a veiled actress: she cannot kiss or embrace her own "son" or "husband." Even when sitting at home with only "her relatives" around or alone in her bedroom, she is still unable to unveil. Soheir al-Babli was ridiculed because she refused to kiss "her youngest son" when he returned from a long journey. This criticism needs qualification: she allowed for kisses, but only on her hand, forehead, or shoulder. Soheir al-Babli explained, though, that she insisted on her "husband" being written out of the script and only accepted the role of a widow in order to avoid compromising scenes.[22] This might also explain the preference of Hanan Turk to play the role of an "unprotected" strong character. 'Afaf Sho'ib allegedly refused to look her "husband," the religiously committed actor Hassan Yusif, in the eyes during the series about Sheikh al-Sha'arawi. This was deemed improper and against Islam.[23] I did not check all scenes of the thirty episodes for potential eye contact, but a preference for positioning male and female bodies at right angles to each other is noticeable.

The secular producers I interviewed refused to work with veiled actresses, although they did not mind occasionally producing films in which a veiled character is portrayed. This role should be played by a nonveiled actress. Other secular critics argued that the veil is not the problem, but the veiled actresses' position on art. They argue that the veiled stars had first declared art *haram* and now only permit a restricted form of art. It is this limited and restricted vision of art's permissibility that makes their productions so poor, the secular critics claim.[24] Secular producers also blamed the productions for their "commanding good and forbidding wrong" style.[25] "If we like sermons we watch religious programs, not soaps," several producers and journalists said. They considered these purposeful art productions unrealistic, boring, and preachy.

Criticism did not come only from the secular adversaries of *fann al-hadif*. I heard critical voices also within the circles of pious producers, journalists, and fans. Several veiled fans had high hopes with regard to the return of the veiled actresses, but were disappointed by the results. First, like the secular critics, they disapproved of the unnatural situations—actresses who remained veiled while resting in their bedroom—for not reflecting their own reality at all. Second, they criticized the image of the veiled character as a flawless creature for its lack of representativeness. Veiled actress Soheir Ramzi starred as a nearly perfect and saintly character enacting with her veil all the goodness and beauty of Islam. Her role as a virtuous wife who continually and patiently corrected her mischievous husband was perceived as unrealistic. This flawless, angelic representation of the veiled character was felt to impede the development of a natural image of veiled women in Egypt. Finally, they also blamed the veiled actresses for using too much makeup, wearing very expensive accessories, and putting on "ridiculous amounts and layers of veils." They did not feel represented as normally veiled Egyptian women. The veiled fans longed for veiled characters who more closely approached their daily realities, including (minor) mistakes, without casting doubt on their religious intentions and morality. The veil for them is not a condensed symbol of Islam and female virtue, but rather a daily reality and a way of dressing. The veil, according to them, should be recaptured from a hyper(un)real symbol of religion into a sign of normal religiosity. They felt the need for pleasant forms of religious representation of veiled women in soaps, not too boring, preachy, or moralizing, but still retaining Islamic aesthetics. Only Hanan Turk, in her role as one of the street children, was liked for her sober outfit and simple makeup, and was able to connect to the "normal life"—indeed, even to the poor strata of Egyptian society.[26]

The veiled actresses' embodiment of piety and moral virtue for women restricted their artistic possibilities. The way the fans wanted to deal with the artistic obstacles differed. Most fans did not have clear solutions for the unnatural situations except for shooting almost all scenes outside the home so that veiling is required and realistic, an option that worked well in the soap *Children of the Street*.[27] Other fans suggested that the veiled actresses should wear light shawls inside the house. The veiled character should also be allowed to make some mistakes. The editor-in-chief of *al-Zuhur* magazine maintained that the veiled character can make mistakes as long as she immediately repents. In this way she remains a role model without becoming an unrealistic character.[28] The stricter religious critics preferred that the veiled actress keep away from the soaps altogether and present children's programs instead. Actor Wagdi al-ʿArabi doubted whether the presentation of the veiled actresses, with their makeup, accessories, and shiny, colorful dresses, had done any good for veiled women in Egypt. Although he acknowledged each individual's freedom to veil or not to veil, he thought that, once veiled, the actress has a great responsibility to spread the "right image of Islam."[29]

The heavy criticisms directed at the soap productions of the veiled actresses, specifically those related to the veil, make the choice of Sabrin to come back with a wig understandable. They also offer a background to the decision of ʿAbir Sabri to come back unveiled. As she stated, with probable justification, even if she had stayed on working with a veil, she would still have evoked critical responses. For that reason she preferred that her "situation with the people was correct."[30] It was better to be criticized as an unveiled actress than as a veiled one, due to the responsibility of being a role model of virtuous womanhood in Islam, she maintained. The "veiled-thus-flawless" format, leading to unrealistic imagery and flat story lines dictated by moral categories, made it difficult to depict a veiled character in a more natural way. The producer ʿImad al-Bahad, for instance, provoked tension when his veiled character had her—realistic—periods of doubts and unveiled.[31] The number of roles and also the characters that could be played by veiled actresses were limited. The symbolic import of the veil proved to be a heavy responsibility not only in real life but also on stage or on screen.

The soaps with the veiled actresses as leading characters were thus generally seen as a flop, and this probably explains the lack of a follow-up in this moral-preachy format. With the exception of Hanan Turk, who works with a veil in a nonmoralistic genre, and Sabrin, who downplays the religious imagery or—where deemed necessary—wears a wig, the veiled stars have not come back as leading actresses. This does not mean that the veiled actresses have had no influence with regard to messages and visual imagery. As we have seen previously, they have been influential in making veiling fashionable. Although they were criticized for the layers of shawls, excessive accessories, and makeup, they were also admired for the way they have made veiling chic and stylish. They have also been successful in conveying the message that the veil is a common sight in the Egyptian streets and that this should be reflected in soaps and cinema. The number of films with a veiled character, played by a nonveiled actress, is increasing. Recent soaps also show a mix of veiled and unveiled characters and actresses. These soaps contain a less dominant religious imagery than that in purposeful productions, since the veiled person is just one of the characters amid others, but this is still a remarkable development that contrasts with the total lack of religious visual imagery in previous mainstream soaps. ʿAfaf Shoʿib, for instance, has returned in *al-Hara / The Alley* (2010), in which she figures as one of many characters in a populous neighborhood. She is married to a strict local sheikh, *ustaz* Tammam, while her son works as a musician and is chased from home by his strict father. *Ustaz* Tammam initially refuses to allow a TV to enter his home. However, eventually, he develops into a charismatic preacher and enters the tempting world of media himself. The alley is populated with many other, predominantly poor, families, and shots of the alley show a variety of styles of veiled and unveiled women, close to a natural depiction of lower-class neighborhoods.

The veil has entered mainstream productions, and veiled characters—though not necessarily veiled actresses—have become part of the visual imagery in the field of art. Several of the committed artists, however, also perceived being part of the mainstream market as a danger. How to retain the moral-religious message? The tension between conserving moral-religious aesthetics and meeting market demands is an issue that will be discussed in the final section.

ISLAMIC AESTHETICS: BETWEEN ETHICS AND THE MARKET

Just as Islamic wedding bands developed certain ethics and aesthetics that marked them as religious, or purposeful, art—such as, for instance, proper wording of the songs, the absence of certain instruments in addition to (partial) segregation, veiling, no mixed dancing, and specified time of performance (see Chapter 8)—so have the soaps. The soaps provide a positive representation of Islamic values and intend to promote religious morals and proper family values. These Islamic values, moral messages, and pious aesthetics are expressed by several means, which vary between the different genres I have distinguished in the previous section—the overtly religious, the purposeful, and the clean.

First, the soaps "normalize" religious conduct. The abundant use of religious expressions and religious home decorations, and the positive image of (moderate) religious personalities, communicate the normality of pious lifestyles. No weird beardy religious fanatics who have lost touch with ordinary life, the usual representation of religious people in mainstream soaps (Armbrust 2002), are to be found here, but lenient, good people who can be one's uncle or nice neighbor, such as, for instance, Habiba's brother. Praying, reading the Qur'an, and veiling are normal acts, not those of "fundamentalists." This holds true for explicitly religious, as well as purposeful, productions. For instance, the strict local preacher in *The Alley*, *ustaz* Tammam, is mildly mocked for his narrow-mindedness. The clean genre merely avoids religious themes or sensitivities.

Second, the soaps have a clear moral message. This is particularly communicated by a strong separation between "good" versus "bad" characters, behavior, or ways of living. Good and bad personalities are clearly distinguishable by religious, moral, and family values, such as filial love, modesty, patience in the face of bad luck, and "striving for the good and warding off evil." The good and the bad are also easy to recognize through religious aesthetics with regard to apparel, such as wearing revealing dresses versus modesty. Excess marks women's poor moral qualities. Whether excessive makeup or loud laughter, it is always considered bad for women (see also Yiğit 2011). Bad things are shown as long as the ultimate aim is to improve offensive conduct and particularly as long as the bad person finally repents for the evil behavior. The bad character can be transformed into a good person by the process of repentance and sincere remorse—for instance, Badriyya's repentance of her life as a nightclub Madame, the "bad" son Mawas repented of his greed, and the pregnant secretary, who was a Christian, converted to Islam. The process of repentance shows the several stages of soul searching, remorse, and falling back into the old habits before at last repentance takes place. We thus see the different states of the *nafs*, most clearly the one that blames itself for misconduct and finally the "contented self."

Third, the soaps particularly revolve around representations of proper familial relations and gender norms. The explicitly religious soaps emphasize conservative role models for women and stress the importance of complementary sex roles. Virtuous women are particularly portrayed as forgiving mothers and patient wives. In the religious soaps, several religious issues related to women, such as polygamy, arranged marriage, education, and work outside the home, are discussed, mostly confirming traditional religious views. An example of this is the proposal by Sheikh 'Abd al-Halim's mother to help her husband out of a delicate matter by having him take a cowife—with whom she will then live peacefully together. In the purposeful productions, we can see different moral-religious representations of female virtue. The soap *Habiba's Heart* promotes conservative constructions of femininity by stressing the importance of marriage and having children, modesty, obedience, and patience. In *Sweetheart*, Ruh is a capable doctor and businesswoman who combines her job with taking proper care of her family. Hanan Turk shows, in *Hanim Bint Basha*, a tougher "masculine" role model of female virtue, close to the character of "the daughter of the country." Chaste and virtuous, but a product of lower-class working conditions, the *bint al-balad* is forced to defend her honor verbally or physically. The clean genre can play with role reversal, such as in *Lady Mayor*, although this reversal is of a temporary nature and ultimately the proper relations between the sexes are confirmed.

In addition, the religiously inflected soaps are distinguishable from mainstream productions by the way intimacy and love are represented in a form appropriate to Islam. The explicitly religious soaps show "respect" between husband and wife and do not hint at intimacy. They respectfully address each other and talk together about familial affairs, but bodily closeness is avoided. As mentioned before, the male and female bodies representing intimacy are not put next to each other or closely opposite, but are often positioned at right angles, providing space between the bodies and preventing close (eye) contact. In the purposeful moral productions, sexual feelings are hinted at between the "bad" characters, the less-than-perfect protagonist and his second wife or secretary, rather than between the faithful wives and their husbands.

Whereas the secretary dances with her lover, the faithful wife—played by the veiled actress—keeps her distance. The clean genre intends to avoid indecencies and is chaste rather than pious. In the latter genre, comedy is used to allude to sexual intercourse without actually showing any form of intimacy. As Tartoussieh argues (2007), comedy or the slapstick genre is an appropriate vehicle for modesty because of the comic's sexual innocence and chasteness. For instance, in the soap *Lady Mayor*—in which women took over the tasks of their lazy husbands—the wives repeatedly prepared tea and turned on the electric fan in the evening, indicating their preparation for sexual intercourse, but they were always called to duty before any intimacy could take place. Romance and sexuality are thus not shown, but made clear in indirect ways. Director Dawud 'Abd al-Sayyid called this "*hubb bi al-yafta,*" "love by signboard." He ridiculed the clean cinema's avoidance of romantic scenes or its passionless way of imagining romance. "You're better off putting a signpost on their breast saying 'I love you' than showing any signs of tenderness," he said mockingly.[32] Cameraman Ahmad Hussein, who prefers a moderate clean genre, explained that you can show intimacy, but it should not necessarily be a long shot of thirty seconds; three seconds will do.[33] Many people criticized the "clean actors" in the "love scenes" for acting like brother and sister rather than lovers. The erasure of these kinds of scenes in the overtly religious genres was less under attack. The removal of kisses and embraces from the scripts not only was negotiated by the veiled actresses as a condition for their return, but also evaluated as appropriate for the religious genres by audiences. Although the clean character of male-female interactions is the hallmark of the *sinima nidifa*, the genre's close resemblance to mainstream productions invites expectations of and comparison with mainstream aesthetics.

Moreover, the Islamic aesthetics are also communicated by the representation of the body. The general bodily comportment, the way of dressing, and the way the body moves enact piety (Stellar 2011). The religious and purposeful soap productions are not simply pious performances, but also perform piety. In particular, the soap *Habiba's Heart* shows lengthy shots of Habiba, motionless, mumbling Qur'anic expressions, or moving serenely when in action. The body is not simply a chaste body, but foremost a pious body. Whether performing the daily prayers or a supplicatory prayer, holding and reading the Qur'an, or consoling women and advising them to be patient and obedient with gestures of submission and patience, the body avoids restlessness and agitation. This pious body in motion appears to embody the religious values of calmness, *sakina*, and patience, *sabr*. There is a complex set of contrasts between heaviness and lightness, slowness and rapidity, restlessness

and calmness, excess and austerity in moral-religious terms. In the Middle
East, more generally, the relationship between movement and morality is apparent. Heaviness signifies moral solemnity and lightness connotes triviality
in Persian (Bayat 2007a, 438). Algerian men are considered "heavy," that is,
in control of their movement, whereas women have to overcome their natural tendency to be light (Jansen 1987, 183). Lightness of movement stands for
lightness in morals. Whereas in the religious and purposeful genre the accent
is on the pious body, in the genres more akin to the clean productions the
chasteness of the body is emphasized. In the lighter version of *fann al-hadif*,
such as the soaps of Hanan Turk, the leading actress is also more active. Due
to the specific circumstance of being fugitive or on the street, the female character is moving around, defending herself and her honor verbally as well as
physically. In the clean genre, women's bodies are not only chaste, but can
also be somewhat frivolous. According to Tartoussieh, in the clean cinema,
women's bodies have to be "silenced, sanitized and their sexuality erased."
Clean cinema actresses "inhabit a body that is at once chaste, ascetic, and
overwhelmingly appealing, even prurient in its modesty and morality" (Tartoussieh 2007, 37).

Finally, the veil is an obvious element of religious aesthetics. As we have
seen, the veil is contentious and can have different shapes. There is, for instance, quite a difference in the apparel and veiling among the different genres
of the soaps I have described in the previous section. In the religious genre
and in *Habiba's Heart*, situated in a rural religious setting, most "respectable" women wear a full *higab* or a black outfit, whereas in the more mundane upper-class setting of *Sweetheart*, Soheir Ramzi wears a lot of makeup,
accessories, and different styles of fashionable veiling. Sabrin has recently ex-
changed her veil for a small sharp, or wig, at least during those scenes that in
her view demand unveiling.[34] Miyar al-Bablawi has also opted for this solution in a shot—taking place in her bedroom—in the Saudi soap opera *Ayam
al-Sarab / Days of Mirage*. Initially she defended Sabrin's choice as well as her
own step, but eventually "repented" of wearing a wig due to her responsibility as a veiled actress to provide a good role model for her veiled fans.[35] Her
"repentance" points to the great importance attached to the veil as a crucial
ingredient of religious aesthetics, at least from the point of view of the religiously committed artists themselves. Without the veil, the aesthetics of the
soaps become difficult to distinguish from those of mainstream productions
and lose the religious reference. Most of my interlocutors do not consider
"clean" productions part of the art-with-a-mission project because of the absence of veiling or religious messages. In order to get a better understanding

of the importance of the veil as one of the most crucial elements of art with a mission, I will make a short detour into the attacks on the wig, the *baruka*, by religious artists and scholars.

The choice to unveil, and perhaps even more so, to wear a wig instead of the veil, has caused quite some debate among the veiled actresses. Akin to what we have seen in the field of songs, the encapsulation in mainstream productions is felt to endanger the mission of *fann al-hadif*. Whereas 'Abir Sabri's choice to unveil is regretted by religiously committed artists, she has fallen beyond the scope of purposeful productions into mainstream "*fann al-habit*," lowbrow art, again. Yet the selection of a wig instead of the *higab* brings nonreligious aesthetics into the religious domain, making its moral message confusing and unclear.[36] Sabrin intended to opt for the wig only if it was not "logical" within the scene to be veiled, such as inside the home. In all other scenes, she wears the veil or a shawl and confirms her identity as a veiled actress. Her choice to wear a wig is linked to the lack of roles for veiled actresses. She argued that acting is her single source of income and is accordingly necessary for providing a living. She thus offered a religious legiti-macy—"necessity," or "*darura*"—for her action. She was surprised at the fuss the wig has given rise to, even to the extent that some people demanded the removal of the series during Ramadan. Some scholars backed her argument by stating that it is possible to cover the hair by any means as long as the real hair is not visible, under the condition that it is a necessity. The necessity argument could be based on either "making a living" or on "the great im-portance for the future," as with, for instance, schoolchildren in France, or previously in Turkey, who were denied access to education if they insisted on veiling. Most scholars, however, denied the legitimacy of the "necessity argu-ment." Acting as a profession does not belong to the category of "*darura*." Besides, the wig is a form of embellishment (*zina*), which is not allowed. Also, several of the veiled actresses denied the legitimacy of the "*baruka*." They held that the wig is generally *haram* and it is possible to earn a living as a veiled actress. Accordingly, there is no urgent reason to "cover the veil."[37] Some of the scholars feared the spread of this "solution," not only to all scenes in acting, but more important, to all veiled women in the street. They might imitate the artists and use the argument of either necessity or the sufficiency of covering the hair by any means to "visually unveil." Miyar al-Bablawi "re-pented" from wearing the wig when she realized the great impact she could have on other veiled women to cover their veils. She once more concluded that as a veiled actress she carried a heavy responsibility.[38] The veil is thus cru-cial to mark the productions as religious and purposeful. Without this visible marker of religiosity, they lose their clear religious message.

In the different genres of soaps produced by the religiously committed artists and veiled actresses, we thus see various combinations of morals, messages, and entertainment, obtained by varying the degree to which religious aesthetics dominate them. The purposeful art project has resulted in different forms of art that can be placed on a continuum ranging from pious to clean art. On the left pole we can position artists who remained on the safe side of the religious discourse regarding the permissibility of art. They produced art that was overtly religious in content and missionary in purpose. The middle part is the heart of the *fann al-hadif* project, trying to produce moral art, although within the fashionable formats such as soaps and contemporary songs that are also entertaining. At the other extreme of the continuum we can group popular art productions that have superficial references to religion and morality, such as clean cinema, or have moved beyond the scope of art with a mission. The "lighter" versions draw a broader audience and are in that sense "more successful"; however, they are close to losing the religious inspiration. The overtly missionary productions have a difficult time finding and sustaining a large market.

It proved difficult to find a good balance among morals, messages, and the market. The preachy, overtly moral religious soaps were often dismissed as unrealistic or boring. The explicitly moralizing soaps were perceived as not very successful and did not capture the fancy of audiences beyond an initial curiosity. The attempt to lighten up the soaps by less-moralizing messages or by making their religious imagery more subtle was satisfying to a broader audience, but left the religiously committed artists and fans uncertain about the fulfillment of the productions' missionary objective. Did the "lite" version still communicate its religious purpose, or did it lose its sting? The clean soaps were felt to lose their religious reference. Clean productions were, according to several producers, artists, and art critics, not that much a product of morals, but more of the market. Clean cinema must largely cater to the market in the Gulf and thus has to adapt to the conservative morality of these societies. This light, comical, and clean genre, although related to the morally conservative climate and growing religious sensibility, is not seen as *fann al-hadif*. According to many people I interviewed, it is to be characterized as empty and without any purpose other than superficial, momentary entertainment. There are no messages involved, let alone religious messages. The clean productions reflect the changing sensibilities among the public and actors, but, although more respectable than the usual "indecent" productions, have no clear purpose.

Pious artists and producers are searching for popular productions that still retain their religious relevance. They have discovered that art with a "pulpit style" is not successful in transmitting its message to the public, except for those who are most devout. However, the need to balance morals and the market has had ambiguous results for the *fann al-hadif* project. It has partly changed its former explicitly Islamic content into the post-Islamist *al-din al-laziz* format, a nice and pleasurable form. We thus see a relaxation on the part of several Islamist artists. The gap that had existed between strict Islamists and the general public was partially bridged. The religious message was packaged in an enjoyable form by preachers and performers. It was successful in its aim to reach out to more people. It also addressed upper-class people, who were pleased by the message of *al-din al-laziz*. The new religiosity among the upper classes was an important condition for the further development of Islamist art into *fann al-hadif*. The eventual success of purposeful art, however, had a price. The more success it had, the more it lost its original message. It was imitated and transplanted outside its original frame and purpose. It spilled over to the non-*hadif* field of art production. It could "halalify" ordinary productions, and a diluted version, seen as an even more enjoyable than *fann al-hadif* productions, came into being. The pious upper class increasingly tended to prefer the famous prestigious singers who gained respectability through an occasional religious song or to watch a clean production without a clear religious mission.[39] In a way, the art-with-a-mission project thus seems to have been buried by its own success.

The balance between ethics and the market is a delicate one. Whether the *fann al-hadif* project of Islamists managed to successfully balance these tensions is in the end connected to how we analyze the ultimate aim of the project: Is the fundamental purpose to popularize Islam or Islamize popular culture? Some thoughts about the balance between the mission and the market, as well as the possible future and challenges of Islamism through art, will be discussed in the Afterword.

Afterword

E gypt is presently going through a turbulent time, full of potential
and tensions. During the time of writing this book, I was only able
to visit Egypt for a few days in October 2010 and December 2011.
For that reason, I cannot go into all the current transformations in Egypt and
what they mean for the Islamist movement and its art project, because the up-
heaval postdates the period I collected my material. Yet I managed to interview
the media man Ahmad Mursi Abu Haiba during my last two visits shortly before
and after the revolution.[1] Ahmad Abu Haiba was in 2010 selected by the American network CNBC World as one of the top seven media leaders in the world.
His most recent endeavor was to open the channel Tahrir, which broadcast all
events from Tahrir Square to the whole world. The ordeals of his career within
the Islamist movement and the media are an excellent illustration of what this
book has sketched. Starting as a playwright within the Islamist Student Union,
and writing religio-political satirical plays that were thwarted by the government
for their "fundamentalist" leanings, he moved on to media. He worked with
ʿAmr Khalid, worked for al-Risala with the veiled actresses, launched the first
Islamic video clip channel 4Shbab, which was obstructed by Saudi funders for its
open-mindedness, and has now opened the channel Tahrir, an endeavor which,
like the revolution, appears to be wavering. His story thus neatly illustrates the
developments in Egypt over the last thirty years that I have reconstructed in this
book and provides glimpses into the postrevolutionary period as well.

THE CAREER OF AHMAD ABU HAIBA

Ahmad Mursi Abu Haiba described himself as a very religious youngster
and would now call himself at that period "a fundamentalist, or an extremist."

10.1. *Ahmad Abu Haiba in his office at 4Shbab (photograph by author)*

Like many other young Muslims in his environment, he considered everything *haram*: art was deemed illicit and watching TV was not permissible.
Despite his rejection of his previous views, he is happy that he went through
this stage, because it now helps him to understand and argue against those
strict religious interpretations.

Upon entering the faculty of engineering, Abu Haiba started to open up
his views in general and toward art in particular. He began to read a lot of
books and to discuss religion with open-minded friends such as 'Amr Khalid,

AFTERWORD (*261*)

who lived in the same neighborhood and with whom he used to play soc-
cer. They came to the conclusion that they could use art to deliver a message.

Characteristic of other student-artists of the Islamic groups, he started
with plays that remained on the safe side of contemporaneous religious interpretations. He related with a smile that his first plays were "very bad plays:
boring, historical plays in standard Arabic. I remember there was a competition of bands and play teams. The judges that came to our show actually
slept during the show, they literally slept! Because it was so boring! I myself
was about to sleep."[2] The actors were not chosen for their acting skills, but
for their piety and commitment. Yet Abu Haiba developed his views on art,
maintaining that art is not only a message or a tool, but has a value in itself.
The plays greatly improved, and, eventually, his group's "Islamic theater play"
won the university competition in the year of their graduation.

Abu Haiba divides his artistic development into three periods, which
were closely tied to political developments in Egypt as they have been described in this book. His first period as a playwright was at university: "It
was without women and without music. It had a clear Islamic message. We
were speaking about something historical or political issues. When I would
like to make a justification for that period I would say the usual theater was
just only about women and partly about music."[3] He intended to develop an
alternative to this kind of "lowbrow" art.

The second period came after graduation from, 1991 to 1996, when Abu
Haiba and his company started to use music:

> It was a strange coincidence, the biggest theater in Egypt at that time,
> Ramsis, was controlled by the Syndicate of Engineers. It was hired by ʿAdil
> Imam [one of the most famous Egyptian actors, also known for his anti-
> Islamist critiques] for the previous ten years. The strange coincidence was
> that his contract ended at the same time I graduated from the faculty, and
> the syndicate was controlled by the Muslim Brothers. So they decided not
> to renew the contract. It was a historical moment; everything was just in
> front of me: there was a theater, and the people who controlled the theater
> would like to have a kind of Islamic theater. We are the winners of the fes-
> tival and we are all engineers. So everything fitted.[4]

They started to perform in the theater of the Syndicate of Engineers and became known by that name, although they named themselves "Al-Ghad Team
Theater." They produced three plays. The distribution of the plays on videotape spread their fame to wider Islamist circles. Yet in 1995, changing political

fortunes, which had helped them to gain access to the theater, turned against them: The Egyptian government began a crackdown on radical and moderate Islamist movements, and the Muslim Brothers were kicked out of the syndicate. The team fell apart, and Abu Haiba started a career in the media.

Yet in 2000, during the Palestinian *intifada*, some of the team members decided it was time to show their support during a special week for Palestine. Abu Haiba wrote a play, which they performed for two weeks. This motivated them to professionalize the team, a project that demarcates the third phase of his artistic career. He wrote a play that became a great success within Islamist circles and was to become the first of a trilogy of "resistance theater": *Isha Ya Basha*, or *Wake Up*, a political play about Palestine. It was successful for two years, and they toured with it in the countryside. The second play, called *Vietnam 2*, was a political comedy about the invasion of Iraq, which was even more successful. The third play of the resistance trilogy was *al-Shifra*, or *The Code*. *The Code* was meant as a political comedy about Egypt, a tricky play that was obstructed by the authorities and eventually closed down due to its political sensitivity:

> *The Code* [big sigh] was a very big problem. We were speaking about Egypt! Just like the first time, there was another coincidence. Just before we were about to perform the play, some young students of the Muslim Brotherhood made a parade in al-Azhar University. Newspapers picked that up and made a big propaganda: "the Muslim Brotherhood is making a militia and invading the society." A journalist came to my theater and interviewed me. He wrote, "The Muslim Brotherhood is invading the theater." I was astonished. They took all our permits. Everything was legal. Actually, the play was defending the president! *Al-Shifra* is about strangers, robots, invading Egypt. The president likes to lead the nation and to defend the nation, but the people don't want it. They say, "As long as I eat my food and listen to Umm Kulthum it is fine, I don't mind." But they made a big noise in the newspaper: "This is a play of the Muslim Brothers."[5]

The government canceled the permits, deleted half of the script, and forbade the sale of tickets at profitable venues such as schools and government offices, which had proved to be such a good marketing strategy for *Vietnam 2*. The security police were present almost every night, which intimidated people. Many performances of *al-Shifra* were canceled on short notice, as I also experienced when I tried to watch this play in 2008, to no avail. Abu Haiba decided to stop and devote all his energy to visual media, in which he had been working since the early 1990s.

As a playwright, Abu Haiba faced opposition from the national level of the government, secular journalists, and colleagues for his plays' preponderantly religious character. In the global media world, however, he was attacked by Salafi opponents who disagreed with his "open Islamic message" and especially with the "Western" formats he used. He was also attacked for financially exploiting the Islamic message by using a commercial MTV format. After graduation, he worked for Japanese TV as a producer, and in several other companies until 1998. He then started his own company, Sana al-Sharq:

> At that time there were only religious programs on state TV, such as those of Sheikh al-Shaʿarawi, or just some satellite channels such as Iqra that started in 1995. A lecture in the mosque: that was the concept of religious TV or Islamic media at the time. When I started my company I raised this question: "Why should it be so traditional? We can make good music, a good talk show." So we started our new program, *Kalam min al-Qalb / Words from the Heart.* That was the beginning of ʿAmr Khalid. But no one decided to buy the program. For the tenth time I felt that I failed. For one year we tried to promote this program, but we were unsuccessful. It was something new to them. This is not a religious program, so they were afraid. [. . .]. So we lost a lot and I decided to cover up my losses by selling the tapes. Once we sold the tapes everything opened. People started to know ʿAmr and to buy the tapes. That was a good time. We both went to Iqra. I stayed less than six months and left because they asked me to choose between my company and Iqra.[6]

With his own company he produced a social program with the veiled actress-singer Mona ʿAbd al-Ghani. The talk show *Mona and Her Sisters* was bought by the Iqra channel for three years. Abu Haiba was then approached to start the new channel al-Risala.[7] This was the chance he had hoped for: "Al-Risala channel was exactly what I was dreaming of. But, as usual, after six months . . . The majority of the production was from Egypt and they were criticizing that it was outside their standard. Salafi people started to attack the channel, so it was decided to stop the production in Egypt. Al-Risala was the first, what I would consider good channel, with an Islamic face."[8] But after a short period it was turned into a regular channel, that is, a religious channel with preachers.

And then—*l'histoire se repète*—4Shbab, his new endeavor, began on February 1, 2009. This time it took a year before the investors decided to halt production and change the channel "back again to distant time [. . .]. So I am fed up!" Abu Haiba initially tempted the Saudi investors by confronting them with the "lewd" video clips Muslim youth eagerly watch. He selected some provocative videos that the investors had never seen before, as they generally avoided satellite TV and certainly music channels. They immediately recognized the necessity of providing an alternative. The channel was successful and received three Oscars at the Best Video Clip Award Festival of 2009 for the clip "If You Forget Allah." Yet Abu Haiba's concept of "showing Islamic values in the language of the twenty-first century and with the use of the most attractive media techniques" was soon attacked. Several Saudi sheikhs protested 4Shbab's editorial line and advised the investors in the channel to review their support.[9] Within a year, one million riyals was withdrawn from the channel, which meant a cut of 20 percent of the budget. Whereas it used to produce fourteen clips every three months, it now only produced one clip a season, all of them about male Saudi singers.

Abu Haiba concluded the first interview by summing up his expectations for the near future: "Do what you like till they stop you and when they stop you, look for another venue." He had accurately anticipated actual events, as I was to learn during the second interview in December 2011. I asked him— reiterating this final phrase—what had happened next and he related how he left 4Shbab and opened the Tahrir channel.

> I felt so oppressed at the time. It seems like my goals are not achievable. I was searching for another place to find funders, to make my own channel. [. . .] Then I started to work as a political activist till it happened . . . the revolution . . . I was one of the people who started on the 25th of January. I was on the street the 25th. I was arrested during the morning of the 25th. They arrested us, we were about fifteen people, eight men and seven women. We were arrested for four, five hours and they released us again. We went back to Tahrir. We did not know or expect that the regime would finally respond. By the 5th of February I got connected to Ibrahim 'Issa [see Chapter 5 for his anti-Salafi stance and his critiques on the Sauditization of Egypt]. [. . .] He was the only one who criticized the president before. He is a fighter. [. . .] Of course he is against the Islamists. I became one of his fans, although he is against the Islamists.[10]

Later on during the interview he reflected, "I am an Islamist, he is a liberal, but we are sharing ideas as everyone is doing now in Egypt." He continued:

The revolution connected us together. [. . .] Ibrahim said we need to express our voice, the Tahrir voice, because the regular channels express their
own point of view, the state's point of view or the private channel express
the businessmen's point of view. So we need to have a neutral, objective,
our own channel. I told Ibrahim, "I can do this." I told a friend I need a
frequency for the revolution. I told him, "I am going to pay myself but
give me time." They respect me so they gave me the frequency at once.
At my laptop I started to take the videos from the Internet, from Face-
book, and reedited it and sent it by e-mail to a satellite in Bahrain. [. . .]
I prepared everything and we decided it is going to be on air on Thursday
the day before Mubarak stepped down [February 11, 2011]. We came on
air that day, the second day he stepped down, so actually we became the
channel of the revolution. We started to broadcast everything, the people
shot in the street, on Tahrir, the martyrs, interviews with activists. [. . .]
The channel became so popular. [. . .] We try to be objective as much as
we can, we support the revolution, we are against the SCAF [Supreme Military Council of the Armed Forces], we care a lot about freedom, about
human rights, about freedom of expression. [. . .] We care about building
the New Egypt on a strong basis.[11]

Everything went fine with the channel until September 2011. The channel attracted a lot of stars, because — as Abu Haiba explains — "a lot of people
wanted to be cleansed on our channel." The Tahrir channel chose those stars
who were not directly connected to the regime, like Mahmud Sa'd, who was
the first anchor to resign from the Egyptian state TV. In a very short time,
Tahrir became a leading channel: "Many people were calling us; the SCAF is
trying to get close to you; you are starting to feel that you are controlling
the streets!" He presented a talk show that was favorably reviewed.[12] Good
fortune continued "[t]ill September, then we started suddenly to suffer financially." The channel had made a deal for an advertising campaign that
underwrote all expenses and salaries. But after Ramadan, the agency that
had bought the airtime lost money and withdrew. So Tahrir had to look for
other sponsors, but now facing the problem that the channel had become a
symbol for a revolution not for sale to the highest bidder, whether foreigners
or businessmen connected to the old regime. "I don't want to take any action
that makes the people feel that Tahrir is sold to the regime." Other factors
impacted the prospects of the channel as well: "Other channels have opened
that can pay the stars huge numbers. The impact of the revolution started to
decay and people started to question the revolution. It did not become like

it started." So when I conducted the interview, Ahmad Abu Haiba was just facing a huge dilemma with regard to the future of the channel. He also got offers to work for other channels: "People think that having me on will give them the credibility of Tahrir."

One of the offers he thought would interest me was an offer to run the channel of the Muslim Brothers, Masr 25 / Egypt 25.[13] Ahmad Abu Haiba's program in Ramadan, in which he sharply argued against dogmatic views, was well received by the Muslim Brothers; "therefore, they asked me to run their channel." In this program he tried to raise those questions that secularists would throw at Salafists.

> We talked about religion not from a ritual point of view, but from an ideological point of view, as ideas and thoughts. It was a provocative program. I put question marks from the basis. Does Allah exist? Shari'a, women's rights, everything. I argue as if I am against those ideas. I play the devil's advocate. The people accepted this because they know me and my background. I am not against them, I play this role. Usually in these kinds of debates sheikhs and secularists do not finish the debate. They start to shout at each other and the presenter ends the program. So you do not have the possibility to follow the discussion to the end. I went to the secular side; I tried to get their point of view and tried to play their role. Even secular friends said: "You asked the questions that were in our heads. We are not totally convinced, but we are happy to finally find someone discussing the ideas of the Muslim Brothers and Salafi ideas."[14]

His former mentor Hazem Salah Abu Isma'il, now head of the Salafi political party al-Nour and potential Salafi presidential candidate, was interrogated by Ahmad Abu Haiba in one of the episodes about the obligation of all women, including Copts and nonbelievers, to wear a headscarf, were he to become president. He proclaimed it mandatory under Islamic law, after which his rating in the opinion polls started to go down. Nevertheless, Ahmad Abu Haiba is still on good terms with his former mentor.

Ahmad Abu Haiba had not yet decided whether to accept the offer of the Muslim Brothers to run their channel. He respects the Brothers and described their unique system: "We call it *tarbiyya*, 'life education.' When I was still with the Brothers we lived together. We go on trips together; our leaders would come with us. We played together; we went on demonstrations together and found our leaders in the front. They were the courageous people cheering in the front. Even if you go out [of the movement], like me, we still respect them, we honor them. [. . .] The Muslim Brothers did not call for the revolution, but also did not go against it. They said it is your personal choice. But on the 28th, they called for a march. I think this was a turning point when the Muslim Brothers called for the march and decided to go for the streets." Ahmad Abu Haiba might decide to work for them: The Islamists are pushing him to leave Tahrir and work for Masr 25, which is still of a poor quality and needs to be professionalized.

> I told them that I will make drama, social programs, I will bring women, and music, and everything! They said, "We are OK with that." They want to show the whole world that they can cope with modern life. [. . .] The Muslim Brothers are heading towards authority, they are so influential. They have the power of the street. So, it might be useful if you are asked to be inside the cockpit. Why not go there and try to influence the direction? On the other hand maybe you need to be outside the focus to give them the other opinions and ideas and the things they do not see. It is the dilemma of being inside or outside; which gives you a clearer vision?[15]

POPULARIZING ISLAM OR ISLAMIZING POPULAR CULTURE

Although Ahmad Abu Haiba has had no time to further his *fann al-hadif* project because of his political activism, he intends to resume this project in due time. Generally, it is clear that art and protest go hand in hand. Zakia Salime argues that culture, aesthetics, and politics have never become more intertwined than during the current uprisings in the Middle East and North Africa.[16] The revolution has inspired the creation of new songs. Especially among youth, rap and hip-hop flourish. Ramy Donjewan's song "Against the Government" was adopted as the protesters' "official" rap song. "This music, in turn, has inspired its listeners to reclaim their neighborhoods, vocalize their frustrations, and demand their rights. After nearly two decades of underground activism in alternative spaces, the region's revolutionary music has finally come to the surface."[17] Daniel J. Gilman has noted the emergence of a new subgenre of musical videos after the revolution, which he labeled "Martyr Pop."[18] Egyptian popular singers, even those initially not very supportive of the revolution, such as Muhammad Fu'ad, who praised Mubarak during the early days of the revolution, and Tamir Hosni, who tried to convince the protesters to go home, have produced a song and clip commemorating the people who were killed during the eighteen days of protest. I have no clue what the recent transitions will mean for the Islamist cultural productions, as my fieldwork was mainly conducted in 2005, 2006, and 2008, but the examples above and the career of Ahmad Abu Haiba, just reviewed, show the great entanglement of Egypt's historical transformation and the field of art.

Islamists were largely absent during the initial stage of the revolution. The religious establishment of al-Azhar had ties of allegiance with the regime. Salafists condemned the protest and aligned with the view of Saudi Arabia's Wahhabi clerics that "all protest movements in the Arab world are western machinations against the Muslim community."[19] The Muslim Brothers' position evolved under pressure from the street, and the group initially joined the demonstrations "only in a symbolic way, sending some very restrained groups from their youth movement."[20] On the "Day of Rage" on January 28, the Brothers reportedly mobilized about 100,000 people. A dialogue and disagreement emerged between some of the young Brothers mobilized in the streets and the Brotherhood elite. *Time World* reporter Bobby Ghosh perceived a tendency toward moderate Islamism, finding that "Islamists of all stripes—extremist Salafis to members of more orthodox groups like the Muslim Brotherhood—say they are breaking with the past and reinventing themselves as the moderate mainstream."[21] *Masry al-Yawm* reporter Khalil al-Anani noted the familiar antagonism, or "Salafobia," from liberals toward the Islamists, making effective coalition building during the months after the revolution a near "mission impossible."[22] 'Amr Khalid, however, the person "everyone had thought to be the least inclined to get involved in politics," supported the protest movement openly from the start, and appeared on Tahrir Square several times, calling on the regime to "listen to the demands of the young."[23] At the time of the interview, the first results of the parliamentary election of 2011 showed a victory for the Brothers and the Salafists. Ahmad Abu Haiba expected that the Salafists would soon vanish, as they have kept segregated from society for a long time, have no clear ideology, and lack unified leadership. The real danger, in his opinion, comes from the side of the old regime forces: "They have the keys of the country. What we have done is to take the banner of the house. The house of Mubarak is now the house of Egypt, but the keys of every single door are still with them. We have to get the keys or we have to make our own keys."[24] As a result of the May 2012 presidential elections, the keys are entrusted to the candidate of the Muslim Brothers, President Morsi.

Piety was clearly visible in the streets and squares during the uprisings, whether in the form of veiling or praying. Not as a prominent organizing principle or motivating factor, but as part of daily practices. Will the moderate turn of small fractions of the Muslim Brothers be broadened? Will the post-Islamist turn among youth be extended? It is not clear what the recent turbulences in Egypt will mean for the Islamist movements and how this will be translated in artistic terms. Will the purposeful productions, with their overtly religious messages and aesthetics prevail, or will "lighter" versions gain dominance? I will not speculate about the future prospects of Egypt's transition and its translation into the field of popular art production. However, as has been argued in this book, mutual influence between the two is to be expected, because art not only reflects historical transformations, but is also intimately intertwined with them. Art productions are powerful vehicles for debating, challenging, and sustaining regimes of power.

This book has described and analyzed the history of Egypt, and particularly of the pious Islamist currents, over the last three decades through the lens of performing arts. In the 1980s, Egypt witnessed a growing revival of religiosity, among large lower- and middle-class sectors of the population, ranging in form from militant to pietistic. Artists were just one of the groups affected by the religious spirit in Egypt in those days. They were, however, also special—not only with regard to their affluent backgrounds and lifestyles, but also with regard to their influential status as celebrities. They celebrated piety and "celebritized" piety—that is, they cultivated pious lifestyles and provided pious role models for emulation among millions of fans. The pious stars retired from art, "repented" from "sinful" activities, and dedicated themselves to worship, religious knowledge, charity, and other religious activities. We have seen the profound impact of their religious turn on even the smallest details of their comportment in their daily lives. Piety was ingrained into their bodies and minds, and became a habitual part of daily practices, practices that also constituted their pious selves. Dreams, visions, the pilgrimage, and death or illness have been powerful transformative experiences in their lives. However, continuous repentance, praying, and veiling as habitual daily practices were equally influential in sustaining and nurturing their religious selves in their striving to come close to God. The stars have also become active in spreading religious lifestyles through Islamic preaching and teaching, Islamic salons, and Islamic charity. They have enabled the spread of pious sensibilities into the upper-middle and upper classes. The moral-religious engagements and pious lifestyles were part and parcel of the growing Islamist strands and parallel Islamic sector in Egypt but also had in their pietistic quest commonalities with Sufism. The moral politics of piety was empowering for women, providing them with moral agency that enabled them to enter into the field of religious preaching, teaching, and other public arenas. Because of its growing influence and visibility, the pious current was politicized—perhaps not in its aims, but certainly in its effects—and was increasingly perceived as a threat by the state.

In the 1990s, we see the ambiguous politics of the state, trying to con-

tain, co-opt, and repress the diverse varieties of Islamists, increasingly blurring distinctions between them and enforcing total repression. Confrontation
of Islamists by the state was also carried out within the cultural arena with the
help of the secular cultural players. The Islamists capitalized on the "repentance" of the pious stars to promote their ideals. In the intense deliberations
in the emergent public sphere in Egypt of the 1990s, the "repentant" artists
became one of the touchstones for debating the different cultural and national
visions of Islamists and secularists. Gender, art, and Islam, condensed in the
symbol of the veiled actresses, proved a perfect way to delineate the opposing
ideals of secularists and Islamists in which the religious idiom nevertheless
became inescapable, strengthening the Islamization of the public sphere. This
Islamization was also due to the space allowed by the state to conservative
religious forces within the state-controlled religious establishment. While
intended to counter Islamists, the leverage accorded the conservatives resulted in an attack on the secular cultural field that supported the state. The
repulsive forces of secularists and Islamists of all sorts were strategically manipulated by the state. The 1990s thus witnessed an entanglement of factions
and forces that could not be classified as counterpublics independent of the
state. The notion of counterpublic, not as independent debate and reasoning
by oppositional groups, but as an ethical counterworld crafting moral dispositions and taste cultures in opposition to secular liberal sensibilities proved,
however, to be valuable in understanding the development toward pious art
that emerged around the turn of the century.

   In the new millennium, the fragmentation of religious authority increasingly took form in the popularity of young lay preachers who had a pleasant, "lighter" version of the Islamic messages, which was well received by
the middle and upper classes. The post-Islamist turn by part of the Islamist
movement enabled the Islamization of the upper classes of Egypt, although
the meaning and practice of Islam also changed upon reaching the higher
echelons. The "repentant" artists have been influential in spreading piety to
the upper classes; the Islamization of the upper classes in turn enabled the
development of pious markets for leisure and art, thus facilitating the return of artists as veiled actresses or religiously committed performers. The
pious artists were also backed by the change in religious discourse on art and
entertainment, in particular by the emergence of the discourse on art with a
mission. There thus developed an extensive field of religiously inflected art
accommodating to religious sensibilities and promoting pious taste cultures.
The development of religious aesthetics proved to be a contentious issue.
The moralizing forms with explicitly religious references did not cater to the

evolving post-Islamist sensibilities. The religious taste cultures of the affluent classes were influenced by global cosmopolitan forces coming from both the West and the Gulf. "Lighter" forms of *halal* or clean art productions were closer to their taste. The pleasant post-Islamist style has in the meantime become available as an alternative to all audiences. There thus developed a fragmented market that balances different combinations of religious mission and pleasant recreation.

It appears that Islamist players in the cultural field, who are internally divided, have difficulty controlling the balance between moral messages and market forces as well. The more successful pious art productions tend to lose their original message. As we have seen in Chapters 8 and 9, the religious originals are copied and transplanted outside their original frame and purpose. Pious audiences increasingly tend to invite to their weddings prestigious singers who have gained credibility through an occasional religious song, or watch a clean production without a clear religious message. In a way, art with a mission thus seems to be buried by its own success. However, this observation needs qualification, as the process worked out differently for the songs and the soaps. The songs have apparently been more successful in bridging the gap between morals and the markets. When the artists experimented beyond the strictly religious *anashid*, singers of *halal* songs began by cutting words and replacing them with clean alternatives, mimicking the clean cinema strategy. Yet, with this further development, the songs have become successful in attracting a large following and inspiring imitation. They were admired for quality and piety. The songs had a ripple effect, leading to religious songs by performers with a normally not-so-Islamic repertoire. This development is related to market forces outside the control of Islamist circles, which also affected the soaps, but the *fann al-hadif* artists have been able to bring the religious songs and their content into the popular art scene. These songs have thus extended piety into the popular realm. The soaps were less successful in bridging faith and fun. The soaps stuck to the message and could not that easily shake off the preachy image. The Islamist message remained visible, for instance, in the form of the veil, and imposed limits on creative forms. The soaps and historical productions that have remained truthful to the original message were seen as unrealistic and moralizing. The alternative clean productions did not offend religious sensibilities, but contained no religious messages or references. They were mainstream productions evaluated by the usual criteria for assessing art, not for their pious nature. Some of the productions have brought nonreligious elements—for instance, the wig instead of the veil—into the religious genre. These productions lost part of their markers of piety instead of moving piety into the popular realm. Why have the songs done better than soaps in bridging morals and the market while retaining the religious message?

First, it is remarkable that the success in singing is mainly awarded to male singers, whereas the failure in the field of acting is related in large part to veiled women. The clean cinema's success was mainly based on male actors. Gender is thus an important dimension. In performing arts, whether on the stage, the small screen, or the large screen, the body is focal. As we have seen, the body is a highly gender-sensitive issue. Particularly, the female body on stage remains a difficult issue. For a pleasing female body, it is difficult to avoid sexual connotations while performing in front of the male gaze. The sexual dimension of the female body was contained by veiling and other forms of pietization. Religious comportment and ways of being expressive, as well as covering the female body, have the intent of changing the sexualized body into a religious body. However, this neutralizing strategy did not produce a balanced form of pious pleasure. Exposing "pleasing" female bodies on stage appeared difficult to combine with the piety of the project. The range of male behavior between piety and pleasure is much larger than for women. The formats for pleasant forms of pious performances by female bodies are still not well developed. Second, it is interesting to link the divergent success of the songs versus the soaps to a difference in the sensorium related to each genre. Using Charles Hirschkind's ideas (2006) on the location of the Islamist counterpublic in its alternative soundscape, it could be argued or imagined that the aural is a more fruitful foundation for an alternative, yet Islamic, message. Listening to cassettes has long been an oppositional activity within the Islamic Revival. This could have led to a better adaptability of the aural to the Islamist art project. The visual media to which the soaps belong have been largely dominated by the state and the secular artistic field. For that reason, they might less easily adapt themselves to alternative pious art or easily lose their religious references and become mainstream. I discussed this theory with some of my interlocutors, but they pointed to the different material structure of the aural versus the visual media. The soundscape is more accessible and cheaper, in a sense more democratic, than the visual media. The latter need a lot of money and are dominated by market forces outside the scope and intentions of the actors, actresses, and producers involved. These remarks by my interlocutors thus affirm the counterpublic status of the aural and the hegemonic character of the visual, not so much at the level of the sensorium, but rather at the level of the market.

How should we evaluate the efficacy of the pious art project? Should we interpret the new "lite" trend in Islamist art as an extension of the Islamist political project by attractive means? Or does it indicate a change of direction away from political activism toward consumerism and hedonism? Has the Islamist art project been co-opted by global markets? Or have the "market Islam" versions of art spread among wider audiences, thus enabling the propagation of the Islamic message? Have market forces engulfed the moral mission? Or do the moral missionaries use the market to reach out to a larger clientele? The answers to these questions depend on how we evaluate the ultimate aim of the Islamist art project. Is its aim to Islamize popular culture and art or to popularize Islam? This question will probably have different answers aligned with the fragmentation within the Islamist movement more generally, which is mirrored in the divisions among the players in the field of pious art. The "hard core" of Islamist actors aims at Islamizing art, popular culture, and the public sphere in general. These Islamists do not want to spread Islam by all means, but only by Islamically appropriate means. The moderate mainstream intends to bring moral-religious messages and provide an alternative pious taste culture to secular sensibilities. Mainstream Islamists are eager to popularize Islam by Islamizing popular culture. If the popularization of Islam is benefited by less missionary moral messages or less explicit forms of Islamization, they can live with that. The clean marketeers' purpose is to sell by not offending religious sensibilities, but they have no aim to either Islamize art or to popularize Islam. Market Islam has, however, become prominent and has been able to accommodate these diverse taste cultures. Although clean markets do not necessarily support or spread religious lifestyles, they do abide by the growing dominance of religious taste cultures.

This fragmentation in the market of artistic productions that is able to accommodate diverse religious taste cultures is probably an important factor in the pious art project's future prospects. This religious-clean market enables lifestyles offering alternatives to secular taste and sensibilities. It is capable of catering to diverse audiences, from strict Islamist to pleasant post-Islamist. Despite the different trends, aims, and content, the diverse segments of the market encourage a moral-clean, albeit not necessarily explicitly religious, climate. Yet even the clean genre abides by and affirms religious sensibilities. The diversification of pious-clean arts thus ultimately nourishes pious taste cultures in Egypt.

Notes

INTRODUCTION

1. Most of my material has thus been collected before the 25th of January Revolution (2011), and I can therefore not deal with the recent developments that have swept over Egypt. Only in the Afterword do I go into the latest developments based on my last short visit to Egypt and interview with media man Ahmad Abu Haiba.
2. I dealt with similar questions in my study on female converts to Islam in the Netherlands (Van Nieuwkerk 2006a).

PART ONE

1. The "secular" and the "religious" or "spiritual" domains are constructed as opposites in the Egyptian debates around the celebrities. Although I do not intend to reproduce this dichotomy, in describing the debates between "secularists" and "Islamists" in the Egyptian public sphere these oppositions are widely used (see Part Two).

CHAPTER I

1. Kariman Hamza retired before Shams al-Barudi, but she was a TV presenter and not a performer; see Malti-Douglas (2001) for an interesting analysis of Hamza's autobiography *Rihlati min al-sufur ila al-hijab / My Journey from Unveiling to Veiling* (1986).
2. In addition to her autobiography several other sources are relevant: Nasif and Khodayr (n.d.), *Fannanat Ta'ibat / Repentant Artists*, pp. 47–63; Kamil (1993), *Fannanat wara' al-Hijab / Artists behind the Veil*, pp. 61–65; 'Abdallah (sha'aban 1425/2004), *Dumu' al-Ta'ibin / Tears of the Repenters*, pp. 218–223; al-Sayyid (n.d.), *Nisa' 'A'idat ila Allah / Women Returning to God*, pp. 64–65; al-Juhayni (1989), *Min 'Alam al-Shuhra ila Rihab al-Iman / From the World of Fame to the Acceptance of Faith*, pp. 32–45; al-Sangri (1999), *al-'A'idun*

ila Allah | People Returning to God, pp. 89–104; Abu Dawud and Bayumi (1994), *Hiwar ma'a al-Fannanin wa al-Fannanat al-Ta'ibin wa al-Ta'ibat | Conversations with Male and Female Artists Who Repented*, pp. 13–41.

3. See section 2 of Chapter 2 for further elaboration on the notion of repentance.

4. See http://www.yallacinema.com and http://entertainment.filbalad.com for information on the films in which she acted (accessed January 15, 2006, but no longer available). See also *Awraq Shams al-Barudi* (Siraj al-Din, 1993) for the view of the author on the bad influence of Hollywood and British sexual morals on the Egyptian film industry.

5. Interview with Hassan Yusif published on http://islamna.org (n.d.) (accessed January 15, 2006, but no longer available).

6. See also Amal Khodayr's interviews published on the website "Our Islam" (http://islamna.org [no longer available]) and Nasif and Khodayr (n.d., 50–51).

7. Nasif and Khodayr (n.d., 50–51); translation taken from Abu Lughod (1995, 55).

8. Ibid.

9. Interview in *al-Kawakib*, August 2, 1979, quoted in Siraj al-Din (1993, 30).

10. Interview in *Ruz al-Yusif*, March 7, 1988, quoted in Siraj al-Din (1993, 66–67).

11. Reproduction of a tape in which Shams al-Barudi tells her story, quoted in magazine *Ruz al-Yusif* (November 18, 1996, pp. 49–52).

12. Nasif and Khodayr (n.d., 51); translation taken from Abu Lughod (1995, 55–56).

13. See also Malti-Douglas (2001) on the importance of the female body in revivalist literature.

14. The order of the spiritual events slightly differs among several versions of her story. Whereas the poem comes first, followed by the devil, and finally a short, almost passing, mentioning of the vision in Khodayr's reconstruction, in *Awraq Shams* by Siraj al-Din (1993), first the experience of reading the *fatiha* for the first time, then the poem about the veil, and finally the vision of the Prophet are presented. Her later retelling has no devil, but the vision of the Prophet in greater detail as the turning point. This probably has to do with the great importance that is generally attached to visions of the Prophet as the epitome of veracious dreams and visions. Despite the differences in the reconstructions, they all convey a strong image of the immense change accompanied by turbulent bodily sensations.

15. Online at Ishrinat, September 1, 2005, http://www.20at.com (no longer available), taken from journal *Migallit al-Ahram al-'Arabi* (accessed January 15, 2006).

16. Interviews on http://www.al-eman.com, taken from Internet source *Muheet al-Akhbariyya*, December 20, 2002 (accessed January 15, 2006, but no longer available); *Kolenas*, no. 174, September 9, 1992.

17. See Fahd 1978.

18. A new term is "post-Islamism," which describes the recent trend from the mid-1990s onward. I will come back to this notion in Chapter 7.

CHAPTER 2

1. This story is also used in Van Nieuwkerk (2008b).

2. Interview with author, February 3, 2006.

3. Ibid.

4. Ibid.

5. Ibid.

6. That is, as explained above, "repentant artists, retired artists, or veiled artists."

7. Interview with Wagdi al-'Arabi took place on February 22, 2008.

8. See also *"A Trade like Any Other"* (Van Nieuwkerk 1995). An important reason for female artists to retire is when their children start to feel embarrassed by the mother's profession.

9. In some interviews the tone is slightly negative, in some neutral, but in general the message is that despite her adherence to rules she lacked a real understanding of Islam. This was also confirmed during an interview with her half brother, actor Wagdi al-'Arabi, on February 22, 2008.

10. In most stories it is mentioned that from the moment of the *hajj*, her wish to veil grew steadily until her final decision to veil in Ramadan 1989 (interview in *al-Nur*, September 18, 1996). Nasif and Khodayr, however, relate that she actually veiled after her *hajj*. She returned to the television building as a *muhagaba*, but was not allowed to continue working as a presenter. Then the "mean devil" started whispering in her ear that it is only the intention that counts, that she could not do without her work in the media and that she could use her position as a presenter as a form of Islamic outreach. She later on deconstructed these excuses and arguments as "beautifying devices of the devil" (Nasif and Khodayr n.d., 114–115). This account is supported by an interview in *al-Nur* in which she says she gained the knowledge of veiling and veiled. However, after that insight the devil played with her until the aforementioned evening in Ramadan (*Al-Nur*, April 1, 1992).

11. Untaped interviews with Sheikh al-Matar on January 26 and January 31, 2005.

12. See al-Ghazali 1933 (see also French translation by Bousquet [1955], *Ihya 'Ouloum Ed-Din ou Vivification des Sciences de la Foi* [Paris: Besson], or English translation, Stern 1990). See also Stern (1979); Wilzer (1957, 1958, 1959).

13. Scholars such as Roy (2004) and Bayat (2002a, 2005b) coined "post-Islamism" to describe this new tendency within the Islamic Revival. Lauzière (2005) alternatively labeled it post-Salafism. Post-Islamism will be discussed in more detail in Part Three, which deals with the period after the turn of the century. The roots of the spiritualization can already be found, however, in the 1980s.

14. See, for instance, the ideas of Ibn al-'Arabi as described by Khalil (2006).

15. Stern 1990, 32. All English translations will be taken from Stern 1990.

16. Ustadh Amru Khalid, lesson "al-Tawba," *Kalam min al-Qalb* (Cairo: Sana al-Sharq, n.d.), videotape; Ustadh Amru Khalid, *Silsila: Aslah al-Qulub, al-Tawba* (Abu Dhabi: RDI, 2000), CD-ROM.

17. See also Chapter 9, section 1 on the negligent soul (*al-nafs al-ghafila*).

18. Khalid, lesson "al-Tawba."

19. Reproduction of a tape in which Shams al-Barudi tells her story in magazine *Ruz al-Yusif*, November 18, 1996.

20. I will use *daʿiyya* as a generic label.

21. See Cook (2000) for an overview of this concept.

22. Interview in *Ruz al-Yusif*, March 7, 1988, reprinted in Siraj al-Din (1993).

23. I interviewed journalist Kamal Masri on February 17, 2005.

CHAPTER 3

1. Interview took place on March 3, 2005.

2. Other sources on her life story include Nasif and Khodayr (n.d.). Although her story is mentioned in *The Repentant Artists and the Sex Stars*, several pages are dedicated to her objections to being included in the book. Khodayr finally succeeded in making an interview by telephone, but was asked not to publish it. Another source is the book *al-Shaʿarawi . . . wa al-Fannanat* (Abu al-ʿAynayn 1999, 49–67), which focuses on the relationship of Sheikh al-Shaʿarawi with artists. Although Abu al-ʿAynayn mentions that the interview with al-Shaʿarawi took place in the summer of 1995, he does not mention when he spoke with Yasmin al-Khiyyam. He presents her story, however, as an interview and first-person narrative by Yasmin.

3. al-Shaykh Mahmud Khalil al-Hosari, *Ahkam Qiraʾit al-Qurʾan al-Karim* (Cairo: Maktabit al-Turath al-Islamiyya, 2002).

4. The tape is named *Asmaʾ Allah al-Hasana; Ya Rasul Allah / Names of God; Oh Messenger of God* after two of the most important religious songs on it.

5. See also interview with Yasmin al-Khiyyam on the program *Muwajihat* on television channel Iqra (n.d.).

6. Abdo (2000, p. 143) is a former correspondent of *The Guardian* and *The Economist*. Unfortunately, her references to sources are very scarce. Wise, in her master's thesis (2003, 48) refers to the Abdo book as her source.

7. The article is entitled "Tatawurat gidida li al-ʿamal al-khayriyya / New Developments in Charity Work," *Islam Online*, November 29, 2004, available online at (www .islamonline.com), first published in *al-Bayan*, December 3, 2003 (accessed February 15, 2006).

8. Amira Howeidy, "Flight no. 1 to Baghdad," *Al-Ahram Weekly Online*, no. 504 (October 19–25, 2000), available online at http://weekly.ahram.org.eg/2000/504/eg3.htm (accessed December 27, 2011).

9. Interview with Yasmin al-Khiyyam, February 17, 2006, at Filbalad.com (accessed March 21, 2006).

10. Interviews with author, February 20, 2005, and February 5, 2006.

11. See documentary by Ismail El-Mokadem, *Pop Goes Islam* (abbreviated version at http://www.youtube.com/watch?v=NR99ivKP_MY; on sale at http://sales.arte.tv/detail Fiche.action?programId=2435).

12. "Tatawurat gidida."

13. Interview with author, March 8, 2006.

14. "Tatawurat gidida."

15. His conversion is documented in his autobiography *Rihlati min al-shakk ila al-iman / My Journey from Doubt to Faith* (Cairo: Akhbar al-Yawm, 2001).

PART TWO

1. The opposition between "secular-liberals" and "Islamists" is very strong in the Egyptian debate to the present. I use these categories as discursive constructions and do not contend they represent personal religious convictions or practices. Sherine Hafez (2011) has argued that the female Islamic activists of her research reproduce a sharp opposition between religion and secularity in their discourses. In their daily practices as activists, however, they are affected by both religious and secular discourses as well as lifestyles.

2. The formation of an ethical counterworld in the field of art will be the topic of Part Three.

CHAPTER 4

1. Interview in *al-Mawed*, November 1992, pp. 24–28. I interviewed Shahira on February 13, 2006.

2. Interview took place on February 15 and March 8, 2005.

3. Interview with author, February 15, 2005.

4. Other sources on her life story or interviews with her are published in Kamil (1993), pp. 91–95; al-'Aynayn (1999), pp. 131–140; *al-Mawed* (November 1992), pp. 24–28; *al-Kawakib* (December 17, 1998), pp. 22–24; *al-Nur* (October 21, 1992); *al-Bayan* newspaper (May 22, 2008).

5. The serial is made in Saudi Arabia and is entitled *Elazee ahtado / Those Who Are Guided* (Sana Production Company, n.d. [ca. 1995]). Because of the ban it was difficult to locate the serials. It was generously sent to me for free by the production company. The two videos also include lengthy interviews with former dancer Zizi Mustafa, actress Madiha Hamdi, and actor Hamdi Hafiz. The interviews are conducted by Islamist poetess 'Aliya Go'ar, who has also been influential in the veiling and retirement of the famous singer Shadia (see volume Introduction).

6. Interview with censor Abu Shadi in *al-Kawakib*, December 17, 1998.

7. Interview with author, February 15, 2005.

8. *Elazee ahtado.*

9. Interview with author, February 15, 2005.

10. Interview published online at website Islamna (accessed January 15, 2004, but no longer available).

11. Signed by retired artists Shams al-Barudi, Hala Fu'ad, Kamilia al-'Arabi, Madiha Kamil, Nisrin, Hana' Tharwat, Shahira, Hala al-Safi, and Amira.

12. Signed by Shadia, Shams al-Barudi, Nisrin, Madiha Kamil, ʿAfaf ʿAbdelraziq, Amira, Hala Fuʾad, Hala al-Safi, Kamilia al-ʿArabi, ʿAfaf Shoʿib, Hanaʾ Tharwat, and Shahira.

13. Stories of, among others, Cat Stevens, Hanaʾ Tharwat, Shams al-Barudi, and the late Hala Fuʾad are read from the book of al-Misnid *Those Who Return to God* (no date or publisher mentioned on the tape).

14. For instance, the website Islamna (accessed January 15, 2004, but no longer available).

15. See Chapter 5 for the story of Soheir al-Babli, who was invited to ʿAmr Khalid's show.

16. These are huge topics, but I will only analyze how the case of the "repentant" artists is used by these Islamist authors to oppose the "enemies of Islam" and promote their ideas of the "common good." The religious discourses on women, art, and veiling as important for the veiling of artists, by religious scholars such as Sheikh al-Shaʿarawi, Sheikh al-Ghazali, and Dr. ʿUmar ʿAbd al-Kafi, as well as the changes in the religious discourse at the end of the century, will be analyzed in Chapter 6. Here I focus more narrowly on the debates unleashed by the "repentance" and veiling of female artists.

17. *The International Jew, the World's Foremost Problem* is a collection of his largely anti-Semitic articles, which had been published in the journal issued by Ford, *The Dearborn Independent* (1920).

18. Bayat lists the following (1998, 156): *Al-Shaʿb* of the Islamist Labor Party and *Al-Nour* of the Liberal Party / Muslim Brotherhood. *Al-Moslimoun* and *Al-Moslim Al-Moasir* are international dailies. Other periodicals were *Al-Liwaʾa Al-Islami*, of the National Democratic Party; *Aqidati*, an al-Azhar–sanctioned journal; and *Liwaʾ Al-Islam* (published weekly). Periodicals included: *Al-Mukhtar Al-Islami* (MB), *Minbar El-Sharq* (Labor Party), *Al-Tasawaf Al-Islami* (the Sufi Council), *Minbar Al-Islam* and *Al-Azhar* (al-Azhar Institute), and *Al-Muslim Al-Saqir* (Islamic children). In addition, a number of dailies and weeklies were published by the leading Islamic political organizations and parties. They included: *Al-Ahrar* (daily), *Al-Aharar* (weekly), *Al-Haqiqah* (weekly), *Al-Nour* (weekly), and *Al-Osrat el-Arabi* (weekly). There were also over thirty specialized or region-based publications, such as *El-Orouba*, *Shabab el-Aharar*, *Ahrar el-Saiid*, and *Ahrar El-Hilwan*.

CHAPTER 5

1. The interview took place on March 11, 2006.

2. I am grateful to Amani ʿAli for providing me with these—as well as other—media fragments on the veiled artists. It is a talk in Arabic for the 22nd Annual Convention of the Muslim Arab Youth Association (MAYA) in Los Angeles, entitled "From Heart to Heart." There is no date provided, but it was probably recorded in 1999, as she mentioned that she retired six years before. It is detailed and consistent with other interviews she gave in newspapers and magazines. Yet in other interviews, she was often interrupted with new

questions. The listener feels that she was just about to tell a story or did not complete one already begun because a new issue was raised, as in, for instance, the one-and-a-half-hour interview at al-Jazeera conducted by Mahir 'Abdallah (January 28, 2001). They are interesting material for her views on issues like art and Islam, but less so for her life story.

3. The expression "*rabbina yitob 'alayya*," meaning "to stop working," was also regularly used among the performers who were subjects of my previous research on Muhammad 'Ali Street. It conveys the awareness of sinfulness accorded to the profession, but meant "leaving the trade," not necessarily as a result of spiritual experiences or being born again, but also because of their age and being less in demand (Van Nieuwkerk 1995).

4. Interview with Mahir 'Abdallah on al-Jazeera (January 28, 2001).

5. According to the Arab Wikipedia, on February 14. A portrait of Soheir al-Babli in *al-Ahram Hebdo* (October 12, 2005) mentions February 7 without the year of birth, but dates her appearance in the film *Seduction* to 1957. It also mentions Mansura as her place of birth, whereas other sources mention Faraskur. At the age of thirteen, Soheir al-Babli moved with her family to Cairo. The Arabic Wikipedia website mentions four husbands; the portrait in *al-Ahram Hebdo*, five.

6. From other interviews I conclude that this is probably Dr. 'Umar 'Abd al-Kafi (*Ruz al-Yusif*, November 14, 2005, pp. 82–83). See Chapter 6 for his views on art.

7. Shahira is a well-known actress and wife of the famous actor Mahmud Yasin. She veiled and retired in 1992. I interviewed Shahira on February 15, 2006.

8. Not the lesser pilgrimage, the *'umrah*, which can be done in any month of the year but in the month, prescribed for the *hajj*, Dhu al-Hijj. After performing this pillar of Islam, the pilgrim is called Hagg (male) or Hagga (female).

9. Ashraf al-Sirgani, a merchant in jewelry. Mahmud Ghanim was probably her fourth husband.

10. See, for similar story, 'Amr Khalid, *Kalam min al-Qalb / Words from the Heart* (Cairo: Sana' al-Sharq, n.d.), videotape.

11. Exact date is not clear, due to bad quality of the copy.

12. Interview, March 11, 2006.

13. See Afterword for the story of Ahmad Abu Haiba, the playwright of these theater plays.

14. See Afterword for his remarkable cooperation with the Islamist actor, playwright, and media man Ahmad Abu Haiba during the 25th of January Revolution.

15. Other fields of art production, such as the film industry—with the exception of 1960 when it was nationalized by Nasser—have been mostly privately financed.

16. In Morocco and Syria, Sufism is promoted as the tolerant "good," or "moderate," Islam. I am not aware of a clear state-induced promotion of Sufism in Egypt similar to those in Syria and Morocco (see Shannon 2011).

CHAPTER 6

1. The interview took place on February 22, 2005.

2. Interview with author, February 22, 2005.

3. Ibid.

4. Ibid.

5. Mahmud Khalil, "'Abir Sharqawi," *Hamasna*, 2006, http://www.hamasna.com /articles/abeer1.htm (accessed April 27, 2010).

6. *Al-Sharq al-Awsat* 23, no. 8077 (January 8, 2001): 2; *al-Sharq al-Awsat*, January 12, 2001; later interviews in *al-Arabiyya*, April 9, 2005; Khalil, "'Abir Sharqawi."

7. Interview with author, February 22, 2005.

8. Ibid.

9. Ibid.

10. Ibid. She refers to the effects of "street censorship" (see Chapter 5).

11. Interview with author, February 22, 2005.

12. *Al-Arabiyat*, April 23, 2004, http://www.arabiyat.com/node/888 (accessed April 27, 2010); *al-Arabiyya*, April 9, 2005; Khalil, "'Abir Sharqawi."

13. *Al-Arabiyya*, April 9, 2005; Khalil, "'Abir Sharqawi."

14. Interview with author, February 22, 2005.

15. *Al-Arabiyya*, April 9, 2005.

16. Ibid.

17. Interview with author, February 22, 2005.

18. Interviews with Mona 'Abd al-Ghani and Hanan took place on the March 5, 2005. Sources on the other veiled artists of the younger generations are many, among others: *Kamal 'Azab* (n.d.), a book that collected many interviews with them; *al-Hayat al-Fann*, September 30, 2002, on Nashwa Mustafa; *Ayan* newspaper, April 19, 2002, on Wafa' 'Amer; *al-Watan al-Islami*, November 7, 2003, on Mona 'Abd al-Ghani.

19. The interview took place on February 3, 2006.

20. When I asked her about the religious scholars or sheikhs she found inspirational with regard to art and religion, she mentioned several books of al-Ghazali, chief among them *al-Sunna al-Nabawiyya, Bayn Ahl al-Fiqh wa Ahl al-Hadith / The Prophet's Sunnah between the People of* Fiqh *and the People of* Hadith (Dar al-Shuruq, 1st printing, 1989). She also mentioned Dr. Muhammad 'Imara (1991), *Al-Islam wa al-Funun al-Jamila / Islam and the Fine Arts* (Dar al-Shuruq); al-Qaradawi (1997a), *Fiqh al-Ghina' wa al-Musiqa fi Dhu' al-Qur'an wa al-Sunna* (Maktabit Wahbah). She also arranged an interview with Dr. Muhammad 'Abdul, sheikh of al-Azhar University and head of the al-Falah Foundation, which translates and publishes religious literature (interview with author, March 5, 2005).

21. See Chapter 3.

22. Also one of her guests that day, Reda Ta'ima, preacher-cum-actor-cum-writer-cum-producer, extensively and repeatedly talked to me about his ideas of Islam as a loving and merciful religion. He considered himself to be more influential with regard to new ideas on combining art and religion than 'Amr Khalid. See also interview with him in *al-Shabab*, no. 332, March 2005.

23. Interview took place on March 5, 2005.

24. See Chapter 8.

25. See also Mahmud Gamiʿ (2005, 108–114) and Abu al-ʿAynayn (1999).

26. Madiha Hamdi, interview with author, March 8, 2005.

27. Mona ʿAbd al-Ghani, interview with author, March 5, 2005.

28. Hamdi, interview with author, March 8, 2005.

29. See story of Soheir al-Babli, Chapter 5.

30. Interviews with Abu Haiba took place on November 4, 2010, and December 19, 2011; see also Afterword.

31. See also Chapter 7 on post-Islamism.

32. It was quite popular and sold out at the time of my research. I received it as a gift from the bandleader of Al-Andalus, because he greatly admired ʿAmr Khalid's approach to art. Khalid (2005) also wrote a short essay, "Culture: The Distinguishing Feature of a People," in *Transnational Broadcasting Studies*.

PART THREE

1. This introduction is based on Van Nieuwkerk (2011a).

2. Lecture given May 17, 1934, at a meeting of the Société de Psychologie.

3. Aristotle's notion of estheses is understood as organizing "our total sensory experience of the world and our sensitive knowledge of it" (see, e.g., Meyer 2006, 19).

CHAPTER 7

1. The first interview took place on February 20, 2005, the second interview on February 5, 2006.

2. Ahmad (Mursi) Abu Haiba, interview with author, November 4, 2010, see also Afterword.

3. Interview with author, February 20, 2005.

4. Ibid.

5. In this context pilgrimage is often the initial point for retirement and veiling. See the stories of the other retired and veiled actresses.

6. Interview with author, February 20, 2005.

7. Ibid.

8. See Chapter 3, where I have used her story as an example of habituation to veiling.

9. Interview with author, February 20, 2005.

10. Ibid.

11. Ibid.

12. Ibid.

13. Ibid.

14. Ibid.

15. Ibid. The year after, during the second interview (February 5, 2006), I asked about her endeavors, but nothing had come of her attraction to this man. According to several newspapers she eventually got married to a Saudi producer and businessman, left him in silence, returned to him, but recently was divorced again.

16. The speakers were editor-in-chief of *al-Zuhur* magazine, Nur al-Huda Sa'ad, whom I also interviewed on February 7, 2008; Dr. Muhammad 'Imara, a noted *wasatiyya* thinker who also wrote about Islam and art in *Al-Islam wa al-Funun al-Jamila* (Cairo: Dar al-Shuruq, first published 1991); actress Samira 'Abd al-'Aziz; the preacher *ustaz* Muhammad Hamid; poet Dr. Muhammad Siyam; actor Tariq 'Abd al-'Aziz; playwright, actor, and producer Ahmad Mursi Abu Haiba, whom I interviewed on November 4, 2010, and December 19, 2011 (see Afterword); actor 'Abd al-'Aziz Makhyun; veiled singer, actress, and presenter Mona 'Abd al-Ghani, whom I interviewed on March 5, 2005; young preacher Khalid 'Abdallah; actor Wagdi al-'Arabi, whom I interviewed on February 26, 2008; Dr. Gaber Qamar al-'Arabi, a specialist in English literature. In addition, I interviewed one of the guests, actor Samih al-Sariti, on February 10, 2008. I would like to thank Joseph Alagha for translating the CD copy of this conference, which was sometimes of a very bad audio quality. Most information in this section is also available in Van Nieuwkerk (2011b).

17. I became intrigued by the theory of the conservative climate in Egypt being the result of returning migrants from Saudi Arabia. I therefore interviewed 10 persons who had spent their youth in Saudi Arabia and discussed with them their views on Islamic entertainment such as religious weddings and the soaps of the veiled actresses.

18. For instance, I interviewed director Dawud 'Abd al-Sayyid (February 2, 2008); 'Imad al-Bahad (February 11, 2008); Attiyat al-Abnudi and her daughter, the actress Asma Yihya (both on February 18, 2008); and Dina 'Abd al-Rahman, a presenter of Dream TV (February 15, 2008).

19. Interview with author, February 2, 2008.

20. See Chapters 4 and 5 for their self-understanding as competing publics.

21. *Al-Zuhur* conference, actor Ahmad Mursi Abu Haiba, and interview with him on November 4, 2010.

22. *Al-Zuhur* conference, actor 'Abd al-'Aziz Makhyun.

23. Nur al-Huda Sa'ad, interview with author, February 7, 2008.

24. Ahmad Mursi Abu Haiba, interview with author, November 4, 2010.

25. Wagdi al-'Arabi, interview with author, February 26, 2008.

26. *Al-Zuhur* conference, actor 'Abd al-'Aziz Makhyun.

27. Ibid.

28. *Al-Zuhur* conference, *wasatiyya* intellectual Muhammad 'Imara.

29. Ibid.

30. Ibid.

31. *Al-Zuhur* conference, preacher Muhammad Hamid.

32. *Al-Zuhur* conference, Muhammad 'Imara.

33. *Al-Zuhur* conference, Nur al-Huda Sa'ad.

34. *Al-Zuhur* conference, Muhammad Hamid.

35. *Al-Zuhur* conference, Ahmad Mursi.

36. *Al-Zuhur* conference, Muhammad 'Imara.

37. *Al-Zuhur* conference, Ahmad Mursi.

38. Samih al-Sariti, interview with author, February 10, 2008.

39. *Al-Zuhur* conference, 'Abd al-'Aziz Makhyun.

40. Dawud 'Abd al-Sayyid, interview with author, February 2, 2008.

41. Muhammad al-Baz, interview with author, February 12, 2008.

42. See also Afterword for his story.

43. Interview took place February 2, 2008.

CHAPTER 8

1. The interview took place on January 22, 2005.

2. Muhsin, interview with author, January 22, 2005.

3. See also Van Nieuwkerk (1995) for an elaboration of the difference between the social and moral evaluation of male and female performers in Egypt.

4. The interview took place on February 26, 2008.

5. The interviews took place on November 4, 2010, and December 19, 2011.

6. The interview took place on February 1, 2005.

7. As observed in *al-Masry al-Youm*: "When the popular band Wust El-Balad played . . . at the outdoor theater in Al Azhar park, the audience was full of young *muhajjabat*, some of whom were dancing. Those same fans probably couldn't attend the band's regular performances at After Eight" (http://www.almasryalyoum.com/en/node/4519 [accessed March 23, 2011]).

8. The interview took place on February 12, 2008; see also article about him on the website Islam Online (June 10, 2004), available online at http://www.islamonline.net (accessed February 15, 2006).

9. Mustafa Mahmud, interview with author, February 12, 2008.

10. It is also common in Egypt, but then in an informal way, as a nickname, not as a formal name.

11. See also Frishkopf (2009) for the kind of covers used in *anashid*.

12. Mustafa Mahmud, interview with author, February 12, 2008.

13. Ahmad Zayn, June 10, 2004, also available on the website of Islam Online, http://www.islamonline.net (accessed February 15, 2006).

14. Mustafa Mahmud, interview with author, February 12, 2008.

15. Ibid.

16. Ibid.

17. Ibid.

18. Website www.islamonline.net contains, among others, the following interesting articles on Islamic songs: Ahmad Zayn, "al-mughaniyyun al-Islamiyyun . . . qariban satanafus / Islamic Singers Will Soon Be Competitors," July 8, 2001 (accessed March 28, 2006); Dr. Magdi Sa'id, "Hikayit al-funun bi 'uyun mutafariga / The History of Arts through Various Viewpoints," March 13, 2001 (accessed July 2, 2006); Hashim 'Abd al-

Salam al-Kafawin, "Asbab ti'aththar al-Ghina' al-Islamiyya / Factors That Influence Islamic Songs," June 24, 2001 (accessed February 7, 2006); Hussam Tammam, "al-Ikhwan wa al-fann: min al-mufid al-hadif li al-mumti'al-nadhif / The Brothers and Art: From the Purposeful Mission to Clean Enjoyment," July 5, 2004 (accessed February 18, 2006); Rabab Sa'fan, "Firqit banat li al-aghani . . . islamiyya! / Female Bands for Islamic Songs!," February 9, 2004 (accessed March 28, 2008); Dr. Magdi Sa'id, "'al-sinima al-islamiyya': hal hiyya mumkina? / 'Islamic Theater': Is This Possible?," July 4, 2004 (accessed February 7, 2006); Wafa' Sa'dawi, "'Aghani al-Banat': 'Alehum al-alhan wa 'alena al-kalimat! / 'Girls' songs': Upon Them the Melody, Upon Us the Words," March 14, 2006 (accessed March 28, 2006).

19. It is a common idea that the mothers of the bride and groom should dance to show their happiness (Van Nieuwkerk 1995).

20. The interview with the bandleader of Basmit Andalus took place on February 12, 2006.

21. Muhammad al-Naggar, bandleader of Basmit Andalus, interview with author, February 12, 2006.

22. The interview took place on February 11, 2006.

23. The interview took place on February 12, 2006.

24. Common expression used by performers at all kinds of weddings (Van Nieuwkerk 1995).

25. Muhammad al-Naggar, interview with author, February 12, 2006.

26. Ibid.

27. Muhammad Sa'id, of al-Hayah Company, interview with author, February 7, 2006.

28. The interview took place on February 11, 2006. See also Sa'fan (2004) and Tammam and Haenni (2005).

29. The interview took place on February 11, 2006.

30. The interview with Tamir 'Abd al-Shafi' took place on November 7, 2010.

31. The same type of argument is heard with regard to veiling, which was initially seen as a lower-middle-class phenomenon, but has since become widespread among all classes, including the affluent strata of Egyptian society.

32. See also Bayat (2007b, 147): 67 percent of the female visitors to a shopping mall in Zamalek, a Westernized neighborhood, were wearing a veil.

33. This is an imagery we can also observe in soaps of the veiled actresses, such as *Qalb Habiba* for the new rich and *Habib al-Ruh* for the professional cosmopolites (see Chapter 9).

CHAPTER 9

1. Of course, they could be confronted with tabloid stories and gossip, but these are generally not considered reliable sources.

2. For more information on Sawsan Badr, see, e.g., http://www.enigma-mag.com

/interview_archives/2011/06/sawsan-badr-february-2011/ (accessed June 8, 2011, but no longer available).

3. "Abir Sabri: The Last Egyptian Belly Dancer," http://current.com/news/88998100 _abir-sabri-the-last-egyptian-belly-dancer.htm (accessed June 1, 2011).

4. http://www.danceanddance.com/dancers/dancer_details.php?dancer=Abir_Sabri &dancerid=211 (accessed June 1, 2011).

5. ʿAbir Sabri, interview with author, February 19, 2005.

6. http://us.moheet.com/asp/report/hewar_abeer2.htm (accessed May 15, 2011, but no longer available).

7. See also entry "*nafs*," *Encyclopaedia of Islam*, 2nd ed. (Leiden: Brill).

8. See al-Ghazali 1933, pp. 38–40 (see also French translation by Bousquet [1955], *Ihya ʿOuloum Ed-Din ou Vivification des Sciences de la Foi* [Paris: Besson], or English translation, Stern 1990).

9. Adham al-Saʿid, interview with author, February 6, 2008.

10. ʿAbir Sabri, interview with author, February 19, 2005.

11. Ibid.

12. Interview with Muhammad al-Baz, *al-Fajr*, February 12, 2008.

13. "Abeer Sabri Takes Off Her Hijab," http://www.albawaba.com/star-news-and -gossip/abeer-sabri-takes-her-hijab (accessed June 2, 2011).

14. http://us.moheet.com/asp/report/hewar_abeer2.htm (accessed May 15, 2011, but no longer available).

15. They have produced a third one on the former sheikh al-Azhar, Mustafa al-Maraghi, which I have not seen.

16. I interviewed Madiha Hamdi on March 8, 2005.

17. Sabrin returned in *Kashkol li kull Muwatin | A Notebook for Every Citizen*, but I have not been able to locate this serial on the market yet.

18. Ahmad Hussein, interview with author, February 2, 2008.

19. There are more soaps of this kind, but this is the only one I know of with the participation of a veiled actress. Most veiled actresses act in the more overtly religious or moral productions.

20. In 2008, I discussed the soaps with, among others, ten youngsters who had been raised in Saudi Arabia (see Chapter 8), four producers, five journalists, three singers, and five actors.

21. See also Chapter 5 on the secular cultural field and its attacks on the "repentant" artists: secularists did not attack the veil per se.

22. Interview, Dream TV, *Yata Salon*, available online at YouTube (accessed July 20, 2009).

23. Link 007, December 24, 2006, available online at http://www.link07777.com (accessed February 18, 2008).

24. *Al-Ahali*, no. 1299, October 18, 2006, available online at http://www.al-ahaly.com (accessed February 18, 2008).

25. Ibid.

26. In a TV interview she herself, however, deemed her scarf in *Children of the*

Street a not yet proper *hijab* and has returned in productions with a less revealing style of veiling. Future TV Lebanon, available on YouTube, http://www.youtube.com /watch?v=I5N5wwmMn2c (accessed January 12, 2009).

27. Also in the other soaps of Hanan Turk, the street scenes are quite dominant.

28. Interview with author, February 7, 2008.

29. Wagdi al-ʿArabi, interview with author, February 26, 2008.

30. Talk show al-Qahira wa al-Nas, available online at http://www.youtube.com /watch?v=w-cOZAeHwbk&feature=related (accessed May 2011).

31. ʿImad al-Bahad, interview with author, February 11, 2008.

32. Dawud ʿAbd al-Sayyid, interview with author, January 2, 2008.

33. Ahmad Hussein, interview with author, February 25, 2008.

34. March 17, 2008, available online at http://www.alarabiya.net/save_print.php?print =1&cont_id=47410 (accessed March 1, 2010); and September 2, 2009, available online at http://nogoom.akhbarway.com/news.asp?c=2&id=33118 (accessed March 1, 2010).

35. See, e.g., http://lahamag.com/printArticle.asp?articleId=10991 (accessed March 12, 2011).

36. ʿAbir Sabri explained her choice to unveil as due to, among other reasons, her feeling that her *higab* limited the variety of artistic roles to "the *muhagaba.*" Some of the older "repentant" artists, such as Shams al–Barudi and Yasmin al-Khiyyam, whom we have met in Part One, reacted with the remark that the veiled person would be better off completely leaving the field of art than looking for solutions that compromise the veil. Soheir al-Babli and ʿAfaf Shoʿib, whose stories were narrated in Part Two, have returned themselves, but stick to the idea that acting with a veil is part of bringing a message. So-heir al-Babli further remarked that the actress should respect herself before she respects her *higab.* She indicated that in this sense there is no difference between a veiled and a nonveiled actress: if she respects herself she refuses to kiss or embrace. In short, the veil cannot be compromised, and the corresponding moral conduct should be extended to all productions. Interview with ʿAbir Sabri is available online at http://www.mbc.net/portal /site/mbc/menuitem .cec41c4faec6734497b11b101f10a0a0/?vgnextoid=724fbd912a0c7110 VgnVCM1000008420010aRCRD&vgnextchannel=380ee30e61801110VgnVCM100000f 1010a0aRCRD (accessed March 1, 2010).

37. See, e.g., http://lahamag.com/printArticle.asp?articleId=10991 (accessed March 12, 2011).

38. See, e.g., http://www.elbashayer.com/news-117702.html (accessed June 15, 2011); http://www.alanba.com.kw/AbsoluteNMNEW/templates/art2010.aspx?articleid=147283 &zoneid=15&m=0 (accessed June 15, 2011).

39. See the interview with Mustafa Mahmud, which took place on February 13, 2008.

AFTERWORD

1. The interviews were conducted in English on November 4, 2010, and December 19, 2011. See also El-Mokadem (2008), Chammah (2010), Wise (2005), Shenker (2009), and

Awad (2009). See also the interesting documentary by El-Mokadem, *Pop Goes Islam*, about Ahmad Abu Haiba and the Islamic fashion model Yasmin Muhsin (abbreviated version at http://www.youtube.com/watch?v=NR99ivKP_MY; on sale at http://sales.arte .tv/detailFiche.action?programId=2435).

2. Ahmad Mursi Abu Haiba, interview with author, November 4, 2010.

3. Ibid.

4. Ibid.

5. Ibid.

6. Ibid.

7. See also Chapter 7.

8. Ahmad Mursi Abu Haiba, interview with author, November 4, 2010.

9. See documentary *Pop Goes Islam*.

10. Ahmad Mursi Abu Haiba, interview with author, December 19, 2011.

11. Ibid.

12. See, e.g., "Ramadan Talk Show Questions Salafi Dogmas," *al-Masry al-Yawm*, August 21, 2011, http://www.almasryalyoum.com/en/node/488604 (accessed August 22, 2011). This link was sent to me by Ahmad Abu Haiba, who commented, "Nice article about my new show!!!"

13. The number 25 obviously refers to the January 25 Revolution.

14. Ahmad Mursi Abu Haiba, interview with author, December 19, 2011.

15. Ibid.

16. Zakia Salime, "Rapping the Revolution," *Muftah*, May 28, 2011, http://muftah .org/?p=1071 (accessed June 20, 2011).

17. Ibid.

18. Daniel J. Gilman, "'Martyr Pop'—Made in Egypt," *Norient*, May 19, 2011, http:// norient.com/video/martyrpop/ (accessed May 25, 2011).

19. Husam Tammam and Patrick Haenni, "Egypt: Islam in the Insurrection," *Religioscope*, February 22, 2011, http://religion.info/english/articles/article_519.shtml (accessed February 24, 2011).

20. Ibid.

21. Bobby Ghosh, "The Rise of Moderate Islam," *Time World*, July 14, 2011, http:// www.time.com/time/world/article/0,8599,2082964,00.html (accessed July 14, 2011).

22. Khalil al-Anani, "Salafobia," *Egypt Independent*, May 8, 2011, http://www.al masryalyoum.com/en/node/483504 (accessed August 6, 2011).

23. Tammam and Haenni, "Egypt: Islam in the Insurrection."

24. Ahmad Mursi Abu Haiba, interview with author, December 19, 2011.

Glossary

abaya, coat
adhan, call for prayer
afrah baladi, popular weddings
ajr, spiritual recompense
alam, pain
al-din al-laziz, pleasant religiosity
al-dunya, this world (as opposed to the afterlife)
al-fann, art (see also *fann* entries)
al-ibda', creativity
'alim, religious scholar
'almaniyya, secularization
al-nafs, the soul (see also *nafs* entries)
al-sahwa al-islamiyya, the Islamic Awakening
'amal, deeds
amr bil ma'ruf wal-nahi 'an al-munkar, to command what is good and to prohibit what is evil
anashid, religious songs
'awra, taboo
ayat, divine signs
'azab al-qabr, the horrors and suffering in the grave
baruka, wig
bint al-balad, daughter of the country
da'a, to call or to summon
da'i, male (lay) preacher (s.)
da'iyya, (lay) preacher (general term) or female preacher (s.)
da'iyat, female preachers (pl.)
darura, necessity
da'wah, Islamic outreach, propagation
dish, the satellite

du'a, supplicatory prayer

du'at, male preachers (pl.)

duff, tambourine

durus dinniya, religious lessons

'eb, shameful

fajr, prayer, early morning prayer (sunrise)

fann al-badil, alternative art

fann al-habit, lowbrow art

fann al-hadif, art with a mission or purposeful art

fann al-islami, Islamic art

fann al-mabadi', art based on principles

fann al-multazim, pious art

fann al-nadif, clean art

fann raqi', uplifting art

fannanat muhagabat, veiled artists

fannanat multazimat, religiously committed artists

fannanat mu'tazilat, retired artists

fannanat ta'ibat, repentant artists

farah, wedding party

farah islami, Islamic wedding

farida min al-fara'id, personal duty

fatiha, the opening verse of the Qur'an

fatwa | fatawa, religious ruling(s)

fawahish, obscenities

fiqh, Islamic jurisprudence

fitra, nature or disposition

galabiyya, long gown

ghafla, inattentiveness

hadith, the authoritative record of the Prophet's exemplary speech and actions

hagga, honorific title for a female pilgrim (colloquial)

hajj, pilgrimage to Mecca

halal, that which is religiously permissible and legal

haram, that which is religiously forbidden and unlawful

hasana(t), meritorious deed(s)

higab, veil (colloquial)

higg, pilgrimage to Mecca (colloquial)

hisab, the final account

hubb Allah, God's love

hubb lilaah, love for God

'ibadat, acts of worship

ijtihad, independent interpretation

ikhtilat, mixing of the sexes

'ilm, knowledge

iltizam, (religious) commitment

imam, worship leader of a mosque

iman ʿaqil, rational belief

infitah, opening

istikhara, special prayer for guidance

i ʿtidal, moderation

jihad, struggle

kafir, unbeliever

khalas, finished, enough

khashiya, anxiety

khauf, fear

khushu ʿ, humility before God

khutaba ʾ, official preachers (pl.; s. *khatib*)

kuttab, the religious village school

maghrib, prayer, evening prayer (sunset)

maskhara, shamelessness

masrah al-hadif, purposeful theater

masrah al-qima, value theater

masrah multazim, religiously committed theater

masrah raqi ʿ, uplifted theater

midalla ʿ, spoiled

mollat, shopping malls

mubaligha, spokesperson (f.)

mufti, juridical consultant

muhagaba / muhagabat, veiled person (s./pl.)

muhtashima, modest, shy

mulid, saint's day celebration

multazim(a), (religiously) committed (m./f.)

mu ʾmin, pious believer

munaqaba(t), face-veiled person (s./pl.)

muqadis(a), holy

musawwaratiyya, female photographers

musharaka, partnership in profit or loss

mutadayin, religious, pious

mutadayinin, religious or pious people

nadam, regret

nadr, vow

nafs, soul

nafs al-ʿamara, the evil-inciting soul

nafs al-ʿamara bi al-su ʾ, the evil-inciting soul

nafs al-ghafila, the negligent soul

nafs al-lawwama, the reproachful soul

nafs al-masula, the tempted soul

nafs al-mutma'inna, the serene or tranquil self
nidif, clean
niyya, intention
niqab, face veil
nu'ta, tips
qal'a, unrest
raha, calmness
raka'at al-tawba, special prayers for repentance
raqs sharqi, Oriental dance
rawshana, cool, hip, or fashionable
rugu' al-nafs, comeback of the self
ru'ya, sight or vision
sabr, patience
sadaqa, voluntary donations
sakina, tranquillity
sala, venue
salat, prayer
salat al-'asr, afternoon prayer
salat al-tarawih, special Ramadan evening prayers
salit al-munasabat, venue for special occasions
shar'i, Oriental
shar'i, in accordance with the Shari'a
shari'a, Islamic law
sinima nidifa, clean cinema
subu', the celebration for a seven-day-old baby
sunna, following the example of the Prophet
sunniyyin, colloquial expression for strict Muslims
sura, verse of the Qur'an
tabla, drum
tablighi, missionizing
tafsir, exegesis of the Qur'an
ta'ibat, female penitents
tanazulat, concessions
tannura, whirling dance
taqi, devout person
taqwa, piety or virtuous fear
tarab, enchantment
tarbiyya, (life) education
targhib ("awakening desire"), style of preaching based on trust on God's mercifulness
tarha, shawl
tarhib, style of preaching that makes people fearful
tashaddud, strictness
tawba, repentance

tawba nasuha, sincere repentance

'ulama', religious scholars

'umdah, mayor

ummah, community (of believers)

'umrah, lesser pilgrimage (on a date other than that of the official *hajj*)

urfi, secret marriage

urg, electric organ or synthesizer

ustaz, honorific title, literally, "professor"

'uzla, withdrawal

wa'd, promise

wasatiyya, center, mainstream, middle ground

wudu', ritual ablution before prayer

yitaqi, to be devoted

zaffa, wedding procession

zaffa islamiyya, Islamic wedding procession

zakat, alms

zawiya, prayer room

zayy islami, Islamic dress

zina, embellishment

Bibliography

Abaza, M. 2005. "Today's Consumption in Egypt." *ISIM Review* 15 (1): 38–39.

———. 2006a. *The Changing Consumer Cultures of Modern Egypt: Cairo's Urban Reshaping.* Leiden: Brill.

———. 2006b. "Egyptianizing the American Dream: Nasr City's Shopping Malls, Public Order, and the Privatized Military." In *Cairo Cosmopolitan: Politics, Culture, and Urban Space in the New Globalized Middle East,* ed. D. Singerman and P. Amar, pp. 193–221. Cairo: American University in Cairo Press.

———. 2010. "The Trafficking with *Tanwir* (Enlightenment)." *Comparative Studies of South Asia, Africa and the Middle East* 30 (1): 32–46.

ʿAbdallah, Muhammad Bin ʿAbdallah A. Shaʿaban 1425/2004. *Dumuʿ al-Taʾibin / Tears of the Repenters.* Cairo: Maktabit al-Iman.

Abdelrahman, M. 2006. "Divine Consumption: 'Islamic' Goods in Egypt." In "Cultural Dynamics in Contemporary Egypt," special issue of *Cairo Papers in Social Science* 27 (1/2): 69–79. Cairo: American University in Cairo Press.

Abdo, G. 2000. *No God but God: Egypt and the Triumph of Islam.* Oxford: Oxford University Press.

Abu al-ʿAynayn, S. 1999. *al-Shaʿarawi . . . wa al-Fannanat / al-Shaʿarawi . . . and the Female Artists.* Cairo: Akhbar al-Yawm.

Abu Dawud, S., and L. Bayumi. 1994. *Hiwar maʿa al-Fannanin wa al-Fannanat al-Taʾabin wa al-Taʾibat / Conversations with Male and Female Artists Who Repented.* Alexandria: Dar al-marwa li al-tawziʿ.

Abu Lughod, L. 1989. "Zones of Theory in the Anthropology of the Arab World." *Annual Review of Anthropology* 18:267–306.

———. 1993. "Islam and Public Culture: The Politics of Egyptian Television Serials." *Middle East Report,* no. 180, 25–30.

———. 1995. "Movie Stars and Islamic Moralism in Egypt." *Social Text* 13 (1): 53–68.

———. 1998. "The Marriage of Feminism and Islamism in Egypt: Selective Repudiation as a Dynamic of Postcolonial Cultural Politics." In *Remaking Women: Feminism and*

Modernity in the Middle East, ed. L. Abu Lughod, pp. 243–270. Princeton, NJ: Princeton University Press.

———. 2005. *Dramas of Nationhood: The Politics of Television in Egypt.* Cairo: American University in Cairo Press.

Ahmed, L. 1992. *Women and Gender in Islam: Historical Roots of a Modern Debate.* New Haven, CT, and London: Yale University Press.

Amin, G. 2000. *Whatever Happened to the Egyptians?* Cairo: American University in Cairo Press.

Armbrust, W. 1996. *Mass Culture and Modernism in Egypt.* Cambridge: Cambridge University Press.

———. 2002. "Islamists in Egyptian Cinema." *American Anthropologist* 104 (3): 922–931.

———. 2006. "When the Lights Go Down in Cairo: Cinema as Global Crossroads and Space of Playful Resistance." In *Cairo Cosmopolitan: Politics, Culture, and Urban Space in the New Globalized Middle East,* ed. D. Singerman and P. Amar, pp. 415–445. Cairo: American University in Cairo Press.

Asad, T. 2003. *Formations of the Secular: Christianity, Islam, Modernity.* Stanford, CA: Stanford University Press.

Auslander, P. 2008. *Theory for Performance Studies: A Student's Guide.* London and New York: Routledge.

Awad, M. 2009. "Muslim Music Channel Islamizes Pop Culture." *Al-Arabiya News Channel.* Also available online at http://www.alarabiya.net/articles/2009/03/10/68148.html (accessed January 5, 2011).

al-Awadi, H. 2004. *In Pursuit of Legitimacy: The Muslim Brothers and Mubarak, 1982–2000.* London and New York: Tauris Academic Studies.

'Azab, S. K. n.d. *Fannanat Ta'ibat fi Maglis Amru Khalid / Repentant Artists in the Presence of 'Amr Khalid.* Cairo: Dar al-Rawda.

Badawi, H. S., and S. A. Mourad. 1994. "Observations from the 12 October 1992 Dahshour Earthquake in Egypt." *Natural Hazards* 10 (3): 261–274.

Bakas, A., and M. Buwalda. 2006. *De Toekomst van God / The Future of God.* Schiedam, the Netherlands: Scriptum.

Baker, R. W. 2003. *Islam without Fear: Egypt and the New Islamists.* Cambridge, MA, and London: Harvard University Press.

———. 2005. "Building the World in a Global Age." In *Religion, Social Practice, and Contested Hegemonies: Reconstructing the Public Sphere in Muslim Majority Societies,* ed. A. Salvatore and M. LeVine, pp. 109–132. New York: Palgrave Macmillan.

Barbas, S. 2001. *Movie Crazy: Fan, Stars, and the Cult of Celebrity.* New York: Palgrave.

Baron, B. 2005. *Egypt as a Woman: Nationalism, Gender, and Politics.* Berkeley: University of California Press.

Bayat, A. 1998. "Revolution without Movement, Movement without Revolution: Comparing Islamic Activism in Iran and Egypt." *Comparative Studies in Society and History* 40, no. 1 (January): 136–169.

———. 2002a. "Activism and Social Development in the Middle East." *International Journal of Middle East Studies* 34, no. 1 (February): 1–28.

————. 2002b. "Piety, Privilege and Egyptian Youth." *ISIM Review*, no. 10, 23.

————. 2005a. "Islamism and Social Movement Theory." *Third World Quarterly* 26 (6): 891–908.

————. 2005b. "What Is Post-Islamism?" *ISIM Review*, no. 16, 5.

————. 2007a. "Islamism and the Politics of Fun." *Public Culture* 19 (3): 433–460.

————. 2007b. *Making Islam Democratic: Social Movements and the Post-Islamist Turn.* Stanford, CA: Stanford University Press.

————. 2009. *Life as Politics: How Ordinary People Change the Middle East.* Stanford, CA: Stanford University Press.

Berman, Sh. 2003. "Islamism, Revolution, and Civil Society." *Perspectives on Politics* 1 (2): 257–272.

Blackman, L. 2008. *The Body: The Key Concepts.* Oxford and New York: Berg.

Bourdieu, P. 1977. *Outline of a Theory of Practice.* Cambridge: Cambridge University Press.

Brooks, G. 1998. *De Dochters van Allah / The Daughters of Allah.* Amsterdam: Ooievaar.

Calhoun, C., ed. 1992. *Habermas and the Public Sphere.* Cambridge, MA: MIT Press.

Carlson, M. 2004. *Performance: A Critical Introduction.* New York and London: Routledge.

Chammah, M. 2010. "Cosmopolitan Islamism and Its Critics: Ahmed Abu Haiba, 4Shbab TV, and Western Reception." *Arab Media and Society*, March 30, 2010. Also available online at http://arabmediasociety.sqgd.co.uk/articles/downloads/20100330113056_Ch ammah.pdf (accessed January 5, 2011).

Cook, M. 2000. *Commanding Right and Forbidding Wrong in Islamic Thought.* Cambridge: Cambridge University Press.

Csordas, Th. J. 1999. "The Body's Career in Anthropology." In *Anthropological Theory Today*, ed. H. L. Moore, pp. 172–234. Cambridge and New Malden: Polity Press.

Deeb, L. 2006. *An Enchanted Modern: Gender and Public Piety in Shi'i Lebanon.* Princeton, NJ: Princeton University Press.

De Koning, A. 2006. "Café Latte and Caesar Salad: Cosmopolitan Belonging in Cairo's Coffee Shops." In *Cairo Cosmopolitan: Politics, Culture, and Urban Space in the New Globalized Middle East*, ed. D. Singerman and P. Amar, pp. 221–235. Cairo: American University in Cairo Press.

————. 2009. *Global Dreams: Class, Gender, and Public Space in Cosmopolitan Cairo.* Cairo: American University in Cairo Press.

Denis, E. 2006. "Cairo as Neo-Liberal Capital? From Walled City to Gated Communities." In *Cairo Cosmopolitan: Politics, Culture, and Urban Space in the New Globalized Middle East*, ed. D. Singerman and P. Amar, pp. 47–73. Cairo: American University in Cairo Press.

Denny, F. 2000. "Tawba." In *The Encyclopaedia of Islam*, new ed., p. 10:385. Leiden: Brill.

Eickelman D. F., and J. W. Anderson. 1999. "Redefining Muslim Publics." In *New Media in the Muslim World: The Emerging Public Sphere*, ed. D. F. Eickelman and J. W. Anderson, pp. 1–19. Bloomington and Indianapolis, IN: Indiana University Press.

Eickelman, D. F., and J. Piscatori. 1996. *Muslim Politics.* Princeton, NJ: Princeton University Press.

El-Guindi, F. 1981. "Veiling Infitah with Muslim Ethic: Egypt's Contemporary Islamic Movement." *Social Problems* 28, no. 4 (April): 465–485.

———. 1983. "Veiled Activism: Egyptian Women in the Contemporary Islamic Movement." *Peuples Méditerranéens*, no. 22–23, 79–89.

El-Mokadem, I. 2008. "Islamic Music Videos, All the Time." *Daily News Egypt*, July 27. Also at http://www.thedailynewsegypt.com/islamic-music-videos-all-the-time.html (accessed December 13, 2010, but no longer available).

Elsheshtawy, Y. 2006. "From Dubai to Cairo: Competing Global Cities, Models, and Shifting Centers of Influence?" In *Cairo Cosmopolitan: Politics, Culture, and Urban Space in the New Globalized Middle East*, ed. D. Singerman and P. Amar, pp. 235–251. Cairo: American University in Cairo Press.

Fabian, J. 1990. *Power and Performance: Ethnographic Explorations through Proverbial Wisdom and Theater in Shaba, Zaire*. Madison: University of Wisconsin Press.

———. 1998. *Moments of Freedom: Anthropology and Popular Culture*. Charlottesville and London: University Press of Virginia.

Fahd, T. 1978. "Istikhara." In *Encyclopaedia of Islam*, ed. E. van Donzel, B. Lewis, and Ch. Pellat, pp. 259–261. Leiden: Brill.

Farag, F. 2002. "Shaken, Not Stirred." *Al-Ahram Weekly*, no. 601 (August 29–September 4). Available online at http://weekly.ahram.org.eg/2002/601/eg4.htm (accessed February 5, 2010).

Farhat, Y. 1993. *Ma'raka al-Hijab: Asrar wara' al-hijab al-madfu'/ The Campaign against the Veil: Secrets behind the Paid Veil*. Cairo: Dar al-Rawda.

Fawzi, M. 1993. *al-Sheikh al-Sha'arawi: Al-'Ilag bi al-Qur'an wa 'umur al-dunya / al-Sheikh al-Sha'arawi: Treatment by the Qur'an and Matters of the World*. Cairo: Dar al-Nashr Hatiyya.

———. n.d. *'Umar 'Abd al-Kafi, Fatawa sakhina / 'Umar 'Abd al-Kafi, Spicy Fatwa's*. Cairo: Matabi' Ruz al-Yusif al-Gidida.

Foucault, M. 2003. "Technologies of the Self." In *The Essential Foucault*, ed. P. Rabinow and N. Rose, pp. 144–170. New York: New Press.

Fraser, N. 1990. "Rethinking the Public Sphere: A Contribution to the Critique of Actually Existing Democracy." *Social Text*, no. 25/26, 56–80.

Frishkopf, M. 2009. "Mediated Qur'anic Recitation and the Contestation of Islam in Contemporary Egypt." In *Music and the Play of Power in the Middle East, North Africa and Central Asia*, ed. L. Nooshin, pp. 75–115. Farnham, Surrey, England; Burlington, VT: Ashgate.

———. 2011. "Ritual as Strategic Action: The Social Logic of Musical Silence in Canadian Islam." In *Muslim Rap, Halal Soaps, and Revolutionary Theater: Artistic Developments in the Muslim World*, ed. K. van Nieuwkerk, pp. 115–149. Austin: University of Texas Press.

Gaffney, P. 1994. *The Prophet's Pulpit: Islamic Preaching in Contemporary Egypt*. Berkeley: University of California Press.

Galal, E. 2009. "Yusuf al-Qaradawi and the New Islamic TV." In *Global Mufti: The Phe-

nomenon of Yusuf al-Qaradawi, ed. J. Skovgaard-Petersen and B. Gräf, pp. 149–181. London: Hurst & Company.

Gamiʿ, M. 2005. *Wa ʿArafit al-Shaʿarawi | Testimonies of al-Shaʿarawi*. Cairo: Dar al-tawziʿ wa al-nashr al-islamiyya.

Gamson, J. 1994. *Claims to Fame*. Berkeley: University of California Press.

Gazzah, M. 2008. *Rhythms and Rhymes of Life: Music and Identification Processes of Dutch-Moroccan Youth*. Amsterdam: Amsterdam University Press.

Gestrich, A. 2006. "The Public Sphere and the Habermas Debate." *German History* 24 (3): 413–431.

Ghannam, F. 2006. "Keeping Him Connected: Globalization and the Production of Locality in Cairo." In *Cairo Cosmopolitan: Politics, Culture, and Urban Space in the New Globalized Middle East*, ed. D. Singerman and P. Amar, pp. 251–267. Cairo: American University in Cairo Press.

al-Ghazali, Abu Hamid Muhammad. 1933. *Ihya ʿUlum al-Din (Fourth Book on Tawba | Repentance)*. Cairo: al-Maṭbaʿa al-ʿUtmaniyya al-Miṣriyya.

Gilsenan, M. 1973. *Saint and Sufi in Modern Egypt: An Essay in the Sociology of Religion*. Oxford: Clarendon Press.

Gräf, B. 2009. "The Concept of *wasatiyya* in the Work of Yusuf al-Qaradawi." In *Global Mufti: The Phenomenon of Yusuf al-Qaradawi*, ed. J. Skovgaard-Petersen and B. Gräf, pp. 213–239. London: Hurst & Company.

Gräf, B., and J. Skovgaard-Petersen. 2009. "Introduction." In *Global Mufti: The Phenomenon of Yusuf al-Qaradawi*, ed. J. Skovgaard-Petersen and B. Gräf, pp. 1–17. London: Hurst & Company.

Graw, K. 2005. "Culture of Hope in West Africa." *ISIM Review*, no. 16, 28–30.

Green, N. 2003. "The Religious and Cultural Roles of Dreams and Visions in Islam." *JRAS*, 3rd ser., 13:287–313.

Gwilliam, S. 2010. "The Rise of 'Pop Islam' in Britain." Available online at http://www.wm .edu/as/globalstudies/documents/european/Sarah%20Gwilliam%20ESconf08.pdf (accessed January 15, 2011).

Haenni, P. 2002. "Au-delà du repli identitaire . . . Les nouveaux prêcheurs égyptiens et la modernisation paradoxale de l'islam." *Religioscope*, Novembre. Also available online at http://www.religioscope.com/articles/2002/029_haenni_precheurs.htm (accessed May 15, 2012).

———. 2005. *L'islam de marché. L'autre révolution conservatrice*. Paris: Seuil.

Hafez, Sh. 2003. *The Terms of Empowerment: Islamic Women Activists in Egypt*. Cairo Papers in Social Science 24, no. 4. Cairo: American University in Cairo Press.

———. 2011. *An Islam of Her Own: Reconsidering Religion and Secularism in Women's Islamic Movements*. New York and London: New York University Press.

Hamza, K. 1986. *Rihlati min al-sufur ila al-hijab | My Journey from Unveiling to Veiling*. Beirut: Dar al-fath li al-tabaʿa wa al-nashr.

Hatem, M. 1998. "Secularist and Islamist Discourses on Modernity in Egypt and the Evolution of the Postcolonial Nation-State." In *Islam, Gender & Social Change*, ed. Y. Yazbeck Haddad and J. Esposito, pp. 85–99. Oxford: Oxford University Press.

Hermansen, M. 1997. "Visions as 'Good to Think': A Cognitive Approach to Visionary Experience in Islamic Sufi Thought." *Religion* 27, no. 1 (January): 25–43.

Herrera, L. 2001. "Downveiling: Gender and the Contest over Culture in Cairo." *Middle East Report*, no. 219 (Summer): 16–19.

Hirschkind, C. 2001. "The Ethics of Listening: Cassette-Sermon Audition in Contemporary Cairo." *American Ethnologist* 28 (3): 623–649.

———. 2006. *The Ethical Soundscape: Cassette Sermons and Islamic Counterpublics*. New York: Columbia University Press.

Hoffman, V. 1997. "The Role of Visions in Contemporary Egyptian Religious Life." *Religion* 27, no. 1 (January): 45–64.

Hoffman-Ladd, V. J. 1987. "Polemics on the Modesty and Segregation of Women in Contemporary Egypt." *International Journal of Middle East Studies* 19, no. 1 (February): 23–50.

Holtrop, T. 2004. "Amr Khalid, de chique shayk." *Sharqiyyat* 16 (1): 5–21.

ʿImara, M. 1991. *Al-Islam wa al-Funun al-Jamila / Islam and the Fine Arts*. Cairo: Dar al-Shuruq.

Ismail, S. 1998. "Confronting the Other: Identity, Culture, Politics, and Conservative Islamism in Egypt." *International Journal of Middle East Studies* 30, no. 2 (May): 199–225.

ʿIssa, I. 1993. *al-Harb bi al-Niqab / War with the Face Veil*. Cairo: Dar al-Shabab.

Jansen, W. 1987. *Women without Men: Gender and Marginality in an Algerian Town*. Leiden: E. J. Brill.

al-Juhayni, A. Abu Bakr. 1989. *Min ʿAlam al-Shuhra ila Rihab al-Iman / From the World of Fame to the Acceptance of Faith*. Cairo: Maktabit Ibn Sina.

al-Kafawin, H. ʿAbd al-Salam. 2001. "Asbab tiʾaththar al-Ghinaʾ al-Islamiyya" / "Factors That Influence Islamic Songs," June 24. http://www.islamonline.net (accessed February 7, 2006).

Kamil, M. 1993; 2nd ed., 1994. *Fannanat waraʾ al-Hijab / Artists behind the Veil*. Cairo: Markaz al-raya li al-nashr wa al-ʿilam.

Katz, J. 1997. "An Egyptian Sufi Interprets His Dreams: ʿAbd al-Wahhab al-Shaʿrani 1493–1565." *Religion* 27, no. 1 (January): 7–24.

Kepel, G. 2000. "Islamism Reconsidered: A Running Dialogue with Modernity." *Harvard International Review* 22 (2): 22.

Khalid, ʿA. 2005. "Culture: The Distinguishing Feature of a People." *Transnational Broadcasting Studies* 1:30–33.

Khalil, A. 2006. "Ibn al-ʿArab on the Three Conditions of Tawba." *Islam and Christian-Muslim Relations* 17 (4): 403–416.

Kılıçbay, B., and M. Binark. 2002. "Consumer Culture, Islam and the Politics of Lifestyle Fashion for Veiling in Contemporary Turkey." *European Journal of Communication* 17, no. 4 (December): 495–511.

Kirshenblatt-Gimblett, B. 2004. "Performance Studies." In *The Performance Studies Reader*, ed. H. Bial, pp. 43–56. London and New York: Routledge.

Lauzière, H. 2005. "Post-Islamism and the Religious Discourse of ʿAbd al-Salam Yasin." *International Journal of Middle East Studies* 37, no. 2 (May): 241–261.

LeVine, M. 2008. "Heavy Metal Muslims: The Rise of a Post-Islamist Public Sphere." In "Creating an Islamic Cultural Sphere: Contested Notions of Art, Leisure and Entertainment," ed. Karin van Nieuwkerk, special issue, *Contemporary Islam* 2 (3): 229–251.

MacLeod, A. E. 1991. *Accommodating Protest: Working Women, the New Veiling, and Change in Cairo.* New York: Columbia University Press.

Mahmood, S. 2001a. "Feminist Theory, Embodiment, and the Docile Agent: Some Reflections on the Egyptian Islamic Revival." *Cultural Anthropology* 16 (2): 202–236.

———. 2001b. "Rehearsed Spontaneity and the Conventionality of Ritual: Disciplines of Salat." *American Ethnologist* 28 (4): 827–853.

———. 2005. *Politics of Piety: The Islamic Revival and the Feminist Subject.* Princeton, NJ, and Oxford: Princeton University Press.

Malti-Douglas, F. 2001. *Medicines of the Soul: Female Bodies and Sacred Geographies in a Transnational Islam.* Berkeley and Los Angeles: University of California Press.

Marshall, D. 1997. *Celebrity and Power.* Minneapolis: University of Minnesota Press.

Marsot, A. Lutfi al-Sayyid. 1984. "Religion or Opposition? Urban Protest Movements in Egypt." *International Journal of Middle East Studies* 16, no. 4 (November): 541–552.

———. 1991. "Survey of Egyptian Works of History." *American Historical Review* 96, no. 5 (December): 1422–1434.

Mauss, M. 1979. "Body Techniques." In *Sociology and Psychology: Essays,* pp. 95–124. London, Boston, and Henley: Routledge and Kegan Paul.

Mehrez, S. 2001. "Take Them out of the Ball Game: Egypt's Cultural Players in Crisis." *Middle East Report* 31, no. 219 (Summer): 10–15.

———. 2008. *Egypt's Culture Wars: Politics and Practice.* New York: Routledge.

al-Messiri, S. 1978. *Ibn al-Balad: A Concept of Egyptian Identity.* Leiden: E. J. Brill.

Meyer, B. 2006. *Religious Sensations: Why Media, Aesthetics and Power Matter in the Study of Contemporary Religion.* Amsterdam: Vrije Universiteit.

Mitchell, T. 1999. "Dreamland: The Neoliberalism of Your Desires." *Middle East Report* 29, no. 210 (Spring): 28–33.

Moll, Y. 2010. "Islamic Televangelism: Religion, Media and Visuality in Contemporary Egypt." *Arab Media and Society,* no. 10 (Spring). Also available online at http://www.arabmediasociety.com/?article=732 (accessed August 10, 2010).

Mostyn, T. 2002. *Censorship in Islamic Societies.* London: Saqi Books.

Munson, Z. 2001. "Islamic Mobilization: Social Movement Theory and the Egyptian Muslim Brotherhood." *Sociological Quarterly* 42 (4): 487–510.

Murphy, C. 2002. *Passion for Islam.* New York: Scribner.

Nasif, ʿI., and A. Khodayr. n.d. *Fannanat Taʾibat / Repentant Artists.* Cairo: n.p.

Navaro-Yashin, Y. 2002. "The Market for Identities: Secularism, Islamism, Commodities." In *Fragments of Culture: The Everyday of Modern Turkey,* ed. D. Kandiyoti and A. Saktanber, pp. 221–254. London: I. B. Tauris.

Nicholson, R. 1911. *The Tarjuman al-Ashwaq: A Collection of Mystical Odes by MuhyiʾDdin Ibn al-ʿArabi.* London: Theosophical Publishing House Ltd.

Nelson, K. 2001. *The Art of Reciting the Qurʾan.* Cairo: American University in Cairo Press.

Nooshin, L. 2009. "Prelude: Power and the Play of Music." In *Music and the Play of Power in the Middle East, North Africa and Central Asia*, ed. L. Nooshin, pp. 1–33. Farnham, Surrey, England; Burlington, VT: Ashgate.

Possamai, A. 2005. *Religion and Popular Culture: A Hyper-real Testament*. Brussels: Peter Lang.

al-Qaradawi, Y. 1997a. *Fiqh al-Ghina' wa al-Musiqa fi Dhu' al-Qur'an wa al-Sunna*. Cairo: Maktabit Wahbah.

———. 1997b. *The Status of Women in Islam*. Cairo: Islamic Printing and Publishing Company.

———. 1998. *Diversion and Arts in Islam*. Cairo: Islamic Printing and Publishing Company.

———. 2001. *The Lawful and the Prohibited in Islam*. Cairo: El-Falah.

Racy, A. J. 2003. *Making Music in the Arab World: The Culture and Artistry of Tarab*. Cambridge: Cambridge University Press.

Rambo, L. 1993. *Understanding Religious Conversion*. New Haven, CT: Yale University Press.

Ramzi, K. 1994. *From Extremism to Terrorism: The Relationship between Religious Groups and the Arts*. Cairo: LRRC. Also at http://www.geocities.com/CapitolHill/Lobby/9012 /Freedom/kamalmain.htm (accessed November 18, 1999, but no longer available).

Randall, A. J. 2005. *Music, Power, and Politics*. New York and London: Routledge.

Renard, J. 2008. *Friends of God: Islamic Images of Piety, Commitment, and Servanthood*. Berkeley and Los Angeles: University of California Press.

Rojek, Ch. 2001. *Celebrity*. London: Reaktion Books.

———. 2006. "Celebrity and Religion." In *The Celebrity Culture Reader*, ed. P. David Marshall, pp. 51–102. New York and London: Routledge.

Rosaldo, M. 1974. "Woman, Culture and Society: A Theoretical Overview." In *Women, Culture and Society*, ed. M. Rosaldo and L. Lamphere, pp. 17–42. Stanford, CA: Stanford University Press.

Roy, O. 2004. *Globalized Islam*. London: Hurst and Company.

Rugh, A. B. 1986. *Reveal and Conceal: Dress in Contemporary Egypt*. Syracuse, NY: Syracuse University Press.

Sa'dawi, W. 2006. "'Aghani al-Banat': 'Alehum al-alhan wa 'alena al-kalimat!" / "'Girls' Songs': Upon Them the Melody, Upon Us the Words," March 14. http://www.islam online.net (accessed March 28, 2006).

Sadek, S. 2006. "Cairo as Global/Regional Cultural Capital?" In *Cairo Cosmopolitan: Politics, Culture, and Urban Space in the New Globalized Middle East*, ed. D. Singerman and P. Amar, pp. 153–191. Cairo: American University in Cairo Press.

Sa'fan, R. 2004. "Firqit banat li al-aghani . . . islamiyya!" / "Female Bands for Islamic Songs!," February 9. http://www.islamonline.net (accessed March 28, 2008).

Sa'id, M. 2001. "Hikayit al-funun bi 'uyun mutafariga" / "The History of Arts through Various Viewpoints," March 13. http://www.islamonline.net (accessed July 2, 2006).

———. 2004. "'al-sinima al-islamiyya': hal hiyya mumkina?" / "'Islamic Theater': Is This Possible?," July 4. http://www.islamonline.net (accessed February 7, 2006).

Salamandra, C. 2008. "Creative Compromise: Syrian Television Makers between Secularism and Islamism." In "Creating an Islamic Cultural Sphere: Contested Notions of Art, Leisure and Entertainment," ed. Karin van Nieuwkerk, special issue, *Contemporary Islam* 2 (3): 177–191.

Salvatore, A. 2000. "Social Differentiation, Moral Authority and Public Islam in Egypt: The Path of Mustafa Mahmud." *Anthropology Today* 16, no. 2 (April): 12–15.

Salvatore, A., and D. F. Eickelman, eds. 2004. *Public Islam and the Common Good.* Leiden: Brill.

Salvatore, A., and M. LeVine, eds. 2005. *Religion, Social Practice, and Contested Hegemonies: Reconstructing the Public Sphere in Muslim Majority Societies.* New York: Palgrave Macmillan.

Sandikci, O., and G. Ger. 2010. "Veiling in Style: How Does a Stigmatized Practice Become Fashionable?" *Journal of Consumer Research* 37 (1): 15–36.

al-Sangri, ʿAbd al-Rahman. 1999. *Al-ʿAʾidun ila Allah / People Returning to God.* 5th ed. Beirut: Dar al-Bashaʾir.

al-Sayyid, M. F. n.d. *Nisaʾ ʿAʾidat ila Allah / Women Returning to God.* Cairo: Maktabit al-Tawfiqiyya.

Schechner, R. 2002. *Performance Studies: An Introduction.* London and New York: Routledge.

Schielke, S. 2008. "Boredom and Despair in Rural Egypt." In "Creating an Islamic Cultural Sphere: Contested Notions of Art, Leisure and Entertainment," ed. Karin van Nieuwkerk, special issue, *Contemporary Islam* 2 (3): 251–271.

———. 2009. "Being Good in Ramadan: Ambivalence, Fragmentation and the Moral Self in the Lives of Young Egyptians." In "Islam, Politics, Anthropology," ed. Filippo Osella and Benjamin Soares, special issue, *Journal of the Royal Anthropological Institute* 15 (May): 24–40.

Schimmel, A. 1998. *Die Träume des Kalifen: Träume und ihre Deutung in der islamischen Kultur.* München: Verlag C. H. Beck.

Shafik, V. 1998. *Arab Cinema, History and Cultural Identity.* Cairo: American University in Cairo Press.

———. 2001. "Prostitute for a Good Reason: Stars and Morality in Egypt." *Women's Studies International Forum* 24 (6): 711–725.

Shahine, G. 2002. "Piety for the Young and Affluent." *Al-Ahram Weekly,* no. 614 (November 28–December 4). Available online at http://weekly.ahram.org.eg/2002/614/fe1 .htm (accessed January 15, 2011).

Shannon, J. H. 2011. "Suficized Musics of Syria at the Intersection of Heritage and the War on Terror; Or 'A Rume with a View.'" In *Muslim Rap, Halal Soaps, and Revolutionary Theater: Artistic Developments in the Muslim World,* ed. K. van Nieuwkerk, pp. 257–275. Austin: University of Texas Press.

Shehata, D. 2010. *Islamists and Secularists in Egypt: Opposition, Conflict, and Cooperation.* New York and London: Routledge.

Shenker, J. 2009. "Rapping for Allah: The New Channel for the Muslim MTV Generation." *The Guardian,* March 7.

Singerman, D. 1997. *Avenues of Participation: Family, Politics, and Networks in Urban Quarters of Cairo.* Cairo: American University in Cairo Press.

Singerman, D., and P. Amar. 2006. *Cairo Cosmopolitan: Politics, Culture, and Urban Space in the New Globalized Middle East.* Cairo: American University in Cairo Press.

Siraj al-Din, S. 1993. *Awraq Shams al-Barudi | The Dossier of Shams al-Barudi.* Cairo: Maktabat ihya al-kutub al-islamiyya.

Sirriyeh, E. 2000. "Dreams of the Holy Dead: Traditional Islamic Oneirocriticism versus Salafi Scepticism." *Journal of Semitic Studies* 45, no. 1 (Spring): 115–130.

Skovgaard-Petersen, J. 2009. "Yusuf al-Qaradawi and al-Azhar." In *Global Mufti: The Phenomenon of Yusuf al-Qaradawi,* ed. J. Skovgaard-Petersen and B. Gräf, pp. 27–55. London: Hurst & Company.

Solomon, Th. 2011. "Hardcore Muslims: Islamic Themes in Turkish Rap between Diaspora and Homeland." In *Muslim Rap, Halal Soaps, and Revolutionary Theater: Artistic Developments in the Muslim World,* ed. K. van Nieuwkerk, pp. 27–55. Austin: University of Texas Press.

Stacher, J. A. 2002. "Post-Islamist Rumblings in Egypt: The Emergence of the Wasat Party." *Middle East Journal,* June 22.

Stack, L. 2009. "'Islamic MTV' Takes on Brash World of Arab Pop Videos." *Christian Science Monitor,* March 17. Also available online at http://www.csmonitor.com/World/Middle-East/2009/0317/p04s01-wome.html (accessed January 5, 2011).

Starrett, G. 1995a. "The Hexis of Interpretation: Islam and the Body in the Egyptian Popular School." *American Ethnologist* 22 (4): 953–969.

———. 1995b. "The Political Economy of Religious Commodities in Cairo." *American Anthropologist* 97 (1): 51–68.

———. 1998. *Putting Islam to Work: Education, Politics and Religious Transformation in Egypt.* Berkeley and Los Angeles: University of California Press.

Stellar, Z. 2011. "From 'Evil-Inciting' Dance to Chaste 'Rhythmic Movements': A Genealogy of Modern Islamic Dance-Theatre in Iran." In *Muslim Rap, Halal Soaps, and Revolutionary Theater: Artistic Developments in the Muslim World,* ed. K. van Nieuwkerk, pp. 231–257. Austin: University of Texas Press.

Stern, M. S. 1979. "Al-Ghazzali, Maimonides, and Ibn Paquda on Repentance: A Comparative Model." *Journal of the American Academy of Religion* 47 (4): 589–607.

———. 1990. *Al-Ghazzali on Repentance.* New York: Sterling Publishers Private Limited. Also available online at http://www.ghazali.org/books/gz-repent.pdf (accessed March 15, 2009).

Stewart, P. J., and A. Strathern. 2002. *Gender, Song, and Sensibilities.* Westport, CT, and London: Praeger.

Stowasser, B. Freyer. 2009. "Yusuf al-Qaradawi on Women." In *Global Mufti: The Phenomenon of Yusuf al-Qaradawi,* ed. J. Skovgaard-Petersen and B. Gräf, pp. 181–213. London: Hurst & Company.

Strathern, A., and P. J. Stewart. 2008. "Embodiment Theory in Performance and Performativity." *Journal of Ritual Studies* 22 (1): 67–72.

Stratton, A. 2006. *Muhajababes.* London: Constable.

Sullivan, D. J. 1994. *Private Voluntary Organizations in Egypt: Islamic Development, Private Initiative, and State Control*. Gainesville: University Press of Florida.

Sullivan, D. J., and S. Abed-Kotob. 1999. *Islam in Contemporary Egypt: Civil Society vs. the State*. London; Boulder, CO: Lynne Rienner Publishers.

Swedenburg, T. 2001. "Islamic Hip-Hop versus Islamophobia: Aki Nawaz, Natacha Atlas, Akhneton." In *Global Noise: Rap and Hip-Hop outside the USA*, ed. T. Mitchell, pp. 57–85. Middletown, CT: Wesleyan University Press.

Tadros, M. 1994. *Women: The Perspective of Fundamentalist Discourse and Its Influence on Egyptian Artistic Creativity and Cultural Life*. Cairo: LRRC. Also at http://www.geo cities.com/CapitolHill/Lobby/9012/Freedom/marlynmain.htm (accessed November 18, 1999, but no longer available).

Tammam, H. 2004. "al-Ikhwan wa al-fann: min al-mufid al-hadif li al-mumti⁽ al-nadhif" / "The Brothers and Art: From the Purposeful Mission to Clean Enjoyment," July 5. http://www.islamonline.net (accessed February 18, 2006).

———. 2009. "Yusuf al-Qaradawi and the Muslim Brothers: The Nature of a Special Relationship." In *Global Mufti: The Phenomenon of Yusuf al-Qaradawi*, ed. J. Skovgaard-Petersen and B. Gräf, pp. 55–85. London: Hurst & Company.

Tammam, H., and P. Haenni. 2003. "Chat Shows, Nashid Groups and Lite Preaching: Egypt's Air-Conditioned Islam." *Le Monde diplomatique*, September 3.

———. 2005. "Daqat al-duff al-islamiyya / The Beat of Islamic Drums." *Wajhat Nazr* 73:45–57.

Tartoussieh, K. 2007. "Pious Stardom: Cinema and the Islamic Revival in Egypt." *Arab Studies Journal* 17 (1): 30–44.

Tibi, B. 2008. "Islamist Parties: Why They Can't Be Democratic." *Journal of Democracy* 19, no. 3 (July): 43–49. Also at http://libarts.wsu.edu/philo/faculty-staff/Snyder/Why%20 They%20Can't%20Be%20Democratic%20Tibi.pdf (accessed January 15, 2011, but no longer available).

Turner, Bryan S. 2008. "Introduction: the Price of Piety." *Contemporary Islam* 2 (1): 1–6.

Turner, G. 2004. *Understanding Celebrity*. London: Sage Publications.

Utvik, B. 2005. "*Hizb al-Wasat* and the Potential for Change in Egyptian Islamism." *Critique: Critical Middle Eastern Studies* 14 (3): 293–306. Also available online at http:// www.tandfonline.com/doi/abs/10.1080/10669920500280672 (accessed January 15, 2011).

———. 2006. *The Pious Road to Development: Islamic Economics in Egypt*. London: Hurst & Company.

Van den Bulck, H., and S. Tambuyzer. 2008. *De celebritysupermarkt / The Celebrity Supermarket*. Berchem, Belgium: EPO.

Van Nieuwkerk, K. 1995. *"A Trade like Any Other": Female Singers and Dancers in Egypt*. Austin: University of Texas Press.

———. 1996. *Dochters van de Volle Maan / Daughters of the Full Moon*. Amsterdam: Jan Mets.

———. 2006a. "Gender and Conversion to Islam in the West." In *Women Embracing Islam: Gender and Conversion in the West*, ed. K. van Nieuwkerk, pp. 1–17. Austin: University of Texas Press.

————. 2006b. "'Islam is your Birthright.' Conversion, Reversion and Alternation: The Case of New Muslimas in the West." In *Cultures of Conversions*, ed. J. N. Bremmer, W. J. Bekkum, and A. L. Molendijk, pp. 151–165. Leuven, Belgium: Peeters.

————, ed. 2006c. *Women Embracing Islam: Gender and Conversion in the West*. Austin: University of Texas Press.

————. 2007. "Werken aan vroomheid: Religieuze lessen voor Marokkaanse vrouwen in Rotterdam." In *Uit en thuis in Marokko: Antropologische schetsen*, ed. M. Buitelaar, pp. 146–158. Amsterdam: Bulaaq.

————. 2008a. "Creating an Islamic Cultural Sphere: Contested Notions of Art, Leisure and Entertainment. An Introduction." In "Creating an Islamic Cultural Sphere: Contested Notions of Art, Leisure and Entertainment," ed. Karin van Nieuwkerk, special issue, *Contemporary Islam* 2 (3): 169–176.

————. 2008b. "Piety, Repentance and Gender: Born-again Singers, Dancers and Actresses in Egypt." *Journal for Islamic Studies* 28:37–65.

————. 2010. "Cultiver la pieté: Cours d'instruction religieuse pour les Marocaines de Rotterdam." In *Le Maroc De Près et de Loin: Regards d'antropologues Néerlandais*, ed. M. Buitelaar, pp. 133–143. Rabat: Marsam.

————. 2011a. "Introduction. Artistic Developments in the Muslim Cultural Sphere: Ethics, Aesthetics, and the Performing Arts." In *Muslim Rap, Halal Soaps, and Revolutionary Theater: Artistic Developments in the Muslim World*, ed. K. van Nieuwkerk, pp. 1–27. Austin: University of Texas Press.

————. 2011b. "Of Morals, Missions, and the Market: New Religiosity and 'Art with a Mission' in Egypt." In *Muslim Rap, Halal Soaps, and Revolutionary Theater: Artistic Developments in the Muslim World*, ed. K. van Nieuwkerk, pp. 177–205. Austin: University of Texas Press.

Verrips, J. 2008. "Offending Art and the Sense of Touch." *Material Religion: The Journal of Objects, Art and Belief* 4, no. 2 (July): 204–225.

Vignal, L., and E. Denis. 2006. "Cairo as Global/Regional Economic Capital?" In *Cairo Cosmopolitan: Politics, Culture, and Urban Space in the New Globalized Middle East*, ed. D. Singerman and P. Amar, pp. 99–153. Cairo: American University in Cairo Press.

Wickham, C. R. 2002. *Mobilizing Islam: Religion, Activism, and Political Change in Egypt*. New York: Columbia University Press.

Wilzer, S. 1957–1959. "Untersuchungen zu Gazzalis Kitab at-Tauba." *Der Islam* 32 (1957): 237–309, *Der Islam* 33 (1958): 51–120, *Der Islam* 34 (1959): 128–137.

Winegar, J. 2006. *Creative Reckonings: The Politics of Art and Culture in Contemporary Egypt*. Stanford, CA: Stanford University Press.

————. 2008. "Purposeful Art: Between Television Preachers and the State." *ISIM Review*, no. 22, 28–30.

Wise, L. 2003. "'Words from the Heart': New Forms of Islamic Preaching in Egypt." Master's thesis, Oxford University. http://users.ox.ac.uk/~metheses/Wise.html (accessed November 28, 2006).

————. 2005. "Whose Reality is Real? Ethical Reality TV Trend Offers 'Culturally Authentic' Alternative to Western Formats." *Transnational Broadcasting Studies*, no. 15

(Fall). Also available online at http://www.tbsjournal.com/Archives/Fall05/Wise.html (accessed January 5, 2011).

Wynn, L. L. 2007. *Pyramids & Nightclubs*. Austin: University of Texas Press.

Yiğit, A. 2011. "Islamic Modernity and the Re-enchanting Power of Symbols in Islamic Fantasy Serials in Turkey." In *Muslim Rap, Halal Soaps, and Revolutionary Theater: Artistic Developments in the Muslim World*, ed. K. van Nieuwkerk, pp. 207–231. Austin: University of Texas Press.

Zayn, A. 2001. "al-mughaniyyun al-Islamiyyun . . . qariban satanafus" / "Islamic Singers Will Soon Be Competitors," July 8. http://www.islamonline.net (accessed March 28, 2006).

Zeghal, M. 1999. "Religion and Politics in Egypt: The Ulema of al-Azhar, Radical Islam, and the State (1952–94)." *International Journal of Middle East Studies* 31:371–399.

Zubaida, S. 2002. "Religious Authority and Public Life." *ISIM Newsletter* 11 (December): 19.

Zuhur, S. 1992. *Revealing Reveiling: Islamist Gender Ideology in Contemporary Egypt*. Albany: State University of New York Press.

Index

Oriental (*raqs sharqi;*), 45, 214; whirling (*tannura*), 219
dancer/s, 1–6, 8, 30, 44–46, 65, 90, 103,
130–131, 156, 185, 206–207, 212, 215–
216, 219, 234–235, 279; belly, 130, 215,
236; male folklore, 219
da'wah, 18–20, 36–37, 43–44, 59–66,
72–73, 94–95, 108, 115, 133, 159, 164,
168, 188, 220. *See also* Islamic: outreach; propagation; *tablighi*
devil/s, 26–29, 32–33, 35, 46–47, 50, 64,
109–110, 123, 125–126, 134, 149, 153, 155,
163, 202, 266, 276–277
devout, 3, 123–124, 162, 181, 239, 241, 243,
258
devoutness, 53, 180
din al-laziz, al-, 173, 199, 203, 258. *See also*
religiosity
director/s, 10, 23, 121–122, 125, 131, 146,
150, 184–185, 191–192, 196–197, 203,
248, 254
discourse/s, gender, 25, 162, 168–169; on
art, 10, 145–146, 152–153, 157–158, 162,
164; on art with a mission, 173, 270; on
gender and art, 25, 162; religious, 9, 78,
233, 280; on veiling, 77, 158–159
domesticity, 92–93, 155, 159–160, 164
drama, 122, 141, 151, 182, 189, 240, 244–
245, 267
dream/s, 11, 22–23, 30–35, 45–46, 49,
52–53, 100, 107, 125, 147, 237, 244, 263,
269, 276; interpretation, 30, 32
Dream TV, 133, 158, 170, 173, 225, 236
du'a, 28, 65, 77, 189. *See also* prayer
duff, 1, 211, 215, 217, 219–221
dunya (al-dunya), 99, 101–102, 125, 128
durus dinniya, 60. *See also* religious lessons

earthquake, 6, 29–30, 83, 89, 98, 100–101,
114, 119, 131
'eb, 49, 124
economic, crisis, 39, 114, 117; liberalization, 39, 224

empowerment, 34, 82, 85–87
entertainer/s, popular, 3, 204
entertainment, 1–3, 5, 15–17, 38, 90, 94,
116, 133, 167, 176–177, 181, 192, 196,
199–200, 212, 215–216, 219–222, 224,
228, 242, 257, 270; popular, 94, 176;
wedding, 219. *See also* wedding/s
ethical: self-making, 14, 18–19, 65–66, 88,
107, 180–181, 201, 238; sensibilities, 85
ethics, 138, 180–181, 195–197, 233, 252, 258;
Islamic, 175, 181; moral-religious, 175;
pious, 37; religious, 11–12, 178
etiquette, 38, 213, 222
extremism, 60, 89–90, 109, 131–132, 140,
164
extremist/s, 69, 89–90, 113, 120, 132–133,
135–136, 140–141, 165–166, 194, 259,
268

fann, al-. *See fann*
fann: *al-badil*, 193; *al-habit*, 193–194, 196,
256; *al-hadif*, 10, 172, 181, 190–197,
210–211, 213, 222, 232, 249, 255–258,
267, 271; *al-islami*, 193, 208; *al-
mabadi'*, 193; *al-multazim*, 193; *al-
nadif*, 193; *raqi'*, 193. *See also* art; pious
fannanat: *muhagabat*, 20, 47; *multazimat*,
19; *mu'tazilat*, 19, 47; *ta'ibat*, 47, 52,
171, 275–276, 280
fans, 3–4, 9–11, 15–17, 66, 81, 109, 186, 191,
201, 208, 229, 234, 248–250, 255, 257,
264, 269
farah, 10, 209; *islami*, 206, 215. *See also*
wedding/s
farida min al-fara'id, 56
fatiha, 29, 276
fatwa / fatawa, 127, 135, 142, 144, 149–150,
160, 169
fawahish, 194
female, artist/s, 20, 80, 91, 108, 112–113,
135, 153, 160–161, 172, 207, 235, 276,
277, 280; band, 210, 213–214, 216–217,
219–222, 286; body/ies, 134, 249, 253,